UNDERSTANDING
SUBSTANCE
ADDICTIONS

Elizabeth,
What a wonderful
gift you are to
our field.

Also available from Lyceum Books, Inc.

MENTAL HEALTH IN LITERATURE: LITERARY LUNACY AND LUCIDITY, by Glenn Rohrer

INTRODUCTION TO SOCIAL WORK: THE PEOPLE'S PROFESSION, 2E, by Ira C. Colby and Sophia F. Dziegielewski

GENERALIST PRACTICE IN LARGER SETTINGS, 2E, by Thomas M. Meenaghan, W. Eugene Gibbons, and John G. McNutt

USING EVIDENCE IN SOCIAL WORK PRACTICE: BEHAVIORAL PERSPECTIVES, by Harold E. Briggs and Tina L. Rzepnicki

CASE MANAGEMENT: AN INTRODUCTION TO CONCEPTS AND SKILLS, 2E, by Arthur Frankel and Sheldon Gelman

SOCIAL WORK WITH FAMILIES: CONTENT AND PROCESS, by Robert Constable and Daniel B. Lee

ENDINGS IN CLINICAL PRACTICE: EFFECTIVE CLOSURE IN DIVERSE SETTINGS, by Joseph Walsh

NAVIGATING HUMAN SERVICE ORGANIZATIONS, by Margaret Gibelman

MODERN SOCIAL WORK THEORY: A CRITICAL INTRODUCTION, 3E, by Malcolm Payne, foreword by Stephen C. Anderson

CROSS-CULTURAL PRACTICE: SOCIAL WORK WITH DIVERSE POPULATIONS, by Karen Harper and Jim Lantz

WORKING WITH CHILDREN AND THEIR FAMILIES, 3E, by Martin Herbert and Karen Harper-Dorton

SCHOOL SOCIAL WORK: PRACTICE, POLICY, AND RESEARCH PERSPECTIVES, 5E, by Robert Constable, Shirley McDonald, and John Flynn

Foreword by Gabriel Mayer, MD

UNDERSTANDING SUBSTANCE ADDICTIONS

Assessment and Intervention

Edited by
Sophia F. Dziegielewski

LYCEUM
BOOKS, INC.

5758 South Blackstone Avenue
Chicago, Illinois 60637

Published by

LYCEUM BOOKS, INC.
5758 S. Blackstone Ave.
Chicago, Illinois 60637
773+643-1903 (Fax)
773+643-1902 (Phone)
lyceum@lyceumbooks.com
http://www.lyceumbooks.com

Library of Congress Cataloging-in-Publication Data

Dziegielewski, Sophia F.
    Understanding substance addictions : assessment and intervention / Sophia
Dziegielewski
        p. cm.
    Includes bibliographical references (p.   ) and index.
    ISBN 0-925065-41-2 (paperback : alk. paper)
    1. Substance abuse. 2. Substance abuse—Treatment. I. Title.
RC564.D95   2005
616.86—dc21
                                                            2003011689

Dedication

Problems with substance addiction have touched the lives of so many people whom I have loved dearly. This book is dedicated to all of these incredible individuals, especially the ones who have been able to beat the "addictions dragon." These wise individuals celebrate their victory by using what they have learned to help others, while staying forever mindful of how easy it is to relapse and once again get scorched by the flames.

Contents

Foreword

When I first read *Understanding Substance Addictions*, I was happily reminded of holding one of those "must have" pocket reference books that my colleagues and I carried during our internships at Boston City Hospital. However, this book can serve not only as a quick reference and guide for practitioners but also as a significant resource for a larger audience.

I wholeheartedly recommend *Understanding Substance Addictions* to a wide spectrum of practitioners, from social workers and psychologists to physicians and nurses. In addition, other groups of concerned professionals ought to possess this text. Among these, I would include emergency medical services personnel, school teachers, and government administrators whose work deals with substance abuse. The first group can benefit and learn from the book's succinct science, while the latter can obtain vital information about the epidemiology of addictions.

The presentation of *Understanding Substance Addictions* is both elegant and simple. The conceptual outline is a perfect roadmap, starting with general diagnostic and epidemiological issues and then dealing specifically with eleven of the substances of abuse identified by the American Psychiatric Association. The final chapters move beyond single-substance addictions to polysubstance addiction, dual diagnosis, and their attendant dilemmas. Each chapter begins with just enough history and science to provoke and intrigue before moving on to specific intervention concerns. The case histories, *DSM-IV-TR* guidelines, and treatment considerations at the conclusion of each chapter provide a didactic experience for the reader.

I would like to call special attention to three chapters: chapter 2, which addresses the complexities of diagnosis; chapter 4, which speaks to the difficulty of managing cocaine addiction; and chapter 12, which deals with the pediatric issues surrounding inhalant abuse. I also commend chapters 5 and 6 for openly addressing caffeine and nicotine abuse. Chapters 8 and 9 deal with opiate and sedative addictions, and tongue in cheek, I recommend these for any self-respecting news reporter who wishes to cover the recent spate of celebrity prescription drug abuse.

As a medical doctor, academician, and addictions researcher, I realize the need to own this book. At the same time, I see *Understanding Substance Addictions* as a valuable tool in the hands of many, above and beyond the professions previously mentioned, including parents, relatives, and friends of those with addictions. In assisting those parents, relatives, and friends, I would first direct them toward one of the twelve-step self-help groups now found in all communities, as well as professional counseling, and then I would add, "Please read this book."

My concluding opinion is that, as a reader, you are holding in your hands not only an academic resource but also a potential best seller.

Gabriel Mayer, MD
Fellow of the American Academy of Family Physicians
Certified by the American Society of Addiction Medicine

Preface

Although there are many types of addiction, this book focuses on those related to substance use. Substance use leading to abuse and dependence can have devastating effects on individuals, families, and society. Each chapter highlights specific substances and how easily individuals can be lulled into believing that legal substances cannot be as harmful as those that are illegal. Yet nothing could be further from the truth. As the reader will see, particularly in the chapter on caffeine, commonly used substances, when used excessively, can have life-altering effects.

Substance use and subsequent dependence has become a significant problem for society, and 82 percent of Americans list it among their top health concerns (Leshner, 2001). As the number of individuals suffering from addictive disorders continues to increase, professionals as well as the lay public must reevaluate their negative assumptions about the individuals who develop substance-related disorders (Kaplan, 2001). Substance abuse and addiction is a complex phenomenon that involves changes in brain chemistry, and the authors of this text unanimously support efforts to abandon the notion of the "typical addict." Many professionals believe that the term *addiction* has been overused and in some ways trivialized. This term has been employed to describe a multitude of social problems, from television addictions to sex addictions to money addictions. In this book, however, the term *addiction* will refer specifically to the eleven substance areas listed in the *DSM-IV-TR*. The purpose of examining the substances individually is to highlight the unique characteristics each has as the primary substance of abuse.

Each chapter summarizes the most up-to-date practical advice available to practitioners. Because clients need careful, individualized assessment, screening, intervention planning, and service delivery, each chapter takes a how-to approach that challenges the professional to provide a comprehensive assessment that will lead to the best intervention outcomes possible.

Chapter 1 introduces the reader to the area of substance addictions and provides a summary of some of the salient issues. Chapter 2 supports the positive advancement of professional work in the field by urging professionals in the area of substance addictions to complete comprehensive yet standardized diagnostic assessments of their clients. Information to support and coordinate the assessment process is gleaned from two major sources—the *Diagnostic and Statistical Manual of Mental Disorders*, Fourth Edition, Text Revision (*DSM-IV-TR*), published by the American Psychiatric Association (2000), and the *International Classification of Diseases*, Tenth Edition (*ICD-10*), published by the World Health Organization (1992). The information on abuse, dependence, intoxication, and withdrawal presented in chapter 2 is then applied in the subsequent chapters.

Each of the remaining chapters relates to a specific substance or group of substances and is designed to provide professional practitioners with a quick, simplified source for major issues in assessment and intervention. Each chapter gives an overview of the substance in question, citing common problems that occur with use of and addiction to that substance and highlighting special issues that result when the substance is used in combination with other substances. Furthermore, each chapter emphasizes the importance of recognizing the behavior patterns that can lead to abuse and includes case presentations and direct intervention recommendations. In closing, each chapter notes any special considerations for intervention and suggests future directions for research.

Chapters within the section covering central nervous system stimulants address amphetamines (chapter 3) and cocaine (chapter 4), which are widely considered the most dangerous substances of this type, as well as caffeine (chapter 5) and nicotine (chapter 6), the effects of which are often underestimated.

Chapters in the section on central nervous system depressants introduce the reader to some of the most common substances of this type that practitioners in the field of addictions may encounter. These include alcohol (chapter 7), heroin and other opiates (chapter 8), and prescription sedatives, hypnotics, and painkillers (chapter 9). Each chapter stresses that these substances, whether legal or not, can have disastrous effects when misused or abused.

Chapters in the section entitled Other Addictive Substances include information on cannabis (chapter 10), LSD, PCP, and ecstasy (chapter 11), and inhalants (chapter 12). The potential side effects that can result from misuse (the most extreme resulting in death) are discussed. Although almost any use (or improper use in the case of inhalants) of these substances is currently considered illegal, information is presented on how the negative view of some of these substances, especially cannabis and ecstasy, may be changing in the future.

In the last section of the book, two complicating factors—polysubstance addiction (chapter 13) and dual diagnosis (chapter 14)—are addressed. These chapters highlight the complexity of treating individuals with addictive disorders.

Each chapter of this book supports the claim that problems with substance addiction are growing rapidly. In the United States, these frequently occurring substance disorders are an increasingly costly major public health concern that cannot be ignored (Sloves, 2000; McCaffrey, 2000). The book is designed to increase professional knowledge of proper assessment techniques, the characteristics of the major substances of addiction, and the most up-to-date practice strategies in order to help close the gap between the need for and the availability of appropriate substance addiction services (National Institute on Drug Abuse, 2001c).

ACKNOWLEDGMENTS

My coauthors and I would like to extend special thanks to colleagues in the field who commented on or contributed to earlier drafts of the chapters: Mark Arost; Jeanie Bondy; Rita Michelle Barrett; Vanessa Brown; Ida Cook; Kimberly

Crawn; Joy Dann; Valerie Gay; Alison Grant; Cheryl Green; Lolly Green; Carolyn Heymann; Elaine Marie Harnandez; Amy Kryszan; Beverly Matthews; Melodee McAfee; Michelle Miller; Nita Pierre; Nancy Puntheive; Patty Renga; Angie Rogowski; Kyle Satterthwaite; Deborah E. Shirley; Nancy Suris; Emily Tow; Krystal Wald; and Jan Vaughan.

References

Kaplan, A. (2001). Trying to solve the prescription drug abuse equation. *Psychiatric Times.* Retrieved September 3, 2003, from http://www.psychiatrictimes.com/p010201a.html

Leshner, A. (2001). Understanding and treating drug abuse and addiction. *Business and Health, 19*(7), 23–30.

McCaffrey, B. (2000). Methadone treatment. *Vital Speeches of the Day, 66*(15), 450–54.

National Institute on Drug Abuse (NIDA). (2001c). *Principles of drug addiction treatment: Scientifically based approaches to drug addiction treatment.* Retrieved March 4, 2002, from http://www.nida.nih.gov/PODAT/PODAT9.html

Sloves, H. (2000). Drug treatment for drug addiction: Surmounting the barriers. *Behavioral Health Management, 20*(4), 42.

Chapter 1

Understanding Substance Addictions: An Overview

Sophia F. Dziegielewski

THE INCREASING PREVALENCE OF SUBSTANCE USE IN THE UNITED States, especially when it results in substance abuse and dependence, has become a major public concern, and helping professionals can now neither ignore nor deny the important role substance addiction plays in their ability to provide efficient and effective client services. As a backdrop for the rest of the book, this chapter discusses broadly the history of substance abuse; recent public and professional debate and policies related to substance abuse; the current prevalence of substance abuse and the associated health and economic costs and issues, including insurance coverage for its treatment; the care of special populations, including children and adolescents, women, and the elderly; and an overview of the complicating factors inherent in a dual diagnosis of substance abuse and mental illness.

A BRIEF HISTORY OF SUBSTANCE ABUSE

Problems related to substance abuse have been known among men and women since antiquity. For the most part, however, it was not until the early nineteenth century that the active elements of these substances were openly identified, extracted, and marketed as drugs. Some of these drugs such as morphine, laudanum, and cocaine were prescribed freely by physicians. Morphine and heroin were even recommended as early remedies for alcoholism. Morphine was also widely used during the civil war, and historical reports show that veterans returned home with kits containing morphine and hypodermic needles. Opium dens also thrived in the nineteenth century, and from the 1870s until the early twentieth century, the patent medicine industry sold concoctions containing opiates, cocaine, and other drugs, making extravagant claims that these remedies would cure all manner of ills. Public acceptance of these substances contributed to the rise in addiction, yet few individuals knew of the extent of problems that could come from use (National Clearinghouse for Alcohol and Drug Information, n.d.).

After the Harrison Narcotic Act of 1914, subsequent Supreme Court decisions made it illegal for doctors to prescribe narcotics to clients with substance addictions. As a result, many doctors who prescribed maintenance doses as a part of addiction treatment were jailed, but there was still no penalty for those who consumed the substance.

Soon, however, the magnitude of this problem could no longer be ignored, and laws were passed to control drug use and to make certain drugs illegal. Yet some argue that, rather than being motivated by a concern for the problem, this move toward legal penalty for drug use had classist and racist overtones. For example, although the spirit of temperance is generally credited for the passage of the Eighteenth Amendment prohibiting alcohol in the United States in 1919, some believe that legislators took this action partly in response to the drinking practices of the new lower class of European immigrants. Similarly, it is argued that because cocaine and opium were the favored drugs among the middle and upper classes, cocaine did not become illegal until after Reconstruction, when it was associated with African Americans, and smoking opium (not opium itself) became illegal in San Francisco in 1875, after it became associated with Chinese opium dens (National Clearinghouse for Alcohol and Drug Information, n.d.). Marijuana, too, was legal until the 1930s; it became illegal after numerous reports showed that Mexicans were profiting from its importation. And finally, it was not until LSD became directly associated with the "hippie" counterculture of the 1960s that efforts to make it illegal were supported (National Clearinghouse for Alcohol and Drug Information, n.d.).

In the 1970s, as problems related to addictive behaviors continued to develop, greater regulation of illegal drugs was introduced. Efforts to secure a clear differentiation between legal and illegal drugs resulted in the passage of the Controlled Substances Act. This act classified drugs according to their medical use, their potential for abuse, and their likelihood of producing dependence. It also established maximum penalties for the illegal manufacture and distribution of these drugs. These efforts to control drug use behavior continued with the creation of the U.S. Drug Enforcement Administration (DEA) in 1973. Federal control of illegal substances was further strengthened with the passage of the Anti-Drug Abuse Act of 1988 (National Institute on Drug Abuse [NIDA], 2001).

Despite increased legislation related to addictions during this period, intervention efforts focused more on establishing treatment programs than on the effectiveness of treatment they provided. The twenty-eight-day inpatient program became the benchmark for treatment. Later, in the 1970s and 1980s, this treatment model was questioned, especially because outpatient care appeared to be just as effective as inpatient care. Today, recent research evidence once again supports a shift in treatment efforts. This time the emphasis is moving away from programmatic structure to individualized client care (Pacione & Jaskula, 1995).

CURRENT PREVALENCE OF SUBSTANCE ABUSE AND ITS COSTS

Mental and addictive disorders are some of the most serious health problems facing the United States today, with almost one-third of those persons between fifteen and fifty-four years of age experiencing one or more mental or addictive disorders in a given year (Marwick, 1998). The annual cost of various services, disability subsidies, and lost productivity due to untreated mental illness and abuse or dependence disorders exceeds $150 billion (Budgar, 2001). In the 1997 National Household Survey on Drug Abuse, the primary source of statistical information on alcohol, tobacco, and illicit drugs, 13.9 million Americans (6.4%) reported being current users of illicit drugs, 111 million (51%) stated that they used alcohol, and 64 million identified themselves as current cigarette smokers (NIDA, 2001).

Mental health problems such as depression and anxiety, whether they occur coincidentally or are caused by substance abuse, often further complicate the psychological suffering associated with an addictive disorder. The resulting symptoms can become so severe that individuals may become unable to perform necessary activities of daily living like eating and sleeping.

The sociological and economic effects of substance addiction include but are not limited to the dissolution of families, the creation or perpetuation of a multigenerational cycle of addiction, loss of employment, loss of worker productivity, increased health care costs, and an increase in criminal activity and incarceration related to substance-seeking behaviors. Such daunting effects make knowledge of these addictive substances and the implementation of appropriate treatment interventions imperative.

According to many professionals, substance abuse is the number one public health problem in the United States, leading to greater morbidity and mortality than any other single health problem. For example, estimates indicate that between 25 and 40 percent of hospitalized clients have diseases related to alcoholism (Marcus, Rickman, & Sobhan, 1999). Barriers to treatment such as the lack of health insurance, the high cost of pharmaceuticals, and the stigma surrounding substance abuse further complicate this problem. In 2000, the number of emergency room visits for ecstasy-related problems alone rose 58 percent, while heroin-related visits increased by 15 percent (U.S. Department of Health and Human Services, 2001). The United States spent $1.1 trillion dollars on health care in 1997, yet less than 25 percent of people in need of substance abuse treatment received it. Although alcohol-dependent and drug-dependent individuals are among the most frequent recipients of medical care, only 5 to 10 percent of these costs are directly related to substance abuse treatment (Zywiak et al., 1999). Reasons for this inconsistency include lack of funding for this type of treatment, and many clients in need of service do not qualify for insurance coverage (Garcia, McGeary, Shultz, & McCoy, 1999).

Because psychiatric and substance abuse treatment costs are rising at approximately twice the rate of medical inflation, cost control methods have been employed to decrease the high relapse rates for individuals with these often chronic conditions (Pearson, 1995). Consequently, these cost-cutting efforts have lead to growing restrictions on the approval of treatment, in particular the expensive inpatient stays that specialized behavioral health companies provide (Dayhoff, Urato, & Pope, 2000).

The Mental Health Parity Act of 1996 compels insurance companies to provide the same coverage for mental illness as they do for physical illness if they choose to offer mental health coverage as a benefit. Implemented in 1998, the act took effect September 30, 2001, and was recently upheld in court. Those who opposed the act claimed that adoption of the bill would increase the costs of HMOs, thus harming small businesses. Because employers with fifty or fewer employees are exempt from the legislation, there is also a concern that these companies might elect not to offer any substance addiction mental health coverage or might eliminate their mental health coverage from their health plans altogether (Leshner, 2001).

There is still no firm decision on whether this legislation will also mandate the provision of substance abuse insurance coverage. Failure to provide accessible and effective substance abuse treatment presently costs U.S. taxpayers up to $276 billion per year. Even as the relevant legislation is being developed and written, however, such cost estimates fail to include foster care and social service expenses for children of addicted parents (Amaro, 1999). At present, the efforts toward convincing Congress to keep the Mental Health Parity Act are not expansive enough to provide the full array of services needed for those who are suffering from the addictive disorders. Full parity mental health coverage would include the full range of treatment options for the addictive disorders.

CURRENT SUBSTANCE ABUSE DEBATE AND POLICY

The problems related to substance addiction are deeply rooted in the past, but these substances still pose a public health threat that directly affects millions of people nationwide. Today, there is considerable debate between those who believe that the responsibility for addressing this problem rests with public law enforcement and those who believe it is a health issue. The former would try to control addiction through criminal punishment and denial of benefits; the latter would treat addiction through the medical/mental health system (Segal & Brzuzy, 1998).

Each chapter of this book will attempt to answer two important questions fundamental to this debate: What are the critical factors related to the development of an addictive disorder? And, once these factors are identified, what is the best way to assess and intervene?

The answers to these questions are not clear-cut because different disciplines approach substance abuse in different ways. For example, politicians may consider drug abuse and dependence to be a problem of self-control. For those whose view of addiction is based on the twelve-step model of Alcoholics Anonymous and Narcotics Anonymous, the opposite is true—the individual has lost control over his or her addiction (has become powerless) and cannot stop using without help. For sociologists, problems with addiction are best related to issues of poverty. For biologists, they are partially explained by heredity. For psychiatrists, psychologists, and many mental health professionals, they are related to a combination of personality and character traits. For practitioners who specialize in cognitive-behavioral approaches, addiction is the development of a conditioned response. And finally, for social workers, the interplay of all these factors with the individual's situation or environment is key.

Taking these multiple perspectives into account makes it easy to see how complicated understanding and solving the problem of addictions has become. The authors of this book recognize these varied perspectives and recommend strongly that, regardless of the type of substance addiction, the best intervention efforts will always be specific to the individual. There is no such thing as a completely standardized protocol—designed for a standardized client. A one-size-fits-all approach simply cannot accommodate the diversity, depth, and breadth of the problems that the individual with an addictive disorder can encounter. Practitioners must consider all of these perspectives in order to provide the best assessments and interventions possible.

To support the great efforts that have been made to change the professional conversation, the authors of this book suggest that caution be used when referring to an individual with a substance disorder as a "substance abuser," preferring the phrase "individual with an addiction." Using this terminology can help avoid labeling and stereotyping the entire person and instead supports the notion that addiction does not describe the whole person. Perhaps in the long run, using this terminology will help change the way that these varying professions view and treat the substance-addicted individual.

From a policy perspective, efforts to address the problems associated with addictive disorders have resulted in three recent changes in legislation that make it more difficult for individuals with substance addictions to get financial assistance from the government. These policies stem from a belief that the most effective deterrent for excessive use of illegal substances is the anticipation of negative consequences. Therefore, withholding government funds that may be misused to purchase illegal drugs is considered to be an effective intervention. Effective or not, taxpayers often support these types of policies because they object to having their tax dollars spent on illegal drugs or expenses incurred due to the use of illicit substances rather than on the purposes for which they were earmarked.

As a result of the first legislative change, those with addictive disorders (with the exception of alcohol-related disorders) are ineligible for educational loans if they have had a drug conviction, even if the conviction occurred in the distant past. Taxpayers feel that their dollars are not well spent on an education obtained while a student is under the influence of illegal substances. Many may feel similarly about alcohol abuse, which is a significant problem within the college community, but because it is a legal substance, measures toward control and sanction are not pursued to the same extent.

Second, changes in Supplemental Security Income (SSI) benefits and other welfare reforms have significantly limited the financial assistance that persons with addictive disorders can receive. A mentally or physically ill person's SSI benefits cease when he or she is institutionalized, even if only for a day. With passage of the Contract with America Advancement Act of 1996, SSI applicants are no longer eligible for benefits if drug addiction or alcoholism is a major factor in their disability, unless they qualify on some other basis. Benefits approved for these individuals prior to the act were terminated as of January 1, 1997, regardless of the cause of the disability (Social Security Administration, n.d.).

The third legislative change also addresses eligibility for welfare benefits. Between 6 percent and 37 percent of welfare recipients have addictions problems. From this statistic, one can estimate that one in five women receiving welfare has an addictions problem. Intervention efforts could provide a viable way of moving these substance-using women off of welfare subsidies and back into the workforce (Metsch, McCoy, Miller, McAnany, & Pereyra, 1999). But under the Welfare Reform Law of 1996, Temporary Assistance for Needy Families (TANF) recipients convicted of drug-related felonies after August 1996 are ineligible for cash welfare benefits or food stamps (Metsch, McCoy, Miller, McAnany, & Pereyra, 1999). Furthermore, any drug offender with dependents, regardless of the charge, is ineligible for public assistance.

Many claim that individuals with substance addictions are mentally ill and therefore are not stigmatized and punished in society. In fact, these individuals are directly punished when they are dropped from or made ineligible for certain types of funding such as SSI. Even those who are no longer abusing substances are affected. For example, an individual recovering from an alcohol addiction, in full remission for years, who develops liver disease secondary to his alcoholism, could be denied SSI benefits.

Employment policies regarding employee drug use have also changed in recent years. Employers face increased liability pressure to provide a safe and hazard-free employment environment because insurance companies will deny injury claims related to drug or alcohol use. As a result, individuals addicted to substances who are capable of performing a job can be excluded from potential employment if they fail to pass a drug screening.

And finally, individuals involved in drug-related dealings cannot expect protection from law enforcement nor dispute resolution by the courts if disagreements arise. Illegal drug use may involve violence, compounded by a diminished likelihood of reporting the incidence (DeSimone, 2001). Recently, new "drug courts," which forge working relationships with judges, treatment providers, and offenders, have been attracting attention. Drug Court programs advocate using positive and negative incentives to encourage compliance. These courts offer treatment to persons whose truant behaviors are rooted in mental health or addiction disorders, or both. For some individuals, it appears that these drug courts are effective in reducing drug abuse levels, incarceration, and recidivism (Tauber, 1995). Some professionals argue, however, that drug courts are not sensitive to various substances as being part of treatment. For example, if a heroin user is receiving methadone as part of treatment, he or she may not be able to graduate from drug court, even if that treatment appears to be effective (see chapter 8 for more information on the use of methadone as a treatment approach for heroin addiction).

WORKING WITH SPECIAL POPULATIONS

The problems that surround the substance addictions can be extensive. Not only is the individual with the substance problem directly affected, but so are their children and other family members. Furthermore, if a traditional "male" treatment model is used, the special needs of other populations (e.g., women and the elderly) may be overlooked.

Children and Adolescents

Some research studies have found disturbing relationships between substance abuse and mental health. An estimated 22 million children are currently being raised in homes with parents who abuse substances (McGaha & Leoni, 1996). Severe emotional problems can occur in a child as a result of the psychological effects of parental substance abuse. Research indicates that children raised in chemically abusive homes are rarely exposed to nurturing interactions. This lack of attention can result in an inability to trust others, presently and in future relationships (Feaster, 1996). Other studies have associated traits of early childhood behavior to later substance abuse. The more disruptive or troublesome the behaviors exhibited in childhood, the more likely the use and misuse of alcohol and other substances (Lynskey & Fergusson, 1996).

Surveys focusing on adolescents suggest that nearly one-third of high school seniors experiment with illegal drugs. Many adolescents admit to drinking alcohol regularly, even though they are aware that the purchase, possession, and use of alcohol is illegal for persons under the age of twenty-one (American Academy of Pediatrics, 1996). In a recent survey of college students, 44 percent of a nationally representative sample indicated binge drinking in the two-week period prior to completing the survey, and 24 percent reported the use of marijuana in the last year (Feigelman, Gorman, & Lee, 1998).

In another study on substance abuse and suicide, researchers found that 70 percent of youths who committed suicide had either a drug problem or an alcohol problem (Trammel, Kurpius, & Robinson, 1998). Increasingly, evidence links suicide attempts with substance abuse; and individuals who abuse alcohol and other drugs are five times more likely to attempt suicide than nonabusers (Buelow & Buelow, 1998).

Women

Many treatment programs treat women using methods developed for men. The inappropriateness of this is evident when one considers how gender differences can effect even the diagnosis of alcoholism. Women who are suffering the effects of alcohol abuse are often misdiagnosed because the definition of a heavy drinker (twelve to twenty-one drinks per week) does not take into consideration differences in body weight, water content, and fat content, all of which affect the rate and process by which the body metabolizes alcohol (McNeece & DiNitto, 1998). If the definition were adjusted appropriately, more women would be classified as heavy drinkers and would be receiving the treatment necessary for recovery. At present, however, men are nearly ten times more likely to enter treatment than are women, and when in treatment, men have longer lengths of stay and greater rates of completion (Scott-Lennox, Rose, Bohlig, & Lennox, 2000).

The choice of chemical substances abused also varies by gender. Women are more likely to have a preference for and an addiction to tranquilizers and diet pills. And because women are less likely than men to report psychoactive substance abuse disorders, their substance abuse as well as their alcohol abuse continues to be minimized and ignored (McNeece & DiNitto, 1998). For the most part, gender differences are not currently addressed in substance abuse treatment protocols.

Those arguing from a feminist perspective believe that women who are addicted to substances are more stigmatized by society than are addicted men. They find that this is partly because more is at stake—a child born to a mother who suffers from an addictive disorder can be negatively affected by the mother's addiction. In addition, many services developed for women, like domestic violence shelters and homeless shelters, exclude substance-addicted women. Few residential drug and alcohol programs have provisions for accepting children or for childcare (Hall, Baldwin, & Prendergast, 2001). The general public perceives that women addicted to substances are involved in more unacceptable behaviors such as child neglect and abuse, engage in prostitution, and because of these addictive behaviors, exhibit unnecessary economic dependency on the welfare system (Goldberg, 1996). When Hall et al. (2001) examined the problems that addicted women face while on parole, they found high recidivism rates. Many of the issues these women faced involved unemployment, illiteracy, mental illness, and homelessness.

Many of these women who have been victims of sexual abuse or domestic violence are more likely to suffer from a higher incidence of substance abuse (Goldberg, 1996). In an examination of domestic violence, one-fourth to one-half of domestically abusive men were found to have substance abuse problems, and the perpetrator or female survivor had consumed alcohol prior to or during at least half of all incidents of domestic violence (Bennett, 1996). Among women involved in domestic violence, substances are often used to inhibit normal sanctions, thereby effecting changes in thinking, emotion, and motivation. Substance abuse and domestic violence have been shown to have a high correlation, but surprisingly, few studies report findings or treatment efforts that deliberately link the two. Addiction treatment and the cessation of substance use can directly decrease violent behaviors. Treatment programs teach anger management, communication skills, and ways to improve interpersonal relationships, but they can sometimes neglect the relationship between stopping substance use and decreased episodes of violence.

Pregnancy is also a problem for women who are addicted, though outlawing substance use during pregnancy continues to be protested as a violation of a woman's personal rights. Many questions surround this debate, including what rights the fetus has in this situation.

In summary, women appear to constitute a special population not only because of the characteristics of their substance abuse but also because of their likelihood of suffering from sexual abuse, victimization, and emotional dependency and the consequences their abuse may have for their children. A discussion of all the intervention issues salient to women is beyond the scope of this text. However, recognizing that women constitute a special population clearly requires continued attention and study within the context of intervention.

The Elderly

Society has difficulty recognizing the elderly as a population with chemical dependency problems, despite the fact that older people use three times as many prescription drugs as the general population. The incidence of heavy drinking (twelve to twenty-one drinks per week) is estimated to be between 3 and 9 percent among older adults (Patterson, Lacro, & Jeste, 1999). Depression among the elderly remains a significant mental health problem that is frequently associated with physical symptoms and illness (Rhodes, 1988). But depression is not always situational or reactive; it also can be related to internal causes (endogenous)or may result from a combination of situational and internal factors. For example, many of the chronic medical conditions often found among the elderly are accompanied by depression. These conditions include hypothyroidism, Addison's disease, idiopathic Parkinson's disease, and congestive heart failure. Symptoms of depression also may be the side effects of medications being taken for other conditions (Belsky, 1988). Furthermore, the symptoms of depression—especially loss of interest and pleasure in one's usual activities, disorientation, and memory loss—can also mimic an addictive disorder.

The use and misuse of prescription medication with older individuals can present particular problems and should be an area of practice for professionals in the field of addictions and physical medicine (Dziegielewski & Leon, 2001). Medications and various dosages prescribed may produce different reactions in an elderly individual than in a younger person. Elderly individuals often have slower metabolic rates, possibly related to decreased activity or physiological losses (Belsky, 1988). In addition, medications used to treat chronic conditions such as arthritis, ulcers, heart conditions, and hypertension can cause depression when taken alone or with other medications. Commonly prescribed medications can also present side effects such as irritability, sexual dysfunction, memory lapses, and a general feeling of tiredness (Dziegielewski & Leon, 2001).

Faced with complex medical regimens and diminished tolerances for alcohol, many elderly Americans run the risk of falling into the trap of substance abuse. With aging, there is a higher incidence of chronic, painful physical difficulties, often treated with medications that are addictive and have a potential for misuse and abuse. If medications for pain are no longer effective, a client should be informed not to "double dose" his or her medication but rather to seek the advice of their physician (NIDA, 2001). Feelings of anxiety, anger, depression, and resentment of being or becoming dependent because of physical disabilities also make the aging population vulnerable to addiction.

Unfortunately, medical professionals often have little knowledge of substance abuse or use. This can lead to misdiagnosing the aging population because the many changes and declines associated with aging produce similar symptoms. As the baby boomer generation ages, addictions professionals in every setting will increasingly find themselves working with clients who are taking medications as well as dealing with potential problems created by substance abuse.

But even medical professionals familiar with issues of substance abuse among the elderly may not be aware of the potential for a problem. Frequently, elderly individuals see more than one physician, and each one may not be aware of what the others have prescribed. In addition, especially when taking multiple prescriptions, it is not uncommon for older individuals to simply forget not to eat or drink prohibited foods that can lead to a toxic drug reaction. (Wolfe, Hope, & Public Citizen Health Research Group, 1993). Therefore, it is of the utmost importance for addictions professionals to be aware of all the medications that an elderly client is taking. Before beginning any type of intervention for an addictive disorder, the practitioner needs to explore whether the symptoms exhibited might be medication related (Dziegielewski & Leon, 2001).

DUAL DISORDERS

Assessing and screening an individual with a substance addiction who also suffers from another major mental illness (e.g., major depressive disorder, schizophrenia) is never easy. But when the individual exhibits the symptoms of another type of mental illness and the potential for a co-occurring substance addiction is ignored, a great injustice occurs (Loneck & Way, 1997).

For example, an estimated 50 percent of the chronically mentally ill suffer from alcoholism and other drug dependence, and approximately 75 percent of young mentally ill clients either abuse or are addicted to alcohol or other drugs (Buelow & Buelow, 1998). Individuals with schizophrenia may also abuse alcohol or other drugs, and at times use these substances in addition to prescription medications. This combined use can create reactions to intervention regimens as well as increase or decrease the effectiveness of certain medications (Dziegielewski & Leon, 2001; National Institute of Mental Health, 1999).

Adolescents diagnosed with dual disorders are most often depressed and using alcohol and marijuana, both of which intensify depression and anxiety. Among more severely disabled chronically mentally ill youth, alcohol and marijuana use may result in psychosis and amphetamine abuse will more often increase symptoms of schizophrenia (Buelow & Buelow, 1998).

For the most part, traditional mental health services often are not well prepared to deal with clients who have a co-occurring substance abuse disorder. This short-sightedness can result in only one of the two problems being identified and treated. If both problems are not identified and addressed simultaneously, the individual may be bounced back and forth between services for the mental illness and those for the substance addiction. Furthermore, because one disorder could be considered a complicating condition for the other, the individual may be refused admission by one or both types of treatment program, even though neglecting one disorder could precipitate a recurrence of the other.

Comprehensive evaluation and screening for issues beyond the presenting problem can lead to more positive outcomes for the client, the practitioner, and the agency. Unfortunately, the decision to take these actions is often influenced by managed care organizations that may not be familiar with the individual needs of the client being served. Also, making accurate diagnoses, especially during emergencies, can be difficult because the effects produced by some drugs are very similar to the manifestations of psychoses and manic episodes (McNeece & DiNitto, 1998).

Because of the differences in treatment for individuals suffering from addictive disorders and for those who are mentally ill, as well as the complications that arise in their co-occurrence, serving clients with dual disorders is particularly complex. This special population is therefore discussed in greater depth in chapter 14.

CONCLUDING COMMENTS

Why does substance abuse occur? According to the "self-medication hypothesis," an individual's decision to abuse a particular substance is not random. Rather, it is made in part to alleviate a specific distressing symptom or affect (Maxmen & Ward, 1995). A National Institute on Drug Abuse experiment revealed that environmental cues (e.g., the sights, sounds, or physical surroundings that a person associates with drug use) can also trigger a nearly irresistible urge to use drugs (Zickler, 2001). Therefore, understanding both the individual and the environment as well as identifying known and possible unknown factors is crucial to the completion of a comprehensive assessment.

In professional practice, the medical model for understanding the causes of substance abuse remains prominent. From this disease-based perspective, it makes sense that individuals who suffer from addictive disorders may have the same problems as those who suffer from other chronic and incurable disorders. Therefore, harm reduction (palliative care) should be part of these individuals' long-term treatment (Willenbring, 2000). In this, the authors of this book all agree: harm reduction should be the premise underlying all assessment, process, and intervention principles.

As the number of individuals suffering from addictive disorders continues to increase, society will need to reevaluate negative assumptions about individuals who are victims of the substance disorders (Kaplan, 2001). In the past, degenerate morals were believed to be the underlying cause of alcoholism and drug addiction. For addictions practitioners, moral advice will always fall short. Current medical science supports that addiction changes brain chemistry, and notions that there is a "typical addict" have been challenged. Each of the subsequent chapters suggests that addictive disorders, and the problems associated with addiction, result from a combination of known and unknown factors. An assessment of each of the known possible factors is crucial, including the identification of biochemical, genetic, familial, environmental, and cultural dynamics (Straussner, 1993). To identify the unknown factors, the practitioner must be sensitive to variables in the client's situation. If left unidentified, these unknown factors may impede or be counterproductive to the intervention process. Efficient, effective client service therefore requires careful, individualized assessment, screening, intervention planning, and service delivery. This book presents the most up-to-date practical advice available for practitioners and others who strive to help individuals with addictive disorders achieve a better life.

References

Amaro, H. (1999). An expensive policy: The impact of inadequate funding for substance abuse treatment. *American Journal of Public Health*, *89*(5), 657–60.

American Academy of Pediatrics. (1996). The role of schools in combating substance abuse. *Pediatrics*, *95*(5), 784–86.

Belsky, J. (1988). *Here tomorrow: Making the most of life after fifty*. Baltimore: Johns Hopkins.

Bennett, L. (1996). Substance abuse and the domestic assault of women. *Social Work*, *40*(6), 760–72.

Budgar, L. (2001). Is your mental health coverage about to improve? *Psychology Today*, *34*(6), 20.

Buelow, G. D., & Buelow, S. A. (1998). *Psychotherapy in chemical dependence treatment: A practical and integrative approach*. Pacific Grove, CA: Brooks Cole.

Dayhoff, D., Urato, C., & Pope, G. (2000). Trends in funding and use of alcohol and drug abuse treatment at specialty facilities, 1990–1994. *American Journal of Public Health*, *90*(1), 109–11.

DeSimone, J. (2001). The effect of cocaine prices on crime. *Economic Inquiry*, *39*(4), 627–36.

Dziegielewski, S. F., & Leon, A. M. (2001). *Psychopharmacology and social work practice*. New York: Springer.

Feaster, C. (1996). The relationship between parental chemical abuse and children's behavior disorders. *Preventing School Failure*, *40*, 155–60.

Feigelman, W., Gorman, B., & Lee, J. (1998). Binge drinkers, illicit drug users, and polydrug users: An epidemiological study of American collegians. *Journal of Alcohol and Drug Education*, *44*(1), 47–69.

Garcia, L., McGeary, K., Shultz, J., & McCoy, C. (1999). The impact of insurance status on drug abuse treatment completion. *Journal of Health Care Finance*, *26*(1).

Goldberg, M. (1996). Substance abusing women: False stereotypes and real needs. *Social Work*, *40*(6), 789–99.

Hall, E., Baldwin, D., & Prendergast, M. (2001). Women on parole: Barriers to success after substance abuse treatment. *Human Organization*. Retrieved January 21, 2004, from http://proquest.umi.com/pdqw

Kaplan, A. (2001). Trying to solve the prescription drug abuse equation. *Psychiatric Times*. Retrieved January 5, 2004, from http://www.psychiatrictimes.com/p010201a.html

Leshner, A. (2001). Understanding and treating drug abuse and addiction. *Business and Health, 19*(7), 23–30.

Loneck, B., & Way, B. (1997). Using a focus group of clinicians to develop a research project on therapeutic process for clients with dual diagnoses. *Social Work, 42*(1), 107–12.

Lynskey, M., & Fergusson, D. (1996). Childhood conduct problems, attention deficit behaviors, and adolescent alcohol, tobacco and illicit drug use. *Journal of Abnormal Child Psychology, 23*(3), 281–303.

Marcus, M., Rickman, K., & Sobhan, T. (1999). Substance abuse education liaisons: A collaborative continuing education program for nurses in acute care settings. *Journal of Continuing Education in Nursing, 30*(5), 229–34.

Marwick, C. (1998). Parity for mental health and substance abuse treatment. *Journal of the American Medical Association, 279*(15), 1151–52.

Maxmen, J. S., & Ward, N. G. (1995). Substance-related disorders. In *Essential psychopathology and its treatment* (pp. 132–72). New York: W. W. Norton.

McGaha, J., & Leoni, E. (1996). Family violence, abuse, and related family issues of incarcerated delinquents with alcoholic parents compared to those with nonalcoholic parents. *Adolescence, 30*(118), 473–83.

McNeece, C. A., & DiNitto, M. D. (1998). *Chemical dependency: A systems approach.* Boston: Allyn & Bacon.

Metsch, L. R., McCoy, C. B., Miller, M., McAnany, H., & Pereyra, M. (1999). Moving substance-abusing women from welfare to work. *Journal of Public Health Policy, 20*(1), 36–55.

National Clearinghouse for Alcohol and Drug Information. (n.d.). *A short history of the drug laws.* Retrieved June 6, 2004, from: www.druglibrary.org/schaffer/library/shrthist

National Institute on Drug Abuse. (2001, April 10). NIDA and partners announce national initiative on prescription drug misuse and abuse. *NIDA News Release*, 1–2.

National Institute of Mental Health. (1999). *Schizophrenia.* Retrieved January 5, 2004, from http://nimh.gov/publicat/schizoph.htm

Pacione, T., & Jaskula, D. (1995). Quality chemical dependency treatment in an era of cost containment: Clinical guidelines for practitioners. *Health and Social Work, 19*(1), 55–63.

Patterson, T. I., Lacro, J. P., & Jeste, D. V. (1999). Abuse and misuse of medications in the elderly. *Psychiatric Times*. Retrieved January 4, 2004, from http://www.psychiatrictimes.com/p990454.html

Pearson, J. (1995). Controlling treatment costs of substance abuse and psychiatric problems. *Personnel, 66*(10), 12–15.

Rhodes, C. (1988). *An introduction to gerontology: Aging in American society.* Springfield, IL: Charles C. Thomas.

Scott-Lennox, J., Rose, R., Bohlig, A., & Lennox, R. (2000). The impact of women's family status on completion of substance abuse treatment. *Journal of Behavioral Health Services & Research, 27*(4), 366–79.

Segal, E. A., & Brzuzy, S. (1998). *Social welfare policy, programs and practice.* Itasca, IL: F. E. Peacock.

Social Security Administration. (n.d.). *Social Security on-line.* Retrieved January 6, 2004, from http://www.ssa.gov

Straussner, L. A. (1993). *Clinical work with substance abusing clients.* New York: Guilford Press.

Tauber, J. (1995). Drug courts: Treating drug-using offenders through sanctions and incentives. *Corrections Today, 56*(1), 28–35.

Trammel, R., Kurpius, S., & Robinson, A. (1998). Suicide and substance abuse among student teachers. *Journal of Alcohol and Drug Education, 43*(2), 64–74.

U.S. Department of Health and Human Services. (2001). *Monitoring the future survey released: Smoking among teenagers decreases sharply and increase in ecstasy slows.* National Institute on Drug Abuse Press Office.

Willenbring, M. (2000). Harm reduction for substance abuse in the psychiatric setting. *Psychiatric Times, 17*(2), 19–25.

Wolfe, S. M., Hope, R., & Public Citizen Health Research Group. (1993). *Worst pills, best pills II: The older adult's guide to avoiding drug induced death or illness.* Washington, DC: Public Citizens Health Research Group.

Zickler, P. (2001). Cue-induced craving linked to brain regions involved in decision-making and behavior. *NIDA Notes, 15*(6), 9–10.

Zywiak, W., Norman, G., Hoffmann, R., Stout, S., et al. (1999). Substance abuses cost offsets vary with gender, age, and abstinence likelihood. *Journal of Health Care Finance, 26*(1), 33–39.

Chapter 2

An Introduction to Formal Diagnostic Assessment and Documentation

Sophia F. Dziegielewski

BECAUSE ASSESSMENT AND INTERVENTION EFFORTS FOR INDIVIDUALS who suffer from addictive disorders involve a multitude of client problems, all practitioners can expect to work for agencies that either directly or indirectly serve the substance-addicted person, their significant others, or their family members (Gassman, Demone, & Albilal, 2001). Whether the treatment of these disorders constitutes the primary or secondary mode of practice, practitioners must develop proper skills in formal diagnostic assessment and documentation.

For social workers and other mental health professionals, reaching agreement on how to best complete a diagnostic assessment will never be an easy, straightforward process. A complete and relevant diagnostic assessment will always be somewhat flexible, relating both subjective and objective criteria in the formulation of a diagnostic impression (Dziegielewski, 2002). Furthermore, everything that the professional does will always be subject to interpretation—the art located within the science. This process is complicated even further because the professional must take into consideration agencies' standards such as those required by the Joint Commission on Accreditation of Healthcare Organizations (JCAHO) and the Health Insurance Portability and Accountability Act of 1996 (HIPAA). Regardless of these complicating factors, however, some level of agreement must be achieved with respect to diagnostic assessment if advancement in the field of addictions is to continue.

Therefore, to encourage uniformity of assessment within the field, this chapter highlights formal diagnostic assessment and documentation methodology as it applies to the treatment of substance disorders. Diagnostic information is presented from the two books most commonly used in mental health settings across the United States: the *Diagnostic and Statistical Manual of Mental Disorders*, Fourth Edition, Text Revision (*DSM-IV-TR*) (American Psychiatric Association, 2000), and the *International Statistical Classification of Diseases and Related*

Health Problems, Tenth Revision (*ICD-10*) (World Health Organization, 1992). This information is applied directly to the substance-related disorders. The general criteria that these books designate as constituting abuse, dependence, intoxication, and withdrawal for all substances are outlined in this chapter; information on particular substances and the most common modes of intervention will be presented in chapters 3 through 13.

Since the beginning of the nineteenth century, after substance-related disorders were identified as a medical condition, clinicians have followed what is often referred to as the *medical disease model* of substance abuse (McGrady & Epstein, 1999). This model supports the contention that changes in the body and brain need to be understood using a biomedical approach to practice (Dziegielewski & Green, 2004). This model for understanding disease is based on a biomedical paradigm wherein approaches to mental health problems such as those related to addiction are based on scientific facts derived from empirical evidence (Engel, 1977; Gilbert, 2002; Rock, 2002; Spraycar, 1995). This paradigm has helped practitioners understand the origin, signs and symptoms, medical diagnosis, treatment procedures and protocol, and the prognosis for physical health conditions (Carlton, 1984).

Professionals in the field of family medicine and the supporting disciplines have long argued, however, that this approach is limited because it places the clinical emphasis on curing or resolving the physical problems experienced and does not take into account the systemic and interrelated factors that also contribute to the true nature of the problem. That is, an emphasis on what constitutes physical and empirically verifiable phenomena, such as weight loss, falls short when the factors related to the client's situation that contribute to those phenomena are not highlighted (Dziegielewski & Green, 2004). Consequently, various helping professionals believe that to effectively serve their clients, it is necessary to acknowledge and understand the clients' perceptions, including their values, thoughts, feelings, and fears, when evaluating their current lifestyle patterns and behaviors (McWhinney, 1989). Because the medical disease model is limited in its consideration of these psychosocial factors, the effectiveness of any diagnostic assessment and treatment of addiction and dependence based on this model may also be limited (McGrady & Epstein, 1999).

In reaction to this need for a more expansive scope of practice, much of today's intervention strategy is based on a biopsychosocial/spiritual model . From this perspective, the "person in environment" is highlighted, with a recognition and respect for the spiritual needs of the individual. (Here the term *spiritual* refers to the meaning the individual attaches to his or her life and the values and priorities he or she holds, with no reference to organized religion.)

IDENTIFYING SUBSTANCE ADDICTIVE DISORDERS

It was not until 1980, with the introduction of the third edition of the *DSM* (*DSM-III*) and the eighth revision of the *ICD* (*ICD-8*), that the concepts of substance abuse and dependence were clearly introduced as part of formal assessment. In these earlier versions, however, the impairment an individual experienced was labeled as abuse when symptoms representative of tolerance or withdrawal were not generally present. The obsessive-compulsive element experienced by individuals suffering from addiction to increase their amount of consumption was not included (McGrady & Epstein, 1999). But the definitions provided in subsequent clinical updates of these two texts were influenced by the identification of Alcohol Dependence Syndrome (ADS). This condition prompted a multidimensional approach in which the degree of severity was noted. The consequent separation of dependence and abuse into two different assessment categories had an impact on all future editions of the *DSM* and *ICD* (McGrady & Epstein, 1999).

The fourth edition of the *DSM* (*DSM-IV*), published in 1995, established the diagnostic criteria for substance abuse, dependence, intoxication, and withdrawal. In the text revision of that edition (*DSM-IV-TR*), published in 2000, no changes were made to these four categories, but some supporting information was updated. Examples were added for clarification of diagnostic classification of substance intoxication or substance withdrawal versus a substance-induced disorder with onset during intoxication or with onset during withdrawal.

In their review of the most recent revision of the *ICD* (*ICD-10*), McGrady and Epstein (1999) point out that the harmful use category identifies both physical and psychological symptoms of harm to the user. This differs slightly from the *DSM-IV-TR*, which combines the notion of harmful use and abuse while highlighting socioenvironmental consequences.

THE DSM-IV-TR MULTIAXIAL DIAGNOSTIC ASSESSMENT SYSTEM

The current standard for formal diagnostic assessment and documentation is the *DSM-IV-TR* multiaxial diagnostic assessment system. The remainder of this chapter provides a practical introduction to this system as it applies to substance disorders. (For a more complete explanation of how to use this system with other mental disorders, see *DSM-IV-TR in Action* [Dziegielewski, 2002].) This system, when used as part of professional record keeping, provides quality assurance and improvement (Browning & Browning, 1996; Dziegielewski & Leon, 2001; Dziegielewski & Powers, 2000; Frager, 2000; Rudolph, 2000; Wambach, Haynes, & White, 1999). For the addictions professional, training in the use of this system constitutes a functional building block for effective, efficient, and cost-controlled service provision and is invaluable in managing the legal, ethical, and fiscal concerns inherent in all client services (Mitchell, 1991; Sheafor, Horejsi, & Horejsi, 1997).

When using the *DSM-IV-TR* multiaxial assessment system, the practitioner must first determine the presence or absence of numerous possible disorders and conditions that the client may be experiencing. These disorders and conditions are divided into five major categories, or axes:

Axis I: All clinical and pervasive disorders, including the substance addictive disorders
Other conditions that may be the focus of clinical attention
Axis II: Personality disorders
Mental retardation

Axis III: General medical conditions
Axis IV: Psychosocial and environmental problems
Axis V: Global assessment of functioning (GAF)

To facilitate this process, the *DSM-IV-TR* provides codes that represent each of the possible disorders and conditions that the client may be experiencing. These codes allow for quick and consistent recording that will lead to prompt service recognition and reimbursement. These codes also simplify descriptions of the injuries or illnesses from which a client suffers; are helpful in gathering prevalence and research information; and assist other health care professionals in providing continuity of care (Rudman, 2000). In addition, these codes must be used when completing insurance claim forms. To standardize this coding process, the creators of the *DSM-IV-TR* and the clinical modification of the ninth revision of the *ICD* (*ICD-9-CM*) collaborated to establish similar codes for each text's diagnostic system. Thus, when mental health practitioners use *DSM-IV-TR* codes for reimbursement, they are, in effect, also using the *ICD-9-CM* codes. (A clinical modification of the *ICD-10* is currently in preparation.)

There are two primary types of codes: diagnostic (what a client suffers from) and procedural (what will be done with it). The *DSM-IV-TR* and the *ICD-9-CM* are most concerned with diagnostic codes. *Current Procedural Terminology* (*CPT*) is an annual publication of the American Medical Association that provides codes for the services that mental health practitioners often use. Although these codes are closely linked to the *ICD-9-CM* codes, they correspond to procedures rather than diagnoses.

AXIS I

On Axis I, the practitioner should cite clinical disorders as well as any "other conditions that may be a focus of clinical attention"—that is, any other conditions that are not attributable to a clinical disorder but will be a focus of intervention. The specific disorders and conditions that that are coded on Axis I are listed in box 1.

Included in the clinical disorder subcategory are disorders related to eleven substances: alcohol, amphetamines, caffeine, hallucinogens, inhalants, nicotine, opioids, phencyclidine (PCP), sedatives, hypnotics, and anxiolytics. In fact, what constitutes a substance that may lead to a disorder or the actual effect that substance has on the body can be as varied as the social, biological, and psychological phenomena that influence it. But the diagnostic assessment process must start with agreement on a common definition of a substance disorder, and the definition most widely accepted by clinicians is that outlined in the *DSM-IV-TR*.

When citing substance disorders, the practitioner must first identify the substance being used and then relate the client's symptoms to the appropriate substance disorder subcategory. The two substance disorder subcategories are substance use disorders and substance-induced disorders. There are two possible categories for the substance use disorders—abuse and dependence; and there are

Box 1: Axis I Categories

Clinical Disorders
    Disorders Usually First Diagnosed in Infancy, Childhood, and Adolescence
        Learning Disorders
        Motor Skills Disorders
        Communication Disorders
        Pervasive Developmental Disorders
        Attention-Deficit and Disruptive Behavior Disorders
        Feeding and Eating Disorders of Infancy or Early Childhood
        Tic Disorders
        Elimination Disorders
        Other Disorders of Infancy, Childhood, and Adolescence
    Delirium, Dementia, and Amnesic and Other Cognitive Disorders
        Delirium
        Dementia
        Amnesic Disorders
        Other Cognitive Disorders Not Otherwise Specified
    Mental Disorders Due to a General Medical Condition Not Elsewhere Classified
        Substance-Related Disorders
        Alcohol-Related Disorders
        Amphetamine (or Amphetamine-like)-Related Disorders
        Caffeine-Related Disorders
        Cannabis-Related Disorders
        Cocaine-Related Disorders
        Hallucinogen-Related Disorders
        Inhalant-Related Disorders
        Nicotine-Related Disorders
        Opioid-Related Disorders
        Phencyclidine (or Phencyclidine-like)-Related Disorders
        Sedative-, Hypnotic-, or Anxiolytic-Related Disorders
        Polysubstance-Related Disorder
        Other (or Unknown) Substance-Related Disorders
    Schizophrenia or Other Psychotic Disorders
    Mood Disorders
        Depressive Disorders
        Bipolar Disorders
    Anxiety Disorders
    Somatoform Disorders
    Factitious Disorders
    Dissociative Disorders
    Sexual and Gender Identity Disorders
        Sexual Dysfunctions
        Paraphilias
        Gender Identity Disorders
    Eating Disorders

Sleep Disorders
    Primary Sleep Disorders
    Sleep Disorders Related to Another Mental Disorder
    Other Sleep Disorders
Impulse Control Disorders Not Otherwise Specified
Adjustment Disorders
Other Conditions That May Be a Focus of Clinical Attention
Psychological Factors Affecting Medical Condition
Medication-Induced Movement Disorders
    Neuroleptic-Induced Parkinsonism
    Neuroleptic Malignant Syndrome
    Neuroleptic-Induced Acute Dystonia
    Neuroleptic-Induced Acute Akathisia
    Neuroleptic-Induced Tardive Dyskinesia
    Medication-Induced Postural Tremor
    Medication-Induced Movement Disorders Not Otherwise Specified
    Other Medication-Induced Disorder
Relational Problems
    Relational Problems Related to a General Medical Condition
    Parent-Child Relational Problem
    Partner Relational Problem
    Sibling Relational Problem
    Relational Problems Not Otherwise Specified
Problems Related to Abuse or Neglect
    Physical Abuse of a Child
    Sexual Abuse of a Child
    Neglect of a Child
    Physical Abuse of an Adult
    Sexual Abuse of an Adult
Additional Conditions That May Be a Focus of Clinical Attention
    Noncompliance with Treatment
    Malingering
    Adult Antisocial Behavior
    Child or Adolescent Antisocial Behavior
    Borderline Intellectual Functioning[a]
    Age-Related Cognitive Decline
    Bereavement
    Academic Problem
    Occupational Problem
    Identity Problem
    Religious and Spiritual Problem
    Acculturation Problem
    Phase of Life Problem

Source: Compiled from the *DSM-IV-TR* (American Psychiatric Association, 2000).
[a]This condition can also be listed on Axis II.

two possible categories for the substance-induced disorders—intoxication and withdrawal (see table 1). When a client uses more than one substance and the criteria for abuse or dependence for any one of those substances is not met but the criteria for abuse or dependence *is* met when combined, the designation of polysubstance dependence is given. Therefore, when a client meets the criteria for dependence on at least three substances separately, then all three should be listed on Axis I and the designation of polysubstance abuse should be used. Table 2 provides a quick reference showing which of the eleven substances, according to the *DSM-IV-TR*, are associated with abuse, dependence, intoxication, and withdrawal.

Table 1: Highlights of the Substance Disorders Subcategories and Their Definitions

Subcategory	*DSM-IV-TR* highlights
Substance use disorders	
Abuse	Individual continues using a substance with the knowledge that it is causing harm (does not apply to caffeine and nicotine).
Dependence	Individual needs to take larger amounts of a substance to achieve the same effects and has made unsuccessful attempts to quit using.
Substance-induced disorders	
Intoxication	Individual has developed a substance-specific (reversible) syndrome or a condition related to recent ingestion of a psychoactive substance.
Withdrawal	Individual experiences cognitive and behavioral declines due to a reduction in the use of a substance. (This category is most often associated with dependence.)

Abuse

When using the term *abuse* to describe a client's substance disorder on Axis I, the practitioner should be aware that the term can take on different meanings in other contexts. For example, in reference to curative agents such as benzodiazepines or morphine, the term applies to any nonmedicinal use or to overuse that results in health risks. In the *Encyclopedia of Drugs, Alcohol, and Addictive Behavior* (2001), *abuse* refers to the overuse of noncurative substances such as alcohol. The *Encyclopedia* also employs the term *abuse* to describe use of a substance in an amount that results in potentially harmful or destructive situations for either the user or those around the user. For the helping professional, however, the general criteria that define *abuse* in the *DSM-IV-TR* (pp. 198–99) apply to all substances, even those that have no standard medical purpose such as phencyclidine (PCP), heroin, methamphetamines, ecstasy, and mescaline.

Table 2: Substances Associated with Abuse, Dependence, Intoxication, and Withdrawal

	Abuse	Dependence	Intoxication	Withdrawal
Alcohol	X	X	X	X
Amphetamines	X	X	X	X
Caffeine			X	
Cannabis	X	X	X	
Cocaine	X	X	X	X
Hallucinogens	X	X	X	
Inhalants	X	X	X	
Nicotine		X		X
Opioids	X	X	X	X
Phencyclidine (PCP)	X	X	X	
Sedatives, Hypnotics, or Anxiolytics	X	X	X	X
Polysubstance		X	X	X

Source: Compiled from the *DSM-IV-TR* (American Psychiatric Association, 2000).
Note: This table is designed to help the reader become familiar with the substances the *DSM-IV-TR* lists as being associated with abuse, dependence, intoxication, and withdrawal. It is not meant to be inclusive of all substances and the individual reactions that may occur. Note that, according to the *DSM-IV-TR*, neither caffeine nor nicotine is a substance of abuse, and caffeine is not a substance of dependence.

Fundamentally, the terms *drug abuse* and *substance abuse* (including alcohol abuse) are synonymous, and in many professional settings these terms are used interchangeably. The helping professional, however, should be more cautious. For example, many individuals in the lay community may perceive the term *drug* to mean only a substance that is used for medicinal purposes. Other individuals may hear the word *substance* and immediately think of alcohol or of illegal activity. Furthermore, although either term can be used to refer to any manufactured psychoactive substance, either can also be used to refer to a natural substance such as the angel trumpet flower, which is hallucinogenic but has no known medicinal purpose.

In order for the practitioner to cite abuse on Axis I, the client's symptoms must meet one or more of the following *DSM-IV-TR* criteria within a twelve-month period:

1. Recurrent use resulting in a failure to fulfill major role obligations . . .
2. Recurrent use in situations in which it is physically hazardous . . .
3. Recurrent substance abuse-related legal problems . . . and
4. Continued use despite persistent or recurrent social or interpersonal problems.

"The essential feature of substance abuse is a maladaptive pattern of substance use manifested by recurrent and significant adverse consequences related to the repeated use of substances" (American Psychiatric Association, 2000, p. 198). This includes exhibitions of poor judgment, as when a pregnant woman continues to consume alcohol despite her physician's warnings that alcohol use could result in fetal damage or injury or when a college student continues excessive use of alcohol or cannabis despite its resulting in missed classes, bad grades, or traffic accidents (*Encyclopedia*, 2001).

For comparative purposes, table 3 lists the *DSM-IV-TR* and *ICD-10* criteria for a diagnosis of substance abuse and aspects of the *Encyclopedia* criteria for a diag-

Table 3: Comparison of Diagnostic Criteria for Substance Abuse and Harmful Use

	DSM-IV-TR and *ICD-10* criteria for substance abuse	*Encyclopedia* criteria for harmful use
Criteria	A. The individual has a maladaptive pattern of substance use leading to clinically significant impairment or distress over a twelve-month period. B. The symptoms have never met the criteria for substance dependence for this class of substance.	A. A pattern of psychoactive substance use causes physical or mental damage to health. B. Physical or mental health damage occurs.
Social and environmental circumstances	1. Recurrent substance use resulting in a failure to fulfill major role obligations at work, school, or home; neglect of hildren or household. 2. Recurrent substance use in situations in which it is physically hazardous. 3. Recurrent substance-related legal problems. 4. Continues the substance use despite recurring social or interpersonal problems caused by or exacerbated by the effects of the substance.	1. Harmful patterns of use associated with adverse social consequences and concerns in regard to this pattern of behavior that results in criticism from others. 2. A pattern of substance use that is disapproved by another person or by the culture, or that has led to socially negative consequences such as arrest or marital arguments, is *not* by itself evidence of harmful use.

Sources: Compiled from the *Encyclopedia of Drugs, Alcohol, and Addictive Behavior* (2001), the *DSM-IV-TR* (American Psychiatric Association, 2000), and the *ICD-10* (World Health Organization, 1992).

nosis of harmful use. Similar to *substance abuse*, the phrase *harmful use* denotes a pattern of using one or more substances that causes injury to the physical condition. The primary distinction between the two phrases is that, in harmful use, the experience of unfavorable effects leading to significant harm and impairment may refer to the user *or* to others involved in the user's life. Furthermore, the *Encyclopedia* contends that harmful use is clearly recognizable, and to be such it must first be considered unacceptable by someone other than the user—the individual's support system or others involved in the individual's life. To meet the criteria of substance abuse, the individual must be aware that the dosage levels he or she continues to ingest are harmful. To meet the criteria of harmful use, the dosage levels must be shown to have contributed to mental or physical problems.

A diagnosis of substance abuse should not be applied to chronic substance users who currently demonstrate characteristics of clear dependence on a substance or have a history of dependence (*Encyclopedia*, 2001; Kaplan & Sadock, 1998). In substance abuse, there is limited threat of tolerance, withdrawal, or a pattern of compulsive use.

Finally, it is important to note that in the multiaxial diagnostic assessment system, two of the eleven substances identified in the *DSM-IV-TR*—caffeine and nicotine—cannot be listed as substances of abuse. The reasons for this will be discussed in chapters 5 and 6.

Dependence

A diagnosis of substance dependence as defined in the *ICD-10* and the *DSM-IV-TR* is based primarily on the concept of a dependence syndrome. According to the *Encyclopedia of Drugs, Alcohol, and Addictive Behavior*, a dependence syndrome may be related to use of a class of substances, a wider range of substances, or a specific substance. A diagnosis of dependence does not always entail the existence of psychological, physical, or social consequences, even though some form of impairment is usually present (*Encyclopedia*, 2001). The fundamental concept applies equally to the diagnosis of dependence on all psychoactive substances except caffeine. Caffeine is the only substance to which this diagnosis cannot be applied (American Psychiatric Association, 2000). See table 4 for comparison of the *ICD-10* and the *DSM-IV-TR* criteria for dependence.

The dependence syndrome may be cognitive, behavioral, physical, or physiological (American Psychiatric Association, 2000). In cognitive and behavioral dependence, the means and patterns of obtaining a substance become central to the individual's daily activities. Life events appear to revolve around the substance, with a compulsion to use the substance despite the consequences to the individual's health, safety, or social and support/family system (McGrady & Epstein, 1999; Kaplan & Sadock, 1998).

When the practitioner believes an individual to be substance dependent, he or she must clearly specify the symptoms of physical or physiological dependence pre-

Table 4: Comparison of *DSM-IV-TR* and *ICD-10* Diagnostic Criteria for Substance Dependence

	DSM-IV-TR	*ICD-10*
Tolerance	Need for markedly increased amounts of the substance to achieve intoxication or the desired effect, or markedly diminished effect with continued use of the same amount of the substance.	Evidence of tolerance resulting in increased doses being required in order to achieve the effect originally produced by lower doses.
Withdrawal	Characteristic withdrawal syndrome for the substance or use of a substance (or a closely related substance) to relieve or avoid withdrawal symptoms.	Physiological withdrawal state. Substance use has ceased or been reduced as evidenced by the characteristic withdrawal syndrome for the substance (or use of a substance) to relieve or avoid withdrawal symptoms.
Inability to control use	Persistent desire or one or more unsuccessful efforts to cut down or control substance use. Substance use in larger amounts or over a longer period than individual intended.	Difficulties in controlling substance use at term of onset, levels of use, or termination.
Neglect of activities of daily living	Important social, occupational, or recreational activities given up or reduced because of substance use.	Progressive neglect of alternative pleasure or interests in favor of substance use.
Time related to substance acquisition	A great deal of time spent in activities necessary to obtain the substance. Use of the substance to recover from its effects.	A great deal of time spent in activities necessary to obtain the substance, to use the substance, or to recover from the effects of substance use.
Continued use despite problems	Continued substance use despite knowledge of having a persistent or recurrent physical or psychological problem that is likely to be caused or exacerbated by use. A strong desire to use the substance.	Continued substance use despite clear evidence of overtly harmful physical or psychological consequences. A strong desire or sense of compulsion to use the substance.

Sources: Compiled from the *Encyclopedia of Drugs, Alcohol, and Addictive Behavior* (2001), the *DSM-IV-TR* (American Psychiatric Association, 2000), and the *ICD-10* (World Health Organization, 1992).

sent. The *DSM-IV-TR* does not require that the practitioner distinguish physical dependence from physiological dependence, however, perhaps because it may be impossible to draw such conclusions without further formal diagnostic tests. The addictions practitioner should look for withdrawal symptoms that occur with substance use; these will clearly indicate physical dependence.

Tolerance, as defined in the *DSM-IV-TR,* involves the need for increased amounts of a substance to achieve intoxication (or the desired effect). It can also lead to a markedly diminished effect with the continued use of the same amount of the substance (American Psychiatric Association, 2000). Tolerance categorized as an aspect of dependence reinforces the notion that its effects can be physical, psychological, or behavioral. As stated by Miller (1997), a person is experiencing substance dependence when he or she becomes physically "normal" only with frequent and increasingly larger amounts of the substance. While the body is superficially benefiting from the effects of the drug, it is nevertheless organizing metabolic enzymes and neurological changes that tend to counteract those effects. The individual must therefore maintain higher intake levels to gain the same level of intensity, be it narcosis, elation, stimulus, or to achieve rest and relaxation.

Because tolerance levels will increase over time, an individual who begins to use a substance to obtain a certain effect, say a feeling of euphoria, may change his or her use pattern to one that will help him or her feel "normal" again. In time, the immediate effect of each use will be a craving for the next use, despite the foreign and irritating effect the substance produces on the body. When tolerance is exhibited, the individual must use the substance regularly to avoid withdrawal symptoms or becoming ill (Miller, 1997).

This cycle of addiction can be strong, and according to Miller, it is especially prevalent among individuals who use opiates, barbiturates, alcohol, or a combination of these substances. After becoming tolerant to a substance, the person is physically "hooked." The individual will experience the opposite of the drug's favorable result if his or her usage level is reduced or discontinued. Examples of physical tolerance include individuals addicted to alcohol who can consume amounts of alcohol that would debilitate or kill nontolerant drinkers and substance users who can perform motor functions at modest levels with no impairment. Behaviorally, the tolerant user can also maintain basic, everyday social skills.

Clarification of the powerful relationship between tolerance and the individual can be found in the *Encyclopedia of Drugs, Alcohol, and Addictive Behavior.* The *Encyclopedia* states that the term *tolerance,* while always relating to the degree of sensitivity or vulnerability of a subject to the drug effects, can have a number of different meanings. These meanings are classified as initial tolerance, acquired metabolic tolerance, acquired functional tolerance, and cross-tolerance.

Initial tolerance is defined by the degree of bodily reaction (or lack thereof) displayed during the individual's initial experience with the drug. The amount of consequence formed by a particular amount of the substance is physiologically related to that particular dose, thus the less intense the effect created by the substance, the larger the tolerance. In a clinical setting, it is important to remember that initial tolerance levels can vary individually, due to genetics, physiological factors, or environmental circumstances. Because one cannot predict an individual's exact reaction to a substance, any person ingesting a substance could become vulnerable to dependence. In addition, a person can use for years without knowledge of their abnormal use and/or dependency. The factor to consider in this initial stage is whether the substance interferes with the person's ability to determine whether the substance is affecting or impairing his or her usual level of activity.

Acquired tolerance, the most common meaning, is an amplified ability to resist a substance or an ability to experience a lowered sensitivity to a substance as a result of the body's adaptation to prior exposure to that drug. The development of acquired tolerance can be attributed to two different processes, one metabolic and the other functional. "*Metabolic tolerance* is created by an adaptive upsurge in the degree at which the substance is inactivated by metabolism in the liver and other tissues" (*Encyclopedia*, 2001, p. 25). This results in lower concentrations of the drug in the body after the same dose such that the effect is shorter and less intense. "*Functional tolerance* is formed by a diminution in the sensitivity of the tissues on which the drug acts, primarily the central nervous system, so that the same concentration of drug produces less effect than it originally did" (p. 25). There is a decline in the degree of the outcome produced by the same amount or concentration of the drug or an increased dose or concentration is necessary to facilitate the same amount of effect, and these factors contribute to dependence.

Acquired functional tolerance may occur in one of three forms: *acute, rapid,* or *chronic*. In *acute tolerance*, the individual displays symptoms of tolerance each time the substance is taken, possibly starting from his or her initial exposure to the substance. In acute tolerance, when the substance is introduced, changes in psychological or physiological response occur and can become more pronounced with time. When the effect of a particular concentration of the substance is stronger at first than later, the occurrence is referred to as the *Mellanby effect*. In *rapid tolerance*, the individual experiences increased tolerance shortly after being exposed to the drug a second time. In *chronic tolerance*, the individual constantly desires the effects of the drug and uses the substance regularly. Regardless of the type of tolerance that the individual develops, the use of the substance will always involve significant physical changes in the central nervous system.

The identification of functional difficulties is critical in the identification of substance abuse-related concerns (e.g., daily living skills impaired). According to the *Encyclopedia of Drugs, Alcohol, and Addictive Behavior*, substance-dependence behavior can be related directly to learned behavior and stimuli from the environment, which serve to powerfully reinforce substance abuse patterns or to provoke the renewal of such patterns. Much like Pavlov's dogs, a person can be conditioned to respond to certain cues. When exposed to these cues, often called *triggers*, the brain reacts in the way it has been conditioned to react. This phenomenon is viewed as a primitive survival mechanism. If the conditioning is strong enough, the individual will not be able to override the conditioned response with willpower alone. When this occurs, the person is said to have lost control or to have let go and become unable to resist or control use. The individual's ability to make good decisions and choices regarding use is impaired by the substance itself. Individual differences make it impossible to determine who will react to reinforcers and in what way. Consequently, addiction cannot always be predicted.

The fourth kind of tolerance, as discussed in the *Encyclopedia*, is *cross-tolerance*. If an individual with substance dependence introduces a second substance into his or her pattern of use that creates an effect comparable to the initial substance, he or she may develop a tolerance to the second substance. An individual's propensity for cross-tolerance may be so strong that it may occur during the first exposure to the second substance. A practitioner who suspects an individual of substance dependence should make every effort to anticipate or rule out the possibility of a secondary occurrence of withdrawal symptoms due to cross-tolerance.

Intoxication

The term *intoxication* is broader than the term *abuse*. Intoxication, as defined for use in diagnosis, takes into account context and implies maladaptive behavior (American Psychiatric Association, 2000). For example, the *DSM-IV-TR* describes how tachycardia can occur when an individual suffers from caffeine intoxication. However, if an individual suffers a single occurrence of tachycardia, and this symptom cannot be related directly to maladaptive behavior, there would be no diagnosis of caffeine intoxication (American Psychiatric Association, 2000). Therefore the context, including the social and environmental influences that lead to the social and occupational difficulties related to the symptom or behavior change, must be taken into account when diagnosing substance intoxication.

Furthermore, all of the signs and symptoms the individual experiences during intoxication that are related to the ingestion of the substance are considered reversible, even though these symptoms can last from hours to days. In some cases, the effects of a medication can continue for some time after the substance can no longer be found in the body fluids (American Psychiatric Association, 2000). The exact effect of intoxication on the body's systems is not known, but it is possible that there may be a residual effect related to low concentrations of the substance in the brain. When this residual effect happens and it is significant enough to affect the body's physiological processes, the elimination of the substance takes longer.

One problem that practitioners often encounter when completing diagnostic assessments is whether an individual has a substance intoxication disorder or is suffering from current substance withdrawal. According to the *DSM-IV-TR*, the essential feature of substance intoxication is the development of a reversible substance-specific syndrome due to the recent ingestion of or exposure to a substance (American Psychiatric Association, 2000). According to the *Encyclopedia of Drugs, Alcohol, and Addictive Behavior*, intoxication directly affects functional performance as it reacts with the body's usual methods for maintaining homeostasis.

Substance intoxication can either be acute or chronic. Acute intoxication is defined as the use of a large amount of a substance during one incident. Chronic intoxication is defined as the repetitive use of large amounts of a drug or drugs to uphold an extreme physiological concentration of that drug over an extended period. It is difficult to predict what pattern of intoxication will be characteristic of the substance and its effect on the body. When these substances target the central nervous system, they create physical impairment and maladaptive behaviors that usually develop during or shortly after use (American Psychiatric Association, 2000).

Often the symptoms experienced during intoxication can mimic or resemble a medical disorder. If the symptoms are in fact related directly to a medical condition, a diagnosis of substance intoxication should never be used. Individuals who are intoxicated by alcohol and barbiturates characteristically exhibit instability of muscular control and ability, speech difficulty, dulled sensory capacities, memory impairment, hyper or hypo reaction time, impaired reflexes, poor judgment of speed and distances, and unsuitable management of emotional expression and behavioral performance. Individuals who are intoxicated by amphetamines or cocaine often experience symptoms such as heightened body and blood temperature and increased heart rate. Other symptoms include convulsions and severe hyperactivity and cognitive impairments such as paranoid delusions and hallucinations (*Encyclopedia*, 2001).

In clinical practice, it is not uncommon to see the word *intoxication* used interchangeably with the word *overdose* or *overdosage*. This connection is attributable to the frequently large doses and subsequent symptoms of intoxication that commonly occur among individuals attempting to acquire a desired effect. Table 5 provides a quick reference for deciphering the minimal differences between the *DSM-IV-TR* and *ICD-10* diagnostic criteria for substance intoxication.

Withdrawal

For coding on Axis I, the most important component of substance withdrawal is the progression of negative changes in an individual's behavior that can have physical and psychological consequences when the substance is terminated or reduced, resulting in a pattern of profound and protracted substance use (American Psychiatric Association, 2000). When coding on Axis I, the practitioner must outline the signs of withdrawal that the client experiences. If this combination of symptoms causes a marked impairment in the socioenvironmental, occupational, or other significant areas of an individual's daily functioning, it is referred to as *withdrawal syndrome*. As with abuse, dependence, and intoxication, if the symptoms the individual is experiencing can be attributed to another medical concern or disorder, a diagnosis of withdrawal should not be given.

Table 5: Comparison of *DSM-IV-TR* and *ICD-10* Diagnostic Criteria for Substance Intoxication

	DSM-IV-TR	*ICD-10*
Intoxication	The development of a reversible substance-specific syndrome due to recent ingestion or exposure to a substance. Different substances can produce similar or identical symptoms. Clinically significant maladaptive behavior or psychological changes due to the effect of the substance on the central nervous system that develop during or shortly after taking the substance. The symptoms are not due to a general medical condition and are not better accounted for by another mental disorder.	A transient condition following the administration of alcohol or other psychoactive substances during which the level of consciousness, cognition, perception affect or behavior, or other psychophysiological functions and responses are disturbed. This diagnosis should only be used when intoxication occurs without more persistent alcohol or drug related problems. Disinhibition occurs within the social context.
Acute intoxication	Not specified	Closely related to dose levels. A transient phenomenon. Exceptions to this may occur in individuals with certain underlying organic conditions.
Recovery potential	Not specified	Intensity of intoxication lessens with time, and effects eventually disappear in the absence of further use of the substance. Expected recovery is complete except where tissue damage or another complication has arisen.
Additional information		Symptoms of intoxication may not always reflect the primary actions of the substance. Many psychoactive substances are capable of producing different types of effects at different dose levels.

Sources: Compiled from the *Encyclopedia of Drugs, Alcohol, and Addictive Behavior* (2001), the *DSM-IV-TR* (American Psychiatric Association, 2000), and the *ICD-10* (World Health Organization, 1992).

According to the *DSM-IV-TR*, "*withdrawal* is a maladaptive behavioral change, with physiological and cognitive concomitants, that occurs when blood or tissue concentrations of a substance decline in an individual who had maintained prolonged heavy use of the substance" (American Psychiatric Association, 2000, p. 201). Often, the state of withdrawal can create a situation for the addicted individual that seems exasperating or unbearable (Miller, 1997). A variety of symptoms can be attributed to withdrawal—for example, nervous system rebound from overstimulation, anxiety, diaphoresis, elevated pulse and blood pressure, and a sense of acute physiological distress. If the individual going through substance withdrawal is experiencing extreme physical and psychological suffering, he or she may be at risk for serious permanent physical damage or, in some cases, death. The symptoms and effects of withdrawal vary with each substance, so it is important that the practitioner be able to link particular withdrawal effects to particular substances. These associations are discussed by substance in chapters 3–13.

When a person undergoing medical treatment for another mental health problem is also suffering from substance withdrawal, and that substance cannot be immediately obtained, either legally or illegally, it is not uncommon for the individual to terminate treatment by suddenly signing him or herself out of the hospital against medical advice (also known as AMA). Individuals who stay in treatment may suffer a relapse or an expected delayed response related to the substance withdrawal. Therefore, practitioners need to be keenly aware of the relationship between dependence, withdrawal, and the treatment for not only the present mental health problem but the possibility of other co-occurring mental health problems and disorders. It is often necessary to defer treatment of other mental health problems until the immediate problems that are related to substance withdrawal have been addressed.

Withdrawal is most likely the direct result of substance dependence. The diagnosis of withdrawal is not applied to symptoms associated with the use of caffeine, cannabis, the hallucinogens (LSD, mescaline, MDMA, and other compounds), inhalants, or phencyclidine (PCP) (see table 2) (American Psychiatric Association, 2000). Most individuals experiencing withdrawal report having an insatiable obsession with and a compulsion to obtain the substance. This behavior is directed almost solely at reducing the disturbing substance-specific symptoms that the individual is experiencing. The signs and symptoms of withdrawal are dependent on individual differences and substance classification. The signs and symptoms of withdrawal from use of particular substances are discussed in chapters 3–13.

Patterns of Use Leading to Dependence and Withdrawal

For the practitioner, identifying the patterns of use that could lead to dependence and subsequent withdrawal from a substance is critical. The practitioner is advised to use three key identifiers for a mental health behavioral assessment: *frequency, intensity, and duration*. According to Dziegielewski (2002), *frequency* refers to how often an individual conducts the behavior and, in this case, utilizes the substance; *intensity* refers to the extent that the behavior is affecting the individual's daily functioning and routine; and *duration* refers to the length of time the individual has been using the substance after a previous attempt to discontinue use. The practitioner should keep in mind the importance of recognizing how much of the substance is being used and how long the substance has been used, as well as other factors such as how environmental conditions or supplementary illnesses can affect withdrawal symptoms.

The delineation of abuse and dependency rests on the practitioner's ability to identify the differences between intoxication and withdrawal. Intoxication is reversible and occurs after overingestion of a substance. This may be accompanied by a lower threshold for anger and violence but usually results in generalized inhibition (American Psychiatric Association, 2000; Maxmen & Ward, 1995). Withdrawal is the biophysical reaction to the reduction of a chemical stimulus in the body. Simply stated, substance withdrawal develops when doses of a substance are abridged or terminated. Often, withdrawal is accompanied by tremors, mood instability, physical illness, and in severe cases, seizures and possible death (American Psychiatric Association, 2000; Maxmen & Ward, 1995). In the case of withdrawal, the symptoms get better when more of the substance is received; in the case of intoxication, the symptoms often worsen when more of the substance is received (Miller, 1997).

When working specifically with the substance addictions on Axis I, the practitioner should first note the major psychiatric symptoms a client is displaying. As noted previously, each substance category has specific criteria that are associated with it. Second, the practitioner should clearly note and document these presenting symptoms, especially their frequency, intensity, and duration. To document frequency, the practitioner must record how often the substance-related behaviors are happening (i.e., their rate of occurrence). Are the behaviors happening, for example, once a week or once a day? He or she must also record how the frequency of occurrence of these behaviors directly affects individual, occupational, or social functioning. Many of the diagnostic categories require only that the behaviors occur once or more; others require that they occur frequently. Therefore, the practitioner should always document the frequency of the behavior and relate it directly to how the repeated use of this behavior affects functioning.

To address intensity of use, the practitioner must gather information regarding the strength, power, or force with which a problem behavior is occurring and relate this directly to its effect on daily functioning. To determine duration, the practitioner must document the time between the onset and the offset of the behavior (Ciminero, Calhoun, & Adams, 1986). This measure is very important for the identification of a disorder because the criteria of the different diagnostic categories require specific durations (e.g., for a diagnosis of substance abuse, the symptoms related to active use must last approximately thirty days). Concrete methods, suggested measures, and standardized tools that can assist the mental health practitioner to measure incidents and problem behaviors in terms of frequency, intensity, and duration are presented later in this chapter, along with other rapid assessment instruments.

Box 2: Questions to Guide the Process—Axis I

◆ What are the major psychiatric symptoms the client is displaying?
◆ What is the substance abuse condition the client is suffering from?
◆ What are the frequency, intensity, and duration of the symptoms or problem behavior?
◆ Are cultural, social, or other environmental factors a possible explanation for the symptoms or problem behavior?

AXIS II

On Axis II, the practitioner should report whether the individual suffers from either mental retardation or a personality disorder. Most relevant to this text are the personality disorders, listed in box 3. Although the *DSM-IV-TR* continues to group personality disorders in clusters, the manual urges practitioners to be cautious using the cluster system. This system may be helpful in terms of general categorization of symptoms, but these groupings have not been consistently validated (proven to accurately measure what is expected) in research or in educational settings (American Psychiatric Association, 2000). Practitioners should also note that in the *DSM-IV* and the *DSM-IV-TR*, there are eleven different conditions related to personality. Twelve were reported in the *DSM-III-R*. The personality disorder known as passive aggressive personality disorder was removed from the *DSM-IV* and *DSM-IV-TR* diagnostic categories.

Box 3: Axis II Categories

Personality Disorders

Cluster A: Characteristic of odd and eccentric behaviors
            Paranoid Personality Disorder
            Schizoid Personality Disorder
            Schizotypal Personality Disorder
Cluster B: Characteristic of dramatic, emotional, and erratic behaviors
            Antisocial Personality Disorder
            Borderline Personality Disorder
            Histrionic Personality Disorder
            Narcissistic Personality Disorder
Cluster C: Characteristic of anxious and fearful behaviors
            Avoidant Personality Disorder
            Dependent Personality Disorder
            Obsessive-Compulsive Personality Disorder
            Personality Disorder Not Otherwise Specified

Source: Compiled from the *DSM-IV-TR* (American Psychiatric Association, 2000).

The greatest predictor related to the conditions on Axis II is whether there is a lifelong pattern of behavior or whether the onset of the condition occurred before the age of eighteen. This lifelong pattern is exhibited by most individuals who suffer from mental retardation and by those who suffer from the personality disorders. In cases of mental retardation, the practitioner should immediately look for significantly subaverage intelligence (IQ of 70 or below) with onset before age eighteen. Also, it is critical that the practitioner link findings of subaverage intelligence to concurrent problems in adaptive individual and social functioning.

Individuals with personality disorders will often present with long-standing or enduring patterns of behavior and inner experiences that deviate markedly from expectations within the individual's cultural context. These behaviors remain pervasive and inflexible and cause the individual distress or impairment (American Psychiatric Association, 2000). As with all diagnoses, the symptoms presented must be related directly to either adaptive or functional impairment to be diagnosed as a personality disorder. The practitioner must also assess whether the substance disorder is the primary condition that is being treated and how the personality disorder contributes to the problem behaviors exhibited.

As with Axis I, all presenting symptoms for Axis II conditions should be clearly noted and documented, especially in regard to frequency, intensity, and duration of the problem behavior. That is, be sure to note the rate of occurrence (frequency) of the problem behavior, the strength, power, or force (intensity) with which the problem behavior is occurring, and the length of time (duration) the behavior exists. When the symptoms exist but do not create marked distress, nor do they disturb or impair functioning, application of any diagnostic category is inappropriate.

Some beginning professionals assume that an Axis I diagnosis is the most serious diagnosis, especially when compared with Axis II. This is simply not true. The multiaxial classification system is based on type of illness, not severity. This point is well supported when viewing the two categories of mental health conditions listed on Axis I. Axis I lists the clinical disorders and the other conditions that may be the focus of clinical attention. Both categories have many similar presenting symptoms, and these conditions can cause problems that are significant enough to affect individual, occupational, and social functioning. However, the other conditions that may be the focus of clinical attention that are also listed on Axis I are not considered mental disorders. Furthermore, although a mental disorder (e.g., alcohol abuse) may coexist with one of these conditions that may be the focus of clinical attention (e.g., bereavement), the mental disorder should not be listed as the focus of clinical attention (i.e., the reason for the visit). For example, if a client suffers from bereavement (formerly known as uncomplicated bereavement)and also meets the criteria for substance abuse, but the client's primary symptoms are related to the death of a loved one, the practitioner should document that bereavement exists, and bereavement should remain part of the diagnostic coding. In summary, all practitioners need to be careful not to assume that because a diagnosis is coded on Axis I, it is the most severe. All diagnostic listings on the multiaxial system are merely for categorizing purposes.

Coding on Axis II involves two areas—the personality disorders and mental retardation. The personality disorder diagnoses, when coded on Axis II, are generally expected to have started in childhood or adolescence and to have persisted in a stable form into adulthood with nonexistent or limited periods of remission. This makes it unlikely, although not impossible, that a child would come in for intervention with a presenting condition that would qualify as a personality disorder. Furthermore, mental retardation (coded on Axis II) is considered a lifelong condition that usually would not in itself constitute the presenting problem. If an individual develops a condition that resembles mental retardation in adulthood and this condition is, for example, related to chronic substance dependence, it would not be diagnosed as mental retardation but rather as a specific type of substance-related dementia or delirium, and the substance related to this development would be identified. In this case, an Axis I diagnosis would most likely result.

Another example would be when an adult is given a principal diagnosis on Axis II such as borderline personality disorder. Individuals diagnosed with this condition often have a pattern of "instability of interpersonal relationships, self-image, and affects and marked instability" that might result in "frantic efforts to avoid abandonment [that] may include impulsive actions such as self-mutilating or suicidal behaviors" (American Psychiatric Association, 2000, p. 706). The individual might also engage in self-harming behaviors, with the presence of a substance addiction simply magnifying the problem. Based on possible threats or actions of self-mutilation or suicide, the client likely would warrant admission for inpatient observation. This would make the Axis II diagnosis of a personality disorder, not the substance abuse disorder, the actual reason for admission. When the principal diagnosis is listed on Axis II, it is always good practice to place the words "principal diagnosis" in parentheses after it.

Regardless of where the practitioner is working, acceptable proficient documentation requires that if more than one diagnosis is noted (on either axis), the principal diagnosis should always be listed first. In addition, whether a diagnosis is

---

Box 4: Questions to Guide the Process—Axis II

◆ Is there a pattern of behavior that develops in either adolescence or early adulthood?

◆ Is there one or more enduring pattern of inner experience and behavior that deviates markedly from expectations of the individual's culture?

◆ Are these behaviors independent of the substance use/abuse problem?

◆ Are the symptoms and behaviors pervasive and inflexible?

◆ How do these symptoms or behaviors relate to occupational and social functioning?

◆ What are the frequency, intensity and duration of the presenting behaviors?

◆ How do these behaviors contribute directly to the primary diagnosis of substance addiction?

noted on Axis I or not, some type of coding will always need to be placed there; even if the primary diagnosis falls on Axis II, Axis I should never be left blank. If there is no Axis I diagnosis, the practitioner should list No Diagnosis on Axis I (code V71.09). If uncertain of what diagnosis to place because of insufficient information, the practitioner should list Diagnosis or Condition Deferred on Axis I (code 799.9).

AXIS III

On Axis III, the practitioner should list the general medical conditions that may be relevant to the condition being addressed (box 5). Because the term *mental disorder* means a condition that is not due to a medical condition, it is important for all mental health practitioners to have some knowledge of the medical conditions that may be listed on Axis III and the relationships that these conditions can have to a mental disorder. Alterations in behavior and mood that mimic a mental disorder may be directly related to a medical illness (Pollak, Levy, & Breitholtz, 1999). Because most addictions specialists and other mental health practitioners do not have extensive training in medical disorders, it is possible that they would not know what to expect when one occurs. Therefore, without adequate attention, the misdiagnosis of a medical disorder as a mental health disorder could become a fairly common occurrence. Clients at greatest risk for misdiagnosis in this area include women who are pregnant or were recently pregnant; indigent individuals (because of limited resources and limited access to health care); individuals who engage in high-risk behaviors; individuals with a medical illness who exhibit symptoms that might be confused with mental illness; and individuals with chronic conditions such as those who suffer from major mental disorders (Hartmann, 1995; Pollak et al., 1999). For example, a client who has a mental disorder such as schizophrenia or a bipolar disorder and masks his or her condition with substance use may be unable to perceive, may misperceive, or may simply ignore the warning signs of a medical problem. Many of the chronic conditions that older adults exhibit may be de-emphasized or ignored as being a normal course of aging or chronic disease progression.

For all clients, misdiagnosis or the absence of a proper medical diagnosis can have devastating effects. When a client is acting extremely agitated and uncooperative, the practitioner should find out if this type of behavior is characteristic of any other time in the client's life. If it is not, it is possible the behaviors could be related to an unknown trauma such as a closed head injury. Furthermore, nonrecognition of the medical aspects of a substance disorder could also result in severe legal, ethical, and malpractice considerations. This makes it essential for non-medically trained practitioners to have some background in the medical conditions and the particular influence these conditions can have on mental health conditions such as the addictive disorders.

To ensure diagnostic assessment and screening inquiries that will help to identify the relationship that medical factors can have on mental health–related behaviors, Pollak et al. (1999) suggest following several guidelines. First, the practitioner

Box 5: Axis III Categories

General Medical Conditions

Diseases of the Nervous System
Diseases of the Circulatory System
Diseases of the Respiratory System
Neoplasms
Endocrine Diseases
Nutritional Diseases
Metabolic Diseases
Diseases of the Digestive System
Genitourinary System Diseases
Hematological Diseases
Diseases of the Eye
Diseases of the Ear, Nose, and Throat
Musculoskeletal System and Connective Tissue Diseases
Diseases of the Skin
Congenital Malformations, Deformations, and Chromosomal Abnormalities
Diseases of Pregnancy, Childbirth, and the Puerperium
Infectious Diseases
Overdose
Medication-Induced Disorders

Source: Compiled from the *DSM-IV-TR* (American Psychiatric Association, 2000). See Appendix B of the *DSM-IV-TR* for the complete list of general medical conditions and their *ICD-9-CM* codes.

should look for risk factors and determine whether the client falls into one of the high-risk groups identified above. This is very important when the individual's judgment might be further clouded by the use of a substance. Second, the practitioner should consider whether the client's presentation of his or her condition looks suspicious or inconsistent, and therefore suggestive of a medical condition. Third, after gathering initial screening information, the practitioner should decide whether further testing is warranted to address a physical or medical basis for the symptoms the client is experiencing. A physical exam should always be considered. If the date of the client's last physical exam cannot be verified, and the practitioner is not sure whether the condition is medically based, referral for a physical exam should be made. As a general rule, whenever a substance addiction is suspected, a medical clearance is needed. Note that, once a referral is made, the physician will need a signed release from the client so that he or she may share patient information with the substance addictions practitioner. Practitioners should also use client information from any previous history and physical exams, medical history summaries, radiological reports, or lab findings in their assessment. Remember that,

---

Box 6: Clinical Presentations Not Reflective of a Medical Disorder

◆ Previous psychosocial difficulties that are not directly related to a medical disorder.

◆ Chronic unrelated complaints that cannot be linked to a satisfactory medical explanation.

◆ A history of relationship problems such as help-rejecting behavior, codependency, and other interrelationship problems.

◆ A puzzling lack of concern on the part of the client as to the behaviors he or she is engaging in, with a tendency to minimize or deny the circumstances.

◆ Evidence of secondary gain where the client behaviors are reinforced by significant others, family, or members of the support system.

◆ A history of or current substance use and dependence problems, including prescription and nonprescription substances.

◆ A family history of similar symptoms or mental disorders.

◆ Cognitive or physical complaints that are more severe than what would be expected for someone in a similar situation.

Source: Adapted from Dziegielewski (2002).

---

although the mental health practitioner can assist in helping to identify and document medical conditions, the original diagnosis of any such medical condition always rests with the physician or other trained medical personnel.

Pollak et al. (1999) offer several additional suggestions that can help the practitioner complete the diagnostic assessment for Axis III. First, give special attention to clients who present with the first episode of a major disorder. In these clients, particularly when symptoms are severe (e.g., the client is psychotic, catatonic, or nonresponsive), close monitoring of the original presentation, as compared with previous behavior, is essential.

Second, note if the client's symptoms are acute (have just started or are relative to a certain situation) or abrupt with rapid changes in mood or behavior. Examples include both cognitive and behavioral symptoms such as marked apathy, decreased drive and initiative, paranoia, lability or mood swings, and poorly controlled impulses.

Third, the practitioner should pay particular attention when the initial onset of a problem or serious symptoms occurs after age forty. Although this is not an ironclad rule, most mental disorders become evident before age forty. Thus, onset of symptoms after forty should be carefully examined to rule out social stressors, situational stressors, cultural implications, and medical causes.

Fourth, note symptoms of a mental disorder that occur immediately preceding, during, or after the onset of a major medical illness. The symptoms may be related to the progression of the medical condition or may be medication or substance related (Dziegielewski & Leon, 2001). Polypharmacy can be a real problem for individuals who are unaware of the dangers of mixing certain medications with substances that they do not consider harmful (i.e., herbal preparations) (Dziegielewski, 2001).

Fifth, when gathering information for the diagnostic assessment, note whether there is an immediate psychosocial stressor or life circumstance that may be contributing to the symptoms the client is experiencing, especially when substance use increases. This is especially relevant when the stressors present are so minimal that a clear connection between the stressor and the reaction cannot be made. Also, if the client presents with extreme symptoms relative to the presenting problem with no previous history of such behaviors, attention and monitoring for medical causes is essential. It is also possible the substance being used may cover up medical problems.

Sixth, pay particular attention in the screening process when a client suffers from a variety of types of hallucinations. Basically, a hallucination is the misperception of a stimulus. In psychotic conditions, auditory hallucinations are most common, but they may also be visual (seeing things are not there), tactile (feeling things that are not there, such as bugs crawling on the skin), gustatory (affecting the sense of taste), or olfactory (affecting the sense of smell). A presentation of multiple types of hallucinations is generally too extreme to be purely a mental health condition. Watch in particular for clients who complain of tactile hallucinations. During withdrawal from alcohol, for example, it is common for such symptoms to occur.

Seventh, note any simple, repetitive, and purposeless speech (e.g., stuttering or indistinct or unintelligible speech), movements of the face (e.g., motor tightness or tremors), and movements of the extremities (e.g., tremors, shaking, or unsteady gait). Also note any experiential phenomena such as derealization, depersonalization, or unexplained gastric or medical complaints and symptoms such as new onset of headache accompanied by physical signs such as nausea and vomiting.

Eighth, note signs of cortical brain dysfunction such as aphasia (language disturbance), apraxia (movement disturbance), agnosia (failure to recognize familiar objects despite intact sensory functioning), and visual constructional deficits (problems drawing or reproducing objects and patterns).

And finally, note any signs that may be associated with organ failure such as jaundice, which may be related to hepatic disease, or dyspnea (difficulty breathing), which may be associated with cardiac or pulmonary disease. For example, if a client is not getting proper oxygen, he or she may present as very confused and disoriented—signs and symptoms that would quickly subside if the oxygen were regulated.

Although practitioners skilled in the area of substance addiction are not expected to be experts in diagnosing medical disorders, being aware of the medical complications that can influence mental health presentations is necessary to facilitate the most accurate and complete diagnostic assessment possible.

All relevant medical conditions should be listed on Axis III. Medical conditions are relevant when (1) the mental disorder appears to have a physiological relationship or bearing on any mental health condition, including the substance addiction disorders coded on Axis I, the personality disorders coded on Axis II, or both; and (2) the medical condition actually causes or facilitates and is part of the reason for the development and continuation of the substance addiction. One sure way to establish this relationship is to discover that when the general medical condition is resolved, the mental health condition is resolved as well. Although conclusive, such a determination does not always happen so easily. For example, the damage from the general medical condition may not be curable. Regardless, it is important to document all related medical conditions when forming a diagnosis. For example, if an individual suffers from dementia of the Alzheimer's type, which is coded on Axis I, then it is expected that a medical cause for the dementia (e.g., Alzheimer's disease) would be coded on Axis III. Similarly, when a mental disorder due to a general medical condition is coded on Axis I, the medical condition that caused it should be reported on both Axis I and Axis III.

When making an Axis III diagnosis, practitioners may find it helpful to receive support from an interdisciplinary or multidisciplinary team that includes a medical professional. Individuals who have training in the medical aspects of disease and illness can be valuable resources in understanding this mind body connection.

In summary, before an Axis III diagnosis is recorded, there should always be some hard evidence to support its inclusion. The practitioner should query whether a recent history and physical has been conducted and when one is available review the written summary, which can be helpful in identifying medical conditions that may be related to the symptoms and behaviors a client is exhibiting. Also, as stated earlier, if a physical exam has not been conducted prior the assessment, it is always a good idea to either refer the client for a physical or suggest that the client see a physician for a routine examination. Furthermore, a review of the medical information available such as lab reports, including drug screens and other findings as well as consulting with a medical professional may also be helpful in identifying disorders that could complicate or prevent the client from achieving improved mental health. When utilizing this axis mental health practitioners should be prepared to inquire into the signs and symptoms of these conditions and to assist in understanding the relationship of this medical condition to the diagnostic assessment and planning process that will evolve.

Box 7: Questions to Guide the Process—Axis III

- Has the client had a recent physical exam?
- Does the client have a summary of a recent history and physical exam that could be reviewed?
- Are there any laboratory findings, tests, or diagnostic reports such as drug screen information that can assist in establishing a relationship between a medical condition and the presenting mental and physiological symptoms?
- Does the client have any problems with hearing or vision?

AXIS IV

The practitioner should use Axis IV to assess the severity of the psychosocial and environmental stressors clients have experienced over the last year. Axis IV is particularly relevant when one considers how these stressors can directly or indirectly influence mental health problems and symptoms. Both the *DSM-IV* and the *DSM-IV-TR* include a list of stressors that contribute to overall life stress. These stressors can be further clarified by listing the specific problem that results. The practitioner should discern how long each stressor has been prevalent. An acute stressor has a better prognosis for recovery. In the area of substance addiction, coding this area is essential because life circumstances can increase the signs and symptoms exhibited.

Box 8: Axis IV Categories

Psychosocial and Environmental Problems

Problems with Primary Support
Problems Related to Social Environment
Educational Problems
Occupational Problems
Substance Use Problems
Economic Problems
Problems Accessing Health Care Services
Homelessness or Lack of Stable Living Situation
Problems Related to Interaction with the Legal System
Other Psychosocial Problems

Source: Compiled from the *DSM-IV-TR* (American Psychiatric Association, 2000).

AXIS V

On Axis V, the practitioner should rate the client's psychosocial and occupational functioning for the last year using a scale known as the Generalized Assessment of Functioning (GAF). Over the years, this scale has gained importance because it can be used to support the diagnostic information (Dziegielewski, 2002). Therefore, an increasing number of professionals are turning to the *DSM-IV-TR* and the GAF independent of the multiaxial diagnostic system as an aid for measuring and documenting client behaviors. Use of the GAF supports the current movement to enhance diagnostic assessments by responding to the pressure to incorporate additional forms of measurement as part of the treatment plan (Dziegielewski, 1997). This pressure to achieve evidence-based practice gears the practitioner toward efforts that go beyond traditional documentation, thereby leading to the incorporation of factors related to the individual and his or her family and social ranking (Dziegielewski & Roberts, 2004). These factors are now included in the GAF, a reporting scale that allows the practitioner to monitor a client's functioning over time and can be clearly supported through direct client observation and recording.

In both the *DSM-IV* and the *DSM-IV-TR*, the GAF is a 100-point scale, with lower numbers indicating lower functioning (e.g., 1 = minimal functioning, 100 = highest level of functioning). But several changes related to the GAF have been made between the *DSM-IV* and the *DSM-IV-TR*. These modifications include (1) changes to the instructions for using the scale; (2) minor changes and clarification in how to record multiple scores on the scale (i.e., past, current, at discharge); and (3) the addition of a function component reflective of the score range (Dziegielewski, 2002).

The GAF can help the practitioner both to quantify client problems and to document observable changes that may be attributable to the intervention efforts by allowing him or her to assign a number that represents a client's behaviors. The practitioner can then track performance variations across behaviors relative to client functioning. Score comparisons can provide helpful diagnostic information. For example, the practitioner can gather information about the client's level of functioning over the last year, upon admission or start of treatment (current level of functioning), and at discharge or termination. Although the *DSM-IV* called for all assessments of a client's functioning, current and past, to record the highest level of functioning observed, the *DSM-IV-TR* encourages practitioners to also note the lowest level of functioning assessed during the weeks prior to hospitalization or initiation of service. When assessing functioning at other times (over the last year or at termination), however, the practitioner should still note the highest level of functioning.

The *DSM-IV-TR* also gives more detailed instructions on how to apply the GAF. First, starting at the top of the scale (with the numbers that denote the highest level of functioning possible), compare the behaviors that the client is exhibiting to the sample behaviors listed in each category. Second, compare the individual's current level of functioning or severity of the behaviors with the category descriptions. (Note that, when working with the substance addictions, special attention must be given to those with dependence and potential withdrawal. These individuals may actually assess better than their true functioning level due to the body having become accustomed to the use of the substance.) If the behaviors are more severe than those outlined in the category description, move to the next lower category. The practitioner should always assign the score most relevant to the client's behavior. If the severity of the symptoms and the level of functioning differ, the score assigned should represent the more dysfunctional aspect. Third, to determine the appropriate number from the range associated with the most relevant category, consider whether the individual's symptoms and level of functioning are at the high or low end of the range. The exact number (e.g., GAF = 45 [current]) identifies the relationship between the symptoms and level of functioning. A GAF score within the range of 41 to 50 is often considered indicative of inpatient admission. According to the criteria for this range, individuals assigned a score between 41 and 50 are experiencing serious symptoms that disturb functioning. When a client exhibits behaviors that fall into this range, the behaviors need to be clearly identified.

Most professionals are not expected to memorize the GAF, and the entire scale is listed in the *DSM-IV-TR*. But practitioners may want to keep a copy of the GAF on hand for quick reference. Also, it is strongly suggested that, when working as part of an interdisciplinary or multidisciplinary team, all members sit down with a copy of the GAF and outline what behaviors would fall into which score range based on the specific population being served. This is especially important when working in the area of addictions. The connection between the behavior and level of functioning needs to be specified because a client's GAF score may be used to justify the need for additional testing or assessment (Pollak et al., 1999).

Supplements to Axis V

In the *DSM-IV* section entitled "Criteria Sets and Axes Provided for Further Study," there are two scales that are not required for diagnosis. But use of these scales can provide a format for ranking function that can be particularly helpful in

---

Box 9: Practice Exercise—GAF, GARF, and SOFAS

One of the hardest problems practitioners confront when using therapist-driven scales such as the GAF, the GARF, and the SOFAS is ensuring that the documented behaviors are relevant to the clients being served. To facilitate documentation of client behaviors in the population you serve, try the following exercise.

1. Ask to host an in-service training or to provide a segment of continuing education for your agency, inviting members of the interdisciplinary team or, if you do not use a team approach, other colleagues and practitioners who work with the same population group as you. If you are working alone, try the same exercise by yourself.
2. Provide a copy of the GAF, the GARF, and the SOFAS for each person who will be attending.
3. Lead the discussion and start with the GAF. For your population group, what behaviors do the majority of the clients served exhibit that represent each category? What are the problem-solving skills these individuals would have? What type of organizational skills would they have? What type of emotional climate would be expected from them? Starting at the top of the scale provides the perfect opportunity for participants to focus on client strengths and what they mean in terms of future progress and success.
4. Once the group has agreed on client behaviors and skills for each category of the GAF, do the same for the GARF and the SOFAS. Because coding on the GAF is considered mandatory, it is best to complete it first before moving on to the other measures.

Source: Adapted from Dziegielewski (2002).

the area of addictions. The first of these optional scales is the relational functioning scale termed the Global Assessment of Relational Functioning (GARF). This index is used to address the status of family or other ongoing relationships on a hypothetical continuum from competent to dysfunctional. The second index is the Social and Occupational Functioning Assessment Scale (SOFAS). With this scale, an "individual's level of social and occupational functioning that is not directly influenced by overall severity of the individual's psychological symptoms" can be addressed (American Psychiatric Association, 1994, p. 760). The complementary nature of these scales for identifying and assessing client problems is evident in the fact that all three scales—the GAF, the GARF, and the SOFAS—use the same rating system. The rankings for each scale range from 0 to 100, with lower numbers representing more severe problems. In the area of addictions, these scales provide a viable framework within which practitioners can apply concrete measures to a wide variety of practice situations. They also provide a multidimensional perspective that permits workers to document variations in levels of functioning across individual (GAF), family (GARF), and social (SOFAS) systems. The same method of scoring as described for the GAF should be applied when using the GARF and the SOFAS.

Standardized Measurements

The GAF, the GARF, and the SOFAS are considered therapist-driven assessments—that is, the practitioner uses clinical judgment to interpret all clinical information regarding symptom severity and level of functioning and to determine the appropriate score. Therefore, it is sound practice to also consider using other standardized assessments to supplement the diagnostic assessment and to provide evidence for the development of operationally based terms and methods that have been empirically demonstrated to be effective (Mullen & Bacon, 2004). During the diagnostic assessment, reporting of symptom behaviors related to substance use, such as stress, anxiety, and depression, are avoided, with a greater emphasis placed on problem behaviors that are clearly and operationally defined. Standardized instruments can assist in this process, and it is the responsibility of the practitioner to select, implement, and evaluate the appropriateness of the measurement instruments. Most professionals agree that standardized scales (i.e., those that have been assessed for reliability and validity) are generally preferred.

In the area of addictions, a greater emphasis is placed on accuracy and objectivity in all attempts to measure commonly encountered clinical problems. The most notable development in this regard has been the emergence of numerous brief pencil-and-paper assessment devices known as rapid assessment instruments (RAIs). As standardized measures, RAIs share a number of characteristics. They are brief, relatively easy to administer, score, and interpret, and require very little knowledge of testing procedures on the part of the clinician. For the most part, they are self-report measures that can be completed by the client, usually within fifteen minutes. They are independent of any particular theoretical orientation and as such can be used with a variety of intervention methods. Because RAIs provide a systematic overview of the client's problem, they often stimulate discussion related to the information they elicit. The score that is generated provides an operational index of the frequency, duration, or intensity of the problem. Most RAIs can be used as repeated measures and thus are adaptable to the methodological requirements of both research design and goal assessment. In addition to providing a standardized means by which change can be monitored over time with a single client, RAIs can also be used to make equivalent comparisons across clients experiencing a common problem (e.g., depression and marital conflict).

One of the major advantages of standardized RAIs is the availability of information concerning their reliability and validity. Reliability refers to the stability of a measure—in other words, the extent to which the questions that make up the instrument mean the same thing to the individual when answering them at different times and the extent to which different individuals interpret those same questions in a similar manner. Unless an instrument yields consistent data, it is impossible for it to be valid. But even highly reliable instruments are of little value unless their validity can be demonstrated. Validity speaks to the general question of whether an instrument measures what it purports to measure. Information concerning reliability and validity, as well as other factors related to the standardization process (e.g., the procedures for administering, scoring, and interpreting the instrument), can help professionals make informed judgments concerning the appropriateness of any given instrument. The key to selecting the best instrument to facilitate the diagnostic assessment is knowing where and how to access the relevant information concerning potentially useful measures (Hudson, 1990). Fortunately, there are a number of excellent sources available to the clinician to facilitate this process.

Two such compilations of standardized measures are *Measures for Clinical Practice*, by Corcoran and Fischer (1999), and *Sourcebook of Adult Assessment Strategies*, by Schutte and Malouff (1995). These reference texts can serve as valuable resources for identifying useful rapid assessment instruments suited for the kinds of problems most commonly encountered in mental health practice. Corcoran and Fischer have done an excellent job, not only in identifying and evaluating a viable cross-section of useful, clinically grounded instruments but also in discussing a number of issues critical to their use. Schutte and Malouff provide a list of mental health–related measures for adults and guidelines for their use with different types of practice-related problems. In addition to providing an introduction to the basic principles of measurement, these books discuss various types of measurement tools, including the advantages and disadvantages of RAIs. Corcoran and Fischer also provide some useful guidelines for locating, selecting, evaluating, and administering prospective measures. Corcoran and Fischer divide the instruments across two volumes in relation to their appropriateness for use with one of three target populations: adults, children, and couples and families. They are also cross-indexed by problem area, which makes the selection process for instruments related to the addictive disorders and subsequent mental health problems very easy.

To assist with the identification of conditions relevant to Axis III (general medical conditions) and Axis IV (psychosocial stressors), it is helpful to outline a detailed family and health history as well as a checklist of neuropsychiatric complaints and symptoms. Health status instruments such as the SF-36 (Ware & Sherbourne, 1992) can be used to identify physical and social functioning difficulties as well as psychiatric problems. The use of these and other similar instruments related to the substance addictions greatly enhances the practitioner's options with respect to monitoring and evaluation practice. Overall, the RAIs can serve as valuable adjuncts for all evaluation efforts.

In summary, working with individuals who suffer from an addiction is complex, and all information gathered as part of the diagnostic assessment needs to provide the basis for the treatment planning and strategy to follow. The practitioner should always consider incorporating RAIs as tools designed to supplement direct behavioral observation techniques.

ETHICAL AND LEGAL CONSIDERATIONS

All professions require that their members' activities and judgments fall within an ethical and legal framework. If a member's activities or judgments fall outside of this framework, he or she may be charged with malpractice—that is, negligence in the exercise of one's profession. Practitioners in the area of addictions, as in any other practice area, should therefore always remain (1) aware of the rules and requirements that govern professional practice activity in their state and (2) well versed in their profession's code of ethics, which represents the moral consensus of the profession. Helping professionals should not assume that their ethical practice will be apparent from their adherence to their professional code of ethics alone.

Client information that is accurate and carefully documented and reflects the nature of the ethical client services provided can be the best way for mental health practitioners to protect themselves against charges of malpractice. Practitioner documents must ensure client confidentiality and privacy. One helpful rule is to remember that at any time, all records may be subpoenaed into a court of law. There, private client information, even information not related to the legal matter under consideration, may be divulged.

Regardless of their employment setting, all helping professionals should consider maintaining personal malpractice insurance in addition to what may be provided through agency auspices. Even with the best of intentions, practitioners may find themselves in legal proceedings defending the content of notes, subjective assessments, or terminology used in the diagnostic assessment. As a rule, practitioners should record objective data and refrain from using terminology that may be subjective in nature (i.e., what they think is happening). When documenting, they should always use direct client statements and never document hearsay or make interpretations based on subjective data. Practitioners need to be familiar with any state statutes that prohibit professionals from eliciting or documenting specific client information. In record keeping, the practitioner will always bear the ultimate legal and ethical responsibility of all written diagnostic and assessment-based notes.

TIPS FOR COMPREHENSIVE DIAGNOSTIC ASSESSMENT FOR SUBSTANCE ADDICTIONS

The first task for completion of a comprehensive diagnostic assessment is to identify the individual's need for treatment. The severity of the condition must then be evaluated. This evaluation must be based on the formal criteria outlined in the *DSM-IV-TR*. The professional should also note other relevant issues presented by the individual being assessed (e.g., medical problems and nutritional status). If a medical condition is suspected or the client has not had a physical exam recently, a referral for one should be made. A medical history should be compiled, including information on previous illnesses, infectious diseases, and physical or medical traumas, as well as past and present history of sexually transmitted diseases. The assessment should include direct questions that focus on high-risk behaviors such as IV drug use and unsafe sex practices. Also important are questions regarding past mental health, such as, Does the individual have a history of depression? Has he or she ever attempted suicide?

The addictions practitioner must also evaluate the client's history of substance use. This evaluation must document his or her use of illicit substances and over-the-counter medications, as well as prescription drugs. The client's use of legal drugs such as alcohol, caffeine, and nicotine should also be evaluated. The practitioner should make sure to document the client's age at onset of the use of these substances as well as the duration of use, pattern of use, and mode of ingestion. He or she should also document whether the client has received substance abuse treatment in the past, including that offered by twelve-step programs such as Alcoholics Anonymous (AA) or Narcotics Anonymous (NA).

In addition to screening for individual and medical issues, the practitioner must recognize the importance of the client's level of peer group, family, and social functioning. Individuals who suffer from addictive disorders often have strained peer and family relationships and do not recognize that these potentially problematic relationships could cause serious setbacks in the intervention process. The practitioner should complete a peer and family assessment that outlines the social dynamics and potential present and future factors that could interfere with or support the recovery process. Questions regarding peer relationships can help the practitioner better understand the client's interpersonal coping skills. Documentation of the client's family history should include information about family members and identified significant others within the client's support system and should indicate whether substance abuse is evidenced within this support system. The practitioner should assess the client's current financial and housing conditions—Does client have stable housing, or is he or she homeless? Does the client have stable and gainful employment? The practitioner should also assess school performance and peer group relationships when dealing with adolescents—What are the client's grades? What do the client's peers/parents think of his or her substance use?

A complete biopsychosocial/spiritual assessment will document the above-mentioned information while also identifying any positive coping behaviors the client exhibits. This includes assessing resiliency factors such as self-esteem, family ties, spirituality, community supports, and motivation for treatment. Once these strengths are clearly identified, they should be applied to the development and implementation of an appropriate treatment plan. The following chapters address assessment and intervention strategies in depth.

Box 10: General Guidelines for Comprehensive Diagnostic Assessment of Substance Addictions

- ◆ Clearly identify the addictive disorder, with particular attention to the severity of the disorder and how it is impairing personal, occupational, and social functioning.
- ◆ Gather a comprehensive history, taking into account medical factors and risk behaviors, as well as peer, family, and social supports.
- ◆ Identify problems or factors that will need to be addressed to ensure client safety.
- ◆ Formulate a plan of action to address the problem areas.
- ◆ Establish a means of monitoring and follow-up for all intervention strategies.
- ◆ Seek to help the individual develop a support system that will assist in addressing problem behaviors.

As contended throughout this book, outcomes-based practice expectations have changed the basis for all interventions with the addictive disorders. Process and outcome evaluations are now routinely performed in professional practice and by supporting agencies. Determinations regarding program continuations are made as a result of evaluative studies. The future of funding decisions and continuing employment now depends on achieving a certain percentage of positive measurable outcomes with the clientele served.

For the practitioner, every effort must be made to assess client problems affecting therapeutic outcome. Untreated or unrecognized addictions can unfavorably affect treatment outcomes. Better education can lead to better evaluation and screening for things other than the presenting problem. This can lead to more control of positive outcomes for the practitioner and the agency, and better services and therapeutic outcomes for the clients.

The field of substance abuse and dependence and the disorders related to these concerns are diverse, with practitioners coming into contact with a multitude of client populations. In practice, most health and mental health practitioners will work for agencies that either directly or indirectly service persons with addictions disorders (Gassman, Demone, & Albilal, 2001). To adequately serve the individual who suffers from a substance abuse or dependence disorder, a proper diagnostic assessment is the crucial starting point for all subsequent interventions.

This chapter is designed to introduce the reader to the general terms related to the substance abuse and use disorders. The categories of abuse, dependence, intoxication, and withdrawal are quite extensive and can be elaborated beyond the boundaries of this chapter. The factors related to substance use and abuse are often varied, as are individual reactions to the use of a substance. Many individuals may be addicted to more than one substance, and thus adequate assessment and intervention will require knowledge of multiple synergistic and interaction effects on the part of the practitioner. The purpose of this chapter is to help the practitioner understand the categories of multiaxial diagnostic assessment, to prepare the practitioner to become knowledgeable in all substances of use, and to form a solid background for the use of diagnostic assessment and subsequent intervention strategies. Each subsequent chapter will provide a more detailed explanation of the categories and foundations of diagnostic assessment and intervention in the area of addictions, establishing fertile ground for greater agreement and future advancement in the field of substance-related disorders.

In the addictions field, depending on the practice setting, the multiaxial diagnostic assessment sometimes may not seem appropriate. For some practitioners, especially those who work with substance-abusing youth in specialized settings such as assisted residential care, formal diagnostic assessment with diagnostic-related treatment plans might not be required. This is particularly true when intervention efforts focus directly on problem solving and on helping individuals gain the resources they need to improve their functioning. When a formal system is not needed, the practitioner can still provide uniform documentation by listing the diagnostic categories that apply to the client, with the principal diagnosis or reason for visit cited first, the substance abuse disorders and other mental disorders that interfere with functioning cited second, and the client's general medical conditions cited third.

CONCLUDING COMMENTS

The underlying premise of this book is that no one makes a conscious, educated decision to be an addict. No person can be certain of what reaction will transpire when he or she takes that first drink, puff, or pill. Effects vary among individuals; some reactions are difficult and in some cases irreversible. All of the authors who have contributed to this book agree that it is critical for professionals not to criticize, judge, or devalue the individuals who suffer from an addictive disorder, just as one would not judge individuals who have serious allergies, cancer, heart disease, or diabetes. For the most part, the latter are medical conditions that do not affect the person's personality, cognitive abilities, or ability to reason. But in the addictive disorders, there is a clear relationship between mind and body, which affects the person as a whole, both in medical and the mental aspects of functioning. In the field of addictions, strides toward helping the individual with a substance addiction will come faster when the barricades of shame, discrimination, and marginalization of services, funds, and support for the victims of addictions are knocked down.

The practitioner skilled in addictions must be aware of how to best proceed with a diagnostic assessment that follows the multiaxial assessment system. All practitioners are being called on to become more knowledgeable in the use of diagnostic tests that support practice strategy (Frances et al., 1991; Frances, Pincus, Widiger, Davis, & First, 1990; Siegelman, 1990). Equipped with a basic knowledge of the use and misuse of the *DSM-IV-TR*, the practitioner can more constructively participate in the consultation process. This knowledge can enhance the client's overall functioning level. Because practitioners often have regular contact with their clients during and even after treatment, they can be essential in helping the interdisciplinary team to reexamine or reformulate original diagnostic impressions and understand the effect these impressions can have on the client's potential for a positive treatment outcome. The addictions practitioner is keenly aware of the client's environment and the importance of building and maintaining therapeutic rapport. On an interdisciplinary team, this makes the practitioner's input in understanding the substance disorder an essential contribution to intervention effectiveness. The practitioner remains in a key position to allay the client's and his or her family's fears as well as elicit their help and support (Bernheim, 1992).

References

American Psychiatric Association. (2000). *Diagnostic and statistical manual of mental disorders* (4th ed., text rev.). Washington, DC: Author.

Bernheim, K. (1992). Supportive family counseling. *Schizophrenia Bulletin, 8.*

Browning, C. H., & Browning, B. J. (1996). *How to partner with managed care.* Los Calamitous, CA: Duncliff's International.

Carlton, T. O. (1984). *Clinical social work in health care settings: A guide to professional practice with exemplars.* New York: Springer.

Ciminero, A. R., Calhoun, K. S., & Adams, H. E. (1986). *Handbook of behavioral assessment* (2nd ed.). New York: John Wiley & Sons.

Corcoran, K., & Fischer, J. (1999). *Measure of clinical practice: A sourcebook. Vol. 1. Couples, families, and children* (3rd ed.); *Vol. 2. Adults* (3rd ed.). New York: Free Press.

Dziegielewski, S. F. (1997). Time limited brief therapy: The state of practice. *Crisis Intervention and Time-Limited Treatment, 3*(3), 217–28.

Dziegielewski, S. F. (2001). Social work practice and herbal medicine. In A. Roberts & G. Greene (Eds.), *Social work desk reference* (pp. 651–57). New York: Oxford.

Dziegielewski, S. F. (2002). *DSM-IV-TR in action.* New York: John Wiley & Sons.

Dziegielewski, S. F., & Green, C. E. (2004). Concepts essential to clinical practice. In S. F. Dziegielewski (Ed.), *The changing face of health care practice: Professional practice in managed behavioral healthcare* (pp. 107–32). New York: Springer.

Dziegielewski, S. F., & Leon, A. M. (2001). *Psychopharmacology and social work practice.* New York: Springer.

Dziegielewski, S. F., & Powers, G. T. (2000). Designs and procedures for evaluating crisis intervention. In A. R. Roberts (Ed.), *Crisis intervention handbook: Assessment, treatment and research* (2nd ed.). New York: Oxford.

Dziegielewski, S. F., & Roberts, A. R. (2004). Health care evidence-based practice: A product of political and cultural times. In A. R. Roberts & K. R. Yeager (Eds.), *Evidence-based practice manual* (pp. 200–205). New York: Oxford.

Encyclopedia of drugs, alcohol, and addictive behavior. (2001). Vol. 2. E–Q (2nd ed.). New York: Macmillan & Gale Group.

Engel, G. (1977). The need for a new medical model: A challenge to biomedical science. *Science, 19*, 129–36.

Frager, S. (2000). *Managing managed care*. New York: John Wiley & Sons.

Frances, A., Pincus, H., Davis, W.W., Kline, M., First, M., & Widiger, T. (1991). The DSM field trials: Moving towards an empirically derived classification. *European Psychiatry, 6*, 307–14.

Frances, A., Pincus, H. A., Widiger, T. A., Davis, W. W., & First, M. B. (1990). DSM-IV: Work in progress. *American Journal of Psychiatry, 147*, 1439–48.

Gassman, R. A., Demone, H. W., & Albilal, R. (2001, Winter). Alcohol and other drug content in core courses: encouraging substance abuse assessment. *Journal of Social Work Education, 37*(1), 137.

Gilbert, P. (2002). Understanding the biopsychosocial approach: Conceptualization. *Clinical Psychology, 14*, 13–17.

Hartmann, D. E. (1995). *Neuropsychological toxicology* (2nd ed.). New York: Plenum Press.

Hudson, W. W. (1990). *The WALMYR assessment scale scoring manual*. Tempe, AZ: WALMYR.

Kaplan, H. I., & Sadock, B. J. (1998). *Synopsis of psychiatry*. Baltimore: Lippincott, Williams, & Wilkins.

Maxmen, J. S., & Ward, N. G. (1995). Schizophrenia and related disorders. In J. S. Maxmen & N. G. Ward (Eds.), *Essential psychopathology and its treatment* (pp. 173–94). New York: W. W. Norton.

McGrady, B. S., & Epstein, E. E. (Eds.). (1999). *Addictions: A comprehensive guidebook*. New York: Oxford University Press.

McWhinney, I. R. (1989). *A textbook of family medicine*. New York: Oxford University Press.

Miller, N. S. (1997). *The principles and practice of addictive actions in psychiatry*. Philadelphia: W. B. Saunders.

Mitchell, R. W. (1991). *Documentation in counseling records*. Washington, DC: American College Association.

Mullen, E. J., & Bacon, W. (2004). Implementation of practice guidelines and evidence-based treatment. In A. R. Roberts & K. R. Yeager (Eds.), *Evidence-based practice manual* (pp. 210–26). New York: Oxford.

Pollak, J., Levy, S., & Breitholtz, T. (1999). Screening for medical and neurodevelopmental disorders for the professional counselor. *Journal of Counseling Development, 77*, Summer, 350–57.

Rock, B. D. (2002). Social work in health care for the 21st century: The biopsychosocial model. In A. R. Roberts & G. J. Greene (Eds.), *Social workers' desk reference* (pp. 10–15). New York: Oxford University Press.

Rudman, W. J. (2000). *Coding and documentation of domestic violence*. Retrieved January 3, 2004, from http://fvpf.org/programs/display.php3?DocID=54

Rudolph, C. S. (2000). Educational challenges facing health care social workers in the twenty-first century. *Professional Development, 3J*(1), 31–41.

Schutte, N. S., & Malouff, J. M. (1995). *Sourcebook of adult assessment strategies*. New York: Plenum Press.

Sheafor, B. W., Horejsi, C. R., & Horejsi, G. A. (1997). *Techniques and guidelines for social work practice* (4th ed.). Needham Heights, MA: Allyn & Bacon.

Siegelman, L. (1990). *Selecting effective treatments*. San Francisco: Jossey-Bass.

Spraycar, M. (Ed.). (1995). *Physician's desk reference: Medical dictionary* (1st ed.). Montvale, NJ: Medical Economics.

Wambach, K. G., Haynes, D. T., & White, B. W. (1999). Practice guidelines: Rapprochement or estrangement between social work practitioners and researchers. *Research on Social Work Practice, 9*(3), 322–30.

Ware, J. E., & Sherbourne, C. D. (1992). The MOS 36-item short-form health survey (SF-36): Conceptual framework and item selection. *Medical Care, 30*(2), 473–83.

World Health Organization. (1992). *The ICD-10 classification of mental and behavioral disorders*. Geneva, Switzerland: Office of Publications, World Health Organization.

Central Nervous System Stimulants

A psychoactive substance is any substance that directly affects the normal functioning of the central nervous system. Stimulants are psychoactive substances that boost the functioning of the central nervous system. Taking these substances usually causes excessive stimulation to the central nervous system that can result in medical problems such as increased heart rate, increased blood pressure, insomnia, decreased need for sleep, and decreased appetite. These effects are not always negative, however; stimulants can be used clinically to treat medical problems such as narcolepsy, obesity, and attention deficit disorder. But when they become substances of addiction, the results can be devastating and possibly lethal.

The chapters in this section provide an overview of the four stimulants that practitioners in the field of substance addictions most commonly encounter, and review the devastating effects that can result from abuse of and addiction to these substances. Chapters 3 and 4 cover amphetamines and their more potent derivative, methamphetamines (aka meth, ice, speed, and crank) and cocaine (aka freebase and crack). These are often considered "top shelf" or "top of the line" stimulants. Although individuals addicted to these strong substances often experience dilated pupils and easily become angry and aggressive, reactions to use are unpredictable. Sometimes the individual may feel more confident, eager, and outgoing. At other times, particularly as the dosages increase, these feelings may change to paranoia, anxiety, an inability to experience pleasure (anhedonia), and confusion. Chronic use of these stimulants can also result in blunted affect, apathy, avolition, and difficulty in abstract thinking. Correspondingly, it can also result in synaptic neuronal sensitivity, manifested by extreme symptoms such as delusions, hallucinations, and disorganized speech or behavior. When used regularly, these substances can exhaust the user and upset the body's natural balance.

Caffeine and nicotine, discussed in chapters 5 and 6, are known as "Bottom shelf" stimulants. Although these stimulants are considered weaker and less dangerous, let the practitioner beware: these less potent substances can cause severe problems. For example, repeated and excessive use of caffeine can lead to problems similar to those created by the stronger stimulants and can easily mimic psychosis. Furthermore, use of tobacco, the source of nicotine, is responsible for more than 400,000 deaths in the United States each year and has been linked directly with cancer, heart disease, stroke, and chronic obstructive pulmonary disease.

Although all stimulant substances share similarities in that they all stimulate the central nervous system, appropriate assessment and intervention efforts are not always the same for each. Each chapter in this section describes a particular stimulant and its psychophysiological effects; points out important considerations for the assessment and intervention phases; outlines the abuse patterns of users; and presents a case example with a sample multiaxial diagnostic assessment and intervention plan. In closing, each chapter notes special considerations regarding intervention for individuals addicted to that particular stimulant and discusses future directions for helping individuals who suffer from substance use disorders associated with it.

Chapter 3

Amphetamines

Carmen P. Chang-Arratia and Sophia F. Dziegielewski

DESPITE THE DEVASTATING EFFECTS OF AMPHETAMINE ABUSE AND ADdiction, recognition of this problem and subsequent intervention efforts remains limited. Often amphetamine addiction is treated similarly to cocaine addiction (National Institute on Drug Abuse [NIDA], 2002), although the differences between these two substances are distinct. To provide a better understanding of the relationship between amphetamines and addiction, this chapter describes the chemical composition of these drugs as it relates to the psychophysiological effects users experience. Differences between amphetamines and methamphetamines, as well as psychostimulants such as cocaine, are explained. After a detailed discussion of the abuse pattern of amphetamine users, a case example and an intervention plan using the multiaxial system are presented. Finally, the chapter highlights special considerations regarding amphetamine and methamphetamine intervention as well as future directions for helping those who suffer from addiction to these substances.

THE ORIGIN AND HISTORY OF AMPHETAMINES AND METHAMPHETAMINES

The first amphetamine was created in 1887 by the German Chemist L. Edeleano, who named the drug phenylisopropylamine (Lukas, 1985). The importance of this drug was highlighted in 1927 when it was suggested that amphetamines would be a cheaper substitute for the stimulant ephedrine, a substance derived from the Chinese herb ma huang (Klee, 1998; Snow, 1998). The first preparation of amphetamines was used in the treatment of nasal congestion and rhinitis and marketed as Benzedrine, an over-the-counter inhalant (Baberg, Nelesen, & Dimsdale, 1996; Murray, 1998). Soon after its introduction, other uses for the medication were discovered, such as treatment for lung congestion, depression, hay fever, asthma, and sleeplessness (Baberg et al., 1996; Lukas, 1985; Murray, 1998).

Pharmaceutical companies (e.g., Smith, Kline & French) developed the first amphetamine tablets in 1935 for the treatment of narcolepsy and Parkinson's disease (Baberg et al., 1996; Lukas, 1985), and by 1937, amphetamine tablets were available by prescription for the treatment of attention-deficit/hyperactivity disorder (ADHD). In the late 1930s, a list of thirty-nine clinical uses for amphetamines was introduced and included treatment of schizophrenia, head injuries, cerebral palsy, low blood pressure, persistent hiccups, seasickness, obesity, tobacco smoking, and morphine and codeine addiction. It was not uncommon for these substances to be prescribed liberally in forms such as Drinamyl, Methedrine, and Dexedrine (Baberg et al., 1996; Klee, 1998; Lukas, 1985; Murray, 1998; Snow, 1998).

In addition to the number of medical uses for amphetamines, a great number of nonmedical applications began to arise. From the 1930s through the 1970s, an increase in the use of the amphetamines occurred among university students, truck drivers, soldiers (during World War II, and later during the Korean War and the Vietnam War), businessmen, and dieters. This class of drugs was also becoming widely used as a performance enhancer (Baberg et al., 1996; Klee, 1998; Murray, 1998). At the end of World War II, stockpiles of the drug in Japan were released for sale without prescription, and it is believed that the availability of this large supply laid the foundation for abuse in that country (Murray, 1998). Japan was one of the first countries to acknowledge that amphetamine abuse had actually reached epidemic proportions among its population. This widespread abuse made it obvious that use could lead to dependence and addiction (Klee, 1998; Lukas, 1985; Murray, 1998). This trend clearly highlighted the potential for trouble, as use of these drugs increased for nonmedical purposes. Furthermore, creating and reproducing this type of stimulant was not difficult because many of its ingredients could be derived from uncontrolled legal supplies (Klee, 1998).

The first significant sign of the abuse of amphetamines in Japan, as well as the United States, occurred with the introduction of intravenous delivery of the drug (Indiana Prevention Resource Center [IPRC], 1998; Lukas, 1985; Murray, 1998). This was further complicated by the introduction of a new and more powerful derivative of the parent chemical compound of amphetamine, known as methamphetamine, which could also be taken intravenously (Koch Crime Institute [KCI], 2002; Lukas, 1985; Snow, 1998).

In 1970, the United States government enacted the Drug Abuse Regulation and Controlled Substances Act in an attempt to limit production, importation, and prescription of amphetamine and amphetamine-related substances. This act enforced the reclassification of amphetamines as Schedule II controlled substances. This means that these drugs have a medical use but only with severe restrictions because they have a high potential for abuse and their use may lead to severe psychological or physical dependence (Baberg et al., 1996; Hargreaves, 2000; IPRC, 1998; KCI, 2002; Lukas, 1985; Murray, 1998; Snow, 1998).

Today, despite the restrictions of this 1970 act, illegal drug trafficking of methamphetamines remains problematic (Hargreaves, 2000; Lukas, 1985). According to the DEA's statistics, more than 99 percent of the clandestine drug labs seized in 1999 were methamphetamine labs, and this number increased in 2000 (DEA, 2001). These labs also create environmental hazards such as explosions and fires, as well as toxic chemicals and fumes. These additional effects cause extensive damage to human health and to the environment. The cost of cleaning up these areas ranges from $3,000 to $100,000 per lab (DEA, 2001; Hargreaves, 2000; KCI, 2002). Methamphetamine production, trafficking, and abuse are predominant in the western, southwestern, and midwestern United States, with availability increasing in the southern and eastern United States (DEA, 2001; KCI, 2002). Because strong odors are produced during manufacturing, the isolation of rural areas is particularly attractive; other desirable areas include moderately sized urban communities (KCI, 2002; Rawson, Gonzales, & Brethen, 2002). Currently, importation of methamphetamine tablets through the mail system from Southeast Asia is increasing, and it is believed that the largest import market for this product in the United States is within the Asian community (DEA, 2001; Lintner, 1997; Vatikiotis, 1995). Because methamphetamine is easy to make and the effects are long lasting (eight to twenty-four hours), the market remains strong. And because it is inexpensive (one can spend 25 percent less for methamphetamine than for cocaine), it remains a powerful contender in terms of demand and marketability (Rawson et al., 2002).

The association of violent crimes, infectious diseases, and amphetamine and methamphetamine use is a focus of investigation for law enforcement and health officials worldwide (Hargreaves, 2000; Klee, 1998; Molitor et al., 1999; Stall, Paul, Barrett, Crosby, & Bein, 1999). Because amphetamines used at high dosages can produce psychotic episodes and paranoid symptoms (similar to those of schizophrenia), potential violence is a serious concern (Borowski & Kokkinidis, 1998; Hargreaves, 2000; Klee, 1998; Murphy, Fend, Russig, & Feldon, 2001; Murray, 1998; Williams, Argyropoulos, & Nutt, 2000). In addition, murder and domestic violence cases have been correlated to methamphetamine abuse (Hargreaves, 2000), and those who use amphetamines are at a greater risk for acquiring sexually transmitted infections, the human immunodeficiency virus (HIV), AIDS, Hepatitis A, B, C, and D viruses, and other blood pathogens (Hutin, Sabin, & Hutwagner, 2000; Molitor et al., 1999; NIDA, 2002; Stall et al., 1999). In the United States, methamphetamines have been associated with Hepatitis A outbreaks, primarily related to intravenous drug use or using fecally contaminated batches of the drug (Hutin et al., 2000), and other diseases related to swapping needles during intravenous drug use. Because amphetamine use has also been associated with stronger sexual excitement (Klee, 1998), individuals abusing this drug may have a greater number of sexual partners, they may be less inclined to use condoms, and they may sell sex for money or drugs. Consequently, HIV infection is three times higher among those injecting amphetamines than among injectors of other drugs (Molitor et al., 1999; Murray, 1998; SAMHSA/CSAP, 2000; Stall et al., 1999).

BIOCHEMICAL COMPOSITION AND PSYCHOPHYSIOLOGICAL EFFECTS

All drugs termed *amphetamines* (including the potent derivative methamphetamine) are chemically related (1-phenyl-2-aminopropane). They are classified as psychostimulants because they stimulate the central nervous system. These drugs are synthetically derived from a colorless liquid consisting of carbon, hydrogen, and nitrogen (Murray, 1998). Current street names for this drug are crystal, meth, speed, go fast, crank, ice, glass, crystal tea, white crosses, ludes, uppers (DEA, 2001; Murray, 1998; Lukas, 1985). Amphetamines can be smoked, snorted, injected, or taken orally (SAMHSA/CSAP, 2000; Snow, 1998). When self-administered, amphetamines increase brain activity by stimulating the excessive release of neurotransmitters (Murray, 1998; NIDA, 2002; Snow, 1998). This produces feelings of euphoria, alertness, and confidence as well as stimulant-induced psychosis, paranoia, hallucinations, mood disturbances, and a greater potential for violent behavior (Lukas, 1985; Murphy et al., 2001; Snow, 1998). Symptoms of amphetamine psychosis closely resemble those of schizophrenia; amphetamine intoxication can produce active symptoms in individuals with no genetic predisposition to the disorder (Flaum & Schultz, 1996; Snow, 1998).

The neurotransmitters most associated with the symptoms of amphetamine use are dopamine, noradrenaline, and serotonin. Dopamine is tied to the regulation of the body's physical movement, emotional behavior (especially in relation to stress), and cognitive functions (e.g., memory and abstract thinking) and to stimulating the body's natural reward system (Drug Text, 2002; KCI, 2002; Lukas, 1985; NIDA, 2002). This neurotransmitter is central to the pleasure sensation an individual experiences when using amphetamines. But with excessive amphetamine use (especially methamphetamine use), dopamine nerve terminals and nerve fibers deteriorate (Snow, 1998). This deterioration can elevate the body temperature, leading to convulsions (NIDA, 2002). Chronic use of amphetamines results in a depletion of dopamine that causes presynaptic neuronal degeneration, which may be manifested as negative symptoms (e.g., blunted affect, apathy, avolition, difficulty in abstract thinking, and social phobia) (Dziegielewski, 2002; Flaum & Schultz, 1996; Williams et al., 2000). Correspondingly, depleted dopamine levels can result in synaptic neuronal sensitivity that is manifested by extreme positive symptoms (e.g., delusions, hallucinations, disorganized speech or behavior) during transient conditions of dopamine availability (Flaum & Schultz, 1996).

Noradrenaline, also known as norepinephrine, is one of the neurotransmitters primarily responsible for the body's fight-or-flight response (Borowski & Kokkinidis, 1998; Drug Text, 2002; Lukas, 1985; NIDA, 2002; Snow, 1998). When combined with the release of the hormone and neurotransmitter adrenaline (a natural form of epinephrine found in the body), increased heart rate, blood pressure, breathing, and body temperature can result. Other effects can include constricted blood vessels, dilated pupils, and the release of sugar and fat into the bloodstream, which energizes the brain (KCI, 2002; Klee, 1998; Snow, 1998). These influences can cause increased alertness, a faster metabolism, and heightened arousal. Other symptoms include anorexic responses (lack of appetite) and restlessness (Drug Text, 2002; Lukas, 1985; SAMHSA/CSAP, 2000; Snow, 1998). It is the release of noradrenaline secondary to amphetamine use that is associated with the precipitation of paranoid psychosis (Murray, 1998).

Serotonin is one of the major neurotransmitters involved in the communication of information between neurons. Serotonin, along with dopamine and noradrenaline, initiates a system of self-regulation that prevents sensory delay while arousing motor relay; therefore, the more active this self-regulating system, the more alert the individual. Disturbances in this self-regulating system have been linked to multiple behavior problems that can lead to a loss of control, including affective disturbances, psychotic symptoms, and hyperaggressiveness (Drug Text, 2002). The disruption of this system has important implications for practitioners. When amphetamines are ingested, snorted, smoked, or injected, short-term physical and psychological effects can emerge. Attention span and activity increase, while feelings of fatigue decrease. Euphoria with a subsequent rush is commonly experienced, especially after injecting or smoking amphetamines (especially methamphetamines). The initial rush can last for five to thirty minutes; the following high can last for four to twenty-four hours (KCI, 2002; Lukas, 1985; NIDA, 2002; SAMHSA/CSAP, 2000). These euphoric effects are long lasting because amphetamines have a long half-life—50 percent of the drug still remains in the body after twelve hours (Zickler, 2001).

The major chemical reason that amphetamines are addictive has to do with their effect on dopamine levels. Like all addictive drugs, the initial pleasurable high is followed by an opposite rebound effect. Amphetamines give almost immediate pleasure. Dopamine plays an important role in the brain's reward system and thus in the biochemical foundation for drug addiction. Amphetamines not only stimulate the release of dopamine but also inhibit its natural reuptake, producing artificial feelings of pleasure (KCI, 2002; Khoshbouei, Sen, Guptaroy, Johnson, & Lind, 2004). In order to keep a balance in the system, the nerve cells adapt to the excess stimulation from amphetamine by shutting down the production of the body's natural stimulating chemistry.

Survival activities such as eating, drinking, sex, and friendship normally stimulate the body's natural dopaminergic reward system. This survival system is short-circuited when the reward center is artificially stimulated by amphetamines. The individual's confidence in the benefits of amphetamine use increases while he or she loses confidence in the normal rewards of life (KCI, 1999–2004).The effects are immediate and long lasting, but tolerance builds up very quickly, causing a need for increasing the dose to get the desired effect. During periods of nonuse, a person will recall the feeling of euphoria amphetamines provide, will crave it again, and will become dependant on the drug to avoid the "down" feeling that occurs once the drug's effects wear off ("Amphetamines," 2002; ADA, 2004).

Although amphetamine use does increase physical activity, this activity is often simple and repetitive—tapping a pencil, assembling and disassembling a project, or excessive fingering of the hair, for example (Lukas, 1985). Other short-term effects of amphetamine use are decreased appetite, excessive talkativeness, impulsivity, quickened respirations, and hyperthermia (DeWit, Crean, & Richards, 2000; Lukas, 1985; NIDA, 2002). Short-term physical symptoms include teeth grinding, dry or itchy skin, acne, sores that will not heal, numbness, impaired speech, and dizziness (KCI, 2002).

THE DEMOGRAPHICS OF ABUSERS

Research statistics demonstrate that individuals who abuse amphetamines cross all socioeconomic backgrounds. High school educated males ranging in age from 14 to 70 years, with a median age of 35.5, are most likely to abuse this substance (Baberg et al., 1996; KCI, 2002). But the median age for individuals who abuse this substance is decreasing. Youth seldom abuse these substances alone and often seek the company of friends when using (Klee, 1998; Yarnold, 1997). Many of them believe that abusing amphetamines is safer that using other drugs. The fact that an amphetamine high is longer than a cocaine high can also be enticing. The use of these substances can be particularly dangerous after drinking alcohol because the effects of inebriation may be delayed by the effects of the amphetamines, possibly creating a false sense of control when large quantities of alcohol are consumed. Without an awareness of the dangerousness of this behavior, sickness or a loss of consciousness may result (Klee, 1998). The feelings of confidence and self-control that amphetamines produce make them more desirable to youths whose main motivation for substance use is social integration and the avoidance of problems associated with alcohol and other drugs (Klee, 1998; KCI, 2002; Pedersen & Wichstrom, 2001; Rawson et al., 2002; Smart & Ogborne, 2000).

European Americans constitute the predominant ethnic group abusing amphetamines, with African Americans most likely to abuse cocaine (West & Templer, 1999). Hispanic Americans and Native Americans are increasingly abusing methamphetamines (Baberg et al., 1996; DEA, 2001; KCI, 2002; Moreales & Sheafor, 2002; SAMHSA/CSAP, 2000). For Hispanic Americans and Native Americans, language and cultural barriers, racism, lack of financial resources, high school dropout rates, and high unemployment rates may support the attractiveness of this substance. For Mexican migrant workers, amphetamines can increase productivity and work performance, and the production and trafficking of the drug from Mexico to the United States is a lucrative business.

Women are at significant risk of abusing this drug, especially because the demands to perform optimally at work and at home may place uncomfortable psychological pressures on women, forcing them to find a way to increase their energy (Chassler, 1998; KCI, 2002; SAMHSA/CSAP, 2000). Compared with men addicted to amphetamines, women who are addicted appear to have higher levels of depression and anxiety syndromes (Gerdner, Nordlander, & Pedersen, 2002). In addition, some research supports that women addicted to amphetamines have a higher incidence of cluster B personality disorders (e.g., antisocial, borderline, histrionic, and narcissistic personality disorders) (American Psychiatric Association [APA], 2000; Gerdner et al., 2002). Some women in small, rural clandestine labs have become entrepreneurs in the production of methamphetamines (DEA, 2001; KCI, 2002). Although the reason for this increased illegal activity is not known, it may be related to the fact that in rural communities, where livelihood is tied to the land, environmental-structural factors play a role for women trapped by lack of finances, lack of skills, and family situations (Moreales & Sheafor, 2002).

PATTERN OF ABUSE

What remains constant among those who abuse amphetamines is that the pattern of abuse progresses through three stages: low-intensity, binge, and high-intensity abuse (Lukas, 1985).

Low-Intensity Abuse

Individuals who are considered low-intensity abusers use amphetamines on a casual basis but are not yet psychologically addicted to the drug (Lukas, 1985). These individuals swallow or snort amphetamines and use them for extra stimulation to stay awake longer, to have the energy to finish a job or task, or to lose weight. The purpose in using the drug is to avoid fatigue, recover from a hangover, or gain energy. This type of abuse is most common among students and truck drivers, for whom the reason for the abuse centers on completion of a task. For the low-intensity abuser, use of the substance is purpose directed, and therefore, it has not yet become a focus for the individual (Lukas, 1985). Those who experience low-intensity abuse of amphetamines often obtain the drug legally with a prescription, as for weight loss, but these individuals generally take three to four times the prescribed dosage (Lukas, 1985).

Binge Abuse

Individuals who binge abuse often smoke or inject amphetamines and are psychologically addicted to the euphoric rush produced by the drug (Lukas, 1985). The process of binge abuse is divided into seven phases: the rush phase, the high phase, the binge phase, the tweaking phase, the crash phase, the normal phase, and the withdrawal phase.

In the rush phase, some abusers experience a euphoric feeling similar to multiple orgasms. This phase can last anywhere from five to thirty minutes.

During the high phase, the abuser feels smarter, more aggressive, and can become argumentative. This phase can last anywhere from four to sixteen hours (Lukas, 1985; NIDA, 2002).

In the binge phase, repeated smoking and injecting of the drug is needed to maintain the high. With each binge, the abuser experiences a rush and a subsequent high until at some point the binge behavior no longer produces the same results. In this phase, the abuser can become mentally and physically hyperactive, and the phase can last anywhere from three to fifteen days (Lukas, 1985).

Feelings of emptiness and dysphoria are experienced in the tweaking phase (NIDA, 2002). Tweaking is an uncomfortable state for the abuser and the most dangerous phase of the abuse cycle because abusers may become violent. In this phase, individual movements may be overexaggerated, quick, and jerky because the user is overstimulated. It is also not uncommon for paranoid thinking, delusions, and hallucinations to occur. Lack of sleep and an inability to recreate the effects of the rush and high phases leave the individual in this phase feeling extremely frustrated. In an effort to help alleviate their discomfort, individuals will often take depressants such as alcohol or opiates such as heroin (or both) (KCI, 2002). Unfortunately, taking this combination of drugs only exacerbates the problem of lowered inhibition levels (DEA, 2001; KCI, 2002).

In the crash phase, the body is depleted of epinephrine due to the previous binging, and the abuser feels an incredible desire for sleep. During this phase, which can last anywhere from one to three days, and after, the abuser may sleep deeply.

The normal phase can last anywhere from two to fourteen days. The abuser returns to a "normal" state—a state slightly deteriorated from the user's state before he or she began taking amphetamines (KCI, 2002; NIDA, 2002).

Binge abusers enter the last phase, the withdrawal phase, slowly, usually thirty to ninety days after their last drug use, making their addiction to amphetamines not as obvious as with other drugs. After this period, the user becomes depressed, lethargic, and loses the ability to experience pleasure. It is at this point that a craving for amphetamines returns and the binge abuse pattern returns, eventually leading to high-intensity abuse (KCI, 2002; Lukas, 1985).

High-Intensity Abuse

High-intensity abusers are individuals addicted to amphetamines. They are often identified by the slang name *speed freaks*. These individuals' only focus is to prevent the crash and perfect the rush experienced by smoking or injecting amphetamines. This is the last phase of the abuse pattern, and the individual is physically and psychologically addicted to amphetamines. Individuals in this stage have often become polysubstance users in their attempts to reduce the uncomfortable side effects of amphetamine withdrawal (KCI, 2002; Zickler, 2001). "These individuals exhibit signs of mental illness such as psychosis, attempted suicide, and other antisocial behavior" (Lukas, 1985, p. 53). The problem becomes so severe that treatment and recovery for these individuals is difficult.

Practitioners working with the substance abuser should keep in mind that the effects of amphetamine use can lead to a false sense of increased self-esteem and self-confidence. Users believe (from their own experience and by word of mouth) that amphetamines enhance their performance even though it appears that the contrary is true (Lukas, 1985; Klee; 1998; SAMHSA/CSAP, 2000). Societal fixations on appearance, sport competition, and winning play an important role in the consumption of amphetamines (Pedersen & Wichstrom, 2001). Eating disorders such as bulimia have a strong correlation with amphetamine use in attempts to maintain an unhealthy body image (Chassler, 1998).

For many individuals, the pressure to be competitive in sports and in the workplace is high. This pressure and intense desire to stay ahead has lead individuals to use anabolic steroids, ephedrine, amphetamines, and methamphetamines to maximize performance and appearance (Lukas, 1985; Pedersen & Wichstrom, 2001). Therefore, those who abuse these substances cross all socioeconomic classes. The desire to increase sociability and decrease inhibitions sets a strong stage for the use of these drugs. For some males, it is believed that use of this substance can increase sexual prowess (Klee, 1998; Molitor et al., 1999; SAMHSA/CSAP, 2000). Some men in the gay community are using amphetamines to stay alert and exhilarated for all-night dance club events; to experience intense, disinhibited sex; and for the self-medication of problems associated with sexual identity, self-esteem, and depression (SAMHSA/CSAP, 2000).

The reality is that sustained use of amphetamines results in addiction to and dependence on the drug, with irrevocable physical and psychological damage to the individual. The physical damage to the individual includes but is not limited to fatal kidney and lung disorders, brain damage, infectious disease (e.g., HIV, AIDS, Hepatitis A, B, C, and D), brain damage, blood clots, immune system deficiency, and malnutrition (Hutin et al., 2000; KCI, 2002; Molitor et al., 1999; NIDA, 2002). Long-term psychological effects of amphetamine abuse are evidenced by psychosis, paranoia with homicidal and suicidal ideation, delusions (e.g., formication—delusions of parasites or insects on the skin), hallucinations, panic, violent and aggressive behaviors, anxiety, chronic depression, confusion, disturbed personality development, social phobia, mood disturbance, repetitive motor activities, insomnia, stroke, weight loss, or death (KCI, 2002; Lukas, 1985; Murray, 1998; NIDA, 2002; Williams et al., 2000). Amphetamine psychosis can also be manifested in the development of stereotypical behaviors as the result of consumed high dosages or usage of the drug over an extended period (Murphy et al., 2001; Murray, 1998). Hallucinations and delusions closely mimic symptoms of paranoid schizophrenia, which makes amphetamine abuse difficult to distinguish from the mental illness (Flaum & Schultz, 1996; KCI, 2002; Murray, 1998). "There is little question that amphetamines can initiate a psychosis that is often clinically indistinguishable from a schizophrenic disorder (especially the paranoid subtype)" (Flaum & Schultz, 1996, p. 814). Paranoid ideation can last up to eight hours after administration of the drug, with paranoid characteristics, ideas of reference, and visual and auditory alterations present (Murray, 1998). Likewise, positive symptoms (e.g., hallucinations and delusions) of amphetamine-induced schizophrenic responses are also associated with withdrawal symptoms and are followed by a state of anxiety, dysphoria, and depression (Murphy et al., 2001). The individual who abuses amphetamines becomes involved in a vicious cycle of dependence and withdrawal.

CASE EXAMPLE

Case History

J is a twenty-two-year-old Caucasian female of average height (5 feet 6 inches) and weighs 109 pounds on assessment. She is a senior in college. She was admitted for an inpatient psychiatric evaluation after expressing suicidal ideation, paranoia, and delusions. J lives with two other female roommates in a house close to campus. J moved to the area four years ago. Her parents still reside in another state. Her roommates were present at the time of J's admission and were able to provide the following information.

According to her roommates, J has experienced some losses recently that may contribute to her feeling suicidal. She was fired from a part-time job as a waitress in a bar approximately two months ago for not attending her scheduled shifts. Her roommates began noticing that her behavior patterns were becoming more erratic and that she was losing weight. She appeared to be more withdrawn, unmotivated, and depressed, and she would skip classes and not attend her scheduled shifts at work. At other times, her behavior appeared almost "manic"—she would talk nonstop and would jump from one subject to another. She was unable to concentrate at work or at school and would become argumentative with coworkers, customers, and friends. J's roommates also stated that she and her boyfriend of six months broke up about three months ago and that this has been difficult for her. As her behavior became more erratic, the roommates claim J became paranoid and delusional, accusing them of hating her, of driving her boyfriend away, and of wanting to destroy her life. J's roommates stated that she has not been herself lately. They described J as "funny, friendly, sweet, and generally a quiet person" who lately "doesn't want to do anything, gets mad, avoids everyone, and stays up all night."

J slept for the first two days on the psychiatric unit and had to be aroused for meals. She reported feeling better after sleeping, still feeling depressed but not suicidal. J reports that she does attend college full-time but that her performance has fallen, and she has recently lost her job. J states she has been unable to sleep for the last four days. She reports using methamphetamines, marijuana, and alcohol, and she attributes her lack of sleep to the "meth." J admits that meth is her drug of choice and that she smokes it daily but is increasingly using marijuana to alleviate her anxiety and to help her get some sleep.

J began using methamphetamines approximately one year ago, when she was a junior. She was introduced to the drug by a previous boyfriend at a party her roommates were throwing. The first time she used meth, she and her friends snorted the drug, and she enjoyed the energy that the drug gave her, claiming it made her more social. J later began using methamphetamines each time she would go out with friends. On these outings, she still only snorted it and had not yet begun to smoke it. She especially liked that the drug took away her shyness. J also states she liked that the drug allowed her to concentrate better at school and at work. She claims attending school and working late left her physically exhausted, and before the drug, she had little time for socializing. J reports that using the drug gave her the energy she needed to be happy and complete her assigned tasks effectively. Use of the drug also took her appetite away. She states that she began losing weight when taking meth, which made her happy because "everyone began noticing how attractive I could be." J believes that the drug allowed her to become a completely different person, and suddenly, guys wanted to hang around her or date her. She claims that she didn't need to do meth all the time, and when she was out she would often use marijuana or have a drink instead. J states she only smoked marijuana or drank alcohol to help her sleep better at nights, but is concerned because she has begun using these substances more often.

J began smoking methamphetamines approximately four months ago. She was out at a dance club with friends, who talked her into smoking it, convincing her that she would love it and that using it caused no harm. She still remembers the rush she got from her first high, and from that moment she was hooked. J smokes the drug first thing in the morning and continues smoking throughout the day. She doesn't like smoking around her friends anymore because she is afraid they may try to harm her. Lately, J reports fear that friends and family are trying to hurt her. J states that she has spent over half of her bank savings because of her need to have drugs and is afraid that before long she won't have any money at all. J reports a good relationship with her mother but lately has avoided talking to her on the phone for fear that she may notice that something is wrong. She also avoids her roommates because they are not aware of her meth use, and she states that she feels ashamed and afraid to confide her problem to them. Her ex-boyfriend was also not aware of her smoking meth and was unable to cope when she became very defensive and paranoid when around him. Their relationship ended on bad terms, with him breaking up with her in front of her roommates and accusing her of being "crazy."

J states that she felt embarrassed, ashamed, and angry with herself and began smoking and abusing meth more than she had previously. She states that she began withdrawing from her friends and felt safer smoking in her room. She reports binging repeatedly and that she is unable to sleep for days at a time. When she does crash, she sleeps for days. When she runs out of "meth," her discomfort is so great that, as J reports, "All I want to do is either die or sleep until the feeling passes." J declares that she wants to quit using drugs, has had previous unsuccessful attempts to quit, and wants to have a normal life, but all she can do is think about using. She reports that she feels like a failure for losing her job and her boyfriend due to her addiction. J wants to continue attending school, but she is concerned because she has missed so many classes and states, "I have a hard time remembering things." J reports feeling lost and that the only thing she has left is school, her relationship with her mother, and her relationship with her roommates. She does not want to lose these too. J would like her mother and her friends to be involved in her treatment. She expresses that they are a source of support for her.

Multiaxial Diagnostic Assessment and Intervention Suggestions

Incorporating information provided by the client and her roommates and the *DSM-IV-TR* gives the following the diagnostic impression of J:

Axis I: Amphetamine Dependence (304.40)
          Amphetamine-Induced Psychotic Disorder (292.84)
          Cannabis Abuse (305.20)
          Alcohol Abuse (305.00)
Axis II: Deferred
Axis III: None
Axis IV: 1. Loss of employment, two months ago.
          2. Loss of relationship with boyfriend, three months ago.
          3. Lack of financial resources due to loss of job and substance use.
          4. Social and interpersonal relationship problems.
          5. Substance abuse problems.
          6. Academic problems secondary to substance abuse.
Axis V: 35

J's intervention plan needs to take into consideration her environment and all the information she has provided. It is essential for J to go through an amphetamine detoxification program before any problems can be resolved. When assessing J, it is important to take into account information regarding her previous attempts to discontinue use of the substance and how this past history might affect current treatment strategy. For J, pharmacological assistance may be necessary because she may begin to experience acute positive and negative symptoms as part of the withdrawal process. When documenting the problems, it is important to make sure that the signs and symptoms that the client has experienced have been documented in the clinical record, creating an individualized intervention plan.

Intervention Plan: Amphetamine Dependence Disorder

Definition.   The continued use of amphetamines despite significant substance-related problems. Pattern of repeated use resulting in tolerance, withdrawal, and compulsive behaviors related to the substance. A physiological and psychological dependence for amphetamines despite adverse psychological and physical consequences. Continued substance use to relieve or avoid withdrawal symptoms. Unsuccessful attempts at stopping or cutting down on use of the substance.

Signs and Symptoms.   Paranoia; weight loss; neglect of responsibilities; delusions; anxiety; relationship problems; withdrawal from friends and social activities; insomnia; memory impairment; absence from school or work.

Goals for Treatment.
1. Help client to abstain from using amphetamines.
2. Acquire a medical and a psychiatric assessment.
3. Educate client on the effects of using. Introduce new coping skills.
4. Enlist family and friends as a support system for continued abstinence. Address underlying issues relating to amphetamine dependency.
5. Link the client to outpatient treatment groups in the community.

Objectives/Interventions.
1. Abstinence. Client will attend an outpatient support group a minimum of three times a week and will keep a journal of her feelings and experiences while participating in the group. Client will discuss issues responsible for amphetamine dependency and self-destructive behaviors. Client will identify triggers that promote dependency and create a plan for combating them. Client will identify withdrawal symptoms and how these affect her recovery process. Client will write a list of personal motivational reasons for not using drugs. Client will compose a list of events, situations, people, places, and things that promote her amphetamine use and will develop positive ways to handle or avoid these.
2. Medical and psychiatric assessment. Client will obtain a medical and a psychological examination to support or rule out the above initial diagnosis. Client will take medications as prescribed by a psychiatrist to ease the symptoms of withdrawal and help prevent relapse. Practitioner will monitor client's medication use or misuse.
3. Drug education. Client will attend outpatient group meetings and discuss their effectiveness in helping her to abstain from amphetamines. Client will become educated about amphetamines and process this information with the practitioner and the group. Client will discuss issues responsible for amphetamine dependency and self-destructive behaviors. Practitioner will educate client on the effects and warning signs of amphetamine withdrawal, as these may arise after use has been discontinued. Client will discuss her substance abuse patterns with her group and her practitioner and identify similarities with others' patterns.
4. Build a support system of family and friends. Practitioner and client will meet with client's family and roommates to educate them about amphetamine addiction. Practitioner and client will enlist the support and encouragement of family and friends. The client and the practitioner will discuss and identify reasons to stop taking amphetamines. Practitioner will assist client in becoming aware of behaviors that affect her and those around her. Practitioner will arrange for family members and friends to attend individual sessions, per client's request.
5. Build a support system in the community. Practitioner will link the client and her support system to outside community support groups. Client will attend an outpatient support group minimum three times a week and will

keep a journal of her feelings and experiences while participating in the group. Practitioner will arrange for family members and friends to attend individual sessions, per client's request.

BEST PRACTICES

Despite the social, environmental, and physical health risks that amphetamines pose, much work remains to be done to formulate the best and most effective intervention for amphetamine addiction. For the most part, research has been unable to establish an optimal duration, frequency, and format of treatment for stimulant addiction (NIDA, 2002). Currently, amphetamine addiction programs follow treatment protocols similar to those used for cocaine-dependent individuals, which can be ineffective for treating individuals with amphetamine-related disorders (KCI, 2002; NIDA, 2002). Although amphetamines and cocaine produce similar mood-altering effects, there are fundamental differences in the patterns of addiction and the psychological and physical effects.

Chapter 4 goes into more depth about the individual who uses cocaine and the central treatments for cocaine abuse. Briefly stated, however, the main difference between cocaine and amphetamines is the duration of the high each drug produces. Cocaine produces a high that usually lasts twenty to thirty minutes; amphetamines produce a high that lasts eight to twenty-four hours (NIDA, 2002). The implications of the duration of the high must be considered in order to properly treat clients—it will be difficult for a client to find positive replacements for a high that can last all day, if not longer, as opposed to one that lasts thirty minutes at most.

The pattern of use of these drugs also has implications for treatment. Amphetamine users typically use the drug first thing in the morning and continue administering the drug every two to four hours during the day (NIDA, 2002). Cocaine users typically engage in recreational use, in which using begins in the evening and continues until the drug has been depleted (NIDA, 2002). One might say that amphetamine users abuse these drugs in a way that resembles taking a medication. Again, this poses difficulties to the practitioner for treatment of the addiction because amphetamines trigger continual use. Consequently, to manage the long-lasting high, many amphetamine users become polysubstance users, which increases the difficulty of living a drug-free life (KCI, 2002; NIDA, 2002).

Research does demonstrate that if an appointment for treatment is made within twenty-four hours of the practitioner's initial contact with a client suffering from amphetamine addiction, the likelihood of effectiveness increases (NIDA, 2002). Also, the frequency of visits is more important than the length of visits. Frequent visits allow the client to establish behavioral accountability and contain impulse-driven behaviors, and they create daily structure. Individual counseling is as effective as group treatment for stimulant-dependent clients, if the client is not experiencing paranoia or hallucinations. The Center of Substance Abuse Treatment at the National Institute of Health speculates that longer treatment durations, of six to twelve months, may produce better outcomes for cocaine-related issues, but this is not consistent with amphetamine-related problems. Other organizations recommend six to eight months for casual amphetamine users and two to three years for regular users and warn practitioners to expect relapses, a common problem with the amphetamine using population (KCI, 2002).

Practitioners need to be aware of the pharmacological treatments available that can help amphetamine users handle the unpleasant and disturbing side effects of withdrawal. For example, pharmacological treatment of positive (hallucinations and delusions) and negative symptoms (lack of goal-directed behavior) of amphetamine-induced schizophrenic responses can be addressed with antipsychotic medication. For some abusers, Risperidone, an atypical antipsychotic medication, alleviates these symptoms. Individuals who underwent Risperidone treatment showed a decrease in hallucinations and cravings for methamphetamines. Overall, symptoms of insomnia, impulsivity, and anhedonia improved, with a reduced craving for the drug (Misra & Kofoed, 1997). Other medications that have been helpful in reducing symptoms related to amphetamine abuse are chlorpromazine and haloperidol, as well as other neuroleptic medications (Flaum & Schultz; 1996; Misra & Kofoed, 1997; Murray, 1998; Snow, 1998).

Anxiety disorders secondary to amphetamine abuse and dopaminergic dysfunctions that are due to dopamine depletion (e.g., social phobia) demonstrate improvement with use of bupropion, a dopamine enhancer (Williams et al., 2000). Benzodiazepines are useful for treating anxiety and agitation involved with amphetamine use, and propanol and clonidine have shown effectiveness in treating sympathetic overactivity (Maxmen & Ward, 1995). Another serious side effect of amphetamine use is depression. Tricyclic antidepressants can be helpful in alleviating the dysphoria associated with withdrawal symptoms (Murray, 1998; Snow, 1998). Medication alone, however, is not enough. These medications should only be considered in conjunction with individual or group therapy.

Pharmacological treatments have shown effectiveness in treating fatigue, irritability, depression, intolerance to stress, reduced attention span, and decreased mental acuity among amphetamine users. Accumulated residues of amphetamines toxins remain in the body for a long time, and this may play a role in the persistence of symptoms.

It has also been suggested that a detoxification program for amphetamine users should incorporate the following: (1) an exercise program designed to stimulate circulation for the abuser while burning fat; (2) low-temperature saunas to promote the sweating of toxins; (3) a regimen of vitamin, minerals, and oils to replace vitamins, minerals, and electrolytes lost during periods of sweating and to correct nutritional deficiencies; (4) niacin doses to assist with the mobilization and elimination of toxins; (5) plenty of liquids and a regular diet with fresh vegetables; and (6) a routine schedule with the normal requirement of sleep. Because the elimination of drugs from an individual's system may continue for up to five weeks and can be detected in both sweat and urine, the possibility of individual differences on tests should always be considered (Maxmen & Ward, 1995).

Although studies suggest that inpatient treatment is needed for rehabilitation of amphetamine and methamphetamine users, especially those who have a history of long-term abuse, one drawback is the cost. An alternative is the Matrix Model, an outpatient approach funded by the Center for Substance Abuse Treatment. This program encompasses a manual-driven, sixteen-week, nonresidential, psychosocial approach used for the treatment of drug dependence for more than a decade. The foundation of the model entails cognitive-behavioral principles and basic goals: (1) stop using the drug; (2) learn the critical issues related to addiction and relapse; (3) obtain education for family members affected by addition and recovery; (4) become familiar with self-help programs; and (5) agree to weekly urine toxicology and breathalyzer alcohol testing. The Matrix Model integrates several interventions into a comprehensive approach tailored to individuals needs. However, this treatment is relatively new, and its success rate leaves much room for improvement (Rawson et al., 2002). Despite the cost-containing draw of outpatient services, individuals who present with severe psychiatric impairment often cannot function safely on an outpatient basis and will be served best by admission to and stabilization in a medically supervised treatment setting.

SUMMARY AND FUTURE DIRECTIONS

The search for improved evidence-based and tested treatments in the area of amphetamine addictions needs to continue. To facilitate improved efforts, practitioners should identify the problems that can occur in the withdrawal phase and share this information with the addicted individual, thereby helping him or her to prepare for what may come. Best practices for this population should not consist of medications alone but rather should include frequent counseling sessions that reinforce accountability for behaviors, the administration of pharmacological aids, and the initiation of a detoxification treatment to eliminate stored toxins. For the practitioner, becoming aware of what specific type of stimulant the client is abusing is of fundamental importance in understanding and planning for the treatment of these addictions. Although these stimulants may induce similar mood-altering effects, their vastly different patterns of addiction should be considered when implementing treatment.

The practitioner should also be aware that symptoms of amphetamine abuse often mimic those of mental illnesses such as schizophrenia. A thorough evaluation of the client during the initial assessment is necessary to correctly identify the cause of the symptoms. Amphetamine abuse can have devastating effects for the individual if it is not properly assessed and treated. The intention of this chapter has been to inform the practitioner about this substance and to assist him or her in developing the best individualized intervention strategies possible.

References
ADA: Division of Alcohol and Drug Abuse. (2004). *Stimulants.* [Pamphlet]. Rockville, MD: National Clearing House for Drug and Alcohol Information.

American Psychiatric Association. (2000). *Diagnostic and statistical manual of mental disorders* (4th ed., text rev.). Washington, DC: Author.

Amphetamines. (2002). Originally published in *Psychology Today*, 20021010. Retrieved June 17, 2004, from http://health.yahoo.com/health/centers/addiction/_96407677.html

Baberg, H., Nelesen, R., & Dimsdale, J. (1996). Amphetamine use: Return of an old scourge in a consultation psychiatry setting. *American Journal of Psychiatry, 153*, 789–93.

Borowski, T., & Kokkinidis, L. (1998). The effects of cocaine, amphetamine, and the dopamine D-sub-1 receptor agonist SKF 38393 on fear extinction as measured with potentiated startle: Implications for psychomotor stimulant psychosis. *Behavioral Neuroscience, 112*(4), 952–65.

Chassler, L. (1998). "Ox hunger": Psychoanalytical explorations of bulimia nervosa. *Clinical Social Work Journal, 26*(4), 397–412.

DeWit, H., Crean, J., & Richards, J. (2000). Effects of d-amphetamine and ethanol on a measure of behavioral inhibition in humans. *Behavioral Neuroscience, 114*(4), 830–37.

Drug Enforcement Administration. (2001). *DEA resources for law enforcement officers, intelligence reports and drug trafficking.* Retrieved September, 27, 2002, from http://www.usdoj.gov/dea/pubs/intel/01020/index.html

Drug Text. (2002). *The neurotransmitters.* Retrieved November 11, 2002, from http://www.drugtext.org/sub/neuro.html

Dziegielewski, S. F. (2002). *DSM-IV-TR in action.* New York: John Wiley & Sons.

Flaum, M., & Schultz, S. (1996). When does amphetamine-induced psychosis become schizophrenia? *American Journal of Psychiatry, 153*, 812–15.

Gerdner, A., Nordlander, T., & Pedersen, T. (2002). Personality factors and drugs of choice in female addicts with psychiatric comorbidity. *Substance Use and Misuse, 37*(1), 1–18.

Hargreaves, G. (2000). Clandestine drug labs: Chemical time bombs. *FBI Law Enforcement Bulletin, 69*(4), 1–6.

Hutin, Y., Sabin, K., & Hutwagner, L. (2000). Multiple modes of hepatitis A virus transmission among methamphetamine users. *American Journal of Epidemiology, 152*(2), 186–92.

Indiana Prevention Resource Center. (1998). *Amphetamines—IPRC factline.* Retrieved October 17, 2002, from http://www.drugs.indiana.edu/publications/iprc/factline/ampet.html

Khoshbouei, H., Sen, N., Guptaroy, B., Johnson, L., & Lind, D. (2004). N-terminal phosphorylation of dopamine transporter is required for amphetamine-induced efflux. *DOI,* 10.1371. Retrieved June 17, 2004, from http://biology.plosjournals.org

Klee, H. (1998). The love of speed: An analysis of the enduring attraction of amphetamine sulphate for British youth. *Journal of Drug Issues, 28*(1), 35–55.

Koch Crime Institute. (2002). *Psychological and physical problems of meth or methamphetamine addiction.* Retrieved October 17, 2002, from http://www.kci.org/meth_info/sites/meth_psycho.htm

Lintner, B. (1997). Speed demons: Asia's newest drug scourge: Mass-produced stimulants. *Far Eastern Economic Review, 160*, 28.

Lukas, S. (1985). *Amphetamines: Danger in the fast lane.* New York: Chelsea House.

Maxmen, J., & Ward, N. (1995). *Essential psychopathology and its treatment* (2nd ed.). New York: W. W. Norton.

Misra, L., & Kofoed, L. (1997). Risperidone treatment of methamphetamine psychosis. *American Journal of Psychiatry, 154*, 1170.

Molitor, F., Ruiz, J., Flynn, N., Mikanda, J., Sun, R., & Anderson, R. (1999). Methamphetamine use and sexual and injection risk behaviors among out-of-treatment injection drug users. *American Journal of Drug and Alcohol Abuse, 25*(3), 475–93.

Moreales, A., & Sheafor, B. (2002). *The many faces of social work clients*. Boston: Allyn & Bacon.

Murphy, C., Fend, M., Russig, H., & Feldon, J. (2001). Latent inhibition, but not prepulse inhibition, is reduced during withdrawal from an escalating dosage schedule of amphetamine. *Behavioral Neurosciences, 115*(6), 1247–56.

Murray, J. (1998). Psychophysiological aspects of amphetamine-methamphetamine abuse. *Journal of Psychology, 132*, 227–37.

National Institute on Drug Abuse. (2002). Comparing methamphetamine and cocaine. *NIDA Notes, 13*(1). Retrieved September 27, 2002, from http://www.nida.nih.gov/NIDA_Notes/NNVol13N1/Comparing.html

Pedersen, W., & Wichstrom, L. (2001). Adolescents, doping agents, and drug use: A community study. *Journal of Drug Issues, 31*(2), 517–42.

Rawson, R., Gonzales, R., & Brethen, P. (2002). Treatment of methamphetamine use disorders: An update. *Journal of Substance Abuse Treatment, 23*, 145–50.

Smart, R., & Ogborne, A. (2000). Drug use and drinking among students in 36 countries. *Addictive Behaviors, 25*(3), 455–60.

Snow, O. (1998). *Amphetamine syntheses: Overview and reference guide for professionals*. Tarpon Springs, FL: Marrakech Express.

Stall, R., Paul, J., Barrett, D., Crosby, M., & Bein, E. (1999). An outcome evaluation to measure changes in sexual risk-taking among gay men undergoing substance use disorder treatment. *Journal of Studies on Alcohol, 60*(6), 837–45.

Substance Abuse and Mental Health Services Administration and the Center for Substance Abuse Prevention. (2000). *A look at methamphetamine use among three populations*. Washington, DC: DHHS Publication.

Vatikiotis, M. (1995). Social climbers: Thai youth look for kicks and status in bottles and pills. *Far Eastern Economic Review, 158*, 52–53.

West, J., & Templer, D. (1999). Sympathomimetic preference and ethnicity in male felons. *Psychological Reports, 85*(3), 1225–28.

Williams, K., Argyropoulos, S., & Nutt, D. J. (2000). Amphetamine misuse and social phobia. *American Journal of Psychiatry, 157*(5), 834–35.

Yarnold, B. (1997). Use in 1992 of amphetamines among Miami's public school students. *Psychological Reports, 81*, 411–17.

Zickler, P. (2001). Methamphetamine, cocaine abusers have different patterns of drug use, suffer different cognitive impairments. *Research Findings, 16*(5). Retrieved September 27, 2002, from http://www.drugabuse.gov/NIDA_Notes/NNVol16N5/Meth_Coc.html

Chapter 4

Cocaine

Sophia F. Dziegielewski and Kimberly Harvey

SINCE THE ADVENT OF CRACK COCAINE IN THE LAST CENTURY, THE INCI-dence of cocaine addiction has risen dramatically in the United States. In 2000 alone, the Drug Enforcement Administration made 16,017 cocaine-related ar-rests—40.4 percent of the total number of arrests the DEA made that year (Office of National Drug Control Policy, 2001). Millions of Americans are affected either directly or indirectly because of cocaine's very high potential for abuse, which re-sults in physical or mental health problems. Historically, cocaine has been used to treat a variety of medical conditions, including depression, chronic fatigue, and asthma. Today, its use is almost entirely nonmedicinal. Individuals ages eighteen to twenty-five tend to report the highest use of cocaine. Significant portions of high school students have also reported cocaine use at least once (Office of Na-tional Drug Control Policy, 2001).

This chapter discusses the effects cocaine, including how these effects vary depending on the form of the substance and the method of ingestion. Recent research studies that suggest frequent past use of this substance can result in impaired cognitive functioning and behavioral impulsivity are explored. Emphasis is placed on traditional and nontraditional interventions that may prove effective in maintaining long-term abstinence from cocaine use, including pharmacological interventions, acupuncture, twelve-step programs, coping skills training, and indi-vidual therapy.

THE HISTORY OF COCAINE USE

Cocaine use has been documented since 3000 BC, when the inhabitants of pre-sent-day South America chewed the leaves of the coca plant to feel its effects. The coca plantations in South America have been active since the 1400s. Spanish ex-plorers brought the plant back to Spain, and from there it made its way through Europe. The medicinal uses of the coca plant were discovered in the early 1700s in Germany. It was at this time that cocaine was first extracted from the coca leaves and made into a powder. This form of the substance became widespread after only a few decades.

In the late 1800s, coca wine became popular. Angelo Mariani advertised his version of this product, Vin Mariani, with the first celebrity endorsements. These promoters included Robert Louis Stevenson, Thomas Edison, and the pope. In the wine he exported, he increased the amount of cocaine in order to compete with the American wines manufactured with the same ingredients (Inaba & Cohen, 2000).

Cocaine was also added to various elixirs and tonics and to topical preparations, such as toothache medications, to achieve a numbing effect. During the latter half of the nineteenth century, European and American physicians and pharmacists cognizant of cocaine's stimulant effect began to use it medicinally. It was also used as an anesthetic prior to the creation of Novocain. During this time, cocaine was thought to be a remedy for everything from gastric disorders to opium and alcohol dependence (Straussner, 1993).

Because of its detrimental effects, cocaine was federally regulated in 1914 with the passage of the Harrison Act, which banned all nonmedical use of cocaine. The act also prohibited the importation of cocaine and advocated for criminal penalties for those either using cocaine or facilitating its use. The same criminal penalties were imposed for cocaine users as for users of opium, morphine, and heroin. For all practitioners able to prescribe medication, strict accounting and limitations were enforced, discouraging the use of cocaine in medical settings (Office of National Drug Control Policy, 2001). Today the use of cocaine in medical settings is limited to use as a local anesthetic for some eye, ear, and throat surgeries.

Injecting cocaine began in the late 1800s for medicinal purposes. Practitioners were then unaware of cocaine's deadly effect, and so overdoses were an unexpected result (Inaba & Cohen, 2000). Also at this time, it became evident that cocaine is highly addictive. Today cocaine is classified as a Schedule II drug—that is, a drug with a high potential for abuse but with some approved medical uses. Although this drug can be also be snorted, drunk, or smoked, it is most often taken intravenously because of the swift and intense effect on the brain. When cocaine is injected, its effects are felt within thirty seconds.

Snorting cocaine became popular in the early 1900s. Since 1910, snorting cocaine has been documented to cause medical problems. This method of ingestion causes constriction of the nasal passages. When the constriction subsides as the effects diminish, the result is a runny or sniffling nose. Persistent cocaine use may also damage the nasal septum, the bone that divides the nostrils. Snorted cocaine reaches the brain within five minutes.

Smoking cocaine began in the early 1900s, when cigarettes first contained refined cocaine. Intense effects were not felt because the high temperature destroyed the psychoactive chemicals. Today cocaine is smokable in two forms: freebase and crack. Popular in the 1970s, freebase cocaine is created by processing cocaine hydrochloride with ammonia and ether so that it can be heated and smoked without the destruction of the psychoactive chemicals. Crack is a rock form of smokable cocaine created by the less volatile method of mixing cocaine hydrochloride with baking soda and water. Crack, so called because of the crackling sound it makes when smoked, is a less pure form of cocaine than freebase, making it cheaper and easier to access.

Crack cocaine made its appearance in the drug world several years after freebase, most notably in Miami, Florida, and Los Angeles, California. In the 1980s, crack use reached epidemic proportions in the United States.

The effects of smoking cocaine are comparable to those of intravenous use. The effects of the drug can be felt within seconds, which increases its desirability and sets the stage for addiction. The Drug Abuse Warning Network (DAWN) study discovered that, in the majority treatment programs in the surveyed cities around the country, clients who named cocaine as their drug of choice preferred smoking crack (National Institute on Drug Abuse [NIDA], 2003).

PSYCHOPHYSIOLOGICAL EFFECTS

All forms of cocaine are highly addictive and, as with any mind-altering substance, their greatest impact is on the brain and how it works. There is a significant amount of research on the effect that cocaine has on the brain and on understanding the way cocaine produces pleasurable effects. According to the National Institute of Health (1999),

> Researchers have discovered that, when a pleasurable event is occurring, it is accompanied by a large increase in the amounts of dopamine released in the nucleus accumbens by neurons originating in the ventral tegmental area. In the normal communication process, dopamine is released by a neuron into the synapse, where it binds with specialized proteins on the neighboring neuron, thereby sending a signal to that neuron. Drugs of abuse are able to interfere with this normal communication process. For example, scientists have discovered that cocaine blocks the removal of dopamine from the synapse, resulting in an increase in an accumulation of dopamine. This buildup of dopamine causes continuous stimulation of receiving neurons, probably resulting in the euphoria commonly reported by cocaine abusers. (p. 4)

Simply stated, dopamine affects the pleasure center of the brain. When cocaine is used, it interrupts the neurons' reabsorption of dopamine, causing the dopamine to remain in the brain for a prolonged period. This in turn causes intense, pleasurable effects. As cocaine use is continued, the amount of dopamine produced by the brain decreases. When cocaine use is discontinued, the brain must reestablish normal levels of dopamine production. In the interim, however, when there are lower than normal levels of dopamine in the brain, the individual will experience intense, unpleasant effects such as fatigue, irritability, and depression.

Some short-term physiological effects of cocaine use are decreased appetite, increased energy, dilated pupils, and constricted blood vessels. Long-term effects of cocaine use include irritability, restlessness, paranoia, auditory hallucinations, and addiction. There are many medical complications associated with cocaine use, including cardiovascular effects, respiratory effects, neurological effects, gastrointestinal complications, and death. Other physical symptoms include nausea, chest pain, blurred vision, muscle spasms, convulsions, and coma. (See boxes 11–14 for the general signs and symptoms of cocaine abuse, dependence, intoxication, and withdrawal according to the *DSM-IV-TR*).

Box 11: Cocaine Abuse

Definition. Indicated by a pattern of maladaptive use. The use must be persistent within the same twelve-month period. With cocaine, abuse may be evident due to episodes of problematic use usually occurring on a special occasion or payday. Cocaine abuse creates interpersonal conflicts and neglect of responsibility. Legal problems may follow from cocaine abuse. Individuals may reject important social, occupational, and recreational activities.

Signs and Symptoms. Impaired occupational functioning; delirium; elevated blood pressure; visual or tactile hallucinations; depression; extreme fatigue; deterioration of physical health; maladaptive behaviors; tachycardia; nausea; anxiety; irritability; paranoia; intense cravings for more cocaine.

Goals for Treatment.

Maintain self as free from cocaine	Change drug-seeking behavior patterns
Learn new coping and refusal skills	Modify environment
Assist client in finding a local NA group	Help link client's family to a local support group

Source: Compiled from the *DSM-IV-TR* (American Psychiatric Association, 2000).

Polysubstance abuse involving cocaine can have deadly results (Office of National Drug Control Policy, 2001). For example, when cocaine and alcohol are consumed at the same time, the liver combines them and manufactures a third substance, cocaethylene. This substance moves to the brain and creates effects similar to those of cocaine, although more harmful. These include increased aggression, anxiety, and violence. Cocaethylene can also cause physiological effects such as high blood pressure, cardiovascular problems, and death. Combining cocaine with other substances such as over-the-counter or prescription medications, marijuana, heroin, ecstasy, or inhalant drugs can also be problematic and, in some cases, fatal (McNeece & DiNitto, 1998). Cocaine combined with other substances complicates the intervention process because of the powerful physiological, cognitive, behavioral, and interpersonal effects that are associated with polysubstances abuse (Levin, 1999).

Substance addiction or dependence remains a serious health problem but also has other significant consequences (Nutt, 1996). These include higher physical and mental health care costs, increased crime, and greater loss of employment. When

Box 12: Cocaine Dependence

Definition. The individual finds it increasingly difficult to resist using cocaine whenever it is available. There is a need for frequent dosing to maintain a "high." The individual may spend large amounts of money on the drug within a very short time. Dependence can develop after a short time of use. Tolerance occurs, as well as withdrawal symptoms.

Signs and Symptoms. Theft, prostitution, or drug dealing to help fund the habit; paranoid ideation; anxiety; weight loss; aggressive behavior; depression; mental or physical complications.

Goals for Treatment.
Abstinence from cocaine
Assist client in dealing with withdrawal
   symptoms
Link client to appropriate services

Medical assessment
Assist client's family in dealing with a
   cocaine-dependent relative

Source: Compiled from the *DSM-IV-TR* (American Psychiatric Association, 2000).

these are coupled with the problems associated with loss of earnings and productivity, the negative societal effects of a highly addictive substance such as cocaine are pronounced. Because of the potential for the development of these problems, reducing the extent of drug dependence has become one of the major goals of the treatment community.

Box 13: Cocaine Intoxication

Definition. The presence of clinically significant maladaptive behavioral or psychological changes (e.g., hyperactivity, restlessness, grandiosity) that develop during or shortly after use of cocaine. Whether acute or chronic, often associated with impaired social or occupational functioning. Severe intoxication can lead to convulsions, cardiac arrhythmia, hyperpyrexia, and death.

Signs and Symptoms. Papillary dilation; rush/euphoria; perspiration or chills; tachycardia or bradycardia; nausea.

Goals for Treatment.
Accept diagnosis of chemical dependence and begin to actively participate in a
   recovery program
Establish and maintain total abstinence while increasing knowledge of the disease in the process of recovery
Medical assessment

Source: Compiled from the *DSM-IV-TR* (American Psychiatric Association, 2000).

Box 14: Cocaine Withdrawal

Definition. The effects of cocaine withdrawal occur with cessation or reduction of heavy and prolonged use. These symptoms can develop within a few hours or up to several days after discontinuance of the substance. These symptoms are independent of any other medical condition and are severe enough to impair occupational functioning.

Signs and Symptoms. Fatigue; insomnia; psychomotor retardation or agitation; vivid, unpleasant dreams; increased appetite.

Goals for Treatment.
Abstinence of cocaine use
Link client to appropriate services
Medical assessment

Source: Compiled from the *DSM-IV-TR* (American Psychiatric Association, 2000).

PREVALENCE OF USE AND DEMOGRAPHICS OF USERS

According to the Office of National Drug Control Policy, medical examiners responding to a DAWN survey reported that they had noted cocaine 4,864 times in drug-related deaths within their jurisdictions during 1999. This made cocaine the drug most frequently mentioned by medical examiners reporting to DAWN in that year. In 2000, problems with cocaine were so extensive that admissions to U.S. hospital emergency rooms for illicit use of this substance reached 29 percent of all substance-related admissions. During the year 2000 alone, there were 174,881 emergency room admissions that, in some way, involved cocaine (Office of National Drug Control Policy, 2001). This trend seems to be continuing: from January to June 2001, there were 96,125 mentions of cocaine in emergency rooms. According to the report of a DAWN survey of emergency room admissions in the first half of 2001, the incidence of cocaine use was higher than that of any other drug in the surveyed areas. This report also indicated that the rate increased significantly within the next year (NIDA, 2003). This makes cocaine the most frequently mentioned illicit substance in medical emergency room settings.

According to the 2000 National Household Survey on Drug Abuse, approximately 11 percent of Americans ages twelve and over reported using cocaine at least once during their lifetime, and 1.5 percent reported that this use occurred within the previous year. This study also found that, in 2000, approximately 0.5 percent (1,213,000) of Americans ages twelve and over were currently using cocaine (Office of National Drug Control Policy, 2001).

In 1999, the Centers for Disease Control and Prevention conducted a survey of U.S. high school students. Of the students surveyed, 9.5 percent reported using cocaine at least once in their lifetime, and 4.0 percent reported that they were current users (Office of National Drug Control Policy, 2001). These figures are supported by another study, conducted in 2000, in which 9.1 percent of college students and 12.7 percent of young adults (ages nineteen to twenty-eight) reported using cocaine at least once in their lifetime. Among these respondents, 4.8 percent of college students and 5.4 percent of young adults reported using cocaine within the previous year, and 1.4 percent of college students and 1.7 percent of young adults reported using cocaine within the previous month (Office of National Drug Control Policy, 2001). The National Institute of Health (1999) reported that cocaine use is highest among men and those persons eighteen to twenty-five years old. Results by ethnicity showed that African Americans had the highest use, followed by Hispanics, with Caucasians using the least (p. 2).

CASE EXAMPLE

Case History

Demographic Information and History of Use. P is a forty-two-year-old, married (separated), unemployed, Caucasian male who was referred to drug treatment by the Department of Corrections. He is currently on probation for possession of cocaine. He violated his probation when he produced a positive urinalysis for cocaine. P related that he started drinking alcohol at age fourteen. He reports drinking sporadically for the next six years. He admits that he drank every day between the ages of twenty-one and thirty-five. He claims that at age thirty-five he digressed to drinking on the weekends until about age thirty-nine. He reports drinking on holidays since he was about forty. P started smoking marijuana at fourteen years old. He reports that he smoked daily while he was in high school and that he quit smoking shortly after graduating. He says he started snorting cocaine at around age thirty-five. He says he used mostly on the weekends for about five years. At age forty, he started smoking crack and smoked every day he could. He admits that he last smoked about a month ago.

Psychological Functioning. P is oriented to person, place, and time, and his memory is within average limits. His thought processes appear logical, coherent, and spontaneous. He denies any suicidal or homicidal ideations. He denies experiencing any type of hallucinations. He relates that he is more irritable as of late and concerned about his legal situation. His insight and judgment seems poor. He seems to struggle with his understanding of his present condition, his self-image, and his impulse control. His affect is within normal limits.

Educational/Vocational/Financial History. P reports graduating from high school without failing any grades. He has been unable to hold a steady job. His last job was in the construction field about three years ago, when he worked as a field supervisor. He reports that he has been working day labor just to get some money.

P relates that he is renting a room from some friends. Due to his lack of work, he is unable to live on his own. He says that he is unable to keep up with his bills and is doing the best he can.

Legal History. P has been arrested once for DUI and once for possession of cocaine. He has been on probation for the last three months. He is in a violation status due to his testing positive for cocaine while on probation.

Social History.   P states that when he was a child, his father left the family household. He says that his mother was never at home because she had to work all the time to support him and his two sisters. He says he has no idea where his father is.

P married when he was twenty-two and admits that the relationship ended due to his use of alcohol. He became involved in another relationship when he was about thirty-five and remarried a couple of years later. He does not have any biological children, but his wife has two children that he was helping to raise. He states that she asked him to leave the residence because of his drug use, anger, irritability, and inability to assist with household expenses. He was living with friends for a while and has since rented a small room. He says that his family doesn't want anything to do with him while he is using drugs.

Physical History.   P relates he experiences headaches occasionally, which he thinks causes his irritability. He denies having any sexually transmitted diseases. He says he has never been hospitalized.

Treatment History.   P reports that he went to an outpatient treatment program when he was arrested for DUI. He admits he knew at that time that he was not going to quit using drugs and alcohol. He felt the program was not helpful but completed the program so that he could regain his driver's license.

He reports that he wants to do something different. He seems aware that he needs to be in treatment in order to rebuild his life. He seems willing to make an effort in treatment, especially because he knows there may be a possibility of jail sentence.

Rationale for Diagnosis.   P's presenting problem warrants a *DSM-IV-TR* diagnosis of cocaine dependence (code 304.20) as evidenced by the following criteria: P has a long history of substance use. In the last couple of years, his primary drug of choice has been cocaine. He continued to use cocaine despite the psychological problems his use created (i.e., separation from his wife and family, trouble with the law, and emotional problems). He has given up important social, occupational, and recreational activities because of his cocaine use as evidenced by his marital separation and his inability to maintain employment and pay his bills. He has experienced withdrawal symptoms in the form of headaches, insomnia, and increased agitation, irritability, and anger. He has had a persistent desire to cut down on his using and has tried to control it by only using on the weekends. P appears to be lacking in coping skills and tends to minimize how unmanageable his life has become. When he does not know how to handle a situation, he becomes angry and abusive. The client is aware that chemical dependency has affected his life. This will make self-help meetings fundamental, allowing him positive assistance in rebuilding his life. He seems aware that, without any intervention, he may go to jail or prison.

Intervention Plan: Cocaine Dependence Disorder

P's treatment plan focuses on abstinence from cocaine, the development of a positive support system to assist him in maintaining that abstinence, obtaining and maintaining stable employment, dealing with his anger appropriately, and reuniting with his family. Present legal problems must also be addressed. Short-term goals include attendance and participation in all group sessions while learning more about the disease of addiction, acquiring techniques to live drug and alcohol free, becoming gainfully employed, and learning how to deal with his anger. He will also attend at least two self-help meetings a week and attend monthly individual treatment appointments.

Rational-emotive therapy and reality therapy as well as a twelve-step approach will be used. Treatment will include two group sessions a week, at least two self-help meetings a week, and monthly individual sessions. Group sessions will stress the progressiveness of the disease of addiction. P will be helped to understand that, although the disease is responsible for his actions, he must learn to take control of his life. This means learning the positive and negative aspects of his reactions to situations and learning how to control his feelings of anger without being hostile. All intervention efforts will be focused in the here and now, with little time spent on understanding past experiences and influences unless they are related to current behavior.

Problem 1.   Client has used mind-altering substances within the last ninety days.

Manifestations.   Client tested positive for cocaine while on probation. Client has difficulty maintaining stable employment.

Goals for Treatment.   Become abstinent within thirty days. Begin to participate in a recovery program. Become gainfully employed.

Objectives	Interventions
Client will abstain from all mind-altering substances.	Client will submit to random urine testing.
Client will identify various ways his life was negatively affected by continued substance use.	Client will attend and participate in all group and individual sessions. He will list and discuss his experiences with substance abuse, noting how the disease progressed along with the negative consequences in his life.
Client will become gainfully employed.	Using classified ads and placement agencies, client will submit three job applications per week.

Review of Treatment Plan for Problem 1.   The client entered group therapy after an introduction process. He seemed willing to orient himself with the group process. Client shared a list of ways his life had become unmanageable, per the counselor's direction, and heard feedback from the group. He attended and participated in all treatment groups and attended at least two self-help meetings each week. He reported for individual sessions, where he reported his progress on finding employment.

Problem 2.   Client is unable to deal with anger and hostility toward others.

Manifestation.   Client yells at his wife and friends and admits being physically and verbally abusive.

Goal for Treatment.   Learn how to understand and express anger and unpleasant feelings appropriately and without hostility.

Objectives	Interventions
Client will complete anger journal.	In every session, client will share from his anger journal and receive feedback from counselor and group members.
Client will practice active listening in groups.	As client listens to group members, he will repeat back to various members what he heard them say.
Client will write down specific instances when he becomes angry between counseling sessions and list how he coped when he felt that way.	Client will share his thoughts and actions during these instances in group and individual sessions and will follow feedback suggestions on how to improve his coping skills and behavior.

Review of Treatment Plan for Problem 2.   Client actively participated in all group sessions. He communicated from his anger journal things about himself, what he had learned about his anger, and how he handled his anger. Client practiced his active listening skills by feeding back to group members what he had heard them say. As treatment continued, he was able to be more aware of his thought processes to the point where he was appropriately confrontational with others.

Problem 3.   Client is estranged from family due to continued substance use.

Manifestations.   Client lives apart from his wife and children. Client's other family members do not want anything to do with him.

Goal for Treatment.   Reunite with family and attend family counseling.

Objectives	Interventions
Client will abstain from all substance use.	Client will submit to and pass random urine tests.
Client will see family counselor to discuss family issues.	Client will sign release of information for family counselor. Client will set, attend, and verify appointment with family counselor.
Client will reestablish positive contact with family and request their attendance in family counseling.	After visiting family counselor and discussing family group sessions, client will contact family and request that they visit the counselor with him.

Review of Treatment Plan for Problem 3.   Client seemed resistant at first to involving his family in the treatment process. As he progressed in treatment, he became more comfortable and in due course contacted his family. They attended several family counseling sessions. Client reestablished a more positive relationship with his family and is working on moving back into the family residence. Client's individual counselor and the family therapist established a line of communication that assisted the client in reaching his goal.

Problem 4.   Client has serious legal problems as a result of substance use.

Manifestations.   Client is presently on probation for possession of cocaine and is facing a violation that may end in a jail sentence.

Goal for Treatment.   Learn to live within the confines of the law.

Objectives	Interventions
Client will remain abstinent from all mind-altering substances.	Client will follow all counselor's directions and test substance free both in treatment and during probation. Client will share in individual and group sessions how his drug use resulted in legal involvement.
Client will attend all required court appearances for pending charge and not go to jail or prison.	Client will arrange his schedule in order to make it to his court sessions. Client will have legal representation and a counselor in court; accept responsibility for actions; and present to the court the positive turn made in life.
Client will prevent any further legal involvement. Client will maintain recovery and live within the confines of the law.	Client will successfully complete treatment and will not incur any new legal charges.

Review of Treatment Plan for Problem 4.   Client maintained abstinence as demonstrated by his clean urinalysis results. In the group and individual sessions, he shared the relationship between his continued drug use and his legal involvement. Client used this experience to change his behavior in order to live within the confines of the law. The client attended his court hearing as instructed. After pleading to the court and relating the changes he had made, the client was reinstated to probation.

Discharge Summary.   P successfully completed the treatment program without any occurrence of relapse while in the program. All tests showed that he was free from mind-altering substances. P met all his treatment plan goals. He worked on his issues and seemed to make progress. The more P learned that he could change his behavior, the more he worked on changing it. His prognosis is fair as long as he continues to abstain from mind-altering substances. He also appeared to make a strong connection with self-help and had obtained a sponsor prior to completing treatment. A plan was established on discharge to help P continue to attend self-help meetings regularly and to be involved in the twelve-step program.

BEST PRACTICES

There have been a variety of treatment options considered for use in cocaine intervention, with studies reporting information on group drug counseling, cognitive-behavioral therapy, supportive expressive therapy, coping and social skills training, acupuncture, contingency management training, twelve-step programs, and pharmacological approaches. Long-term intervention effectiveness has been questioned, with greater results noted within shorter treatment time frames. According to the Harvard Health Publications Group (1999), there is no reliable, lasting, or inexpensive cure for cocaine abuse or addiction. The reason for the lack of long-term efficacy rests in the complicated treatment process—individuals who abuse cocaine often have a multitude of psychological problems and mitigating social system problems that must be addressed as well. Historically, there have been many different approaches to the treatment of cocaine abuse, but because of these mitigating factors, few have proven to be successful in the long term. For many individuals who completed these programs, successful abstinence lasted only a few months.

Crits-Christoph and colleagues (1999) conducted a study comparing four different manual-guided treatments: individual drug counseling plus group drug counseling (GDC), cognitive therapy plus GDC, supportive-expressive therapy plus GDC, and GDC alone. This study involved 487 clients who had a *DSM-IV* diagnosis of cocaine dependence. The clients were randomly assigned to one of the four treatments. The treatment groups all stressed the importance of twelve-step concepts for maintaining abstinence.

The primary outcome measure was obtained from the Addiction Severity Index (ASI). Self-reports and urinalysis results also assessed cocaine use. The ASI was given periodically during the treatment experience: at intake; at the end of the orientation; monthly during treatment; and at nine, twelve, fifteen, and eighteen months after the treatment was completed. Overall, the study showed that those clients who received individual drug counseling and GDC achieved and maintained abstinence more than the other groups. The follow-up data indicated that these clients had the lowest drug use at nine and twelve months. This study also indicated that most clients did not achieve sustained abstinence, but 36 percent of these clients were able to maintain abstinence for a three-month period.

The most commonly known interventions for the treatment of addiction disorders are the twelve-step programs. Although many professionals agree that twelve-step programs are not the answer for everyone, they have been in existence for over sixty years and appear to be successful with a large cross-section of the population. One can easily find twelve-step meetings anywhere in the world. These groups are specific to alcohol, narcotics, or cocaine and provide not only self-help but also a so-cial support network, creating an environment where people can reconstruct their lives and learn to have fun without the use of mind-altering substances.

Fiorentine (1999) examined the effectiveness of twelve-step programs in main-taining abstinence. In this longitudinal assessment of twenty-six outpatient treat-ment programs, each client was given a Client-Needs—Services—Outcomes Ques-tionnaire (CNSQ). This questionnaire was developed by the author and consisted of three parts. Part I of the CNSQ included (1) psychosocial background information; (2) barriers to treatment and treatment utilization; (3) treatment needs; (4) drug and alcohol use; (5) criminal activity; (6) family and social functioning; (7) ancil-lary health and human services needs; and (8) attitudes and values. This portion of the instrument was administered to the client at the treatment center. The areas identified within Part II included (1) treatment needs; (2) services received; (3) drug and alcohol use; (4) criminal activity; (5) employment, vocational training, and education; (6) psychosocial functioning; (7) family functioning; (8) health sta-tus; and (9) pertinent psychological attitudes and constructs. Part II was adminis-tered approximately six months after the initial interview. Part III of the CNSQ in-cluded essentially the same domains as Part II but was administered at a twenty-four-month follow-up.

The results reported included only those participants who completed all three interviews. Nearly 49 percent had attended a twelve-step meeting in the six months prior to the twenty-four-month follow-up. After eighteen months, approximately 27 percent of those participating in any twelve-step meetings had used an illicit drug, compared with 44 percent of those not attending twelve-step meetings. The study supported the idea that participation in twelve-step programs is beneficial in achieving lower levels of drug and alcohol use. Furthermore, those who partici-pated in weekly or more frequent twelve-step meetings had lower levels of drug use than those who participated less than weekly (Fiorentine, 1999). Further results showed that although twelve-step participants may have had slightly higher levels of recovery motivation than nonparticipants, and although they may have had higher scores on the scale related to drug and alcohol abstinence, these differences in motivation accounted for very little, if any, of the more favorable drug or alcohol use outcomes for twelve-step participants. The premise of twelve-step programs is that this type of intervention will work for any addictive behavior because the roots of addiction lie in the character and lifestyle of the user, not in the substance itself (Inaba & Cohen, 2000).

Simpson, Joe, Fletcher, Hubbard, and Anglin (1999) conducted a study of 1,605 cocaine-dependent clients. Three types of treatment program were examined in the study: long-term residential programs, outpatient drug-free programs, and short-term inpatient programs. The clients were split up based on problem severity. Those with more severe problems required a more intensive treatment placement. The Problem Severity Index was used at intake and included seven problem areas: multiple drug use, alcohol dependence, criminal activity, unemployment, low so-cial support, depression or anxiety, and no insurance.

Outcome measures included self-reports and urinalysis results. The results indicated that cocaine relapse rates were highest among clients with more severe problems and early discharge from treatment. Furthermore, longer retention was related to better outcomes for clients who suffered with the highest levels of problem severity (Simpson et al., 1999).

Simpson and colleagues found that long-term residential programs were effective in the treatment of those individuals with a higher problem severity. One limitation of the study is that the researchers did not break down treatment effects into specific areas. Also, each center offered many different techniques, including reality therapy, individual psychotherapy, vocational training, and group counseling, and it is impossible to know if these confounded the results obtained. What is clear, however, is that the only common method of treatment among the three groups was the incorporation of a twelve-step program.

Avants, Margolin, Holford, and Kosten (2000) examined the use of acupuncture as an alternative to the conventional forms of treatment for cocaine addiction. In their report, they commented, "Given the lack of conventional treatments, an alternative therapy-auricular acupuncture, as codified by the National Acupuncture Detoxification Association (NADA)—is in widespread use in drug treatment facilities across the country" (p. 2, 305). This study involved eighty-two participants who were using cocaine and had agreed to participate in a methadone maintenance program. Participants were randomly assigned to one of three treatment conditions: NADA auricular acupuncture protocol, auricular needle insertion control, or relaxation control. At entry into the study and at an eight-week follow-up, participants were given the ASI, the Treatment Credibility Scale, and the Stages of Change Readiness and Treatment Eagerness Scale (SOCRATES). The results supported acupuncture as an effective alternative treatment for cocaine addiction. Caution is warranted, however, because further research on the use of acupuncture is needed.

A study conducted by Margolin et al. (2002), similar to that conducted by Avants et al. (2000), included 620 participants who received weekly individual counseling. The measurement instruments used in this study were the ASI, the Treatment Credibility Scale, the SOCRATES, and the Treatment Services Review (TCR). The researchers stated, "Our study used a research design nearly equivalent to that of a previous, smaller study conducted at the Yale site in which the same four-needle version of the NADA protocol delivered for eight weeks was found to be superior to the two control conditions in reducing cocaine use in cocaine-dependent, methadone-maintained patients. In that study, 54 percent of NADA acupuncture completers provided cocaine negative urine samples in the last week of the study compared to 23 percent of the NADA acupuncture completers in this study" (2002). In conclusion, Margolin and colleagues reported that acupuncture was not found more effective than needle insertion or relaxation control in reducing cocaine use. Based on these study results, acupuncture as a stand-alone treatment falls short as a means for treating cocaine addiction when patients receive only minimal psychosocial treatments.

Higgins, Budney, Bickel, and Badger (1994) examined the effectiveness of an outpatient behavioral treatment program that consisted of contingency-management procedures and counseling according to the Community Reinforcement Approach (CRA). The goal of the study was to identify the predictors of cocaine abstinence and the efficacy of an outpatient behavioral treatment. The contingency-management procedures involved therapists and clients jointly selecting retail items and activities to reinforce abstinence. The CRA procedures were implemented one to two times weekly for one-hour sessions. The goal was to increase the availability of natural reinforcers in the environment so that abstinence could be long term. One of the main goals of the treatment was to involve in the therapy a willing spouse, friend, or relative who was not addicted to a substance. The test group consisted of fifty-two adults who met the *DSM-III-R* criteria for cocaine dependence. The majority of the subjects were Caucasian males. The results of the study revealed that the involvement of a significant other in the therapeutic milieu was a predictor of cocaine abstinence, and social support was recognized as important for improving treatment outcomes.

Monti and O'Leary (1999) examined the use of Coping and Social Skills Training (CSST) in the treatment of substance abuse. According to the authors, CSST originated from social learning theory and now appears to be gaining support for inclusion in addictions prevention and treatment. Based on the premise that many addicted individuals lack the adequate coping skills to function in daily activities, CSST is designed to facilitate social development and teach coping skills. Monti and O'Leary contend that client difficulties can be the result of person-environment interactions, biologic predispositions, precipitating stressful environmental demands, the build up of daily hassles, or peer pressure. These environmental pressures make the development and application of adaptive coping skills difficult for users. CSST focuses on four main themes: (1) interpersonal skills for enhancing relationships; (2) cognitive-emotional coping for affect regulation; (3) coping skills for managing daily life events; and (4) coping with substance-use cues. They emphasize the use of cue-exposure in this form of treatment and consider it an integral part of CSST.

The authors discuss in further detail the rationale and guidelines of CSST in the treatment of alcohol and cocaine abuse. For each substance, they give an assessment, an overview, a rationale, and an outline for treatment. They state that CSST has been an effective treatment for alcohol abuse and that preliminary findings support its promise in treating cocaine addictions. They found that when compared with the control group, the experimental group used less cocaine or used for a shorter time. This study emphasized that, although the use of medication has been successful in treating some addictions, medication alone is never enough, and the use of psychosocial interventions should also be considered.

Crits-Christoph et al. (1999) and Simpson et al. (1999) each studied the effect of the average number of days spent in treatment on relapse rates for cocaine-dependent clients. The results, summarized in table 6, indicate that the lowest

Table 6: Effect of Treatment Length on Relapse Rate among Cocaine-Dependent Clients

Type of group	Average time spent in treatment	Relapse rate
IDC + GDC	46 days	40.4%
CT + GDC	77 days	46.2%
ST + GDC	72 days	48.3%
GDC	56 days	46.7%
LTR	4–9 months	15%
STI	21 days	38%
ODF	90 days	29%

Sources: Crits-Christoph et al. (1999) and Simpson et al. (1999).
Note: IDC = individual drug counseling; GDC = group drug counseling, CT = cognitive therapy; ST = supportive expressive therapy; LTR = long-term residential treatment; STI = short-term inpatient treatment; and ODF = outpatient drug-free program. All groups followed twelve-step program principles.

percentage of relapse occurred among clients who had undergone long-term residential treatment, which required the most time spent in treatment.

The last treatment option, which is almost always used as part of the intervention process, is pharmacological. Because any intervention approach must also seek to achieve sustained abstinence, the medical aspects such as withdrawal symptoms and cravings for cocaine cannot be ignored. The fear of a client substituting one drug for another resounds throughout the literature, but it appears that a combination approach of medications and psychosocial treatments offers the most promise.

SUMMARY AND FUTURE DIRECTIONS

In terms of best practices, the assessment and treatment of cocaine addiction is varied. Straussner (1993) commented that, "based both on current research and on the clinical treatment for cocaine- and other stimulant-dependent clients, it is becoming apparent that an integrated approach addressing each client's substance-related social, psychological, and biological problems is needed if treatment is to succeed" (p. 318). Fiorentine's study suggested that continuous twelve-step participation is a definite predictor of long-term abstinence during and after conventional treatment. Throughout these studies, almost all professionals recommend the integration of a twelve-step program as part of follow-up intervention. Higgins et al. (1994) suggested that the involvement of significant others in treatment, when they are open to participating, is also a predictor of success.

As noted, treatment must be individualized to meet the client's needs. Best practice indicates a thorough assessment of the client to effectively determine the most appropriate treatment for that individual. Abstinence must be the primary goal of any treatment plan, however, whatever the client's needs may be. Those suffering from cocaine addiction often experience one or more of the following symptoms: aggressive behaviors, anxiety, depression, weight loss, neglect of important responsibilities, and paranoid ideation. Once an assessment has determined the specific symptoms from which the client suffers, a treatment plan can then be drawn up that will address those particular needs and therefore, one hopes, will be more effective. The treatment plan for P, an individual diagnosed with a cocaine-related addiction, was individualized to his specific needs, and this is the reason that the case example in this chapter was broken down into such specific areas.

When developing a treatment plan, many things should be taken into consideration. For the most part, it appears that administering a standardized measure such as the ASI could assist in assessing several domains related to substance use, which in turn would be helpful in the development of the treatment plan. Ideally, the practitioner should ensure that the individual being treated has had a proper and thorough medical and psychosocial assessment.

Dependence on drugs and alcohol continues to be a problem in our society, although the drug of choice often changes with the times. Recent research indicates that cocaine use continues to be a problem in the United States. It is also apparent from the research that many people suffer from cocaine dependence simultaneously with other substance dependencies. In addition, more and more adolescents are experimenting with or using cocaine, making early education and intervention critical.

One controversial area in the treatment of cocaine-related addictions that needs further examination is the use of pharmacological approaches to treat cocaine dependence. The debate over replacing one substance with another continues to rage. There does appear to be promise for using these drugs to minimize the cravings, but more research is needed to substantiate the effectiveness of combining pharmacology with psychosocial treatments such as twelve-step programs, coping skills training, and individual counseling.

Because every substance-dependent individual suffers from this disease in a different way, it is helpful to be familiar with a variety of approaches and to be flexible enough to use the approach that best suits the client. This is especially true for clients with mental health issues as well as substance use issues, who will always require assessment and intervention for both.

In terms of future directions, recognition of the importance of family and members of other social support systems in helping clients to be more involved in the intervention process could lead to greater long-term treatment success. The family would also benefit from treatment that teaches them life skills similar to those that are being developed in their recovering loved one. Involving the family can also directly effect the environment to which the client returns during and after treatment. Taking into account the role that environment plays in long-term treatment success, the participation of family and members of other social support systems in treatment is an integral component of intervention success in the inpatient, outpatient, and community settings.

References

American Psychiatric Association. (2000). *Diagnostic and statistical manual of mental disorders* (4th ed., text rev.). Washington, DC: Author.

Avants, K., Margolin, A., Holford, T. R., & Kosten, T. R. (2000). Randomized controlled trial of auricular acupuncture for cocaine dependence. *Archive Internal Medicine, 160*, 2305–12.

Crits-Christoph, P., Siqueland, L., Blaine, J., Frank, A., Luborsky, L., Onken, L., et al. (1999). Psychosocial treatments for cocaine dependence. *Archive of General Psychiatry, 56*, 493–502.

Fiorentine, R. (1999). After drug treatment: Are 12-step programs effective in maintaining abstinence? *American Journal of Drug and Alcohol Abuse, 25*(1), 93–116.

Harvard Health Publications Group. (1999, December). Cocaine abuse and addiction—Part II. *Harvard Mental Health Letter, 16*.

Higgins, S. T., Budney, A. J., Bickel, W. K., & Badger, G. J. (1994). Participation of significant others in outpatient behavioral treatment predicts greater cocaine abstinence. *American Journal of Drug and Alcohol Abuse, 20*, 47–57.

Inaba, D. S., & Cohen, W. E. (2000). *Uppers, downers, all arounders: Physical and mental effects of psychoactive drugs* (4th ed.). Ashland, OR: CNS Publications.

Levin, J. (1999). *Primer for treating substance abusers.* Northvale, NJ: Jason Aronson.

Margolin, A., Kleber, H. D., Avants, K., Konefal, J., Gawin, F., Stark, E., et al. (2002). Acupuncture for the treatment of cocaine addition: A randomized controlled trial. *Journal of the American Medical Association, 287*, 55–64.

McNeece, C., & DiNitto, D., (1998). *Chemical dependency: A systems approach* (2nd ed.). Boston: Allyn & Bacon.

Monti, P. M., & O'Leary, T. A. (1999). Coping skills training for alcohol and cocaine dependence. *Psychiatric Clinics of North America; Addictive Disorders, 22*, 447–69.

National Institute on Drug Abuse. (2003). *Research report series—Cocaine abuse and addiction.* Retrieved June 13, 2004, from http:www.nida.nih.gov/researchreports/cocaine/cocaine.html

National Institute of Health. (1999). *Research report: Cocaine abuse and addiction.* Retrieved July 10, 2002, from http:www.nida.nih.gov/researchreports.html

Nutt, D. J. (1996). Addiction: Brain mechanisms and their treatment implications. *Lancet, 347*, 31–37.

Office of National Drug Control Policy. (2001). *Drug facts: Cocaine.* Retrieved December 26, 2003, from: http://whitehousedrugpolicy.gov/drugfact/cocaine/cocaine_b.html

Simpson, D. D., Joe, G. W., Fletcher, B. W., Hubbard, R. L., & Anglin, M. D. (1999). A national evaluation of treatment outcomes for cocaine dependence. *Archives of General Psychiatry, 56*, 507–14.

Straussner, S. (1993). *Clinical work with substance abusing clients.* New York: Guilford Press.

Chapter 5

Caffeine

Sophia F. Dziegielewski, Jacqueline Swank, and Sara Wienke

CAFFEINE IS ONE OF THE MOST POPULAR AND WIDELY CONSUMED SUBstances in the world (Benshoff & Janikowski, 2000). It has been classified as a psychoactive drug, in the same group as heroin, cocaine, marijuana, nicotine, and alcohol, because it influences mood and behavior. On any given day, caffeine is abused in numerous ways through the ingestion of coffee, tea, soft drinks, and medications. The resulting tolerance, craving, dependence, sensitivity to various doses, and habitual use can have many undesirable effects. Caffeine can cause irregular heartbeat, depression, insomnia, hand tremors, eye twitching, high anxiety, and gastrointestinal upsets (Rogers and Dernoncourt, 1998). Researchers agree that the best treatment for caffeine abuse is a gradual reduction of dosage followed by continued limited consumption (Cherniske, 1998; Mars, 2001). Nutrition education, exercise, homeopathy, and aromatherapy are also suggested to help reduce or replace caffeine habits (Mars, 2001; Reichenberg-Ullman, 2000). For many adults, learning time management skills is essential for reducing their need for caffeine.

This chapter discusses the prevalence of caffeine use and the potential for caffeine dependence, abuse, and withdrawal, despite the fact that there are no classifications for these categories in the *DSM-IV-TR* (American Psychiatric Association [APA], 2000). A case that emphasizes the use of the multiaxial diagnostic system for a client who suffers from caffeine intoxication is presented. Example intervention strategies include self-monitoring, relaxation techniques, and education related to the consequences of caffeine abuse. A review of the literature on the treatment of excessive caffeine consumption is also included, along with a discussion of the need for additional research.

THE ORIGIN AND HISTORY OF CAFFEINE

Caffeine is the most commonly used, freely marketed drug in the world, with more than 80 percent of the population using it daily. *Caffeine* and *coffee* are words of Arabic origin. The roots of caffeine can be traced back to the sixteenth century, and coffee consumption rapidly spread into Europe by the seventeenth century. The white, bitter tasting, crystalline substance was first isolated from coffee in 1820. In addition to coffee, caffeine is consumed in teas, soft drinks, and medications. Across the globe, tea is the most commonly consumed caffeinated beverage. Coffee drinking is the major mode of caffeine consumption in many countries, especially in Europe. In the United States, "more than half a billion cups are consumed daily, with most consumers drinking two or more cups, and more than 10 pounds of coffee per person are consumed yearly" (Haas, 2000, p. 1). One major difference between coffee and tea is the slightly lower amount of caffeine contained in each cup of tea. According to Cherniske (1998), caffeine levels per serving for the most common sources of the drug are as follows: coffee, 90–120 mg; tea, 35–70 mg, soft drinks, 45–72 mg; cocoa, 13 mg; chocolate, 6–35 mg; and medications, 16–200 mg (per dose). Overall, tea and coffee account for 90 percent of the caffeine consumed in the United States, with most of the other 10 percent being consumed through soft drinks.

It is difficult to study the tolerance of human subjects to the various effects of caffeine because nearly everyone in the United States uses it regularly in one form or another. It is well known that caffeine is habit forming, and many people feel that they cannot start their day without that first cup of coffee or other caffeinated beverage. The amount of caffeine needed to produce this wake-up increases with regular use; therefore, larger and more frequent doses will be needed to obtain the same effect (Haas, 2000). Daily use of the drug at a level of approximately 280 mg can cause physical dependence. If this use is interrupted, characteristics of withdrawal such as headaches, drowsiness, jitters, irritability, increased weight, flu-like symptoms, and anxiety will be present anywhere from several days to a few weeks (Cherniske, 1998; Griffiths & Juliano, 2004). Unfortunately, these symptoms can have a variety of causes, which impedes the ability of researchers to pinpoint with confidence the exact effects of caffeine consumption and withdrawal.

PSYCHOPHYSIOLOGICAL EFFECTS

Generally, caffeine is absorbed into the blood and body tissue within five minutes of ingestion, and after about thirty minutes, it has reached its peak within the system. Caffeine has a half-life of four to five hours; that is, only half the dosage of caffeine ingested remains in the body after that time. Caffeine is a central nervous system stimulant that affects the brain, causing increases in neural activity, performance of simple intellectual tasks, and processing of information. Caffeine also increases alertness and the ability to concentrate. It counters fatigue, but in doing so, it can also delay the onset of sleep. When sleep does occur, the substance can affect sleep quality, depth, and length. Through central nervous system stimulation, caffeine increases brain activity, but it also stimulates the cardiovascular system, resulting in a subsequent rise in blood pressure and heart rate (Nehlig, 1999). It generally speeds up the human body, increasing basal metabolic rate, and for many this is a positive side effect, especially when trying to burn more calories (Haas,

2000). Caffeine also stimulates the heart and respiratory systems, causing a temporary increase in breathing, heart rate, and blood pressure. It acts as a mild diuretic and laxative, resulting in the loss of water, vitamins, and minerals from the body. Consumption of large amounts of caffeine may contribute to symptoms of psychosis, anxiety, and insomnia (Kenny, Carlson, McGuigan, & Sheppard, 2000). Depressed body activity may result from the use of large amounts of caffeine (Daly & Fredholm, 1998).

CAFFEINE ADDICTION

When we think of the word *drug*, we are usually referring to illegal narcotics, hallucinogens, or prescription and over-the-counter medications. But caffeine, although legal, is one of the most commonly used drugs of all. This drug is so commonly used that some individuals or refer to it as the drug of choice at Alcoholics Anonymous and other twelve-step meetings (Reichenberg-Ullman, 2000). Caffeine boosts energy and is classified as a psychoactive drug that can have synergistic effects when combined with other substances such as nicotine (Jones & Griffiths, 2003). The ease of consumption makes this type of psychoactive substance so beneficial that the military has evaluated its use to help push human performance even further (Lamberg, 1999).

The action of caffeine on the brain differs from other psychostimulant substances such as amphetamines, cocaine, morphine, and nicotine (Nehlig, 1999). Even at low doses, these drugs trigger activity in the shell of the nucleus accumbens—the part of the brain responsible for addiction. For caffeine, it would take the equivalent of seven or more cups of caffeinated coffee, all consumed in rapid succession, to begin to activate this portion of the brain (Nehlig, 1999). Despite differing opinions on caffeine addiction, researchers do agree that symptoms of withdrawal are present when an individual does not consume his or her usual caffeine intake. Addiction to caffeine is not considered as harmful as addiction to the other substances described in this book; however, it may become a problem for many if they are not fully aware of the symptoms it may be causing. When caffeine is withdrawn, many individuals become keenly aware of the effect this powerful drug is having on their bodies. Tapering off one's use over time will reduce the severity of the withdrawal symptoms that often result (Haas, 2000).

CAFFEINE-INDUCED DISORDERS

According to the *DSM-IV-TR* (APA, 2000), there are four caffeine-induced disorders: caffeine intoxication, caffeine-induced anxiety disorder, caffeine-induced sleep disorder, and caffeine-related disorder not otherwise specified. The *DSM-IV-TR* does not list a diagnosis for caffeine abuse, dependence, or withdrawal. Whether this substance causes abuse remains controversial, but once confirmed in the research, caffeine abuse will most likely be added to the current diagnostic category.

The *DSM-IV-TR* identifies four general criteria for the abuse of any substance: failure to fulfill major role obligations due to recurrent substance use, use in hazardous situations, related legal problems, and continued use despite recurring interpersonal and social problems. Because those who use caffeine, even those who use it regularly, do not experience this level of impairment, caffeine was not included in these categories. According to Hughes, Oliveto, Liguori, Carpenter, and Howard (1998), only 3 percent of the participants in their study of caffeine users met these criteria, supporting the noninclusion of a diagnosis for caffeine abuse in the *DSM-IV-TR*.

Dependence is defined in the *DSM-IV-TR* as the exhibition of any three of the following criteria: tolerance, withdrawal, the use of increasingly larger amounts, inability to quit, a great deal of time spent on obtaining the substance, activities given up due to substance use, and continued use despite knowledge of harmful health effects. Interestingly, caffeine is the only substance listed in the *DSM IV-TR* that cannot be classified under dependence. Nehlig (1999) proposed that the typical method of caffeine consumption—oral consumption gradually throughout the day—could actually reduce the risk of dependence.

Hughes et al. (1998) found that 17 percent of the participants in their study of caffeine users stated that they had to increase the amount of caffeine they consumed to maintain the same effect. In contrast, 45 percent of users in the study had cut down or stopped consuming caffeine for various reasons during the last year and had discontinued their previous pattern of use for various periods. Of the group of users who cut down or stopped their consumption, 11 percent met the criteria for withdrawal. This group accounted for 5 percent of the total number of users in the study. Thirty-eight percent reported consuming more caffeinated beverages than intended, and 28 percent acknowledged that this increased consumption occurred at least once a month. This meets the third criterion for substance dependence—use of increasingly larger amounts of the substance. Fifty-six percent of the individuals in the study reported a persistent desire for caffeine or unsuccessful attempts to cut down or control the use of caffeine. Fifty percent spent large amounts of time obtaining, using, or recovering from caffeine use. Only one person involved in the study reported giving up or reducing activities due to caffeine use. Fourteen percent of the participants continued to use caffeine despite their knowledge of health problems resulting from the use of the substance. Overall, 30 percent of the participants met at least three of the criteria for substance dependence as classified in the *DSM-IV-TR*. Sixteen percent of these individuals qualified for physiological dependence, which is evidenced by tolerance or withdrawal.

The *DSM-IV-TR* lists three criteria for substance withdrawal: a substance-specific syndrome developed due to reduction or cessation of a substance that has been in prolonged or heavy use, a syndrome that causes clinically significant impairment, and symptoms are not accounted for by a general medical condition or another mental disorder. Hughes et al. (1998) determined that 11 percent of the participants in their study met the criteria for substance withdrawal.

Caffeine intoxication, as classified in the *DSM-IV-TR*, includes the recent consumption of caffeine in excessive amounts, usually exceeding 250 mg (more than two to three cups of coffee); symptoms causing clinically significant distress or impairment in functioning; the symptoms are not due to a general medical condition or accounted for by another mental disorder; and the presence of at least five of the following symptoms, developed during or shortly after use: restlessness, nervousness, excitement, insomnia, flushed face, diuresis, gastrointestinal disturbance, muscle twitching, rambling thought and speech, tachycardia or cardiac arrhythmia, inexhaustibility, or psychomotor agitation (APA, 2000, p. 232). Hughes et al. (1998) found that 7 percent of the participants met the criteria for caffeine intoxication, and two-thirds of the participants reported exhibiting at least one of the caffeine intoxication symptoms.

CASE EXAMPLE

Case History

K, a thirty-five-year-old Caucasian female with an average IQ, was referred to a mental health agency by a hospital social worker. She had been discharged from the local hospital the day before, after receiving treatment for injuries resulting from a vehicle accident. She had been admitted to the emergency room after hitting a tree with the truck she was driving to make deliveries for the local newspaper. In the two months prior to the accident, K reported, she drank coffee from a thermos continually during her four-hour delivery route, after always drinking at least two cups before leaving her house. She consumed this caffeine to stay alert during her delivery route. She admitted to usually finishing the thermos, which held four cups of coffee, within the first two hours. She also stated that, on the day of the accident, she took a couple of No Doz tablets before leaving home because she was extremely tired. K complained that as time went on, the delivery route was taking longer to complete because of frequent stops to use the restroom.

K reported that her husband had left for work one day about four months ago and never returned home. She stated that she had a full-time job working as a secretary for an accounting firm, but without her husband's help, she feared her current salary was inadequate to support herself and her two children. K stated that the bills were beginning to pile up, and she had to work the two jobs to try to make ends meet. She reported that she works at her secretary job from 9:00 a.m. to 5:00 p.m. and then delivers newspapers from 3:00 a.m. to 5:30 a.m. K's children are ages five and two. K's mother has moved in with K to help take care of the children.

A friend had suggested that K drink large amounts of coffee and take a few No Doz tablets to stay awake during her work shifts. No Doz tablets contain high doses of caffeine. K had always drunk a few cups of coffee in the morning before going to work, and she decided to just add a little more when she got up for the delivery route instead of taking the No Doz. After doing this for a couple of weeks, she had a difficult time going to sleep due to restlessness after finishing her delivery job.

K had rambling speech patterns when she came home. Her mother reported that she had trouble understanding K and that K's face was always flushed. K reported that she had tried to switch to decaffeinated coffee because she thought it would be better for her health, but she was getting headaches and having difficulty staying awake while driving.

On the morning of the accident, K reported being especially tired because she had been awake for the last two nights with her sick two-year-old. To stay awake, she had taken a couple of No Doz tablets for the first time, along with her usual coffee consumption. She believed the caffeine tablets would give her the extra boost she needed that morning. She stated that she could not remember a lot about the accident, although she was sure she had not fallen asleep at the wheel. K stated that the last thing she could remember was her body twitching and that she was having difficulty steering the truck. She also reported that she swerved after seeing a large animal resembling a dinosaur in the middle of the road. K stated that, previously, she had seen bright lights and other images while driving her paper delivery route. She reported she had not told anyone about her "visions" because she did not want people to think she was crazy.

K appeared to be very restless and nervous during the interview. She stated that she had already drunk several cups of coffee. K reported that she felt compelled to drink the coffee, even though she did not have to drive the route that morning. K stated that she had to drink more than her usual two cups at home because she needed more coffee to feel the same level of alertness. She also stated she would get a headache at work if she did not drink soft drinks or tea during the day.

Multiaxial Diagnostic Assessment

Incorporating information provided by the client and taking into account her resultant actions, the following multiaxial diagnostic impression was formulated:

Axis I: Caffeine Intoxication (305.90)
Axis II: No diagnosis (V71.09)
Axis III: Diuresis (788.42)
Axis IV: 1. Spousal separation
            2. Introduction of multigenerational household
            3. Stressful work schedule
            4. Inadequate finances
            5. Recent hospitalization
Axis V: 55

Axis I.   K met the criteria for caffeine intoxication. She also exhibits symptoms of developing a tolerance for the substance as well as symptoms of withdrawal, which are criteria for substance dependence. According to Larson and Carey (1998), caffeine can affect an individual's psychological state. This could explain the flashes of light and the dinosaur-like animal that K reported seeing during her delivery route after consuming large amounts of caffeine. Kenny et al. (2000) reported similar symptoms of psychosis when the activity of the central nervous system is increased by the combination of consuming large amounts of caffeine and the presence of stress.

According to Rogers and Dernoncourt (1998), headaches, tiredness, and depression are some adverse effects of caffeine withdrawal. Changes in cerebral blood flow also have a connection to caffeine withdrawal. Symptoms of withdrawal disappear soon after the consumption of caffeine (Nehlig, 1999). The symptoms of withdrawal are commonly felt after awakening in the morning due to caffeine deprivation during the night (Lane & Phillips-Bute, 1998). This could provide an explanation for the headache K felt after awakening the morning of her assessment. Interestingly, according to Rogers and Dernoncourt (1998), those who do not use caffeine claim that ingesting caffeine in the morning is "overstimulating" for them. Lane and Phillips-Bute (1998) reported that caffeine deprivation might significantly impact an individual's mood and work performance. K stated that she needed to consume soft drinks or tea at work to avoid headaches. Kenny et al. (2000) have found that, despite the connection between caffeine and maintaining a level of alertness, caffeine use does not improve one's performance of cognitive tasks.

Caffeine has been shown to shorten sleep duration and prolong periods of alertness (Lamberg, 1999; Nehlig, 1999). K experienced insomnia after finishing her newspaper deliveries. Nehlig (1999) noted that it is unclear whether a person's caffeine tolerance level has a correlation to sleeping patterns.

Axis II.   No diagnosis.

Axis III.   The diagnosis of diuresis—excessive urination—is evidenced by K's reports of frequent urination during her delivery of newspapers.

Axis IV.   There are several environmental stressors present in K's life. The absence of her husband has caused a significant amount of stress in several facets of her life. K's financial burdens have increased, causing her to seek another job. The hospital costs from her car accident may increase the financial burden faced by the family. The second job has contributed to a stressful work environment. Finally, the maternal grandmother's inclusion in the household could create stressful conflicts in the house.

Axis V.   The client was given a 55 on the Global Assessment of Functioning scale. This determination was made based on the occurrence of moderate symptoms described by the client. The client's symptoms are stronger than mild symptoms because she currently has a consistent daily pattern of impairment in functioning, but her level of impairment does not appear to qualify for serious symptoms. She has several stressors present in her life, but she continues to maintain a job and did not report suicidal thoughts. The score of 55 lies in the middle of the range for a client exhibiting moderate symptoms.

Intervention Plan: Caffeine Intoxication

The following goals, objectives, and interventions were developed around the current problems identified in K's discussion with the practitioner. The other areas for treatment are related to environmental stressors identified in the client's life that are directly affecting her health and well-being and are correlated to the diagnosis of caffeine intoxication. Through gradual completion of the treatment plan, the prognosis is good that K's level of social and occupational functioning will increase across the time frame of treatment.

A six-month treatment period is estimated, but it is suggested that K have a medical examination prior to any intervention to rule out the possibility of medical problems related to current impairments in social and occupational functioning.

Problem 1.   Excessive consumption of caffeine (caffeine intoxication).

Goal for Treatment.   Reduce caffeine intake.

Objective.   Client will decrease caffeine consumption from six or more cups of coffee/cans of soft drinks to two cups of coffee/cans of soft drinks as measured by a log kept by the client.

Action Tasks.
1. The therapist will assess the role of caffeine in K's level of functioning.
2. With the help of the practitioner, K will identify events that trigger her caffeine use and the positive and negative consequences of that use.
3. K will buy half her current amount of caffeinated beverages and will buy additional decaffeinated beverages to supplement the remaining half.
4. The therapist will provide for K educational materials related to the harmful effects of consuming excessive amounts of caffeine.
5. K and the therapist will explore possible support groups available in the community.
6. The therapist will teach K relaxation techniques.

Problem 2.   Presence of numerous environmental stressors.

Goal for Treatment.   Decrease current environmental stressors.

Objective.   Client will reduce stress related to inadequate finances and a stressful work schedule as measured by stress inventory scales conducted once a month during therapy sessions.

Action Tasks.
1. The therapist will help K explore services for assistance with income, including food stamps and housing assistance.
2. The therapist will work with K to develop a budget.
3. K will discuss with the therapist her stress related to her current employment, and they will develop a plan to create a less stressful work schedule.

Problem 3.   Limited support system.

Goal for Treatment.   Increase interpersonal relationships.

Objective 1.   Client will strengthen relationships within her immediate family as measured by reports from self and family members.

Action Tasks.
1. The therapist will explore with K the possibility of family counseling.
2. K will discuss issues related to role conflicts and household responsibilities with her mother.

3. K will conduct weekly family meetings with her family to discuss issues relating to the well-being of family members.
4. The therapist will discuss with K issues of grief and loss and explore connected feelings related to her separation from her husband.

Objective 2.   Client will develop interpersonal relationships outside of her
immediate family as measured by reports from client on a monthly basis.

Action Tasks.
1. K will create a list of possible sources of support outside of her immediate
family.
2. K will discuss her list of potential sources of support with the therapist.
3. K will join a club/organization identified on her list of potential sources of
support.
4. During therapy sessions, the therapist will work with K on developing relationship skills to enhance her positive reactions with others including her
coworkers.

BEST PRACTICES

Larson and Carey (1998) put forth recommendations for clinicians in mental
health settings related to the impact of caffeine in mental health treatment. The authors stressed the importance of conducting an assessment to accurately identify
the role of caffeine in correlation with mental health issues. For instances of excessive use of caffeine, the authors detail the importance of identifying the triggers
of caffeine use and the consequences, both positive and negative. The authors find
that self-monitoring allows clients to have a better awareness of their caffeine consumption. Because caffeine consumption through coffee and soft drinks is seen as
a normal act in the lives of people around the world, Larson and Carey recommend
educating individuals about the physical and psychological effects that caffeine has
on the body. This education can be provided through the use of psychoeducational
groups. Caffeine consumption problems have been treated with relaxation training
designed to decrease stress and provide an alternative to caffeine consumption
(Hyner, 1979). Overall, evidence-based research documenting the treatment of caffeine consumption is scarce. This is probably why the *DSM-TR-IV* does not identify
a diagnostic category for caffeine abuse, dependence, or withdrawal. Caffeine intoxication is the only classification out of the four categories of substance use that
is diagnosable according to the *DSM-IV-TR*.

It appears that the best treatment practice for reducing or eliminating caffeine consumption is a gradual approach, cutting out one serving of coffee (or
other caffeinated substance) each day until the desired amount of caffeine is eliminated. This can help prevent symptoms of withdrawal such as headaches, fatigue,
and anxiety (Sawynok, 1995). Abrupt cessation will result in withdrawal symptoms
within twelve to eighteen hours (Mars, 2001). Although aspirin or other pain relievers may help to relieve symptoms, the relief is often temporary. When caffeine

is eliminated completely, it may take quite some time before the craving for caffeine is gone.

According to Haas (2000), "for caffeine detoxification, it is important to support ourselves nutritionally while we eliminate or reduce our intake. Breaking the habit by tapering down or going 'cold turkey' will be better handled with a good diet and adrenal support" (p. 6). Maintaining a good diet and adrenal support includes eating fruits and vegetables, decreasing acidic foods, drinking at least six to eight glasses of water daily, and taking vitamin C supplements.

Natural and homeopathic therapies have become popular alternatives to caffeine. These substances can provide supplements when going "cold turkey" or gradually reducing caffeine intake. For example, green tea is suggested as a substitute for coffee or other teas because it contains much less caffeine and offers other health benefits. Herbal therapy is suggested for taking the place of the stimulation one gets from caffeine. Ginseng helps the body adapt to stress and promotes mental and physical alertness, and ginkgo improves circulation. Nutrition therapy focuses on relieving stress by reducing the amount of stimulants in the body. Exercising, eating high-protein snacks, and deep-breathing exercises are all ways to energize without caffeine. Aromatherapy involves inhaling essential oils such as peppermint, lavender, or rosemary to perk one's self up (Mars, 2001). Homeopathy expert Reichenberg-Ullman (2000) reports that "hypnosis, parts therapy, visualization, detoxification diets, fasting and cleansing, and supportive nutritional supplements are all therapies which we find helpful to relieve people of their caffeine habits" (p. 4).

Generally, there are no support groups to help people dependent upon caffeine, nor are there drug treatment programs that focus on caffeine. Yet caffeine can be a powerful substance of addiction and should not be overlooked. Treatment for caffeine abuse is similar for all populations once the caffeinated substance the individual is consuming too much of—coffee, tea, soft drinks, or medications—is identified. Limiting the consumption of caffeinated beverages, foods, and medications is the best way to address caffeine addiction. Substituting decaffeinated forms of beverages may help. One may prevent unwittingly ingesting too much caffeine by becoming aware of the types of foods, medications, and beverages that contain high amounts of caffeine and then limiting their use. Both researchers and clinicians have documented this, from studies and from direct client feedback. Tapering off consumption produces the least amount of withdrawal symptoms.

In this fast-paced society, the popularity of ingesting caffeine in pill form, such as No Doz and Vivarin, which are available without a prescription, has increased. Pills provide a fast and easy way to postpone sleep and stay alert. However, side effects including a numbing/tingling sensation in the arms and legs, nervousness, dizziness, and nausea may occur, causing the individual to feel sick and unable to complete the specific task as desired, despite being awake. Scott et al. (2002) found that giving caffeine to a group of college-age individuals increased their anxiety when completing low-level tasks. Furthermore, long-term use of caffeine can produce tolerance, thereby decreasing some of the effects experienced by the regular user (Sawynok, 1995).

As evidenced in the case example, it is dangerous to take caffeine in high concentrations. The side effect often reported to be of most concern is the disruption of sleep patterns that can leave a person feeling exhausted. Education focusing on developing healthy habits such as time management, avoiding procrastination, and maintaining good health, sleep, and exercise is considered to be an effective treatment. Most individuals do not realize how much caffeine they have ingested after taking a couple of pills in addition to drinking several cups of coffee or soft drinks. Even without the pills, several cups of a caffeinated beverage is plenty to keep an individual alert.

Special Considerations

Caffeine is an accepted drug in society, and there is a lack of awareness related to the potential dangerous consequences that can occur from its use. Even those who are aware of these dangers may ignore the risk of potential side effects and withdrawal symptoms.

In addition to the temporary side effects mentioned earlier, there may be a correlation between the daily use of caffeine across the lifespan and other seemingly unrelated consequences such as premature death due to heart disease (Kenny et al., 2000).

According to a study conducted by Hettema, Corey, and Kendler (1999), patterns of caffeine consumption tend to run in families. This study highlights the importance of including the client's parents, siblings, and other blood relatives in the treatment of a disorder. If patterns of caffeine consumption are similar among family members, it may be difficult to obtain a significant level of support from family members when addressing issues related to caffeine consumption. Family members' knowledge of the large number of people who consume caffeine on a daily basis combined with their own patterns of use may lead them to deny that the client has a problem (Monroe, 1998). They may see even excessive caffeine consumption as "normal."

Client involvement in a support group could be beneficial within the intervention process, but it would be difficult to find or create a group of individuals exhibiting strictly caffeine-related problems. The client would probably have to be grouped with individuals exhibiting other substance-related problems. If the potential problems related to caffeine were more widely recognized, the creation of a support group that deals specifically with this caffeine abuse could be possible. Such a group could help create an awareness of the problem, provide a supportive atmosphere, and serve as a source of accountability for its members by helping them to set and follow through on goals to reduce the amount of caffeine consumed.

SUMMARY AND FUTURE DIRECTIONS

The widespread and increasing use of caffeine worldwide warrants additional research on its short- and long-term effects. According to Kenny et al. (2000), there is a particular lack of research examining the effects of caffeine in children. Such research may show a correlation between caffeine and emotional and behavioral problems in children, such as hyperactivity, or indicate that caffeine consumption by young children may effect their development. Kenny et al. also acknowledge the need for additional research examining the consumption of caffeine by pregnant women and the effects this may have on their unborn children. Rogers and Dernoncourt (1998) acknowledge the importance of research on the effects of caffeine by stating that, even though caffeine may cause a small amount of harm for individuals, it is the "most popular drug in the world" and therefore its overall impact on the physical and psychological well-being of the population may be very large.

The study conducted by Hughes et al. (1998) was limited to 202 participants in one metropolitan county but yielded interesting results. The study revealed a 30 percent rate of substance dependence, with a 3 percent rate of abuse, an 11 percent rate of withdrawal, and a 7 percent rate of intoxication. These figures indicate a need for additional research to determine if there is justification for diagnostic classifications for caffeine dependence, abuse, and withdrawal within the *DSM-IV-TR*.

In summary, consumption of caffeine continues to grow despite research suggesting that it causes both psychological and biological problems. Caffeine affects thinking, mood, social behavior patterns, reactions, and attitudes. Caffeine can also have synergistic effects when combined with other medications, either enhancing the effects of medications such as ibuprofen (Diamond, Balm, & Freitag, 2000) or, when combined with medications such as fluvoxamine, leading to caffeine intoxication (Jeppesen, Loft, Poulsen, & Brsen, 1996). Further research could provide specific data for use in the helping professions. Medical professionals need to be aware of the effects that substances such as caffeine may have on their clients in order to make accurate diagnoses (Dziegielewski & Leon, 2001). Even though caffeine is not a controlled substance, individuals need to be informed of the negative health effects of consuming regular, large amounts of caffeine.

The best treatments for a high rate of caffeine consumption center around the following: (1) awareness of the impact of caffeine, in both physical and psychological terms; (2) gradual reduction of intake; (3) increased exercise or other substitute behaviors; and (4) better time management to allow for more rest and the completion of required tasks in a timely manner. Incorporating each of these four components can help create a healthier lifestyle and reduce the need for caffeine use.

References

American Psychiatric Association. (2000). *Diagnostic and statistical manual of mental disorders.* (4th ed., text revision). Washington DC: Author.

Benshoff, J. J., & Janikowski, T. P. (2000). *The rehabilitation model of substance abuse counseling.* Belmont, CA: Wadsworth/Thomson Learning.

Cherniske, S. (1998). *Caffeine blues: Wake up to the hidden dangers of America's #1 drug.* New York: Warner Books.

Daly, J., & Fredholm, B. (1998). Caffeine: An atypical drug of dependence. *Drug and Alcohol Dependence, 51*(1–2), 199–206.

Diamond, S., Balm, T. K., & Freitag, F. G. (2000). Ibuprofen plus caffeine in the treatment of tension-type headache. *Clinical Pharmacology & Therapeutics, 68*(3), 312–19.

Dziegielewski, S. F., & Leon, A. M. (2001). *Psychopharmacology and social work practice.* New York: Springer.

Griffiths, R. & Juliano, L. (2004). Caffeine addiction. *Psychopharmacology, 176*(1), 1–29.

Haas, E. (2000). Nutritional program for caffeine detoxification. *Staying Healthy with Nutrition: The Complete Guide to Diet and Nutritional Medicine.* Retrieved December 26, 2003, from http://www.healthy.net/asp/templates/article.asp?id=2046&HeaderTitle=Nutritional Programs

Hettema, J., Corey, L., & Kendler, K. (1999). A multivariate genetic analysis of the use of tobacco, alcohol, and caffeine in a population based sample of male and female twins. *Drug and Alcohol Dependence, 57,*(1), 69–78.

Hughes, J., Oliveto, A., Liguori, A., Carpenter, J., & Howard, T. (1998). Endorsement of *DSM-IV* dependence criteria among caffeine users [Electronic version]. *Drug and Alcohol Dependence, 52*(2), 99–107.

Hyner, G. (1979). Relaxation as principal treatment for excessive cigarette use and caffeine ingestion by a college female. *Psychological Reports, 45,* 531–34.

Jeppesen, U., Loft, S., Poulsen, H. E., and Brsen, K. (1996). A fluvoxamine-caffeine interaction study. *Pharmacogenetics, 6*(3), 213–22.

Jones, H.E., & Griffiths, R. R. (2003). Oral caffeine maintenance potentiates the reinforcing and stimulant subjective effects of introvenous nicotine in cigarette smokers. *Psychopharmacology, 165,* 280–90.

Kenny D., Carlson, J., McGuigan, F., & Sheppard, J. (Eds.). (2000). *Stress and health: Research and clinical applications.* Singapore: Overseas Publishers Association.

Lamberg, L. (1999, March 10). Brew it or chew it? Military seeks ways to caffeinate. *Journal of the American Medical Association, 281,* 885–86.

Lane, J., & Phillips-Bute, B. (1998). Caffeine deprivation affects vigilance, performance, and mood. Electronic version. *Physiology & Behavior, 65*(1), 171–75.

Larson, C., & Carey, K. (1998). Caffeine: Brewing trouble in mental health settings? *Professional Psychology: Review and Practice, 29*(4), 373–76.

Mars, B. (2001). *Addiction-free naturally.* Rochester, VT: Healing Arts Press.

Monroe, J. (1998). Caffeine's hook. *Current Health 2, 24*(5), 16–20.

Nehlig, A. (1999). Are we dependent upon coffee and caffeine? A review on human and animal data. *Neuroscience and Biobehavioral Reviews, 23*(4), 563–76.

Reichenberg-Ullman, J. (2000). *Caffeine free.* Retrieved June 3, 2002, from http://www.healthy.net/asp/templates/article.asp?id=466&HeaderTitle=Homeopathy

Rogers, P., & Dernoncourt, C. (1998). Regular caffeine consumption: A balance of adverse and beneficial effects for mood and psychomotor performance. *Pharmacology Biochemistry and Behavior, 59*(4), 1039–45.

Sawynok, J. (1995). Pharmacological rationale for the clinical use of caffeine. *Drugs, 49*(1), 37–50.

Scott, W. H., Coyne, K. M., Johnson, M. M., Lausted, C. G., Sahota, M., Johnson, A. T. (2002). Effects of caffeine on performance of low intensity tasks [Electronic version]. *Perceptual and Motor Skills, 94*(2), 521–32.

Chapter 6

Nicotine

Sophia F. Dziegielewski and Barbara A. Vunk

TOBACCO USE HAS BEEN CITED AS THE NUMBER ONE AVOIDABLE CAUSE OF illness and death in the United States, where it is responsible for more than 440,000 deaths each year. Smoking is clearly linked to diminished health for users (Surgeon General, 2004). Smoking is a known cause of cancer, heart disease, stroke, and chronic obstructive pulmonary disease (Kaplan & Weiler, 1997; Solberg, Maxwell, Kottke, Gepner, & Brekke, 1990; U.S. Department of Health and Human Services, 1996). In addition, the surgeon general's most recent report (2004) identifies numerous other diseases not previously found to be linked directly to smoking, such as cancers of the stomach, pancreas, and kidney; conditions such as acute myeloid leukemia, pneumonia, and abdominal aortic aneurysms; eye problems such as cataracts; and dental problems such as periodontitis. Every day in the United States, six thousand young people start smoking, a 50 percent increase since 1998. Half of these youth who begin smoking will become daily smokers (Committee on Substance Abuse, 2001). Each year, there are more deaths due to tobacco use than from the combined effects of acquired immunodeficiency syndrome (AIDS), suicide, homicide, alcoholism, cocaine, heroin, traffic accidents, and fire (Glynn, Greenwald, Mills, & Manley, 1993; Solberg et al., 1990).

This chapter explores current nicotine addiction and smoking cessation interventions and makes suggestions for an integrated approach to be utilized by practitioners in the area of addictions. The fine line between physiological and psychological addiction is examined. A multi- or interdisciplinary team approach that incorporates pharmacological treatments such as nicotine replacement therapy (nicotine patches or gum); brief treatment using cognitive-behavior modification (including skills training and problem solving); and social support (professional encouragement and assistance) is presented. In closing, recommendations are made for constructing this brief, time-limited model for smoking cessation.

PSYCHOPHYSIOLOGICAL EFFECTS

Phelps and Nourse (1986) describe nicotine as a plant alkaloid, similar in structure to the opium narcotics, that is capable of temporarily satisfying the physiological hunger an addictive person suffers because of a proposed inborn metabolic error. Although any addictive substance "taken into the body ten, twenty, thirty or more times a day is likely to have a potent addicting effect" (Phelps & Nourse, 1986, p. 138), nicotine remains highly addictive. A deadly poison even in very small doses, nicotine is one of the most addictive substances known to humankind (Haustein, 2003). The American Lung Association (1996) suggests that nicotine works on the brain and other parts of the central nervous system simultaneously. When ingested through smoking, nicotine reaches the brain faster than other drugs. It is drawn into the lungs, pumped through the bloodstream, and sent directly to the brain within seven seconds. This sudden burst of nicotine causes an instant high. In addition, nicotine makes the heart to beat faster, which increases the breathing rate and causes the body to use more oxygen. While these reactions are occurring, blood vessels narrow and blood pressure may increase. For years, the tobacco companies claimed that people used cigarettes for sensory pleasure and not to satisfy an addiction. Today, however, scientists, physicians, and the FDA categorize nicotine as a drug and cigarettes as a tool that delivers it. An addiction to nicotine is now recognized as a common consequence to tobacco use (Committee on Substance Abuse, 2001).

According to experts, individuals who are addicted to nicotine show the classic signs of dependence. They want to quit but cannot. They develop a tolerance, having to continually increase their dosage in order to achieve the same effect. When tolerant individuals try to quit, their attempts can be complicated by the symptoms associated with withdrawal (Brautbar, 1995). Furthermore, nicotine directly affects the brain's biochemistry; the levels of neurochemicals such as epinephrine, dopamine, and norepinephrine tend to have dose-related increases (Pomerleau & Pomerleau, 1984). Studies have shown a significant correlation between nicotine and the release of the neurotransmitter dopamine (Came, 1993; "Inside the Addict's Brain," 1994; Nash, 1997; Peck, 1996; "The Science of Smoking," 1996); and the excessive release of neurotransmitters can temporarily prevent the receptors from working. Research continues to suggest that several of the neuroregulators modified by nicotine administration show both positive and negative behavioral reinforcements. Positive behavioral reinforcements center around pleasure enhancement while reducing negative feelings related to tension and anxiety (Brautbar, 1995; Came, 1993). Outside of the brain, nicotinic receptors are found in muscle cells and in the cells of the autonomic nervous system (responsible for the fight-or-flight response). These receptors are stimulated by and respond to nicotine and contribute to physiological responses to tobacco (Cambridge Educational, 2004).

PREVALENCE

Although tobacco smoking has long been known to have negative health consequences, more than one-quarter of the U.S. adult population continue to smoke (Skarr et al., 1992). In the next ten years, it is estimated that smoking-related diseases will kill 4.5 million people in the United States and that more than fifty thousand nonsmokers will die each year as a result of secondhand exposure to tobacco smoke (Kaplan & Weiler, 1997). Secondhand smoke, or, more formally, environmental tobacco smoke (ETS), is classified by the U.S. Environmental Protection Agency as a class A carcinogen (Committee on Substance Abuse, 2001). Chronic exposure to ETS increases the risks of lung cancer and heart disease in adults and increases children's risk for respiratory tract infections, asthma, middle ear disease, pneumonia, decreased pulmonary function, and sudden infant death syndrome (Rigotti, 2000; Committee on Substance Abuse, 2001). Also, exposure to ETS in children before the age of ten increases their risk of developing leukemia and lymphoma as an adult (Committee on Substance Abuse, 2001).

Study after study continues to provide evidence that smoking is not only a danger to health—it can be fatal. Consequently, the surgeon general deems it necessary to put appropriate warnings on all tobacco products. With this in mind, why do one in four American adults continue to smoke? In a 1988 report on the health consequences of smoking, the surgeon general offered evidence that smoking is not only a social habit but also a chemical pharmacological dependency on nicotine as a drug, similar to an addiction to heroin or cocaine (Brautbar, 1995; Moncher, Schinke, & Holden, 1992).

All in all, the scientific community appears to have significant proof that nicotine is a powerfully addictive agent, yet regardless of this proven scientific information, one-quarter of the adult American population continues to ingest nicotine. O'Brien and McLellan (1996) suggest that "after continued repetition of voluntary drug-taking, the drug user loses the voluntary ability to control its use" and becomes addicted with "a compulsive involuntary aspect to continue drug use and to relapse after a period of abstinence" (p. 237). National survey statistics repeatedly indicate high motivation and readiness for change but success can be limited because smoking is a complex addictive behavior. For quitting to be successful, a comprehensive program is needed—one that includes access to self-help guides and programs that teach successful cessation skills.

ASSESSING NICOTINE ADDICTION

According to the *DSM-IV-TR* (American Psychiatric Association [APA], 2000), the essential feature of substance dependence is a cluster of cognitive, behavioral, and physiological symptoms that indicates an individual's continued use of a substance despite significant substance-related problems. Oftentimes there is a pattern of repeated self-administration that usually results in tolerance. After becoming tolerant, the individual must continually increase the dose in order to achieve the desired effect. A dependent individual may also suffer from withdrawal. He or she may use the drug to relieve the withdrawal symptoms that occur when the body is no longer receiving the level of the substance it craves. A desire to avoid withdrawal symptoms can entice the individual to engage in compulsive drug-taking behavior. When an individual is addicted to a substance such as nicotine, he or she may engage in efforts to cut down on the drug or stop using it, but if unassisted, these efforts are typically unsuccessful. The individual will then continue to use the substance despite being fully aware that there is a potential for harm to self or others as a result.

The degree to which tolerance develops varies greatly across substances. A smoker's tolerance will increase over time, creating a need to smoke more in order to achieve the same effect that was once achieved by smoking one cigarette (APA, 2000). Many daily smokers meet the diagnostic criteria for what is termed *nicotine/tobacco dependence* (Committee on Substance Abuse, 2001).

Recovery from this type of addiction can be a tormenting, often lifelong process with no guarantee of success. Research indicates that the nicotine found in cigarettes is the most addicting substance known. Yet, over the last twenty-five years, approximately fifty million Americans have quit smoking (Riessman & Carroll, 1996).

In order to understand why one person can quit but another cannot, it is important to address two different types of addiction: simple and complex. According to Riessman and Carroll (1996), simple addiction is a superficial dependence in that it does not involve physical cravings or withdrawal symptoms when the substance is removed. Complex addiction, however, constitutes a physical and psychological dependency associated with good feelings, loss of control over the addiction, and the compulsion to continue use despite the consequences. Addiction to nicotine is unique because even in its "simple" form, it is one of the most difficult addictions to overcome. As researchers struggle to design smoking cessation programs, practitioners should assess whether the individual suffers from a simple or a complex addiction and use this assessment as a starting point for selecting the best intervention approach.

The first step of the smoking cessation process is often a visit to one's primary caregiver, as nearly three-fourths (74 percent) of Americans make yearly visits to their physician's office. The single most important reason people have to quit smoking is concern over their health, and those who quit for health reasons or in response to their physician's advice are more likely to make repeated attempts to quit and to remain off cigarettes (Orleans, 1985). This places physicians in a strategic position to initiate pharmacological therapy to help their patients quit smoking (Daughton et al., 1998). Although 70 percent of patients who smoke say they would like to quit, only 7.9 percent are able to do so without help. When smokers try to quit on the advice of a physician, however, the smoking cessation rate improves to 10.2 percent (Mallin, 2002).

For many smokers who want to quit, self-initiated willpower isn't enough to beat their cravings. As with other addictive drugs, withdrawal from nicotine can include symptoms of irritability, frustration, anger, anxiety, difficulty concentrating, restlessness, and cravings (Nordenberg, 1997). Fortunately, with the treatment options available today, the client is not forced to rely on willpower alone.

CASE EXAMPLE

Case History

W is a thirty-four-year-old African American female who reports that she smokes approximately one and a half packs of cigarettes per day. W states that she wants to quit smoking cigarettes but has too demanding a schedule, and smoking helps her relax. W is employed by a large law firm as a secretary, and in addition to working twenty hours a week, she also attends college full-time. She is trying to complete her bachelor's degree in elementary education.

W began smoking with other classmates in high school when she was sixteen years old because it was the "cool" thing to do. W states that, as she grew older, she steadily increased the number of cigarettes she smoked due to the need to relieve stressors in her life. Currently, W notes that an upsurge of stress has had a decided effect on how much she smokes. She reports that the two places she is apt to "light up" are on her way to and from work in her car and at night while doing school-work on her home computer.

W is motivated to quit smoking and gives the following reasons. As an intern at a local elementary school, W feels that she is not being a positive role model for her students when she smokes during recess. W is also experiencing upper respiratory infections and other smoking-related health problems, which have caused her to miss work and school. W admits to an unsuccessful attempt to quit smoking after she had bronchitis, when she found herself coughing uncontrollably and smoking at the same time. W states that this was her "wake up call."

W's physician remains concerned about her smoking and at each visit she suggests that W quit smoking because of the health problems she is experiencing. W admits that she is worried about the side effects she may experience when she gives up smoking cigarettes. To address her concerns, W's physician suggested that she consider nicotine replacement therapy, which combines several different types of interventions (i.e., medications and supportive counseling). W also requested information concerning cognitive-behavioral therapy. W's friend successfully quit smoking for a year using this type of psychosocial intervention, which helped him identify and address triggers that led to his smoking behavior.

W began a treatment plan for smoking cessation, which involved three of the interventions mentioned above. She was prescribed the nicotine patch as well as the medication Zyban. In addition, W began seeing a counselor familiar with this type of addiction who provided cognitive-behavioral therapy to help her address the behavioral components of her addiction. W was instructed to keep a smoker's journal to monitor her smoking behavior (Haustein, 2003). Through the use of a journal, she was able to log what situations caused her to want to smoke. In this process she identified situations such as having her morning coffee, driving, and relaxing after meals that prompted her to smoke. Recording these behaviors in her journal helped to boost her motivation because she could see the visible results of the self-monitoring.

To aid W in dealing with her nicotine cravings, W's therapist taught her a relaxation technique, which she was instructed to implement each time she felt the desire to smoke a cigarette. The practitioner continually noted improvements and was quick to help W see the progress she was making. W was also educated on the negative effects smoking was having on her health as well as the dangers her secondhand smoke posed to others within her support system. After eight weeks, W was able to stop using the nicotine patch. She remained on Zyban and completed her psychotherapy sessions. After six months on a maintenance dose of Zyban, W was smoke free. At this time, the Zyban was tapered off and eventually discontinued.

Intervention Plan: Nicotine Dependence and Addiction

Definition.   Nicotine dependence is indicated by an individual's continued use of a substance despite having substance-related problems. As seen in this case example, compulsive drug-taking behavior, tolerance, and withdrawal are common. Tolerance is evidenced by the individual needing increasing amounts of nicotine to achieve the same effect felt at an earlier date with a lesser amount of nicotine. Oftentimes the individual has tried quitting but has been unsuccessful. Nicotine withdrawal symptoms will occur within twenty-four hours of the discontinuance of the substance. Craving for the substance may continue for months after the last ingested dose. Use of this substance is related to multiple medical problems such as cardiovascular diseases, emphysema, and lung cancer. For a diagnosis of nicotine dependence, significant disturbance related to an individual's social and occupational functioning must occur.

Signs and Symptoms.   Withdrawal symptoms include mood changes, difficulty concentrating, restlessness, insomnia, increased appetite, and decreased heart rate. Other symptoms include irritability, frustration, anger, insomnia, anxiety, increased appetite or weight gain, and hand tremors.

Goals for Treatment.
1. Maintain abstinence from nicotine.
2. Utilize new coping methods and build on old coping methods.
3. Obtain a physical exam and obtain medical assistance for withdrawal or while in recovery if needed.
4. Learn to handle stress caused by withdrawal symptoms.
5. Learn new ways of coping and problem solving in a smoke-free environment.
6. Maintain social and occupational functioning.

Objectives	Interventions
Client will abstain from using tobacco.	Client and practitioner will discuss the benefits of remaining tobacco free. Practitioner will educate client about effects of nicotine use and future problems that can arise from nicotine use. Client will self-assess health status and the relationship of health status to current experiences and health problems. Client will cultivate a nonsmoking support system outside of the sessions with her practitioner to help her when cravings arise.

Objectives	Interventions
Client will identify and strengthen coping skills.	Client and practitioner will discuss and list social activities that do not involve the use of tobacco and methods to avoid temptation in situations that do. Client and practitioner will stress the development of problem-solving skills and will set personal goals to avoid relapse. Client will clarify her emotional needs and find alternatives to fulfilling these needs with smoking. Client will keep a smoker's journal to record and break down habits that lead to smoking (e.g., coffee, driving, meals).
Client will learn to deal with symptoms of nicotine withdrawal and its effects.	Client will obtain a physical exam to determine if pharmaceutical assistance is needed in recovery. Client will take medications as indicated, if prescribed. Client will be taught and learn to use relaxation techniques to help deal with cravings.

Intervention Plan: Nicotine Withdrawal

Definition.   Nicotine withdrawal symptoms develop within twenty-four hours after tobacco use is reduced or rapidly stopped. Craving may last months. Use of nicotine is related to illnesses such as cardiovascular diseases, emphysema and lung cancer.

Signs and Symptoms.   Signs and symptoms include mood changes, difficulty concentrating, restlessness, insomnia, increased appetite, and decreased heart rate.

Goals for Treatment.
1. Handle distress caused by withdraw symptoms.
2. Maintain social and occupational functioning.
3. Learn long-term health consequences.
4. Find ways to handle feelings of dependence.

Objectives	Interventions
Client will become educated on health issues related to nicotine use.	Client will be provided with informative brochures and information that outline short- and long-term health related issues. Client will self-assess health status and the relationship of health status to current experiences and health problems.

Objectives	Interventions
Client will identify fears of not being in control of cravings and situations that would enhance cigarette smoking.	Client will clarify the difference between emotional needs and personal desires.
Client will plan ways to avoid cigarette use.	Client will list the pros and cons associated with nicotine consumption.
Client will identify and find ways to manage the discomfort resulting from nicotine withdrawal, craving, and achieving a nicotine-free environment.	Client and practitioner will stress the development of problem-solving skills and will set personal goals to avoid relapse.

BEST PRACTICES

For many clients with nicotine disorders, a combination approach to intervention will be most successful. Such an approach provides a comprehensive treatment package that often consists of nicotine replacement therapy, psychopharmaceuticals, and cognitive-behavioral intervention to address the ingrained patterns of behavior that have been developed and maintained through years of abuse.

Individuals such as W who smoke ten or more cigarettes a day can benefit greatly from nicotine replacement therapy (Committee on Substance Abuse, 2001). Currently, clients undergoing nicotine replacement therapy can choose from the nicotine patch, nicotine gum, nicotine nasal spray, a nicotine inhaler, and nicotine sublingual tablets or nicotine lozenges (Haustein, 2003). These products are licensed as aids to relieve the withdrawal symptoms associated with smoking cessation. Nicotine replacement therapy has been used with nearly thirty million smokers thus far, with success rates of 30 to 40 percent. Users are given a dose of nicotine at the beginning of treatment, which helps to overcome the effects of withdrawal while simultaneously dealing with behavioral side effects that occur from dependence on the substance. After several weeks of use, smokers are more prepared to break their smoking habits (Haustein, 2003). Nicotine replacement products deliver small, steady doses of nicotine into the body to relieve some of the withdrawal symptoms without providing the "buzz" that keeps smokers hooked (Nordenberg, 1997). Transdermal nicotine replacement therapy (the nicotine patch) has been recommended as an efficacious smoking cessation treatment and has proven effective across diverse settings and when used with a variety of psychosocial interventions (Fiore, Smith, Jorenby, & Baker, 1994; Po, 1993; U.S. Department of Health and Human Services, 1996).

It appears that, for most, a NicoDerm CQ 21 mg transdermal nicotine patch can be used successfully as an intervention tool, especially during the initial phases of therapy for smoking cessation. Nicotine replacement therapy acts as a temporary aid to help smokers quit smoking by reducing nicotine withdrawal symptoms, including nicotine craving (Po, 1993). Nicotine patches (and nicotine gums) provide lower levels of nicotine to the body's blood than cigarettes and allow the smoker's body to gradually eliminate its need for nicotine (SmithKline Beecham, 1996). Because nicotine replacement products do not contain the tar or carbon monoxide of cigarette smoke, they do not pose the same dangers as tobacco. However, the main addicting ingredient, nicotine, is still being ingested into the body's system.

Research has been consistent in suggesting that nicotine replacement increases rates of smoking cessation. Studies show that the use of nicotine replacement therapy as much as doubles a person's chances of being able to quit smoking (Nordenberg, 1997). Therefore, except in the presence of a serious medical condition, nicotine replacement therapy should be given serious consideration by clinicians and physicians. Medical precautions, such as monitoring by a physician, may be necessary, particularly for pregnant clients and for particular cardiovascular patients (U.S. Department of Health and Human Services, 1996). Clients should not use nicotine replacement therapy if they (1) have heart disease, irregular heartbeat, or a history of heart attacks (because nicotine can increase blood pressure); (2) have high blood pressure not controlled with medication; (3) take prescription medicine for depression or asthma (unless approved by a physician); or (4) are allergic to adhesive tape or have skin problems (50 percent of those who use transdermal patches experience skin rashes). In regard to skin irritation, a mild itching, burning, or tingling at the site of the patch is normal when first applied, but this should go away in about an hour. Also, after the patch is removed, the skin may be red for a day. If either of these complications worsens or continues past the period considered normal, a doctor should be consulted (Nordenberg, 1997). Clients should be informed that nicotine patches and gum have enough nicotine to poison children and pets and that continuing to smoke while wearing the patch or chewing the gum can result in nicotine overdose (SmithKline Beecham, 1996).

Concerns have been raised regarding the mental health status of persons who quit smoking. Recent studies indicate a link between cigarette smoking and certain psychiatric disorders, particularly depression. The possibility that tobacco use may provide psychological relief for some mental health conditions increases concerns in the health industry about the emotional consequences of smoking cessation (Apgar, 1997). Practitioners should not underestimate the influences of nicotine; it is a powerful drug that behaves similarly to cocaine when it reaches the brain (Nash, 1997). Both of these chemicals are addictive drugs that falsely mimic neurotransmitters in order to induce the body's release of dopamine. This release in turn brings about the desired feelings of pleasure and elation. Pharmacologically speaking, treating nicotine or cocaine addiction is similar to treating depression or anxiety because each involves normalizing the stimulation of the neurotransmitter dopamine (Key, 1994; Nash, 1997).

The second most common intervention is medication. Sequential research initially suggested that nicotine disorders and depression or other psychiatric disorders could be treated simultaneously with the administration of medication. Although numerous drugs other than nicotine (e.g., amphetamine, benzedrine sulfate, methylphenidate, fenfluramine, diazepam, phenobarbital, hydroxyzine, and meprobamete) have been tried to ease the physiological and psychological withdrawal symptoms of cigarette smoking, their usefulness has been limited ("Methods for Stopping Cigarette Smoking," 1986).

In 1989, research found a plausible link between antidepressants and successful smoking cessation when the Food and Drug Administration approved bupropion under the brand name Wellbutrin, a relevant dopamine-specific antidepressant. Since that time, bupropion has been approved for specific use in smoking cessation, and it is now marketed to the general public in a sustained release form known as Zyban (Haustein, 2003; Dunlop, 2000). It is believed that this class of antidepressant aids in smoking cessation by helping to combat the effects of withdrawal and other psychiatric symptoms (Key, 1994).

Several studies have found the success rate for smoking cessation while using Zyban to be as high as 38.8 percent after six months of follow-up and observation (Haustein, 2003; Barringer & Weaver, 2002). But Zyban is not the only pharmacotherapy for smoking cessation. Over the last few years, nearly a dozen other medications have been recognized as helpful for smoking cessation. Among these are the antidepressants nortriptyline, fluoxetine, imipramine, doxepin, and venlafaxine; clonidine; mecamylamine; several types of tranquilizers; buspirone; several opioid agonists; lobeline; and silver acetate (Haustein, 2003). Most of these medications, however, are still in the trial stages for specific use in smoking cessation therapy.

Even with the empirically validated efficacy of pharmacotherapy, however, most professionals discourage the belief that medication alone will solve clients' drug problems. Psychosocial interventions such as psychotherapy and twelve-step programs are typically combined with any pharmacotherapy (Nash, 1997). In addition, cognitive-behavioral therapy may be necessary. The techniques employed in cognitive-behavioral therapy are designed to equip people with new coping skills within a brief treatment context. These learned skills have the potential to change the chemical activities occurring in the brain by increasing the natural release of dopamine through modified thoughts, feelings, and behaviors (Kendall & Panichelli-Mindel, 1995).

This type of modification involves both the external environment and the individual's internal processing of that environment. Professional cognitive-behavioral therapists offer clients ideas for experimentation, help them sort through past experiences, and introduce problem-solving skills, coping skills, and educational tools that influence clients to think for themselves while maximizing personal strengths and altering their problematic thoughts and behaviors. The primary objectives of cognitive-behavioral therapy are to help clients recognize and change the stimulus and response patterns that cause smoking (classical conditioning), to reward clients for not smoking while teaching them how to avoid it (operant conditioning and social learning), or both (*Harvard Mental Health Letter*, May, 1997, June 1997). While cognitive-behavioral therapy is perhaps most successful when professionally designed and administered, self-modification should also be considered as an alternative when professional services are not available or affordable (Dziegielewski & Eater, 2000). For most clients who have a commitment to change, cognitive-behavioral changes can be straightforward and easily implemented.

Dopamine is not just a chemical that transmits pleasure signals, it is the "master molecule of addiction" (Brautbar, 1995; Came, 1993; Nash, 1997; Peck, 1996). Neuroscientists have discovered that almost all of the major drugs of abuse affect a single brain circuit, the mesolimbic pathway, which is mediated by dopamine (Peck, 1996). "The dopamine hypothesis provides a basic framework for understanding how a genetically encoded trait—such as a tendency to produce too little dopamine—might intersect with environmental influences to create a serious behavioral disorder" (Nash, 1997, p. 68).

When treatment options are examined, it is important to remember that neurotransmitters such as dopamine underlie every thought and emotion that leads to memory and learning. The pivotal question appears to be, if neurotransmitters are in fact the carriers of signals between all nerve cells or neurons in the brain, then how can cognitive-behavioral modifications work against such a strong physiological addiction? Given its association with pleasure and elation, dopamine could indeed be elevated by social interactions such as hugs, kisses, or words of praise shared during an evening spent with friends, as well as by the potent pleasures that come from mind/mood-altering drugs (Nash, 1997). Thus, simple cognitive and behavior modifications may naturally increase dopamine release, eliminating the need for long-term pharmaceutical or other drug-related treatments.

One of the first steps in applying cognitive-behavioral treatment involves helping the client to change his or her view of cigarette smoking. Habitually pleasurable thoughts of smoking must be replaced with new thoughts grounded in the reality that smoking often kills. In addition, the smoker must begin to realize that nicotine addiction has another drawback—it is a habit that controls one's life. In order to break the cycle, the user must become aware of and gain some control over his or her dysfunctional thoughts and behaviors. Generally, those who succeed in quitting smoking have clearly defined motivations and expectations, self-management skills, and quitting strategies, and when possible, they have access to social supports and psychosocial resources for both quitting and remaining off cigarettes (Orleans, 1985).

Special Considerations

For success in time-limited cognitive-behavioral treatments, Dziegielewski and Eater (2000) provide the following recommendations for practitioners:

1. *Help the client to find a smoking cessation plan that requires a specific day to stop, and ensure that there is a support group or social network in place to help the client throughout the process.* Although numerous smoking cessation programs exist, they vary greatly in price and proven success rates. The client will need a specific schedule with short-term individual weekly counseling to support and help plan the intervention process.

2. *Help clients realize that in order to fight the desire to smoke, problematic thoughts must be identified and accompanied by a change in thinking.* One of the major concepts of cognitive therapy is cognitive restructuring. This technique in-

volves modifying the thoughts, ideas, and beliefs that maintain the client's abnormal behaviors such as self-statements or self-talk (DeSilvestri, 1989; Dush, Hirt, & Schroeder, 1989). In time-limited cognitive-behavioral therapy, defining the problem, selecting a goal, and generating alternative solutions, all of which alter thoughts and behaviors, are encouraged. A technique called "thought stopping" involves consciously stopping a negative self-talk and replacing it with a positive or more adaptive one. When the smoker faces nicotine cravings, she or he must consciously choose to change thinking patterns. This can be accomplished alone or in combination with other behavioral modifications. For example, the client should be instructed to say no to the craving and then to think about why he or she wants to quit. Constant reminders of how well the client is doing on the plan need to be made available for support in times of weakness. Mixing thought stopping with behavioral intervention is also important. For example, help the client plan to think about something other than smoking that is action related such as getting up, changing positions, taking slow, deep breaths, or simply walking outside. The client needs to identify and plan to become involved in nonsmoking activities such as going to church, the gym, the mall, or just taking a walk.

3. *Always select some type of standardized measurement that can be used to compare pretest/posttest scores, and incorporate some type of self-report instrument to help the client see that progress has been made.* In this type of intervention, standardized measures are essential for determining results. Fischer and Corcoran (2000) provide a rich selection of such measures. Two that might be of particular interest in this area are the Self-Rating Anxiety Scale (SAS) and the Smoking Self-Efficacy Questionnaire (SSEQ). The SAS, a twenty-item instrument consisting of the most commonly found characteristics of an anxiety disorder, is used to assess anxiety as a clinical disorder and to quantify anxiety symptoms (Zung, 1971). The SSEQ, a seventeen-item instrument, is used to measure beliefs about one's ability to resist the urge to smoke (Colletti, Supnick, & Payne, 1985).

4. *In the intervention strategy, never use food as a reinforcer or a substitute.* A primary concern for many individuals who are contemplating smoking cessation is the possibility of gaining weight. In fact, the majority of smokers who quit smoking do gain weight. Most will gain fewer than ten pounds, but a general sense of foreboding about this likelihood can interfere with the cessation motivation process (Williamson et al., 1991). Post-cessation weight gain appears to be caused by both increased food consumption and metabolic adjustments. Regardless of caloric intake, however, once nicotine leaves the system, the body's metabolism will go through a period of temporary gradual arrest until it can rebalance itself naturally (Hatsukami, LaBounty, Hughes, & Laine, 1993; Hofstetter, Schutz, & Wahren, 1986; Klesges & Shumaker, 1992).

Phelps and Nourse (1986) suggest that certain food replacements and exercise can combat the addictive process as long as the smoker is also willing to change his or her patterns of behavior. According to these authors, proper nutrition is essential to beating the body's addictions. Nutritional enrichment based on frequent, sugar-free meals to stabilize blood sugar and large doses of vitamins and minerals to reverse the body's long-standing depletion can help in this process. In addition to better nutrition, daily exercise is recommended as an essential element in both self-treatment and professionally administered programs. Exercise aids in the body's release of natural biochemical neurotransmitters such as dopamine and endorphins, which in turn tone and condition cerebral circulation while acting as powerful antidotes to the depression many recovering addicted persons experience.

Examples of simple behavior-change strategies include changing where and when one eats (e.g., going to different restaurants, always sitting in the nonsmoking section, consciously changing one's diet, and avoiding sugar and caffeine); adding exercise to one's daily routine (e.g., dancing around the house, going for short walks, parking the car in the furthest space; doing isometric exercises while driving and sitting); and learning to use relaxation techniques (e.g., taking at least five deep breaths and then visualizing a soothing, pleasurable situation).

5. *Help the client develop a change strategy that involves real options such as "time out" while giving up feelings of deprivation and the illusion of having "just one."* When examining cognitive-behavioral treatments, simple behavioral modifications that directly address overt behaviors need to be included. Classical conditioning, which consists of identifying existing patterns of stimulus and response, can assist by introducing new stimuli to create new responses. In addition, operant conditioning can also assist by patterning reward and punishment to alter behavior (*Harvard Mental Health Letter*, June 1997). During withdrawal, the smoker can use planned avoidance. For example, the smoker can leave a smoking area and call a family member or friend. Problematic situations can be anticipated by preplanning activities that will keep the client busy and focused during times of cravings. Other behavioral changes can include reading a book, starting a diary, listening to or playing music, gardening, and creating art. In each situation, concentration on either the reward for completion of the successful behavior or the seeking of new stimuli (e.g., calling a friend for socialization) can create new behavioral responses.

6. *Help the client realize that he or she has choices and the decision not to smoke must be self-initiated.* The smoker must embrace choice and remember that the temporary physical discomforts associated with nicotine withdrawal can and will subside in a few days. The client needs to be aware that no one will take his or her cigarettes away, that quitting is entirely voluntary, and that, if failure occurs, the intervention can be resumed. The longer-term psychological dependency can be addressed by changing thoughts and behaviors to increase control of destiny and success.

Even though addiction to nicotine and other drugs appears to be a highly complex brain disorder, the behavioral and social contexts associated with the addiction that have been embedded in the psyche also require complex treatment strategies. This concept is based on what has been called "whole person treatment."

7. *Ensure that the client receives social and professional support during and after the intervention process.* Research repeatedly confirms that physical addiction is only one factor to be considered when designing cessation treatment programs. Many people continue smoking because they enjoy the behaviors that accompany smoking and have become conditioned to "lighting up" in certain

situations. A smoker's entire day is filled with cues that trigger the desire for a cig-arette: the first cup of coffee in the morning, driving to work, sitting down at the computer, or finishing a meal. Although pharmacotherapy and cognitive-behav-ioral interventions may assist in smoking cessation, support from family, friends, and professionals remains a key ingredient in sustaining the will to quit.

When those addicted to alcohol or illicit drugs decide to "get clean," they are often encouraged by family, friends, and professionals to participate in twelve-step programs such as Alcoholics Anonymous or Narcotics Anonymous or to check themselves into supportive in-patient treatment programs. Because nicotine addic-tion is just as powerful (if not more) as other drug addictions, these same strategies need to be implemented into the smoker's daily routine. Further, "flooding" the client with this kind of support can increase the will for abstinence, thus increas-ing the odds for success.

Many smokers who have expressed a desire to quit may resist enrolling in an organized smoking cessation program. This type of participation, however, is par-ticularly important for smokers who have limited social support systems. Physician and other health care providers are in a key position to influence the smoking habits of their patients. According to Hughes (1996), however, many primary care physicians shy away from treating smoking because they feel their training in this area is limited and that the required counseling is too complex and time consum-ing. In addition, it is suggested that other health care professionals such as social workers, therapists, chemical dependency clinicians, and psychiatrists also ignore smoking because nicotine dependence does not cause immediate adverse psy-chosocial consequences or severe intoxication as do alcohol and other illicit drugs. It is also possible that professionals are reluctant to accept the responsibilities of treating smokers who wish to quit because, in spite of a wealth of empirical data, they do not take notice of the severity of this specific addiction. Many experienced addictions specialists fail to see or choose to ignore the need for smoking cessation programs because they believe that most smokers voluntarily choose to quit on their own and are successful in doing so. Many medical professionals often overlook the fact that smoking is a form of drug dependence and should be treated as such.

8. *Help clients understand and address stress.* Many research studies high-light withdrawal symptoms such as irritability, frustration, anger, anxiety, difficulty concentrating, and restlessness. Research suggests that these stress responses can have significant effects on the body. Psychological or physiological stress can affect the immune system by altering the number of white blood cells and by decreasing lymphocyte production (Herbert, 1994). Stress can affect the body in unpredictable ways and can create acutely sensitive reactions. Once a reaction is programmed, even the slightest intimation of stress can trigger chemical reactions in the brain and body (Carpi, 1996).

According to Herbert (1994), stress activates primitive regions of the brain such as the areas that control the immune system. When stress levels begin to rise, the nerve circuits ignite the body's fight-or-flight mechanism. Predominantly, stress attacks the hypothalamus and the pituitary gland. When stress sets off the neurological communications, adrenal glands manufacture and release the "true" stress hormones—dopamine, epinephrine, norepinephrine, and cortisol. This is highly relevant for practice because of the correlation between neurotransmitters and addictions and neurotransmitters and stress. Research also suggests a connection between the duration of the stress and the amount of change to the immune system. Both physiological and behavioral mechanisms provide possible explanations as to why and how emotional states can alter individual immune systems. Furthermore, people under tremendous stress tend to sleep less, exercise less, have poorer diets, smoke more, and use alcohol and other drugs more often than nonstressed people (Carpi, 1996).

Smoking is a complex addictive behavior influenced by powerful physical, emotional, and social factors, making intervention complex. According to Dziegielewski and Eater (2000), professional helping for clients addicted to nicotine needs to include the following: First, medications or other psychopharmacological interventions must remain an important consideration in helping to promote smoking cessation, especially for eliminating the physical craving for nicotine. Second, special attention must be given to what to do when environmental stressors become overwhelming. The importance of environment and family supports cannot be minimized, because they clearly can influence the client's continuation and completion of the intervention process. For practitioners, the "person-in-environment" stance that has long been the cornerstone of professional practice may bring some valuable insight. For many clients, life stressors (e.g., divorce), which are not the focus of the actual intervention, can hamper intervention attempts. Therefore, in the first session of the intervention process, environmental concerns as well as social and family support must be assessed. Clients should be encouraged to attend a nicotine support group, become involved in twelve-step program supports such as telephone therapy, or go through a formal class/support structure (e.g., the American Cancer Society's no-smoking group, Smoke-enders). Also, plans for including the client's friends and family members as supporters in the intervention process should be clearly outlined.

SUMMARY AND FUTURE DIRECTIONS

Even though extensive literature clearly reveals the hazards and harmful effects caused by smoking cigarettes, many helping professionals, including social workers, have virtually no presence in this field. It is critical that the addictions practitioner help all individuals who are vulnerable to the harmful effects of tobacco use. More involvement is also needed in the development of programs and policies related to smoking cessation and other health-related behaviors.

Dziegielewski and Eater (2000) make the following recommendations for practitioners working in this area of addictions:

1. Become better educated in the multifactorial nature of smoking as a form of drug addiction.
2. Utilize supplements to counseling therapy such as pharmacological supports like the nicotine patch or medication intervention.

3. Remain aware that long-term psychological dependencies are possible with this addictive substance as with so many others and that these potential long-term consequences need to be considered as part of the intervention process.
4. Utilize a multi- or interdisciplinary framework for collateral support (e.g., physicians and nutritionists) in the intervention process.
5. To facilitate client adjustment, identify and incorporate social supports such as support groups and indigenous resources such as people in the community who have already quit.
6. Take a preventative stance and be proactive in increasing awareness that nicotine is a powerful substance of addiction. In this way, the profession can act as an industry watchdog.

With nicotine addiction, intervention effectiveness appears to be strongest when the client expresses a desire to quit smoking and helps in designing the intervention plan. Environmental factors that create stress must be identified and ways to address them must be considered. Because increased stress leads to a decreased ability to sustain smoking cessation, decreasing stress can be important for increasing the chances of longer-term success. In the intervention process, psychopharmacological treatment may be critical to addressing physiological dependency by helping to control uncomfortable withdrawal affects, allowing for a greater window of opportunity for behavior change. Cognitive-behavioral therapy can counteract problematic thought processes for the short term; however, longer-term changes must be attempted in tandem with an increased use of social supports. Finally, the importance of clearly evaluating the client's social support and providing access to supportive counseling cannot be underestimated. Support groups are highly encouraged as a means of gaining low-cost support and assistance. Within these groups, recovery techniques borrowed from Alcoholics Anonymous such as telephone therapy, sponsorship, and most importantly the "one drag" versus "one drink" concept should be emphasized. In addition, practitioners need to assist clients in estimating and preparing for "system" difficulties (e.g., clearly identifying problematic marital issues, family situations, and events) that can impede the counseling process. Although more evidence-based research on the treatment of nicotine addiction is needed, it seems clear that a combination approach to intervention offers the most promise.

References

American Lung Association. (1996). *Facts about nicotine addiction and cigarettes* [Brochure]. New York: Author.

American Psychiatric Association. (2000). *Diagnostic and statistical manual of mental disorders* (4th ed., text rev.). Washington, DC: Author.

Apgar, B. (1997). Major depression after smoking cessation. *American Family Physician, 56*(2), 582.

Barringer, T., & Weaver, E. (2003). Does long-term bupropion (Zyban) use prevent smoking relapse after initial success at quitting smoking? *Journal of Family Practice, 51,* 172.

Brautbar, N. (1995). Direct effects of nicotine on the brain: Evidence for chemical addiction. *Archives of Environmental Health, 50*(4), 263–66.

Cambridge Educational (Producer). (2004). *Drugs, uses and abuses: Stimulants* [Video]. Lawrenceville, NJ: Author.

Came, B. (1993). Clues in the brain. *Maclean's, 107*(29), 40–42.

Carpi, J. (1996). Stress . . . it's worse than you think. *Psychology Today, 29*(1), 34–39.

Colletti, G., Supnick, J. A., & Payne, T. J. (1985). The smoking self-efficacy questionnaire (SSEQ): Preliminary scale development and validation. *Behavioral Assessment, 7,* 249–60.

Committee on Substance Abuse. (2001). Tobacco's toll: Implications for the pediatrician. *American Academy of Pediatrics, 107*(5) 794–98.

Daughton, D., Susman, J., Sitorius, M., Belenky, S., Millatmal, T., Nowak, R., et al. (1998). Transdermal nicotine therapy and primary care. *Archives of Family Medicine, 7*(6) 425–30.

DeSilvestri, C. (1989). Clinical models in RET: An advanced model of the organization of emotional and behavioral disorders. *Journal of Rational-Emotive and Cognitive-Behavior Therapy, 7,* 51–58.

Dunlop, H. (2000). Bupropion (Zyban, sustained-release tablets): Update. *Canadian Medical Association Journal, 162,* 106–8.

Dush, D. M., Hirt, M. L., & Schroeder, H. E. (1989). Self-statement modification in the treatment of child behavior disorders: A meta-analysis. *Psychological Bulletin, 106,* 97–106.

Dziegielewski, S. F., & Eater, J. A. (2000). Smoking cessation: Increasing practice understanding and time-limited intervention strategy. *Families in Society: The Journal of Contemporary Human Services, 81*(3), 246–55.

Fiore, M. C., Smith, S. S., Jorenby, D. E., & Baker, T. B. (1994). The effectiveness of the nicotine patch for smoking cessation: A meta-analysis. *JAMA, 271,* 1940–47.

Fischer, J., & Corcoran, K. (2000). *Measures for clinical practice: A source book.* New York: Free Press.

Glynn, T. J., Greenwald, P., Mills, S. M., & Manley, M. (1993). Youth tobacco use in the United States: Problem, progress, goals, and potential solutions. *Preventive Medicine, 22,* 568–75.

Harvard Mental Health Letter. (1997, May). *13*(11), 1–8.

Harvard Mental Health Letter. (1997, June). *13*(12), 1–8.

Hatsukami, D., LaBounty, L., Hughes, J., & Laine, D. (1993). Effects of tobacco abstinence on food intake among cigarette smokers. *Health Psychology, 12,* 499–502.

Haustein, K. (2003). *Tobacco or health: Physiological and social damages caused by tobacco smoking.* New York: Springer.

Herbert, T. B. (1994). Stress and the immune system. *World Health, 47*(2), 4–6.

Hofstetter, A., Schutz, Y., & Wahren, J. (1986). Increased 24-hour energy expenditure in cigarette smokers. *New England Journal of Medicine, 314,* 79–82.

Hughes, J. R. (1996). The future of smoking cessation therapy in the United States. *Addiction, 91*(12), 1797–1803.

Inside the addict's brain. (1994). *Psychology Today, 27*(5), 37–39.

Kaplan, M. S., & Weiler, R. E. (1997). Social patterns of smoking behavior: Trends and practice implications. *Health & Social Work, 22*(1), 47–52.

Kendell, P. C., & Panichelli-Mindel, S. M. (1995). Cognitive-behavioral treatments. *Journal of Abnormal Child Psychology, 23*(1), 107–22.

Key, K. K. (1994, December 5). Smoking issues: Alternative drugs may help kick the habit. *Cancer Research Weekly,* 11–12.

Klesges, R. C., & Schumaker, S. A. (1992). Proceedings of the National Working Conference on Smoking and Body Weight. *Health Psychology*, 11, 1–22.

Methods for stopping cigarette smoking. (1986). *Annals of Internal Medicine, 105*, 281–91.

Mallin, R. (2002, March 15). Smoking cessation: Integration of behavioral and drug therapies. *American Family Physician, 65*, 1107–14, 1117.

Moncher, M. S., Schinke, S. P., & Holden, G. W. (1992). Tobacco addiction: Correlates, prevention, and treatment. In E. M. Freeman (Ed.), *The addiction process: Effective social work approaches* (pp. 222–36). New York: Longman.

Nash, J. M. (1997). Why do people get hooked? Mounting evidence points to a powerful brain chemical called dopamine. *Time, 149*(18), 68–74.

Nordenberg, T. (1997). *It's quittin' time: Smokers need not rely on willpower alone*. Retrieved from http://www.pueblo.gsa.gov/cic_text/health/quittin-time/quitntim.txt

O'Brien, C. P., & McLellan, A. T. (1996). Myths about the treatment of addiction. *Lancet, 347*(8996), 237–40.

Orleans, C. T. (1985). Understanding and promoting smoking cessation: Overview and guidelines for physician intervention. *Annual Review Medicine, 36*, 51–61.

Peck, R. L. (1996). The addicted brain: An era of scientific breakthroughs. *Behavioral Health Management, 6*(5), 33–35.

Phelps, J. K., & Nourse, A. E. (1986). *The hidden addiction and how to get free: Recognizing and breaking the habits that control your life*. Boston: Little, Brown.

Po, A. W. (1993). Transdermal nicotine in smoking cessation: A meta-analysis. *Pharmacology, 45*, 519–28.

Pomerleau, O. F., & Pomerleau, C. S. (1984). Neuroregulators and their reinforcement of smoking: Towards a behavioral explanation. *Neuroscience Behavior Review, 8*, 503–15.

Riessman, F., & Carroll, D. (1996). A new view of addiction: Simple and complex. *Social Policy, 27*(2), 36–41.

Rigotti, N. (2000). A 36-year-old woman who smokes cigarettes. *JAMA, 6*(8), 741–48.

The science of smoking. (1996). *Economist, 339*(7965), 22.

Skarr, K. L, Tsoh, J. Y., McClure, J. B., Cinciripini, P. M., Friedman, K., Wetter, D. W., et al. (1992). Smoking cessation: An overview of research. *Behavioral Medicine, 23*(1), 5–9.

SmithKline Beecham. (1996). NicoDerm CQ stop smoking aid nicotine transdermal system. *Consumer Healthcare, L.P.* Pittsburgh, PA: Author.

Solberg, L. I., Maxwell, P. L., Kottke, T. E., Gepner, G. J., & Brekke, M. L. (1990). A systematic primary care office-based smoking cessation program. *Journal of Family Practice, 30*(6), 647–54.

Surgeon General. (2004). *The health consequences of smoking: A report of the surgeon general*. Washington, DC: National Center for Chronic Disease Prevention and Health Promotion, Office of Smoking and Health. Retrieved October 9, 2004, from http://www.cdc.gov/tobacco/sgr/sgr_2004/chapters.htm

U.S. Department of Health and Human Services. (1996). *Smoking cessation: Information for specialists* (AHCPR Publication No. 96-0694). Rockville, MD: U.S. Government Printing Office.

Williamson, D. F., Madans, J., Anda, R. F., Kleinman, J. C., Giovino, G. A., & Beyers, T. (1991). Smoking cessation and severity of weight gain in a national cohort. *New England Journal of Medicine, 324*, 739–45.

Zung, W. K. (1971). A rating instrument for anxiety disorders. *Psychosomatics, 12*, 371–79.

Central Nervous System Depressants

Depressants are psychoactive substances that suppress, slow, or relax the central nervous system. The most commonly used major depressants are alcohol, the opiates and opioids such as heroin, and the sedatives and hypnotics such as prescription painkillers. Some of these substances, when used to the advantage of the individual, can have great social or therapeutic value. But, although some individuals can use these substances regularly without developing an addiction, others are more vulnerable to developing an addiction or dependence.

When depressants are misused or abused, the outcome can be disastrous. Abuse of these types of substances in combination with other substances such as other depressants (e.g., mixing alcohol and minor tranquilizers) can result in a significant depression of the system or a lethal effect. Medical problems that often occur when the central nervous system becomes depressed range from mild sedation to breathing cessation to coma and possible death. And because these substances are absorbed rapidly into the system, continued use becomes very eductive, resulting in a high potential for abuse.

The chapters in this section provide an overview of the depressants that practitioners in the field of substance addictions most commonly encounter, and review practice strategies designed to help close the gap between the need for and the availability of appropriate drug addiction services. Chapter 7 covers alcohol, the most commonly used depressant. Users often consider depressants such as alcohol and sedatives to be safe because they are legal, but in fact they can have devastating effects for those who become addicted. Excessive use of alcohol, for example, can result in medical problems such as cirrhosis of the liver or substance-related social problems such as unemployment, accidents, and crime. The opiates such as heroin, discussed in chapter 8, can be equally problematic for individuals. As depicted in the case example, some individuals who become addicted to heroin can be forced to give up everything important to them, thereby reducing the multitude of life's urges to one—getting high with the drug. In chapter 9, the reader is introduced to the problems that can occur when prolonged use of prescription medications leads to serious dependence.

To help the reader better understand the relationship between these types of depressant substances and addiction, this section provides a synthesis describing the substances, the psychophysiological effects experienced by the user, and important considerations for the assessment and intervention phases of treatment. Each chapter emphasizes the importance of recognizing the abuse patterns relevant to these types of users, as illustrated with case presentations and supported with direct intervention information. In closing, each of the chapters in this section presents direct information for practitioners to facilitate practice with individuals addicted to depressant substances.

Chapter 7

Alcohol

Cheryl Green, Sophia F. Dziegielewski, and Barbara F. Turnage

ALCOHOL IS REGARDED AS A "STRONG" OR "MAJOR" DEPRESSANT OF THE central nervous system. Although people often consider alcohol to be safe because it is a legal drug, the negative effects this strong depressant can have on individuals and society are extensive. Divorce, child and adult abuse, unemployment, accidents, crimes, hospitalization, loss of workforce productivity, and high economic costs are just some of the problems that can be attributed to alcohol consumption. Alcohol use is further complicated by the fact that 10 percent of all violent crimes in the United States are related to alcohol or other substances of abuse. Indeed, one-third of all federal prisoners and one-half of all state prisoners are considered to be suffering from substance addictions (Milkman & Sederer, 1990). According to Carroll (1997), "each dollar spent on the treatment of alcohol and other drug use disorders saves between $4 and $12 in long term societal, economic, and medical costs" (p. 352).

The problems associated with alcohol addiction can place considerable social and financial burdens on the public. Fields (2001) indicates that alcohol abuse is one of the largest drug problems in the United States. And because most people who consume alcohol began drinking before they reached legal age, alcohol use constitutes one of the earliest forms of rebellion related to substance experimentation. Regardless of the reasons for alcohol use, if alcohol users are underage, they are committing a crime. For many individuals, alcohol becomes a gateway drug leading to the use of other substances. The early and often problematic use of alcohol makes it essential for practitioners to be skilled in recognizing the signs and symptoms of alcohol use and to become aware of the problems and concerns that result when alcohol is abused.

This chapter describes alcohol as a significant addictive substance and examines the multitude of problems that can result from its use. The social problem of alcoholism is discussed, including the definition and description of the adult alcoholic, gender differences that may exist among persons who are alcohol dependent, and the possible causes of alcoholism. Special attention is given to completion of the diagnostic assessment as well as to intervention planning and strategy. Factors in the assessment process are highlighted and treatment strategies are presented, including a biopsychosocial approach, cognitive-behavioral therapy, systems theory, and the traditional self-help approaches. For best practice, an integrated approach that takes into account the individual and his or her support system is suggested. The chapter concludes with a discussion of future directions for practice.

ADDICTION TO ALCOHOL

The severity of the multiple social, biological, and psychological problems related to alcohol abuse is generally proportional to the severity of the abuse itself. For example, in extreme cases, when a large amount of alcohol has been consumed, the resulting physiological damage, physical dependence, and in some cases, withdrawal can be life threatening. Traditionally, the term *alcoholic* is reserved to describe an individual experiencing severe dependence or addiction. It indicates that the person has a cumulative pattern of behaviors, including frequent intoxication, that interferes with socialization, relationships, and employment. The authors of this chapter, however, prefer not to use this term and instead prefer to describe the individual similarly to others with mental health or addictions problems—as an individual suffering from either alcohol abuse, dependence, intoxication, or withdrawal (Dziegielewski, 2002).

For many who drink alcoholically, the desire to use alcohol is so strong that they will risk legal consequences such as being arrested for driving while intoxicated. When an individual suffers from severe alcohol dependence, delirium tremens (the medical term for "the shakes") or cirrhosis of the liver could result, requiring hospitalization. Early detection of alcohol-related disorders is important because the earlier and longer an individual uses alcohol, the more devastating the potential problems related to long-term use (Rotgers, Morgenstein & Walters, 2003).

Dawson (2000) believes that there is probably no single cause of alcoholism. Instead, a combination of many different factors are likely to blame. For the most part, the factors that result in someone becoming dependent on alcohol remain unique to the individual. Nevertheless, there are some common feelings that may be associated with alcoholism, including a generalized sense of inadequacy, insecurity and alienation, isolation, loneliness, shyness, depression, dependency, hostility, and self-destructive impulsivity. Additionally, the experiences of abuse, neglect, and abandonment also appear associated with the development of addiction (Durrant & Thakker, 2003; Van Den Bergh, 1991). Individuals addicted to alcohol frequently have poor family relationships, and this disturbed familial culture also has an effect on alcohol consumption (Lawson, Lawson, & Rivers, 2001; Duncan, Duncan, & Hops, 1998).

PREVALENCE

The National Household Survey on Drug Abuse is the primary source of statistical information on Americans' use of alcohol, tobacco, and illicit drugs. This survey showed that in 1997 approximately 111 million people in the United States (51%) were current alcohol users. According to Marwick (1998), "mental and addictive disorders are among the most prevalent and the most often neglected health problems facing us today in the United States. Almost one-third of those between 15 and 54 years of age experience one or more mental or addictive disorders in a given year" (p. 77). Other sources estimate that 75 percent of all Americans drink and that between 7.5 and 10 percent of those who drink have experienced a problem with alcoholism or alcohol misuse at some time (Fuller & Hiller-Sturmhofel, 1999; Merck, 2000; National Institute of Alcohol Abuse and Alcoholism [NIAAA], 2000).

Problems with alcohol addiction remain pronounced. *Health and Health Care: 2010* (Institute for the Future, 2003) lists alcohol as one of the top ten underlying causes of death in the United States in the 1990s. Between 3 and 9 percent of the American elderly consume twelve to twenty-one drinks per week (Patterson, Lacro, & Jeste, 1999). Fuller and Hiller-Sturmhofel (1999) note that approximately 7.5 percent of the U.S. population engage in the abuse of or are dependent on alcohol. In addition, it is estimated that alcoholism accounts for 15 percent of U.S. medical costs, results in over one hundred thousand deaths per year, and is in some way involved in one-third of all child abuse cases (Treatment of Alcoholism, part 2, 2000). Admissions to programs offering assistance are decreasing, yet the need for intervention remains pronounced because individuals with alcohol-related disorders often experience isolation from family and community activities; a life that revolves around drinking activities; increased frequency of legal problems associated with violence and crime; and extreme financial difficulties (Substance Abuse and Mental Health Services Administration [SAMHSA] 1998).

Substance abuse can cost employers more than $150 billion each year in employee substance abuse treatments and disability payments and in lost productivity due to employees' untreated substance abuse (Budgar, 2001). Many individuals with a substance problem often have poor work histories and may also be the victims of more industrial accidents. Employment data suggest that the majority of individuals with a substance abuse problem have impaired work performance, indicating a high incidence of disability or a co-occurring disorder (SAMHSA, 1998). These types of employee problems make employers keenly aware that addiction exists in the workplace. Of a total U.S. workforce of approximately 198 million, it is estimated that 9 percent have problems with substance misuse (Goff & Cook, 2001; MacPherson, 1998). This estimate is likely to be low, however, because substance abuse is generally a covert activity. Monitoring just the number of employees who seek help for a problem ignores the number of individuals who remain in the workforce but never seek assistance (Goff & Cook, 2001).

GENDER CONSIDERATIONS

According to SAMHSA (1998), men are far more likely (58%) to drink than women, and they drink more heavily than women. Among those suffering from alcoholism, the ratio of men to women is 2 to 1. In terms of treatment, women are underrepresented 3 to 1 in Alcoholics Anonymous and 4 to 1 in treatment centers (NIAAA, 2000). The National Council on Alcoholism reports that, nationally, women constitute less than 25 percent of all treatment center clients, and there is a significant gender disparity between the prevalence of the problem of alcohol addiction and access to care (SAMHSA, 1998; Van Den Bergh, 1991). To some practitioners, this trend may seem unusual because women typically seek out psychotherapy more often than men, although not in the area of substance abuse treatment. One possible reason for this discrepancy is that women break the law less often when intoxicated. Fulfilling the requirements of the court is usually a strong impetus for the men who seek treatment. Also, social stigma might discourage women from seeking intervention assistance. Milkman & Sederer (1990) explain that substance abuse problems among women are often viewed negatively by society—more so than the same problems among men—and women who suffer from alcohol addiction are usually considered less of a person and inadequate as a parent or spouse. Women who are addicted to alcohol are also often victims of aggression and abuse; They may feel that they are to blame and so may hide the problem from others (National Clearinghouse for Alcohol and Drug Information [NCADI], 1995).

Generally, men and women receive the same treatment regime. It is becoming increasingly clear, however, that differences in effectiveness by gender do exist, and gender-specific treatment needs further consideration (Schuckit, Anthenelli, Bucholz, Hesselbrock, & Tipp, 1995). Among other things, life experiences and alcohol-related consequences differ between men and women (Lowinson, Ruiz, Milkman & Langrod, 1997). For example, relevant only to women are the consequences of drinking alcohol during pregnancy. A pregnant women who uses alcohol exposes her child to the drug, which can result in fetal alcohol syndrome or fetal alcohol effects (Christensen, 2000).

ETHNICITY AND GROUP DIFFERENCES

Because the incidence of alcohol addiction and its consequences vary widely among ethnic groups, practitioners need to be careful not to make broad generalizations based on statistics that apply only to specific subgroupings of the population (NIAAA, 2000). Current information indicates that American Indians/Alaskan Natives and Native Hawaiians are comparatively heavier drinkers than African Americans, Hispanics, Asian Americans, and Pacific Islanders, with the most notable increase being observed among Asian Americans. Native Americans are disproportionately affected by alcoholism, at six times the U.S. population rate (NIAAA, 2000). There appears to be a predisposition to alcohol addiction in certain subpopulations that is related to genetically determined variations in the body's ability to metabolize and eliminate alcohol. This predisposition may also lead to an increased degree of vulnerability to alcoholic cirrhosis and alcohol-related fetal damage. Among adolescents, Hispanic individuals appear to have the highest prevalence of heavy drinking, followed by Caucasians (NIAAA, 2000). Environmental and social factors can also play an important role in increased risk of substance use, such as when alcohol sales outlets are readily accessible within the community (Gruenewald, Millar, Ponicki, & Brinkley, 2000). Yet, when sanctions are enforced, such as the local alcohol control laws in remote Alaska Native communities, which prohibited the sale, importation, and possession of alcohol by adults as well as adolescents (i.e., dry communities), alcohol problems are not reduced (Berman, 2000). What may work better, however, is restricting rather than prohibiting the sale and use of alcoholic beverages. Those who emigrate to another country without their families and acculturate through partial or complete adoption of the beliefs and values of the prevailing social system or culture also tend to drink more heavily. Alcohol, with its depressant qualities, may serve as a resource for socialization for many of these individuals.

ELDERLY INDIVIDUALS

Later-onset alcoholism refers to an alcohol addiction that has developed after the age of sixty. The evidence is contradictory as to whether drinking patterns remain stable with increasing age (Wilson & Dufour, 2000). Regardless, individuals have a tendency to increase consumption as a response to age-related stresses, such as loss of employment, widowhood, or other bereavement concerns, and untreated alcohol abuse among older individuals remains a serious problem (NIAAA, 2000).

CONSIDERING THE FAMILY

Individuals addicted to alcohol frequently experience disruptive familial patterns because the addiction affects not only the individual but also the entire family unit. The partner may feel so trapped within the situation that he or she may attempt to hide or deny the problems that exist. Or, the partner may simply take on the other person's responsibilities. This type of "enabling behavior" will only perpetuate the addicted individual's dependence on alcohol. The family may also find it difficult to be open and honest about their feelings of resentment, anger, hurt, and shame. The children may also be at increased risk of developing alcohol dependency and may avoid social peer contacts for fear of embarrassment. When a parent has a substance problem of this nature, the child may feel deprived of emotional and physical support as the parent considers his or her desire and need for alcohol above all else. Although genetic predisposition or linkage may be a factor in the development of alcohol addiction, healthy family relations are important in terms of recovery (Duncan et al., 1998).

UNDERSTANDING ALCOHOL AS A SUBSTANCE OF ADDICTION

In past decades, as professionals have attempted to better understand alcohol as a substance to which people become addicted, various definitions of alcohol addiction have emerged, ranging from moralistic judgments to more concrete attempts at objective and quantifiable description. To identify those persons who drink regularly, as opposed to those who are considered binge or problem drinkers, a classification system was developed. Having had five or more drinks on at least five occasions in the past month qualified a person as a heavy drinker, while having had five or more drinks on only one occasion in the past month identified a person as a binge drinker. An additional category, problem drinker, was used at times to describe the person who drank large quantities for purposes of escape (Cahalan & Cisin, 1968).

Today, most professionals agree that the individual addicted to alcohol will progress through definite stages. The time spent in each stage can vary. Tolerance is a significant factor in the speed of an individual's progression through the early stages. The individual's drinking often starts out as social or controlled behavior and later becomes a method of frequent or constant escape. During these early stages of addiction, the consumption of alcohol is for the specific purpose of easing tensions and everyday cares. As the progression of addiction continues, however, the individual's building tolerance will create a need to consume increasingly more alcohol to achieve the same effect. The advanced alcoholic phase begins with the first "blackout" (temporary amnesia). During a blackout, a person is conscious and aware of his or her activities, but afterward, he or she will have no memory of those actions. Although anyone who drinks too much will pass out, it is said that only an individual who is in the advanced stages of alcohol addiction will experience blackouts (Maxmen & Ward, 1995).

The individual addicted to alcohol will lose control of the amount of alcohol he or she consumes. Other signs of alcoholism include secret drinking, a preoccupation with alcohol, gulping the first few drinks, and experiencing guilt about drinking. The guilt and the effects of alcohol consumption are manifested in various ways. Addicted individuals will avoid talking about alcohol or rationalize their drinking behavior, or they may exhibit grandiose behavior, periods of remorse, or periods of abstinence. A behavior change may occur that results in a shift in drinking patterns. Developments that increase alcohol-centered behavior can have negative effects on family members and lead to unreasonable resentments. The addicted person may begin to hide bottles, neglect proper nutrition, experience a decrease in sexual drive, or begin regular morning drinking. Intoxication during working hours can increase with subsequent task impairment (Maxmen & Ward, 1995).

Two typologies frequently used to describe and differentiate those who are addicted to alcohol are Type A and Type B alcoholics and Type I and Type II alcoholics. A Type A alcoholic has a later onset of drinking and fewer disturbances of psychosocial functioning. A Type B alcoholic has an earlier onset (at twenty-five years old or younger) with increased psychosocial interference. A Type I alcoholic has a later onset of drinking, with a strong genetic effect, and a low probability of risk-taking behavior such as fighting or arrest. A Type II alcoholic has an earlier onset, with gender differences (alcohol use is greater among men), and frequent risk-taking behaviors. There is an ongoing dispute as to ability of either typology to predict patterns of behavior and outcomes. Neither typology appears to be statistically linked to etiology or observed behavioral outcomes (Kirst-Ashman & Hull, 1999; Dawson, 2000).

The definitions of alcohol use disorders most accepted by clinicians are outlined in the *DSM-IV-TR* (American Psychiatric Association [APA], 2000). According to the *DSM-IV-TR*, the alcohol use disorders are earmarked by a consumption of alcohol that exceeds the limits of what the individual's culture considers acceptable and appropriate or that becomes so excessive that health or social relationships are impaired. The *DSM-IV-TR* describes two primary alcohol use disorders: alcohol abuse and alcohol dependence.

A person warrants a diagnosis of alcohol abuse if he or she experiences at least one of the four abuse symptoms—role impairment, hazardous use, legal problems, or social problems—that lead to clinically significant impairment or distress. These symptoms reflect either pathological patterns of alcohol use, psychosocial consequences, or both (American Psychiatric Association, 2000). Alcohol dependence is defined as a constellation of symptoms related to physical dependence as well as compulsive and pathological patterns of alcohol use. To qualify for a *DSM-IV-TR* diagnosis of alcohol dependence, a person must exhibit, within a twelve-month period, at least three of the following symptoms: tolerance; withdrawal or drinking to avoid or relieve withdrawal; drinking larger amounts or for a longer period than intended; unsuccessful attempts or a repeated desire to quit or to cut down on drinking; much time spent using alcohol; and reduced social or recreational activities in favor of alcohol use (American Psychiatric Association, 2000).

In addition to the delineation of abuse and dependency, the practitioner must also identify the differences between two common disorders: intoxication and withdrawal. Intoxication is reversible and occurs when the individual has overingested the substance. Alcohol intoxication may be accompanied by a lower threshold for anger and violence but usually results in generalized disinhibition (American Psychiatric Association, 1994, 2000; Maxmen & Ward, 1995; Zuckerman, 1995). Withdrawal is defined as the biophysical reaction to the reduction of a chemical stimulus in the body. Often withdrawal is accompanied by tremors, mood instability, physical illness, and in severe cases, seizures and possible death (American Psychiatric Association, 1994, 2000; Maxmen & Ward, 1995; Zuckerman, 1995). To avoid withdrawal, many individuals addicted to one substance become cross-addicted, identifying either alcohol or street/pharmaceutical drugs as their drug of choice. Not surprisingly, many of these individuals develop multiple and varied problems (see table 7).

CASE EXAMPLE

Case History

N is a forty-five-year-old male with a twenty-five-year history of alcohol and other drug use. As a child, he was diagnosed with attention-deficit/hyperactivity disorder and received Ritalin from ages eight to ten. At age ten, N was sexually abused by an uncle and began drinking shortly thereafter. By age fifteen, N was

Table 7: Symptoms of Alcohol Abuse and Alcohol Dependence

Alcohol Abuse	Alcohol Dependence
Role impairment Frequent intoxication leading to failure to fulfill major role obligations (e.g., at school, work, or home)	*Tolerance* Need to increase consumption by 50 percent or more to achieve the same effects; markedly reduced effects when drinking the same amount
Legal problems Recurrent alcohol-related legal problems	*Withdrawal* Signs of alcohol withdrawal; drinking to avoid or relieve withdrawal.
Social problems Continued drinking despite knowledge of persistent or recurrent social or inter-personal problems caused or exacerbated by alcohol use	*Inability to control use* Recurrent drinking of larger amounts or for a longer period of time than intended
Hazardous use Recurrent use when it is physically hazardous (e.g., driving while intoxicated)	*Desire to quit* Unsuccessful attempts or a persistent desire to quit or cut down on drinking
No alcohol dependence No diagnosis of dependence in the past twelve months	*Reduced activities; social problems* Much time spent using, obtaining, or recovering from the effects of alcohol; important social or recreational activities given up or reduced in favor of alcohol use
	Psychological/physical problems Continued drinking despite knowledge of a recurrent or persistent psychological or physical problem caused or exacerbated by alcohol use

Source: DSM–IV-TR (American Psychiatric Association, 2000). Adapted from Dziegielewski (2002).

alcohol dependent and had begun experimenting with other drugs such as marijuana and cocaine.

N was raised by both his mother and his father and has four siblings—two older sisters and two younger brothers. Family history reveals that his mother did not use alcohol or drugs but that his father was alcohol dependent and, as adults, his two brothers used alcohol on a regular basis. N got into trouble with the law as a teenager, committing petit theft and burglary. He struggled to complete high school and then entered the army, ostensibly to help him to keep out of trouble. During this period, his alcohol use became more frequent, and he exhibited greater tolerance. Alcohol use preceded every decision to use other types of addictive substances.

In his mid-twenties, N married, and this relationship lasted approximately ten years. At his wife's insistence, he agreed to quit drinking and began attending Alcoholic Anonymous meetings once weekly. He continued to attend over the next seven years but did not completely quit using drugs and alcohol during this time. He and his wife desperately wanted children but were faced with a series of miscarriages, with the last one causing N to go into deep depression that included thoughts of suicide. At this point, he entered therapy and was diagnosed with major depression and prescribed antidepressants. After ten years of struggle, N ended his marriage, stating, "We just fell out of love with one another."

N's work history was fairly stable until age forty, when he received a ticket for driving while intoxicated. He was forced to quit work as a computer programmer and move to another state to stay with relatives. At this time, he felt he was having a "nervous breakdown" and again thought of suicide. He entered a ninety-day outpatient substance abuse treatment program and began attending AA once again. This time, however, he admitted openly that he had a problem and wanted to make every attempt he could to stop it. N successfully completed outpatient therapy and speaks of having a "spiritual awakening" at about that time, which he attributes to his involvement with and support from Alcoholics Anonymous. It has been five years since N took his last drink or drug, and he reports improved relationships, a new job, and a better quality of life. He continues to attend AA meetings three to five times weekly.

What follows are some "words of wisdom" from the individual described in this case example:

The following self-revelation should help you to better understand the true nature and necessity of "Bottoming Out." Alcohol was my greatest "love." When life threw me a curve ball or a great joy it was there to comfort me. In loneliness and despair it gave me hope. In group situations it gave me self-confidence. It was the replacement for a God and faith, which was difficult for me to understand. Then, alcohol betrayed me by not working anymore, as did every conceivable alternative afterwards. Drugs, sex, love, music . . . anything that would take the focus off of me and out into the nether regions no longer worked . . . thus, full betrayal and helplessness and hopelessness.

When you finally "bottom out" you know the truth about all of life's situations. Church, parents, books, crime and punishment, everything that you believed or experienced now becomes crystal clear . . . REAL. You now have the power to decipher crap in a glance (known as "intuitive nature" in the rooms of AA) and you "know" those people who enter your life who are in process for real and those who wish they were. The point of AA is the "process," or so it is said over and over in the rooms. The process for an alcoholic is simple, move closer to God and further from Self.

Intervention Plan: Alcohol Dependence Disorder

Definition. Individuals who are dependent on alcohol exhibit evidence of maladaptive alcohol consumption, which commonly takes up much of their time.

They continue to use despite the negative physical, social, and psychological effects of the drug. These individuals continue using alcohol despite significant substance-related problems. There is a pattern of repeated self-administration that can result in tolerance, withdrawal, and compulsive drug-taking behavior. Individuals who are alcohol dependent may continue to use alcohol despite evidence of adverse psychological consequences (e.g., depression, blackouts, liver disease). They may often continue to consume alcohol to avoid or relieve the symptoms of withdrawal. A minority of individuals who are alcohol dependent never experience clinically relevant levels of alcohol withdrawal (withdrawal symptoms that develop four to twelve hours after the reduction of intake following prolonged, heavy, alcohol ingestion); only about 5 percent of individuals with alcohol dependence ever experience severe complications of withdrawal (e.g., delirium, grand mal seizures). Alcohol-dependent individuals often develop an increasing tolerance over time and consume alcohol with increasing frequency and with a distinctive pattern to use, resulting in life-damaging consequences (e.g., health, legal, family, or work problems). Those who are alcohol dependent often began drinking at an early age in large quantities with high tolerance.

Signs and Symptoms.   Sleep problems; substantial amount of time devoted to obtaining and consuming alcoholic beverages; school or job performance may deteriorate; neglect of role responsibilities; alcohol-related absences from school or job; legal difficulties arising from alcohol-related use; gastritis; psychological and physical dependence; stomach ulcers; impaired immune system; alcohol hepatitis; brain damage; cirrhosis; pneumonia; heart damage; bladder infection; liver cancer; high blood pressure; irregular menses; coma; pancreatitis; colitis; tuberculosis.

Goals for Treatment.
1. Assist client in abstaining from alcohol use.
2. Assist client in getting medical care.
3. Refer client to an in-patient treatment facility.
4. Help link client to socially appropriate AA chapter in community.
5. Address underlying issues of alcohol dependency.
6. Assist family in dealing with the alcohol dependence.

Objectives	Interventions
Client will discuss alcohol dependency issues responsible for self-destructive behavior.	Client, with the assistance of the practitioner, will become fully aware of how his behavior affects him and people around him. Client will identify specific reasons why client will need to stop drinking.
Help client deal with symptoms of alcohol withdrawal and its effects on the body.	Client will receive a physical exam and medical evaluation. Client will be educated as to effects of alcohol dependency and the problems that may arise if client continues to drink.

Objectives	Interventions
Client will discuss experience he has had while attending AA meetings and how it has helped him to become abstinent.	Client will keep a journal of his experiences in AA meetings.
Address the needs of client's family. Encourage client's family to participate throughout program.	Practitioner will arrange for relatives to attend Al-Anon and have sessions to help client's family deal with the alcoholism dependence.
Client will take medications as prescribed for withdrawal/dependency/depression.	Client and practitioner will monitor client's medication use or misuse.
Client will attend therapy.	Client will schedule sessions of appropriate duration at appropriate intervals.
Client will learn about the cycle of addiction.	Client will learn about the cycle of addiction and how behavior could cause situations to get worse and thus lead to addiction.
Client will work to repair relationships with those in support system.	Client will identify individuals in the immediate support system affected by the addiction (e.g., employer, relatives, neighbors, and others) and determine how to best address the problems that have resulted.
Client will admit that he or she has a problem and will agree to attend meetings or participate in activities that will assist in recovery.	Client and practitioner will discuss the common issues and triggers faced in recovery and what resources are available to help in times of need.
Client will develop a daily routine that does not include the use of alcohol.	Client will develop a daily routine that does not include the use of alcohol. Client will keep a journal of daily activities and feelings.

BEST PRACTICES

Considering the debates within the mental health field, the varied attitudes of client populations, cultural considerations, and the variety of intervention models from which to choose, treatment planning can be a complicated process. The most effective plans take into account environment and new approaches to intervention.

Sample treatment goals that can be included in an intervention plan for an alcohol-related disorder include maintaining abstinence, achieving and maintaining sobriety, controlling drinking, resolving legal issues, improving social and coping skills, and enhancing self-esteem. Practitioners should ensure that the selected goals match the assessment and the desires of the client. Additionally, factors such as the client's strengths, support systems, co-occurring disorders, and culture must be incorporated into the treatment planning process.

Objectives for the client with an alcohol-related disorder should be clear and concise. The inherent likelihood of relapse and resistance should be addressed to ensure that the client is not set up for failure. The practitioner should discuss relapse and prevention with the client initially, during the diagnostic assessment, and throughout treatment, regardless of the intervention technique (Dziegielewski, 2002; George & Tucker, 1996). Ascertaining the client's attitudes about treatment is essential in developing a successful plan.

Generally, the first stage of a treatment plan is detoxification. Detoxification is the process during which the client allows his or her body to eliminate the alcohol from its systems. This is typically accomplished through abstinence (often referred to as "going cold turkey"). Most clients will complete this phase as an inpatient. However, some research indicates that, in milder cases of use, detoxification can be done on an outpatient basis under close supervision (Hyashida, 1998). When an individual is detoxing, a medical exam is crucial because withdrawal syndromes often require immediate medical attention (Wesson & Center for Substance Abuse Treatment, 1995; Fuller & Hiller-Sturmhofel, 1999). Withdrawal syndromes are characterized by a continuum of signs and symptoms that usually begin twelve to forty-eight hours after last intake. Mild withdrawal syndrome includes tremors, weakness, sweating, and gastrointestinal symptoms. Some clients have one or two generalized tonic-clonic seizures (sometimes known as "alcoholic epilepsy" or "rum fits") (Wesson & Center for Substance Abuse Treatment, 1995; American Psychiatric Association, 1994, 2000). Because alcohol withdrawal delirium can be life threatening, medical observation is essential in a detoxification program. Often the client will be evaluated to determine the suitability of medications such as thiamine, magnesium sulphate, diazepam, and lorazepam, which can help with this detoxification and withdrawal period (Litovitz, 1987).

The more severe withdrawal syndromes include alcoholic hallucinosis (auditory illusions and hallucinations, frequently accusatory and threatening but usually transient), delirium tremens, anxiety attacks, increasing confusion, poor sleep (with frightening dreams or nocturnal illusions), marked sweating, profound depression, fleeting hallucinations that arouse restlessness, fear and terror, and serious physical distress. These withdrawal symptoms should begin to resolve within twelve to twenty-four hours. Known complications of these severe withdrawal syndromes that may occur in alcohol-addicted individuals are Korsakoff's syndrome, Wernicke's encephalopathy, and cerebellar degeneration. A more serious syndrome is Marchiafava-Bignami disease, a rare demyelination of the corpus callosum that occurs in individuals with a chronic alcohol problem, predominantly men (Wesson & Center for Substance Abuse Treatment, 1995). Pathologic intoxication is another rare syndrome, characterized by repetitive, automatic movements and extreme excitement with aggressive, uncontrolled, and irrational behavior that occurs after ingesting a relatively small amount of alcohol (Miller & Gold, 1998).

INTERVENTION STRATEGIES

For alcohol-related addictions, the debate continues about whether it is better to use an all-or-nothing intervention approach requiring total abstinence or to use moderation. From the traditional perspective of Alcoholics Anonymous, moderation will lead to loss of control. Today, spontaneous recovery, self-change, and motivational therapies seem to support approaches other than abstinence ("Treatment of Alcoholism, Part 2," 2000). It is not surprising that, in a field with so many different theoretical orientations among the involved disciplines, debate centers on the efficacy of nontreatment options. For example, Cunningham (1999) replicated a prior study implemented by Sobel and colleagues and found that reports of natural recovery (without treatment) varied greatly according to the definition used to categorize problem drinking or alcoholism. When the problem was restated to fit more generally accepted definitions of excessive alcohol use, the results showed that a significant proportion (53 percent) of the study participants did recover without seeking treatment. Furthermore, Timko, Moos, Finney, Moos, & Kaplowitz (1999) researched the long-term recovery outcomes of persons who participated in immediate onset, delayed onset, or no treatment groups designed to enhance recovery. They found that individuals who sought treatment declined in success three years posttreatment, but for the most part those who sought treatment had better outcomes than those who did not. Duncan et al. (1998) looked at mild to moderate problem drinkers and found that there was a reduction in drinking behaviors with maturity or in the presence of physical consequences such as blackout.

An important part of understanding intervention approaches is the realization that individuals with alcohol problems score significantly higher on neuroticism and psychoticism scales (Pande, 1987). A study by Chambless, Cherney, and Caputo (1987) indicated that one or more anxiety disorders of a severity comparable to those of 12 socially phobic and 128 agoraphobic clients treated in phobia clinics were diagnosed in 40 percent of adult inpatients who are addicted to alcohol. Individuals who are addicted to alcohol need individualized intervention plans (Caetano, Clark, & Tam, 1998; Tonigan, Conners, & Miller, 1998; Arredondo, 1998). Those with alcohol-related disorders all may have difficulty managing stress reactions such as anxiety, tension, panic, and feeling worried, pressured, and overwhelmed, but they may handle these feelings differently. Given that a person's emotional and behavioral reactions are at least partially determined by a person's cognition and subsequent behaviors.

Pharmacotherapy

In pharmacotherapy, the relationship of the brain and neurotransmitters needs to be examined. The brain consists of multiple neurotransmitter systems that modulate various bodily functions. These neurotransmitters include opioids, glutamate, serotonin, and dopamine. Opioids are pain blockers and have an effect similar to that of morphine or heroin. These peptides appear to increase the sense of reward when alcohol is consumed. Additionally, there appears to be some interaction with dopamine in the creation of this effect. Glutamate is an excitatory transmitter that appears to work with brain receptor sites to increase the effects of intoxication, cognitive impairment, and some symptoms of withdrawal in alcohol consumption. Serotonin affects bodily functioning in varied physiological, cognitive, mood, sleep, and appetite areas. Dopamine is linked to higher brain functioning and the organization of thought and perception (Johnson & Ait-Daud, 1999).

The longest standing pharmacological treatment is aversive medication like disulfiram (Antabuse). This type of medication causes negative physiological reactions after the ingestion of alcohol, including nausea, vomiting, and increased blood pressure and heart rate. However, problems with poor compliance decrease the medication's effectiveness. Supervised administration does improve results, but the outcomes are still lower than originally anticipated (Fuller & Hiller-Sturmhofel, 1999). Two newer drugs being used to treat alcohol dependency are naltrexone and acamprosate. Naltrexone is an opiate-blocking agent, and acamprosate modulates gamma-aminobutyric acid (GABA)/glutamate (Bonne, 1999; Petrakis & Krystal, 1997). Gamma-hydroxybutyric acid (GHB) is also being used to affect GABA (Addolorato et al., 1998). In addition, buspirone (BuSpar), ritanserin (Remeron), and ondansetron (Zofran) are also being used (Johnson & Ait-Daud, 1999; Petrakis & Krystal, 1997). Central nervous system depressants and the benzodiazepines are frequently used to treat alcohol withdrawal. Benzodiazepines in particular are the mainstays of withdrawal therapy. Compared with shorter-acting benzodiazepines (e.g., lorazepam, oxazepam), long-acting benzodiazepines (e.g., chlordiazepoxide, diazepam) provide less frequent dosing and, when the dose is tapered, an easier transition off of the medication. The main problem with benzodiazepines is that they themselves may cause intoxication, physical dependence, and withdrawal in alcohol-addicted individuals and thus create a secondary addiction problem (Myrick & Anton, 1998; Miller & Gold, 1998; Wesson & Center for Substance Abuse Treatment, 1995).

Although this field is developing rapidly, the clinical trials and new developments discussed above are far from being a part of common treatment regimen. The research is promising and shows that most of the drugs have at least some clinical efficacy for reducing cravings and the biochemical impulsivity related to dependence. However, as noted in Bonne's (1999) review of new drugs, these treatments are not cures. They do not eliminate alcohol dependence. Many of those studied continued to drink while on the medications, although with decreased frequency and quantity. The studies reviewed indicated that increased efficacy might be achieved with combination therapy, involving more than one of these medications coupled with behavioral, cognitive, motivational, or self-help intervention.

Behavioral Therapy

Behavioral therapy, a very popular intervention for addictions, rests on the premise that addiction, like all other behavior, is learned and therefore is subject to modification and eventual extinction (Treatment of Alcoholism, part 1, 2000). The principle focus of Skinner's (1953) theory of behavioral therapy is the target behavior, its antecedent behaviors or events, and the consequences that follow the behavior. Once a behavior is targeted for change, an extinction process, or the withholding of a positive reinforcer in response to positive behavior, is used to achieve compliance. The focus of change is observable behavior, not internal mental processes.

Another therapy used in the treatment of addictions is desensitization as developed by Joseph Wolpe. Wolpe's procedures differ from the classical (Pavlovian) technique of systematic desensitization to treat anxiety and phobic disorders. Wolpe's technique teaches a relaxation response using visual imagery to overcome what would normally be an anxiety-provoking situation. Myers (1992) explains that behavior therapists apply well-established learning principles to eliminate unwanted behaviors and replace them with more positive responses.

Studies of the long-term effects of programs designed to help the individual gain insight versus behavioral treatment among those addicted to alcohol resulted in support for the behavioral approach. For example, in one study that examined the relative effects of behavioral treatment involving both covert sensitization and relaxation training versus an insight-oriented treatment, significant differences were noted (Olson, Ganley, Devine, & Dorsey, 1981). For the most part, behavior therapies appear to be strongest when targeting specific fears and problem behaviors (Curtis, 1999).

One effect of alcohol is that it allows the drinker to be less inhibited. This decreased inhibition can reinforce the alcoholic behaviors, thus supporting the need for teaching replacement behavior as well as offering alternative reinforcers to reduce the addiction. In addition, the use of education as a forum to reinforce the consequences of alcoholism is essential in the behavioral therapeutic approach (Moras, 1997).

Multifaceted disorders and possible co-occurring disorders such as depression or a general anxiety condition may best be treated with cognitive processes, utilizing cognitive therapy or behavioral therapy combinations that work toward the development of better coping skills and increased self-esteem (Modesto-Lowe & Kranzler, 1999; Reiss & Center for Substance Abuse Treatment, 1995).

Cognitive Therapy

According to Hepworth, Rooney, and Larsen (1999), cognitive therapies assume that the way a person thinks determines his or her feelings, and cognitive therapists use various approaches to teach clients new, more constructive ways of thinking. According to Hollandsworth (1986), "cognitive therapies assume that (a) human behavior is mediated by cognition (e.g., appraisal) and that (b) emotional disorders are, therefore, essentially a consequence of cognitive deficiencies. These interventions seek to alter cognitions using techniques designed to restore rationality, improve thinking skills, increase problem-solving ability, or enhance self-instructional capabilities" (p. 137).

All cognitive therapy approaches share one common element: they assist the client in reconstructing the problem from a new perspective that is then validated in behavioral assignments (Turner, 1996). As previously noted, an individual addicted to alcohol will commonly report feelings of depression, guilt, and anxiety. The addicted client's goal is often to causally link the addiction with the irrational thinking associated with these feelings. Because denial is a primary factor in this disorder, it will be a primary focus in the initial stages of treatment. If not resolved, denial could be a major obstacle to treatment success in this model. One solution is to pair cognitive approaches with behavioral approaches to elicit a favorable treatment outcome.

The Combination Approach: Cognitive-Behavioral Therapy

Milkman and Sederer (1990) indicate that a person's behavioral repertoire determines the choices that he or she makes regarding alcohol use, which supports the use of a cognitive-behavioral approach to problem drinking. In numerous outcome studies, behavioral therapy has been proven effective for anxiety disorders, sexual problems, psychosis, gerontological problems, depression, obesity, alcohol and drug addiction, and other problems. Treatment rests with education, supportive therapy, and cognitive-behavioral techniques that teach coping skills and give individuals a confident attitude (Anthenelli & Schuckit, 1993; Watson, 1991; Turner, 1996).

The individual suffering from an addictive disorder must first recognize and confront the denial that is commonly associated with addiction. The second goal of treatment could be assisting the individual to identify circumstances that render him or her vulnerable to loss of control. Some clients will be successful when integrating lifestyle changes; others will need to achieve mastery over internal drives (Larimer, Palmer, & Marlatt, 1999). This combination approach helps the client accept the fact that these are really guided self-help steps. The client must work actively to achieve gains, and success will be determined by the degree to which the client accepts responsibility for helping him or herself. The client must take charge of his or her recovery.

The client must identify negative self-statements, private thoughts, or negative self-talk that can inhibit performance of daily activities. Once identified, these thoughts and expressions are cognitively restructured into positive, constructive statements and combined with a perceptual redefinition of the client's reality in the inhibiting situation. The client will learn to use the positive self-statements to reinforce new behaviors as goals are achieved (Turner, 1996).

Expectancies play an important role in cognitive-behavioral therapy. The theory proposes that people act in accordance with expected outcomes, and those expectancies can be positive or negative. When using cognitive-behavioral therapy as an intervention in the treatment of alcohol-related disorders, the practitioner should be familiar with the sources of client expectations. First, the stimuli that have been associated with the effects of drinking may, through classical conditioning, become cues for seeking out anticipated rewards from alcohol or for avoiding the negative consequences of drinking. Second, physiological withdrawal symptoms may, with repeated episodes of heavy drinking, become cues for the belief that more drinking will lead to a temporary reduction in aversive physical symptoms. Third, alcohol outcome expectancies may be determined by physical, social, or environmental factors. For instance, an individual may develop expectancies that are specific to a particular setting. A fourth source of alcohol outcome expectancies consists of the individual's beliefs that affect alcohol use. Cognitive-behavioral theory suggests that people are more likely to abuse alcohol if they lack a sense of self-efficacy in a situation where they expect alcohol to enable them to achieve the desired outcome. Social skills training and the redevelopment of problem-solving pathways, as in the model of cognitive-behavioral coping skills therapy, which is utilized by veterans associations and a number of teaching hospitals throughout the United States, are prime examples of how expectancy modification has evolved in practice with clients who have alcohol use disorders (Longabaugh & Morganstern, 1999).

The Family System Approach

According to the family system perspective, successful treatment of alcoholism requires a multidimensional approach involving the abuser, his or her family, and the environment. The alcohol-addicted individual is viewed as a human system that requires more than one intervention approach, often in combination. The family is viewed as a set of interconnected individuals acting together to maintain a homeostatic balance. The basic premise of this model is to allow each member of the family to achieve a higher level of functioning and emotional security (Curtis, 1999). The view of the family as a system is essential to accomplishing the intended outcome. The alcohol-addicted individual does not exist in a vacuum. Rather, he or she is a living, breathing, interacting element of his or her environment and the environment of his or her family. An exclusionary observation of the person, without consideration of these other factors, is impossible in this model.

Studying a single variable in isolation cannot not reveal the information needed about the system as a whole because the nature of the relationships between components of a system is interactional (Kilpatrick & Holland, 1999). Duncan et al. (1999) agreed with this and stated that a thorough analysis of the cognitive, social, and behavioral aspects of the abuser's drinking behavior has been shown through research to be essential before intervention can be undertaken. Because alcoholism is a psychological, sociocultural, and physical problem, the biopsychosocial approach incorporates the physical with the psychosocial to understand the person as a whole and, in this case, as part of a family system.

Motivational Therapies

DiClemente, Bellino, and Neavens (1999) reported that motivation was an important step toward changing any action or behavior, and they identified five stages for the decision-making process: precontemplation, contemplation, preparation, action, and maintenance. Motivation is critical to initiating a change in behavior and maintaining successful long-term changes in drinking patterns. Determining levels of motivation involves the assessment of internal and external factors that affect change, from within the person or from external or environmental sources.

Different types of motivation include educating the client about the negative effects of alcohol abuse, designed to motivate the client to stop or reduce his or her drinking. This approach is indicated for the nondependent alcohol use disorders and generally entails one to four sessions lasting ten to forty minutes each. The setting is generally substance abuse outpatient or primary care offices (DiClemente et al., 1999). A second type of motivational intervention involves educating the client about the stages of change and informing him or her that denial and ambivalence are natural components of these stages. This knowledge allows the client to work through ambivalence toward sobriety. Techniques include reflective listening, examination of the pros and cons of change, support of client self-efficacy and ability to change, assessment and feedback on problem behavior (abc charting, behavioral counts, etc.), and eliciting self-motivational statements or affirmations from the client. The length of treatment is undefined and can be as long as needed to effect change. Sessions are generally thirty to sixty minutes, once per week (DiClemente et al., 1999).

In another approach, motivational enhancement therapy, practitioners use motivational interviewing within a less intensive setting. The four sessions occur over twelve weeks and are initiated on completion of an intensive assessment process. Evaluation using standardized measures occurs at session one. In session two, a change plan is developed. Session three is used for reinforcing and enhancing the client's motivation and commitment to change. Session four is termination (DiClemente et al., 1999). Clear, concise feedback about the client's addiction behavior is relayed to the client in each session.

It is unclear how effective motivational therapy is compared with other types of therapy. Data is limited on the potential effect of combination therapies, such as cognitive and motivational techniques. It appears that an integrated approach for the treatment of alcohol use disorders is indicated based on these efficacy data sets.

The Traditional Self-Help Approach

The most well known approach in the field of substance addiction is traditional self-help. This approach uses the disease model, provided through Alcoholics

Anonymous (AA), and is a major nonmedical support system available to individuals who suffer from addictive disorders. Individuals with alcohol problems attend meetings in which other previously addicted individuals offer fellowship, emotional support, and practical advice to recovering individuals because they themselves have been in similar circumstances (Mendelson & Mello, 1992; Tonigan et al., 1998). These groups follow the AA twelve-step program and provide peer group support and an added spiritual perspective that is not found in other models presented.

From an evidence-based perspective, AA is difficult to evaluate. AA openly acknowledges that its method does not involve science and proposes that it should not be evaluated from a positivist model. To date, AA has received a number of criticisms, ranging from being nonscientific to being relatively unorganized. The AA approach is not professionally implemented; there are no leaders, only "trusted servants." The Twelve Steps of AA (box 15) promote anonymity of the participants as being of paramount importance. Incorporating a spiritual component, AA differentiates spirituality from religion and bases beliefs in a higher power of understanding. Brown (1985) shared that "educated individuals have trouble accepting the

---

Box 15: The Twelve Steps to Recovery

1. We admitted we were powerless over alcohol—that our lives had become unmanageable.
2. Came to believe that a power greater than ourselves could restore us to sanity.
3. Made a decision to turn our will, and our lives, over to the care of God *as we understood Him.*
4. Made a searching and fearless moral inventory of ourselves.
5. Admitted to God, to ourselves, and to another human being the exact nature of our wrongs.
6. Were entirely ready to have God remove all these defects of character.
7. Humbly asked Him to remove our shortcomings.
8. Made a list of all persons we had harmed, and became willing to make amends to them all.
9. Made direct amends to such people wherever possible, except when to do so would injure them or others.
10. Continued to take personal inventory and when we were wrong promptly admitted it.
11. Sought through prayer and meditation to improve our conscious contact with God, as we understood Him, praying only for knowledge of His will for us and the power to carry that out.
12. Having had a spiritual awakening as the result of these steps, we tried to carry this message to alcoholics and to practice these principles in all our affairs.

Source: Alcoholics Anonymous (1996).

---

inspirational focus of AA. Yet, . . . the suspension of intellectual explanation is essential at certain phases of recovery; it is precisely the intellectual's wish to be able to explain what is happening or to attribute cause that impedes progressive movement into recovery" (p. 12). Despite criticisms, there are many followers of this model, and most professionals agree that for millions of people this model of intervention does work (Alcoholics Anonymous, 1996). AA has been found to enhance the entire treatment system used in work with alcohol-related disorders (Fuller & Hiller-Sturmhofel, 1999; Tonigan et al., 1998; Treatment of Alcoholism, part 1, 2000; Treatment of Alcoholism, part 2, 2000).

SUMMARY AND FUTURE DIRECTIONS

Alcoholism is a multidimensional disease that involves many factors. It results from elements of conditioning and learning as well as neurobiological processes, genetics, cognitive processes, family systems, society, and spiritual and cultural factors (Wallace, 1989; Latorre, 2000). It stands to reason, then, that there will be differences of opinion among professionals in various disciplines concerning the effectiveness of a particular approach to treatment. Turner (1996) warned that practitioners should not adhere strictly to only one practice approach or encourage the exclusion of others because each intervention strategy has its own strengths and limitations. For example, even the best plan of cognitive-behavioral intervention can easily go astray if environmental and family supports are ignored. Incorporating the ideas from family systems theory as part of the intervention process allows the professional to acknowledge the importance of taking into account the whole situation. Intervention needs to include more than just individual and family behavior change strategies, however. It should also involve the sociological, psychological, biological, and environmental elements of the client's situation.

The challenge for the practitioner is to approach the client's entire system in unison with a multidimensional treatment strategy. This involves more than just using the principles inherent in cognitive-behavior therapy, where the role of the practitioner is primarily that of an educator who expects clients to set their own standards, monitor their own performance, and reward or reinforce themselves appropriately. In this approach, the practitioner strives to help the client become his or her own practitioner (Milkman & Sederer, 1990). According to Watson (1991), the preferable strategy is to empower people who feel spiritually and personally empty by giving these areas of living ample attention. Latorre (2000) concurs, stating, "we are dealing with a system, not just a collection of parts, a system that continually strives to balance itself using symptoms as a way to self heal" (p. 67).

The most comprehensive approach appears to be integrated and holistic. In such an approach, exhibited problem behaviors are individualized and related directly to the specific behavior changes needed. Practitioners must have a general understanding of biomedical factors, including the effects of withdrawal, as well as general nutrition, exercise, and the importance of helping the addicted individual to develop and maintain his or her social environment (Wesson & Center for Substance Abuse Treatment, 1995).

Furthermore, an integrated, holistic approach needs to involve family education and support, combined with self-help groups. Alcoholism is a family disease and significant others close to the alcohol-addicted individual typically benefit from treatment themselves. Milkman and Sederer (1990) identify the possible need to restructure the family and the need for the family to adjust to the recovery of the addicted family member. The alcohol-addicted individual's family and other members of his or her support system remain a vital and powerful aspect of the client's ability for recovery. If the intervention strategy does not include the client's family system, the prognosis for long-term recovery from the illness is greatly decreased. Practitioners must also have an understanding of the particular needs of elderly family members and clients (Zimberg, 1996). From the traditional perspective, Alcoholics Anonymous urges family members to participate in Al-Anon, Alateen, Nar-Anon, and Co-Dependents Anonymous. Because the family must be included in treatment, the skilled clinician will be familiar with how to best anticipate and identify potential addiction problems in family members (Steinglass, 1976). Among the tasks of the treatment professional are helping the family accept that alcoholism is the primary problem, recommending treatment options, and instilling a sense of hope for recovery. Therapeutic alternatives are the use of Antabuse, individual therapy, family therapy, and Alcoholics Anonymous. Relapses, when properly handled, can help the alcohol-addicted individual to accept his or her powerlessness over alcohol. King and Lorenson (1989) believe that practitioners should capitalize on their positions to identify individuals suffering from an alcohol-related disorder and guide them to treatment. However, proper training is needed to accomplish this goal.

In summary, alcoholism is a social, psychological, and physical affliction that is difficult to define yet has a profound impact on individuals, their families, and society. The goal of this chapter has been to provide practitioners with information about the best care options available. Whatever the treatment, however, early intervention is critical. If intervention is initiated early enough, it can arrest any additional cognitive and biological deterioration.

References
Addolorato, G., Cibin, M., Caprista, E., Beghe, F., Gessa, G., Stefanini, G. F., & Gasbarrini, G. (1998). Maintaining abstinence from alcohol with gamma-hydroxybutyric acid (Research Letters). *Lancet, 351*(9095), 38.

Alcoholics Anonymous. (1996). *Alcoholics anonymous: The story of how many thousands of men and women have recovered from alcoholism.* New York: Alcoholics Anonymous World Services.

American Psychiatric Association. (1994). *Diagnostic and statistical manual of mental disorders.* (4th ed.). Washington, DC: Author.

American Psychiatric Association. (2000). *Diagnostic and statistical manual of mental disorders* (4th ed., text rev.). Washington, DC: Author.

Anthenelli, R., & Schuckit, M. (1993). Affective and anxiety disorders and alcohol and drug dependence: Diagnosis and treatment [CD-ROM]. *Journal of Addictive Diseases, 12*(3) 73–87. Abstract obtained from *PsychLIT*, AN 81-13797.

Arredondo, P. (1998, July). Integrating multicultural counseling competencies and universal helping conditions in culture-specific contexts (Reconceptualizing Multicultural Counseling). *Counseling Psychologist, 26*(4), 592–602.

Berman, P. (2000). Alcohol control and injury death in Alaska Native Communities: Wet, damp and dry under Alaska's local option law. *Journal of Studies on Alcohol, 61*(2), 311–19.

Bonne, D. (1999). New treatments for alcohol dependency better than old (News). *Lancet, 353*(9148), 213.

Brown, S. (1985). *Treating the alcoholic: A developmental model of recovery.* New York: John Wiley & Sons.

Budgar, L. (2001). Is your mental health coverage about to improve? *Psychology Today, 34,* 6, 20.

Caetano, R., Clark, C. L., & Tam, T. (1998). Alcohol consumption among racial/ethnic minorities. *Alcohol Health and Research World, 22*(4), 233–41.

Cahalan, D., & Cisin, I. H. (1968). American drinking practices: Summary of findings from a national probability sample. *Quarterly Journal of Studies of Alcohol, 29*, 3, 130–51.

Carroll, K. M. (1997, Fall). New methods of treatment efficacy research: Bridging clinical research and clinical practice. *Alcohol Health & Research World, 21*(4). 352–60.

Chambless, D., Cherney, J., & Caputo, G. (1987). Anxiety disorders and alcoholism: A study with inpatient alcoholics [CD-ROM]. *Journal of Anxiety Disorders, 1*(1) 29–40. Abstract obtained from *PsychLIT*, AN 75-26791.

Christensen, D. (2000). Sobering work. *Science News, 158*, 2, 148–50.

Cunningham, J. A. (1999, July). Resolving alcohol-related problems with and without treatment: The effects of different problem criteria. *Journal of Studies on Alcohol, 60*(4), 463.

Curtis, O. (1999). *Chemical dependency: A family affair.* Pacific Grove, CA: Brooks/Cole.

Dawson, D. A. (2000, September). The link between family history and early onset alcoholism: Earlier initiation of drinking or more rapid development of dependence? (statistical data included). *Journal of Studies on Alcohol, 61*(5), 637.

DiClemente, C. C., Bellino, L. E., & Neavens, T. M. (1999). Motivation for change and alcohol treatment. *Alcohol Research and Health, 23*(2), 86–92.

Duncan, T. E., Duncan, S. C., & Hops, H. (1998). Latent variable modeling of longitudinal and multilevel alcohol use data. *Journal of Studies on Alcohol, 59*(4), 399–409.

Durrant, R., & Thakker, J. (2003). *Substance use and abuse.* Thousand Oaks, CA: Sage.

Dziegielewski, S. F. (2002). *DSM-IV-TR in action.* New York: John Wiley and Sons.

Dziegielewski, S. F., & Leon, A. M. (2001). *Psychopharmacology and social work practice.* New York: Springer.

Fields, R. (2001). *Drugs in perspective: A personalized look at substance use and abuse.* Boston: McGraw-Hill.

Fuller, R. K., & Hiller-Sturmhofel, S. (1999). Alcoholism treatment in the United States: An overview. *Alcohol Research and Health, 23*(2), 69–77.

George, A. A., & Tucker, J. A. (1996, July). Help-seeking for alcohol-related problems: Social contexts surrounding entry into alcoholism treatment or Alcoholics Anonymous. *Journal of Studies on Alcohol, 57*(4), 449–58.

Goff, J., & Cook, R. (2001). Coercing addicted employees into treatment: Legal implications. *Review of Business, 22*(1/2), 15–18.

Gruenewald, P. J., Millar, A., Ponicki, W. R., & Brinkley, G. (2000). Physical and economic access to alcohol. In R. A. Wilson & M. C. Dufour (Eds.), The epidemiology of alcohol problems in small geographic areas (pp. 163–212). *National Institute on Alcohol Abuse and Alcoholism Research Monograph 36* (NIH Publication No. 00-4357). Bethesda, MD: National Institute on Alcohol Abuse and Alcoholism.

Hepworth, D. H., Rooney, R. H., & Larsen, J. A. (1999). *Direct social work practice* (5th ed.). Pacific Grove, CA: Brooks/Cole.

Hollandsworth, J., Jr. (1986). *Physiology and behavior therapy: Conceptual guidelines for the clinician.* New York: Plenum Press.

Hyashida, M. (1998, Winter). An overview of outpatient and inpatient detoxification. *Alcohol Health & Research World, 22*(1), 44–47.

Institute for the Future. (2003). *Health and health care 2010: The forecast, the challenge* (2nd ed.). New York: Jossey-Bass.

Johnson, B. A., & Ait-Daud, N. (1999). Medications to treat alcoholism. *Alcohol Research and Health, 23*(2), 99–106.

Kilpatrick, A. C., & Holland, T. P. (1999). *Working with families: An integrative model by level of need.* Boston: Allyn & Bacon.

King, G., & Lorenson, J. (1989, June). Alcoholism training for social workers. *Social Casework*, 375–85.

Kirst-Ashman, K., & Hull, G. (1999). *Understanding generalist practice* (2nd ed.). Chicago: Nelson Hall.

Larimer, M. E., Palmer, R. S., & Marlatt, G. A. (1999). Overview of Marlatt's cognitive behavioral model. *Alcohol Research and Health, 23*(2), 151–60.

Latorre, M. A. (2000, April–June). A holistic view of psychotherapy: Connecting mind, body, and spirit. *Perspectives in Psychiatric Care, 36*(2), 67.

Lawson, G. W., Lawson, A. W., & Rivers, P. C. (2001). *Essentials of chemical dependency counseling.* Gaithersburg, MD: Aspen Publication.

Litovitz, T. (1987). Sedative and opiates. In M. L. Callahan (Ed.), *Current therapy in emergency medicine* (pp. 962–65). Philadelphia: BC Decker.

Longabaugh, R., & Morganstern, J. (1999). Cognitive behavioral coping skills therapy for alcohol dependence: Current status and future directions. *Alcohol Research and Health, 23*(2), 78–85.

MacPherson, N. (1998). The effect of alcoholism on earning capacity. *Expert Witness Newsletter*, 3, 2, 1–3. Retrieved December 28, 2003, from http://www.economica.ca/ew32p1.htm

Marwick, C. (1998). Parity for mental health and substance abuse treatment. *Journal of the American Medical Association, 279*(15), 1151–52.

Maxmen, J. S., & Ward, N. G., (1995). *Essential psychopathology and its treatment.* New York: W. W. Norton.

Mendelson, J., & Mello, N. (1992). *Medical diagnosis and treatment of alcoholism.* New York: McGraw-Hill.

Merck (2000). *The physician guide to diagnosis and treatment.* Whitehouse Station, NJ: Merck.

Milkman, H., & Sederer, L. (1990). *Treatment choices for alcoholism and drug abuse.* New York: Lexington Books.

Miller, N. S., & Gold, M. S. (1998, July). Management of withdrawal syndromes and relapse prevention in drug and alcohol dependence. *American Family Physician, 58*(1), 139–47.

Modesto-Lowe, V., & Kranzler, H. R. (1999). Diagnosis and treatment of alcohol-dependent patients with co-morbid psychiatric disorders. *Alcohol Research and Health, 23*(2), 144–50.

Moras, K. (1997, May). Potential applications of behavioral decision research to treatments for drug abuse, related risky behaviors, and other problems: A comment on Fischhoff and Downs. (Response to article by Baruch Fischhoff and Julie Downs in this issue, p. 154.) *Psychological Science, 8*(3), 159–62.

Myers, D. (1992). *Psychology* (3rd ed.). New York: Worth.

Myrick, H., & Anton, R. F. (1998, Winter). Treatment of alcohol withdrawal. *Alcohol Health & Research World, 22*(1), 38–44.

National Clearinghouse for Alcohol and Drug Information. (1995). Fact sheet on domestic violence and alcohol and other drugs. *National Clearinghouse for Alcohol and Drug Information* (Inventory No. ML001).

National Institute on Alcohol Abuse and Alcoholism. (2000, June). *Tenth special report to congress on alcohol and health.* U.S. Department of Health and Human Services. Retrieved September 3, 2003, from http://www.niaaa.nih.gov/publications/10 report

Olson, R., Ganley, R., Devine, V., & Dorsey, G., (1981). Long-term effects of behavioral versus insight-oriented therapy with inpatient alcoholics. *Journal of Consulting and Clinical Psychology, 49*(6), 866–77.

Pande, P. (1987). Personality patterns of alcoholics [CD-ROM]. *Journal of Psychological Research, 31*(1), 1–3. Abstract obtained from *PsychLIT*: AN 75-36076.

Patterson, T. I., Lacro, J. P., & Jeste, D. V. (1999). Abuse and misuse of medications in the elderly. *Psychiatric Times, 16*(4). Retrieved September 3, 2003, from http://www.psychiatric times.com/p990454.html

Petrakis, I., & Krystal, J. (1997, Spring). Neuroscience: implications for treatment. *Alcohol Health & Research World, 21*(2), 157–61.

Reiss, R. K., & Center for Substance Abuse Treatment. (1995). *Assessment and treatment of patients with coexisting mental illness and alcohol and other drug abuse* (DHHS Publication No 95-3061). Rockville, MD: U.S. Department of Health and Human Services.

Rotgers, F., Morgenstein, J., & Walters, S. T. (2003). *Treating substance abuse.* New York: Guilford.

Schuckit, M. A., Anthenelli, R. M., Bucholz, K. K., Hesselbrock, V. M., & Tipp, J. (1995). The time course of development of alcohol-related problems in men and women. *Journal of Studies on Alcohol, 56*(2), 218–25.

Skinner, B. F. (1953). *Science and human behavior.* New York: Macmillan.

Steinglass, P. (1976). Experimenting with family treatment approaches to alcoholism, 1950–1975: A review [CD-ROM]. *Family process.* 97–123. Abstract obtained from *PsychLIT*: AN 3882.

Substance Abuse and Mental Health Services Administration. (1998). *Treatment episode data set* (TEDS). Retrieved December 28, 2003, from http://www.dasis.samhsa.gov/teds.htm

Timko, C., Moos, R. H., Finney, J. W., Moos, B. S., & Kaplowitz, M. S. (1999, July). Long-term treatment careers and outcomes of previously untreated alcoholics. *Journal of Studies on Alcohol, 60*(4), 437–45.

Tonigan, J. S., Conners, G. J., & Miller, W. R. (1998). Special populations in Alcoholics Anonymous. *Alcohol Health and Research World, 22*(4), 281–85.

Treatment of alcoholism, part 1. (2000). *Harvard Mental Health Letter, 16*(11).

Treatment of alcoholism, part 2. (2000). *Harvard Mental Health Letter, 16*(12).

Turner, F. J. (Ed.). (1996). *Social work treatment: Interlocking theoretical approaches* (4th ed.). New York: Free Press.

Van Den Bergh, N. (Ed.). (1991). *Feminist perspectives on addictions.* New York: Springer.

Wallace, J. (1989). A biopsychosocial model of alcoholism. *Social Casework, 70*(6), 325–31.

Watson, L. (1991). Paradigms of recovery: Theoretical implications for relapse prevention in alcoholics [CD-ROM]. *Journal of Drug Issues, 21*(4), 839–58. Abstract obtained from *PsychLIT*: AN 79-17576.

Wesson, D. R., & Center for Substance Abuse Treatment. (1995). *Detoxification from alcohol and other drugs* [DHHS Publication No. (SMA) 95-3046]. Rockville, MD: Department of Health and Human Services.

Wilson, R. A., & Dufour, M. C. (Eds.). (2000). The epidemiology of alcohol problems in small geographic areas. *National Institute on Alcohol Abuse and Alcoholism Research Monograph* 36 (NIH Pub. No. 00-4357). Bethesda, MD: National Institute of Health.

Zimberg, S. (1996, October). Treating alcoholism: An age-specific intervention that works for older patients. *Geriatrics, 51*(10), 45–49.

Zuckerman, E. L. (1995) *Clinician's thesaurus* (4th ed.). New York: Guilford.

Chapter 8

Heroin and Other Opiates

Sophia F. Dziegielewski and Nancy Suris

THE MISUSE OF OPIATES IS A MAJOR PUBLIC HEALTH CONCERN IN THIS nation. "Five million people in the United States are chronic drug abusers and 20 percent are opiate addicts. . . . Only 2.1 million receive treatment, 179,000 of whom are in methadone treatment" (McCaffrey, 2000, p. 1). These numbers imply a social obligation for treatment focused on closing the gap between the need for appropriate drug addiction services and treatment availability (National Institute on Drug Abuse [NIDA], 2001b).

According to Marks (1998), an estimated 810,000 Americans are chronic heroin users, and more than 900 clinics across the country dispense the drug methadone to 115,000 clients, with an average per-patient cost of thirteen dollars a day. McNeece and DiNitto (1998) asserted that there are approximately 750 to 800 methadone clinics in the United States that serve approximately 100,000 clients. In both estimations, there is a considerable discrepancy between the number of those addicted and the number of individuals receiving treatment. This situation may reflect strict federal regulations regarding entry into methadone maintenance treatment programs and social stigmas associated with drug addiction.

This chapter discusses addictions to heroin and other opiates and describes interventions that seem most helpful in providing treatment. Although the intervention options are few and often used in combination, research studies are highlighted to identify those that have the most promise for treating addiction and helping clients to achieve detoxification with methadone maintenance. A case example and sample treatment plans are provided to help the practitioner in planning intervention strategy.

THE ORIGIN AND HISTORY OF OPIATES

Heroin, a narcotic, is a highly addictive and rapidly acting opiate. Heroin is derived from a product generated from the opium poppy plant and was introduced as an alternative to morphine (Bach & Lantos, 1999). In the 1920s, heroin was frequently prescribed by the medical community but was later avoided for routine medical use because of its extremely addictive qualities.

Heroin in its purest form is a whitish powder that is highly potent. Heroin that is available on the street, however, is typically impure and can vary in color from off-white to dark brown. Depending on the origination of the heroin, the drug comes in various forms, from a tar-like substance to a coal-like substance to a powder. The color variation of street heroin is a result of impurities and the additives that are combined with the narcotic during processing. Additives that serve as fillers commonly found in street heroin include sugar, starch, powdered milk, and poisons such as rat poison. The most common methods of administering heroin include injection, snorting, and smoking. Historically, most addicted individuals have injected heroin. Over the last ten years, however, there has been an increase in smoking and snorting. This change may be related to higher purity levels. Perhaps the greatest reason for this change results from the users' fear of HIV infection from dirty needles.

Although heroin is the opiate most often associated with addiction, there are a variety of opiates, and all have a high potential for both abuse and addiction. Opiates can be broken down into three categories—natural, semisynthetic, and synthetic. Natural opiates such as opium, morphine, and codeine are direct products of the opium poppy. Semisynthetic opiates such as heroin, Diladid, and Percodan are made by modifying the chemicals contained in opium. Synthetic opiates such as methadone and Demerol are chemically produced and made entirely in the laboratory (Carroll, 2000).

Oxycodone is a synthetic opiate that is used in many prescription pain medications such as Percodan, Vicodin, and OxyContin. OxyContin is a relatively new drug, introduced as a pain relief medication by Purdue Pharma in 1995. OxyContin is a potent, time-release pill that has become popular with drug abusers, who chew the tablet or melt it down and inject it. In 2002, Drug Enforcement Administration released an expanded review of autopsy data suggesting that the painkiller OxyContin might have played a role in 464 drug overdose deaths in the previous two years. This figure represents a sharp rise from the agency's previous estimate. According to drug enforcement officials, abuse of OxyContin has grown faster than abuse of any prescription drug in decades (Meier, 2002).

PSYCHOPHYSIOLOGICAL EFFECTS OF HEROIN

Heroin produces a strong euphoric effect. This rush is very powerful because it affects the area of the brain that controls feelings of pain and pleasure. It can also interrupt the functioning of the central nervous system, causing serious repercussions such as drowsiness, decreased respiration and heartbeat, and clouded mental functioning (Texas Commission on Alcohol and Drug Abuse [TCADA], 1997). Generally, the route of administration determines the intensity of this short-term narcotic effect. For most users, the rush sensation is felt in a matter of seconds if the drug is injected and in about fifteen minutes if the drug is either smoked or snorted. The rush sensation is accompanied by various physical effects such as flushed skin, dry mouth, watery eyes, runny nose, constricted pupils, a heavy feeling in the extremities, nausea, vomiting, and severe itching (TCADA, 1997).

Signs and symptoms of prolonged use of opiates (one year or more) include weight loss, low social functioning, drowsiness such as frequent "nodding off" lethargy, slurred speech, unemployment, and recent arrests for possession of heroin. Prolonged heroin abuse can result in long-term heroin addiction. Aside from the development of a severe addiction to the narcotic, the abuser also faces other difficulties that affect the body. The long-term result of injecting heroin can lead to the development of collapsed and scarred veins, bacterial infections, infection of the lining of the heart, abscesses, liver and kidney disease, and pulmonary difficulties. The heroin abuser is also at high risk for contracting HIV as well as Hepatitis B and C and other blood-borne diseases, either by sharing contaminated needles or by engaging in risky sexual behavior.

In addition to these short- and long-term effects of heroin use, abusers also experience withdrawal symptoms. The heroin user generally experiences withdrawal several hours after the last administration of the opiate. Withdrawal symptoms peak at twenty-four to seventy-two hours after use and can last approximately one week, although they may last longer for some individuals. The symptoms may consist of drug cravings, pain in the muscles and bones, restlessness, vomiting, loss of appetite, insomnia, sweats, chills, panic, tremors, cramps, and depression. Withdrawal symptoms may lead to a continuation of heroin consumption in order to avoid experiencing withdrawal.

Heroin is presently classified as a Schedule I controlled substance, which means that heroin users receive significant penalties if convicted for possession, distribution, or use of the drug. Yet the powerfully addictive effects of the drug, combined with users' intense desire to avoid withdrawal by obtaining heroin, make it very problematic for society.

PREVALENCE OF HEROIN ADDICTION

There exists a great deal of controversy regarding the actual prevalence of heroin addiction. This difficulty is partly due to researchers' inability to apply traditional sampling techniques in surveys involving individuals addicted to heroin. Heroin is currently one of the most highly abused drugs in the United States (NIDA, 2002). Heroin addiction crosses all boundaries and affects people regardless of economic status, race, ethnicity, religion, or gender. Although heroin abuse did decrease in the United States with the advent of the HIV/AIDS epidemic, it is steadily increasing once again. According to Mark, Woody, Judary, & Kleber (2001), who took their estimates from the National Institute of Health 1998 Consensus Panel, there were 600,000 individuals addicted to heroin in the United States in 1997. The Office of National Drug Control Policy (2002) estimates that there were 104,000 new heroin users in 1999. Barnett, Rodgers, & Bloch (2001) note that the majority of these new heroin abusers are young adolescents between the ages of twelve and twenty-five.

In the 2000 National Household Survey on Drug Abuse, approximately 2.8 million people reported heroin use in their lifetime. In that same year, according to the Drug Abuse Warning Network (DAWN), heroin was the second most common illicit drug after cocaine to be diagnosed as being a factor in emergency visits—in an estimated 97,000 cases—as reported by participating emergency departments (Office of National Drug Control Policy, 2002).

FACTORS RELATED TO HEROIN ADDICTION

The course of heroin addiction affects many aspects of a person's life. To help practitioners better understand treatment options, Meulenbeek (2000) explored the issues that heroin abusers faced while receiving methadone treatment. The study took place in the Netherlands, where methadone is offered on a voluntary basis to heroin abusers during the withdrawal phase. Participants consisted of four hundred individuals between the ages of seventeen and fifty-five. A rapid assessment instrument known as the Revised Addiction Severity Index (ASI-R) was used during the intake process and follow-up sessions. The ASI-R helped to identify past and present problem severity such as physical health, employment, alcohol use, drug use, legal status, social functioning, and psychological functioning (Meulenbeek, 2000). ASI-R results indicated that the most common problem areas were drug use, employment, psychological functioning, social functioning, and problems with the law and criminal justice system.

In terms of employment and general financial situation, subjects appeared to have limited skills training, carried large financial debts, and relied on the state for financial assistance. A number of participants in the study indicated the need for assistance in the area of psychological functioning and experienced problems with tension, fear, suicidal thoughts, poor concentration, and unresolved past trauma. In the area of social functioning, nearly 75 percent of the participating individuals had serious conflicts between their families or partners and a general dissatisfaction with their own use of free time. Most participants had been involved with the law and had been imprisoned for a variety of different crimes surrounding their drug use. Aside from the heroin abuse, the participants reported use of cocaine, marijuana, and methadone. Meulenbeek (2000) concluded that treating the drug-related aspect of heroin abuse is only part of the solution. Treatment of heroin abuse requires the treatment of the total person and the problems identified as complicating addictive behavior.

ECONOMIC BURDEN OF HEROIN ADDICTION

"Addiction disorders are among the most frequently occurring mental health problems in the United States and impose an enormous cost, totaling some $246 billion per year" (Sloves, 2000, p. 4). This cost analysis takes into account a wide range of services, including various medical and psychological treatments for addiction, legal services associated with drug abuse, and health care costs related to addiction.

Mark et al. (2001) analyzed the economic burden that drug addiction can have on society. They studied two types of fundamental costs related to illness: the direct and the indirect costs resulting from losses in output. They identified direct cost as the amount charged for medical diagnosis and treatment of the addiction, and indirect cost as the loss of income due to various occurrences associated with heroin addiction, such as death, incarceration, and unemployment. They estimated the total cost of heroin addiction in the United States in the year 1996 to be $22 billion dollars. Their analysis revealed that 53 percent of this amount was related to indirect costs associated with the loss of productivity and income due to heroin addiction. Twenty-four percent of the estimated figure was attributed to criminal and legal costs, and 23 percent of the figure reflected medical costs. Criminal and legal costs included police response and involvement in heroin-related incidents, costs to the victims of heroin-related crimes, and the legal and incarceration costs incurred by addicted individuals. Medical costs included the cost of complications resulting from heroin addiction, such as HIV/AIDS and Hepatitis B and C.

CASE EXAMPLE

Case History

The following case history was written in the words of the addicted individual in order to highlight the personal turmoil and intense feelings associated with the desire for a "fix."

I grew up in suburban Philadelphia during the period of great social upheaval that accompanied the Vietnam War. I lived in a chaotic home that featured an abusive father and an anxiety-ridden mother. School was just a different hell for me. I was a scrawny kid and socially inept as well, and this made me an easy target for the school bullies. When I was fifteen years old, someone offered me marijuana and I jumped at the chance to escape. I immediately fell in love with the euphoric intoxication that provided a temporary relief from my unhappy childhood. I began smoking pot morning, noon, and night, and I became submerged in the suburban drug culture, where it seemed that everyone smoked marijuana and experimented with other drugs.

In 1976, when I was twenty years old, I first tried heroin. I was very depressed at the time because of a failed relationship. I felt as if this young woman had ripped my heart right out of my chest. I was in excruciating pain when my dealer offered me a snort of heroin. I needed to lose my heartache, and he insisted heroin would turn that trick. He was right! Heroin wrapped me in its soft, glowing caress. Such a warm, joyous feeling left no room for pain. Heroin felt so good that it scared me. I didn't want to get hooked, so I stayed clear of it for several years.

In 1989 I was again suffering from depression, and a friend introduced me to the Badlands of North Philadelphia, where high quality heroin was sold cheap on the street corner. The Badlands had gotten its name from the Philadelphia news media because this open-air drug supermarket was rife with violence and gunplay.

The area was considered so dangerous that even the police were afraid to enter this dilapidated neighborhood.

That first time I went to the Badlands, I was so frightened I slumped down low in the seat of my friend's car. I wanted nothing to do with the scary mix of dealers, hookers, and hustlers that lined the sidewalks, where they shouted offers of their products and services to the flood of traffic that clogged the streets. The Badlands was an efficient, drive-thru operation. Faster than my friend could say, "burger, shake, and fries," bags of dope were in his hand. That night I was terrified by the macabre street carnival known as the Badlands. Just four years later, I would find myself walking those same streets, alone and unarmed, in a desperate attempt to satisfy my unquenchable thirst for heroin.

Heroin withdrawal is a lot like having a bad case of the flu. Remember what it was like the last time you had a really bad case of the flu? Stuck in bed, buried in blankets, oceans of heat and ice swallow you. You have that really vicious strain of influenza. You're puking one minute and defecating nasty liquids the next. You take more than the recommended dosage of whatever cold medications you can find. The medications do absolutely nothing to stop the faucet that your nose has become. You are too worn out to want to strangle your cheerful caretaker, who keeps offering you chicken soup, which you know you can't possibly keep down. Feeling about as miserable as a person can feel, death suddenly seems like a pleasant option. In your fevered brain you cry out vainly, "Please God, just take me now and be done with me."

That is what it's like to be dope sick, to be strung out on heroin, except there is one difference. A few puffs, a sniff, or a shot of heroin and all that pain and suffering gets instantly traded in for rainbows, warm sunshine, and laughter. Imagine lying in your sweat-soaked bed wanting to die and the doctor says, "The flu will be gone as soon as you jump through these three hoops of fire." ZOOM! Right through those hoops you'd go. The fear of withdrawal combined with the easy access of high purity heroin is what keeps so many addicted.

People talk about addicts needing to hit bottom. All my bottoms had trap doors to places where I did progressively larger amounts of heroin, and as a result, I lost most of my humanity. I relapsed repeatedly during a two-year period that had me bouncing in and out of treatment. Towards the end, I stole from my family and friends. I sold off my possessions, one by one, just to keep from getting dope sick. My dog was my best friend, and I had to give him away because I was no longer able to take care of him. My whole life revolved around heroin and avoiding that dreaded withdrawal. I would go for days without eating and weeks without bathing. Eventually I lost my home and went into long-term, inpatient treatment in order to avoid homelessness.

Getting clean was hard, but staying clean was even more difficult. After the heroin was out of my body, the depression that it had masked rose to the surface. I had to be treated for my depression while at the same time I also had to learn new behaviors and coping skills to deal with the people, places, and things that triggered my frequent urges to use drugs. I've utilized individual therapy as well as self-help groups to aid in my recovery. In the eight years since I last used heroin, I have accomplished much. I have regained the trust of my family and friends and have developed healthy relationships with all of them. I have also returned to school, where I have earned a BA in psychology and am in the process of completing work towards a master's degree in social work. You see, there is life after this addiction, but for all who fall into the seductive web, it will remain a long hard haul.

Sample Intervention Plan: Heroin Dependence Disorder

Definition. The essential feature of substance dependence is a cluster of cognitive, behavioral, and psychological symptoms indicating that the individual continues use of the substance despite significant substance-related problems. Individuals experience a pattern of repeated self-administration that can result in tolerance, withdrawal, and compulsive drug taking behavior (American Psychiatric Association [APA], 2000, p. 192).

Signs and Symptoms. Compulsive behavior; prolonged self-administration of the substance with no medical purpose; if prescribed for a medical condition, use of the substance in excess of prescribed amount; daily activities planned according to possession and administration; false documentation used for substance obtainment.

Goals for Treatment.
1. Maintain active abstinence from heroin and substances of abuse.
2. Develop a planned strategy to prevent relapse.
3. Develop skills to maintain a drug-free life.

Objectives.
◆ The client will be able to verbalize his addiction.
◆ The client will verbalize as well as sign a written agreement to terminate all substance abuse.
◆ The client will participate in detoxification treatment and learn about the various treatment methods.
◆ The client will be able to identify positive traits and skills about self.
◆ The client will identify triggers that lead to relapse.

Interventions.
◆ Take part in an evaluative interview session to assess substance dependence and other factors affected by the addiction.
◆ Attend individual and group sessions.
◆ Partake in a substance abuse treatment program.
◆ Sign an agreement to terminate heroin and other drug use.
◆ Attend rehabilitative classes and develop new job skills if necessary.
◆ Participate in a psychological evaluation and obtain treatment, medication, and/or counseling for any identifiable disorder.

◆ Actively participate in twelve-step meetings or a self-help alternative such as Rational Recovery.
◆ Locate a sponsor who has remained drug free more than two years.
◆ Identify a positive hobby and schedule a time to participate in the hobby.
◆ Obtain employment.
◆ Obtain debt counseling and assistance.

Objectives for MMT	Interventions for MMT
Evaluate appropriate dose level.	Initial medical assessment; monthly urinalysis/medical assessment; daily monitoring of methadone dosage at beginning of treatment to ensure safety and effectiveness.
Establish support system.	Psychosocial assessment; individual, family, and/or group psychotherapy.
Monitor illicit drug use.	Monthly urinalysis; incentive-based program (take-home doses, voucher system).
Case management.	Psychosocial assessment; resources for employment assistance, vocational rehabilitation, legal aid, ensure transportation, basic needs assessment.

METHADONE MAINTENANCE

Methadone maintenance is one form of treatment that can assist individuals similar to the person described in this case history in abstaining from heroin use and prevent the symptoms of withdrawal. Methadone is a synthetic opiate that blocks the effects of other opiates, eliminating cravings for those drugs. It is perceived that clients receiving methadone maintenance treatment (MMT) are able to "function well [during treatment] and become productive members of their communities by returning to their jobs and other activities without experiencing the more debilitating withdrawal symptoms" (Glass, 2000, p. 1). A vast amount of literature exists that examines the role of MMT as the most effective treatment plan for clients addicted to opiates.

During World War II, the Germans used methadone as a pain reliever. After the war, the drug was used in the United States to help individuals withdraw from opiate addictions (NIDA, 2001a). In the mid-1960s, two prominent scientists, Vincent Dole and Marie Nyswander of Rockefeller University concluded that when used on a long-term basis, methadone was beneficial in reducing, and in some cases eliminating, the cravings experienced in addiction (Nadelmann & McNeely, 1996). This led to methadone's use as a treatment method for heroin addiction and as a way to alleviate the social problems associated with heroin use, such as crime among those addicted to the drug (Nadelmann & McNeely, 1996).

The model of MMT originally proposed by Dole and Nyswander consisted of high doses of methadone, long-term treatment, and intensive rehabilitative services (Hall, Mattick, & Ward, 1999). In 1972, the U.S. Food and Drug Administration (FDA) approved the use of methadone for treating opioid addiction (McNeece & DiNitto, 1998). Before long-term studies were performed, the number of methadone treatment centers rapidly increased, reflecting a "quick fix" approach to the problem. At times, the proper guidelines for methadone dosages were not followed, and clients did not receive adequate information regarding treatment goals. In addition, as the interest in methadone grew, so did the potential for its illegal usage. Before long, "methadone acquired a reputation for being part of the drug problem, rather than part of the solution" (p. 3).

After the rapid expansion of MMT clinics and the ensuing problems, extensive federal regulations came into place, which led to methadone now being the most highly regulated drug in the United States (Nadelmann & McNeely, 1996). Both the FDA and the Drug Enforcement Administration (DEA) restrict methadone prescription and oversee treatment facility guidelines. Strict regulations aimed at dictating MMT programs and policies continue to be enforced by federal agencies, as well as by individual states and counties.

With the onset of more recent health risks, such as HIV, methadone has once again become increasingly popular as a treatment option for opiate addiction. Methadone is usually prescribed once a day and serves to block out the rush sensation that the addicted individual craves. It also blocks out withdrawal symptoms for up to thirty-six hours each dose, depending on the dosage amount (Ward, Hall & Mattick, 1999). Methadone is generally taken orally to avoid the use of needles, which can be associated with the contraction of infectious diseases.

In the United States, clients in MMT must submit to urinalysis or hair analysis so that the practitioner can check for illicit drug use and ensure that methadone doses are being taken as prescribed. Incorrect methadone doses may lead to invalid treatment or even death (Hall et al., 1999). Such monitoring, however, may foster a sense of distrust or shame in the client. Treatment facility personnel must take care to establish trusting, therapeutic relationships with clients while never forgetting the deceptive nature of substance-seeking behaviors.

One major issue with MMT is determining what actually constitutes an effective dosage. Dole and Nyswander believed that high doses of methadone lead to a significantly greater decline in illicit opioid use. Strain, Bigelow, Liebson, & Stitzer (1999) concluded from their study that, although both moderate and high dose methadone treatment could result in decreased illicit opioid use, "significantly improved outcomes can be achieved with daily methadone doses greater than 40 to 50 mg, although current federal regulations in the United States discourage methadone doses greater than 100 mg per day" (p. 7).

Other studies, however, disagree. For example, Curran, Bolton, Wanigaratne, & Smyth (1999) examined the "effects of methadone on drug craving, mood, and cognitive and psychomotor functioning in patients on long-term methadone substitution treatment" (p. 1). The study found that "extra methadone increased craving for heroin and drug-seeking behavior has been reported in patients receiving 100 mg per day of methadone" (p. 10).

Regardless of the controversy surrounding use and misuse, or the problems associated with dosing, one of the greatest statements made in support of MMT is that this type of treatment has been shown to decrease criminal behavior among users by as much as 50 percent (NIDA, 2001b). Instead of resorting to criminal activities to support their habit, heroin users have an alternate treatment available that reduces the physical and psychological cravings associated with heroin use. Furthermore, a study by Ward et al. (1999) indicated that methadone maintenance was successful not only in decreasing criminal activity but also in reducing the mortality rate among heroin users and the transmission of HIV among infected heroin users by reducing needle sharing.

Methadone maintenance has also garnered objections in terms of its overall effectiveness. The protests stem from the lack of available research or randomized trial studies that validate effectiveness of and therefore approve the substitution of one opioid type (methadone) for another (heroin) in dependence treatment.

To date, the studies of MMT programs encompass both the enduring benefits and the valid controversies regarding the objectives of treatment and the execution and effectiveness of services provided to clients receiving treatment. It is essential to understand the effects of methadone and MMT for the benefit of both individual clients and the community. Knowledge of optimal treatments will allow for more adequate funding from various sources as well as reduce the stigma associated with MMT and drug addiction. All practitioners need to be aware of the numerous aspects of methadone treatment in order to adequately advocate and link clients to appropriate resources.

INTERVENTION STRATEGIES

According to Nadelmann and McNeely (1996), the "objective of treatment, at least in principle, is to help addicts get their lives together and stop using illegal drugs, not to achieve total drug abstinence" (p. 1). From this perspective, it seems that MMT is an ideal strategy. Maintaining reliance on synthetic drugs for treatment purposes, however, can inadvertently strip addicted individuals of many important freedoms essential to leading productive lives. For the most part, it is accepted that the most effective methadone treatment plans include many components in addition to the administration of methadone (NIDA, 2001c). "For greatest effectiveness, methadone treatment should be coupled with a comprehensive package of health services and behavioral and social counseling, since addicts typically display a wide range of serious medical, psychological, economic, and legal problems in addition to their opiate dependence" (Yarmolinsky & Pechura, 1996, p. 2).

Furthermore, individual treatment outcomes may vary depending on the nature and extent of the client's presenting problems, the appropriateness of treatment, and the level of active involvement by and with the client. In addition, the availability and utilization of supportive services such as informal social support and formal medical, psychiatric, and social services remain important aspects of aftercare transition (NIDA, 2001c).

The following review of strategies highlights both the benefits and the barriers associated with methadone as a maintenance treatment program for opiate-dependent clients. Various MMT methods currently available are described, and a practitioner-friendly MMT plan for opiate-addicted clients is proposed. It is crucial to remember that MMT is not curative in nature. Rather, this type of treatment is designed to attract, retain, and produce positive outcomes for individuals who suffer from heroin addiction. Methadone maintenance treatments are often used in combination with psychosocial approaches. This combination approach is especially popular because of the interconnections between psychosocial problems and issues that often accompany heroin addiction.

Detoxification versus Long-Term Methadone Maintenance

Many professionals agree that the intervention process should begin with a clear method for detoxification. Detoxification is often the first step in the treatment of heroin addiction, with a particular emphasis placed on abstinence. To start the detoxification process, the heroin-dependent individual must go through withdrawal. Yet, even after the completion of the withdrawal phases, the individual is not immune to drug cravings. Therefore, the heroin-addicted individual may require assistance to facilitate abstinence in detoxification in order to meet the overall treatment goals.

Generally, methadone treatment is considered the primary assisted-withdrawal method for narcotic addictions. The client is switched from the opiate of abuse to methadone, which results in milder withdrawal symptoms. Later, the individual is gradually tapered off the substitute medication (NIDA, 2001a). Clients who leave treatment prematurely and do not participate in proper tapering remain at higher risk of relapse to heroin use (Hall et al., 1999). A study performed by Lenne et al. (2001) concluded that the majority of methadone clients exhibit a poor prognosis for withdrawal and should be encouraged to continue treatment to its conclusion.

From a clinical perspective, it is important to note that the side effects from methadone withdrawal are often pronounced. Zajdow (1999) described very negative experiences of withdrawal from methadone, not only for those addicted but also for the people caring for them. Physical aspects of withdrawal included loss of teeth, hair loss, incessant vomiting, and the need for twenty-four-hour care. Zajdow stated that everyone involved should be prepared because helping someone withdraw from methadone can be overwhelming. Zajdow also contends that methadone is as controlling as heroin for some: "Indefinite MMT does not allow for a drug free existence. It means constant surveillance from pharmacists, doctors, nurses, and welfare agencies" (p. 9). Many on MMT must travel great distances to clinics, and this limitation clearly affects employability and other areas of an individual's life. For the client, self-determination and independence may be elusive because control over one's life can be dominated by the need for continued use of the substance.

Psychotherapy

Psychotherapy has numerous benefits for those afforded the opportunity to participate while in drug treatment. For the most part, the purpose of psychotherapy is to make clients feel comfortable talking about their experiences while helping them solve problems in their personal lives without the aid of drugs ("Psychotherapy for Methadone Patients," 1996). This is an important element to addiction therapy, especially if the goal of treatment is total drug abstinence.

Many behavioral therapies have demonstrated usefulness in assisting clients to achieve abstinence from drug use. One frequently utilized approach is cognitive-behavioral therapy for relapse prevention. In this model, clients are taught new ways of acting and thinking that will help them stay off drugs. For example, clients are urged to identify and avoid triggers (people, places, things) that lead to drug use and to practice drug refusal skills (NIDA, n.d. a). According to the cognitive-behavioral strategies, learning processes play a critical role in the development of maladaptive behavioral patterns (NIDA, 2001c). This therapeutic approach also provides assistance to those who have relapsed into substance use, without labeling them as failures.

Supportive-expressive therapy is another psychotherapeutic treatment approach to drug addiction. This type of therapy consists of two main components: supportive techniques designed to help clients feel comfortable while discussing their personal experiences, and the development of expressive techniques designed to help clients identify and address interpersonal relationship issues (NIDA, 2001c). Special attention is placed on the role of drugs in relation to problematic feelings and behaviors and how problem solving can be achieved without the use of drugs. In this model, it is asserted that clients who receive supportive-expressive psychotherapy maintain many of the gains accomplished during the therapeutic process.

Support groups are also an important aspect of psychotherapeutic treatment for drug-addicted individuals. Support groups provide a community in which those addicted can feel a sense of belonging and acceptance while addressing the potential for denial of the causes or extent of the problem. Zajdow (1999) claimed that "12 step groups give many dis-empowered individuals the possibility of meaningful community contact" (p. 9). Many addicts feel socially inept and alone; being part of a support group consisting of people who have the same needs and experiences provides a great level of acceptance and added support.

Voucher System

Voucher-based reinforcement therapy in MMT provides clients with an incentive to abstain from using illegal drugs while receiving addiction treatment. A voucher is provided when a clean urine sample is obtained from the client. Vouchers can be traded in for goods and services consistent with treatment goals (NIDA, 2001c). The goal behind the use of vouchers in MMT is the reinforcement of sustained drug abstinence. Vouchers can be beneficial for behavior reinforcement and monetary-based incentives can assist in the treatment of drug abuse (NIDA, n.d. b).

Office-Based Opiate Therapy

Office-based opiate therapy is one potential solution to the controversy regarding regulations prohibiting private physicians from prescribing methadone. McCaffrey (2000) contended that "drug addiction is a disease and treatment should be part of medical practice. Drug treatment should be available in physicians' offices, which would include detailed assessments of patients with referrals to other services like counseling and psychological support" (p. 5). McCaffrey added that office-based therapy will help reduce the stigma associated with addiction treatment. He also claimed that office-based therapy "will ensure that the training and clinical standards ordinarily applied to medical practice will also pertain to drug treatment" (p. 5).

New regulations that offer a more flexible MMT, involving physicians with approved addiction treatment programs, are scheduled. "The old FDA system focused on controlling the amount of methadone dispensed, which usually forced clients to show up at a clinic every morning. The new regulations will allow physicians to develop individualized treatment plans" (Vastag, 2001, p. 1). This will allow physicians the discretion to prescribe clients several days' worth of methadone doses at a time. This revised prescription schedule will allow clients more personal freedom.

Case Management

Case management provides vital services to clients in MMT. Case management can include linking clients to community resources through appropriate referrals or through on-site delivery. Case management encompasses the provision of services, including transportation, financial and legal assistance, employment services, support groups, and basic needs such as housing and food. Once basic needs have been met, the client has increased opportunities for long-lasting successful treatment outcomes.

Case management services can provide the impetus for effective client participation. Whether a client stays in treatment depends on factors associated with both the individual and the program. Self-motivation is a personal factor related to successful drug addiction treatment. If more aspects of a client's life are functioning well, such as employment options, financial means, and support systems, then the likelihood of treatment success increases. Medical, psychiatric, and social services should be made available to clients, as well as proper after-care to facilitate the transition to a drug-free lifestyle (NIDA, 2001c).

Community-Based Treatment Centers

Community-based treatment centers are vital to addiction recovery because those who are addicted "have to learn to live in communities where illicit drugs are widely available" (Hall, 2000, p. 1). The expense and scarcity of treatment options and specialists to care for addicted individuals make community-based treatment necessary and desirable. Therapeutic communities or hospitals can provide only a temporary retreat for chronic drug users (Hall, 2000).

There are several ways to improve the current trend of prescribing methadone. One method is to increase the availability of other options for treating opiate dependence, such as community-led support groups. Other medications, such as lofexedine or naltrexone, are useful for achieving detoxification from opiates or reducing relapse and should be more widely utilized. Hall (2000) maintained that "a broader range of maintenance options will increase patients' choice, reduce the risk of overdose associated with methadone prescribing, and reduce the difficulty that many users experience in withdrawing from methadone" (p. 1). Wider community acceptance of addiction as a disorder is also important for increasing social tolerance for those addicted to opiates. Many communities are leery of establishing methadone clinics in their area, thus stigmatizing those suffering from addiction, which can damage their self-esteem and hamper their eventual recovery.

Matrix Model

The matrix model provides a framework for engaging abusers in treatment and helping them achieve abstinence. Clients learn about issues critical to addiction and relapse, receive direction and support from a trained therapist, become familiar with self-help programs, and are monitored for drug use through urine testing (NIDA, 2001c). The model also incorporates education for family members affected by drug addiction.

The practitioner holds a pivotal position in this therapeutic model, functioning as teacher and coach while establishing a positive and supportive relationship with the client. The supportive relationship between client and practitioner is used to reinforce positive behavior changes. The interaction between the client and the therapist is critical for directing change. The therapist gives this direction in a non-confrontational or parental way while building the client's self-esteem, dignity, and self-worth. Intervention methods include a variety of other tested approaches, including relapse prevention, family and group therapies, drug education, and self-help participation. According to the National Institute on Drug Abuse (2001c), use of the matrix model has demonstrated statistically significant reductions in drug and alcohol use, improvement in psychosocial indicators, and reduced risky sexual behaviors associated with HIV transmission.

Heroin Substitution Therapy

In a study by Pani, Maremmani, Pirastu, Tagliamonte, & Gessa (2000), the drug buprenorphine was compared to methadone maintenance treatment. Buprenorphine is an opiate drug that does not possess the addictive qualities of other opiates such as heroin. With its lack of addictive qualities, buprenorphine can be easily discontinued even after prolonged use. In a randomized, double-blind design, seventy-two opioid-dependent individuals were studied over a six-month period. The participants ranged in age between eighteen and forty and agreed to routine urine screenings and to reside in close proximity to the facility in order to partake in the daily therapeutic structure of the study. The researchers used instruments designed to gather addiction histories and information on heroin usage. The participants attended individual counseling sessions that covered issues pertaining to addiction, health, psychology, and the law for approximately twenty minutes weekly for six months.

The study separated the groups into the prospective treatment modalities of buprenorphine and methadone. Thirty-four individuals were placed in the methadone group and thirty-eight in the buprenorphine group at the initial stage of the study. Each medication was given at low dosages, increasing until the end of the first week, when threshold was achieved and both groups were receiving the maximum dosage of their respective treatments—8 mg of buprenorphine and 60 mg of methadone. At the end of the study, eighteen individuals remained in the buprenorphine group, and twenty-two individuals remained in the methadone group. Taking into account the limitations of this study (i.e., the limited number of participants, and the conditions of the experimental design), the study indicated that methadone was effective in maintaining a good retention rate among the participants. The study also concluded that buprenorphine was effective in opioid maintenance treatment.

In a meta-analysis comparing buprenorphine and methadone, Fiellin, Rosenheck, & Kosten (2001) postulated that buprenorphine therapy was nearly as effective as methadone maintenance treatment. Buprenorphine therapy provided the potential for reducing harm associated with intravenous drug use. Fiellin et al. (2001b) advocated that, based on the results of their meta-analysis, additional trials were needed to determine the safety, efficacy, medication formulation, and suitability for particular populations.

Overall, the use of buprenorphine provides some advantages for physicians who treat opioid-dependent clients: it is a long-lasting medication, so it can be administered as few as two or three times a week; it has mild withdrawal symptoms compared to methadone; and it can be combined with other opioid antagonists. Other opiate antagonists include naloxone, nalmefene, and naltrexone (Beaini et al., 2000).

RESEARCH SUPPORTS THE NEED FOR ADDITIONAL SERVICES

Six studies were analyzed to compare the effectiveness of methadone treatment methods. The studies examined (1) whether additional services should be provided to clients receiving methadone therapy, (2) appropriate dosage levels, (3) the benefits of detoxification from methadone, and (4) the relevance of office-based therapy for clients receiving MMT. An overview of the comparison follows.

Study 1

The objective of this study by Sees et al. (2000) was to "compare outcomes of patients with opioid dependence treated with MMT versus an alternative treatment of psychosocially enriched 180-day methadone-assisted detoxification." In a controlled trial performed from May 1995 to April 1999, 179 adults diagnosed with opioid dependence were randomly assigned to one of the two treatments. Sees and colleagues concluded that MMT was useful in reducing heroin use and HIV risk behaviors. Although illicit opioid use continued in both groups, the frequency of use was reduced. The researchers further concluded that the results did not support diverting resources from MMT into more long-term detoxification programs. MMT has demonstrated its usefulness in improving life functioning, decline in heroin use and criminal behavior, and a decrease in HIV infection.

Psychosocial services were found to have increased the effectiveness of MMT. The study addressed the concern that MMT amounts to the indefinite provision of a dependence-producing medication by stating that an "effective alternative treatment that did not involve indefinite opioid use would be a valuable addition to the limited array of options available to treat heroin dependence" (p. 2). Short-term methadone detoxification therapy, usually twenty-one days in length, was proposed as an alternative to MMT but was found to have "poor retention and high relapse rates" (p. 2).

Study 2

A study conducted by Lenne et al. (2001) identified the proportion of clients engaged in MMT who have a favorable prognosis for withdrawal, while examining client perceptions and expectations of withdrawal. According to these researchers, the number of clients registered in MMT had steadily increased, yet complaints about the withdrawal process were numerous. To explore the problems associated with the withdrawal process, the research team "identified and operationalized a number of clinical criteria upon which to assess a client's suitability for attempting withdrawal from methadone" (p. 3).

Participating clinicians and clients used Likert scales to rate how likely it was for the client to stay off heroin and methadone for three months if the methadone treatment was withdrawn. Approximately half of the participants surveyed responded that it was "at least considerably likely that they would be able to remain opiate free for three months after methadone withdrawal" (p. 4). Clinician responses were much less optimistic. Overall, the study concluded that "it is only a minority of clients who are likely to benefit from improved withdrawal techniques" (p. 6) and that the majority of methadone clients have a poor prognosis for withdrawal and should not be encouraged to end MMT.

Study 3

Friedman, D'Aunno, Jin, and Alexander (2000) examined the "extent to which linkage mechanisms (on-site delivery, external arrangements, case management, and transportation assistance) are associated with increased utilization of medical and psychosocial services in outpatient drug abuse treatment units" (p. 1). The study asserted that drug addiction produces dysfunction in many facets of an addicted individual's life. This includes mental and physical health, family situations, employment status, legal matters, financial status, and housing. Because of such dysfunctions, the need for appropriate service linkage is crucial to overall treatment success. Results of the study indicated that "transportation is an important linkage mechanism and on-site delivery seems the most reliable mechanism to link drug abuse treatment clients to services" (p. 10). The findings further suggested that "initiatives, grants, and organizational policies to promote the linkage of addiction treatment clients to medical and psychosocial services should emphasize on-site delivery, transportation, and for some social services, on-site case management" (p. 10).

Study 4

Chutuape, Silverman, and Stitzer (1998) conducted a survey assessment of methadone treatment services as reinforcers. The study asserted that MMT outcome can be improved by offering incentives conditional on behavioral change. The study aimed to replicate previous findings regarding the reinforcing potency of previously surveyed clinic privileges (methadone take-home, dose increase, and access to counseling), to test the consistency of response across three instruments on which clients rated these previously surveyed privileges, and to identify additional clinic services that might be deemed desirable by methadone clients.

The 111 participants in this study were enrolled in a MMT program along with a five-week dose-stabilization period. The results of the study demonstrated "that take-homes were consistently ranked higher in preference than both dose increases and extra counseling sessions, and that dose increases were preferred more than extra counseling sessions" (p. 10). Further results suggested that "there exist desirable services other than take-homes that can be delivered at little or no cost to the clinic (control of methadone dose, selection of clinic attendance time, and employment assistance)" (p. 12). The study also pointed out the need for treatment programs to individually tailor reinforcement contingency plans to best suit the needs of each client, while allowing for client empowerment in the treatment process.

Study 5

A study performed by Fiellin, O'Connor, Chawarski, et al. (2001a) aimed to determine "the feasibility and efficacy of office-based methadone maintenance by primary care physicians versus in a narcotic treatment program (NTP) for stable opioid-dependent patients" (p. 1). Fiellin and colleagues asserted that "office-based care of stabilized methadone maintenance patients is a promising alternative, but no data are available from controlled trials regarding this type of program" (p. 1).

The study design consisted of a "six-month, randomized controlled open clinical trial conducted February 1999 to March 2000. The setting included the offices of six primary care internists and an NTP" (p. 1). Participants consisted of forty-seven randomized opioid-dependent clients receiving MMT for one year, with no evidence of illicit drug use. The intervention consisted of randomly assigning participants either to receive office-based MMT from primary care physicians or to continue the usual care at the MMT facility. The physicians participating in the trial had received specialized training in the care of opiate-addicted individuals. The results from the study "support the feasibility and efficacy of transferring stable opioid-dependent clients receiving methadone maintenance to primary care physicians' offices for continuing treatment and suggest guidelines for identifying clients and clinical monitoring" (p. 1).

Study 6

Strain et al. (1999) conducted a study "to compare the relative clinical efficacy of moderate vs. high-dose methadone in the treatment of opioid dependence" (p. 1). Strain et al. asserted that, despite methadone being the most commonly used pharmacological intervention to treat opiate addiction, no controlled clinical trials of higher-dose methadone treatments have been conducted. The study design consisted of a "40-week randomized, double-blind clinical trial starting in June 1992 and ending in October 1995. The setting was an outpatient substance abuse treatment research clinic at the Johns Hopkins University Bayview Campus. There were 192 eligible clinic patients" (p. 1). The intervention was a daily dose of methadone in the dose range of either 40 to 50 mg or 80 to 100 mg, with subsequent substance abuse counseling. Outcome measures included urinalysis testing to see if the individual was opioid positive.

Based on the results of the study, the researchers concluded that "through week 30, patients in the high-dose group had significantly lower rates of opioid-positive urine samples compared with patients in the moderate-dose group" (p. 1). They also determined that "both moderate and high-dose methadone treatment resulted in decreased illicit opioid use during methadone maintenance and detoxification. The high-dose group had significantly greater decreases in illicit opioid use" (p. 1). More specifically, the results from the study "provide evidence that significantly improved outcomes can be achieved with daily methadone doses greater than 40 to 50 mg" (p. 7).

BEST PRACTICES: BENEFITS OF MMT

Methadone is the most studied and accepted medicine for the treatment of heroin addiction. Yarmolinsky and Pechura (1996) state that methadone treatment has been widely shown during the past three decades to help those addicted to heroin free themselves from drug dependency, from a life of crime in support of their habit, and from increased risk of contracting HIV. Indeed, "methadone is far more likely to help heroin addicts regain control of their lives than is any other therapy" (p. 1). Overall, if properly administered, MMT allows drug-dependent citizens to become productive members of society by alleviating health risks and crime related to drug use. Furthermore, Sloves (2000) contends that the "safety and effi-cacy of methadone maintenance treatment has been unequivocally established and that methadone maintenance treatment has received consensual support from the addictions research and treatment communities, if not from society at large" (p. 2).

Several social and individual improvements have been noted as benefits of MMT. First, this treatment can decrease drug use, thus helping the individual to gain increased levels of productive functioning in the family, workplace, and com-munity. Second, MMT has been shown to decrease criminal behavior associated with heroin addiction. Third, the treatment can reduce the risk of contracting or spreading HIV or other infectious diseases by eliminating the use of needles. Lastly, MMT can improve prospects for employment by freeing the addicted person from the frequent physical and psychological cravings for heroin.

Methadone has a less gradual onset than heroin, and so clients stabilized with MMT do not experience any rush. Methadone also wears off more slowly than heroin, so MMT markedly reduces the desire for heroin (NIDA, 2001c). Heroin's ef-fects last four to eight hours, whereas methadone's half-life is approximately twenty-four hours, making once-a-day dosing is possible (Sloves, 2000). Methadone also blocks the euphoric effects of heroin, reducing the likelihood of the combined use of heroin and methadone.

Marks (1998) cites former New York City mayor Rudolph Giuliani's view that "methadone is a mere replacement for heroin. Methadone may get the addict off one fix, but it does not necessarily lead to recovery" (p. 1). Indeed, a great number of studies assert that many components are necessary for addiction recovery, in-cluding counseling, social support, and other community resources. MMT alone does not adequately address the psychosocial issues of drug dependency.

McNeece and DiNitto (1998) disclose several negative aspects of MMT. One drawback is that people taking methadone may develop a dependency to the drug after prolonged use. Taking methadone does not prevent the client from abusing other substances such as cocaine or alcohol, which may hamper treatment goals and desired rehabilitation. Controversies exist over the incidence of clients selling their methadone doses on the illicit drug market. Finally, methadone treatment goals may be perceived as a form of social control rather than as a value to addicted individuals. The stabilization of heroin addiction though the use of a less harmful drug allows addicted individuals to function productively in society. The problem of addiction is not necessarily resolved.

Sadovsky (2000) claims that methadone may have adverse health effects such as "respiratory depression, decreased bowel motility, nausea, and hypotension. Other adverse effects associated with long-term use of methadone can include sweating, constipation, appetite disturbance, sexual dysfunction, abnormal menses, urinary retention, blurred vision, and insomnia" (p. 2). These side effects are sig-nificant and indicate that MMT is not acceptable for everyone. Other effective treat-ment options must be made available. Additional disadvantages to long-term MMT include the stigma associated with addiction, restrictive government regulations, the inadequate number of health care providers and clinics that offer methadone as a treatment, and the recidivism rate after detoxification (Sadovsky, 2000).

Ensuring that proper doses are prescribed by knowledgeable practitioners and are tailored to individual needs is essential. "Methadone may be fatal to non-tolerant individuals in the doses used in MMT, therefore it is important to ensure that patients do not ingest more than their prescribed dosage" (Hall et al., 1999, p. 3). Educating clients about safety issues related to doses and detoxification is crucial.

Restrictive government regulations pose barriers to individuals seeking methadone treatment therapy. Prospective clients must be at least eighteen years of age and must have been dependent on heroin for at least one year before acceptance into an MMT program. Yarmolinsky and Pechura (1996) claim that the FDA and DEA "routinely extend their oversight beyond these boundaries [of regulatory authority]" (p. 1). In addition, the Department of Health and Human Services created special standards determining how and under what circumstance methadone can be used to treat addiction. State and city governments often impose restrictions that are even more stringent. Ten states do not offer MMT programs (1996), denying those populations the freedom to select a viable treatment for heroin addiction.

"Federal regulations rigidly set patient admission criteria, define acceptable methadone dose levels, and limit service sites, which often means that physicians cannot provide treatment in the manner that is best for an individual patient" (Yarmolinsky & Pechura, 1996, p. 1). It is further contended that there is no medical reasoning to back the current regulation of methadone, which has been approved by the FDA. It is believed that current regulative policies place too much emphasis on the limited risk that methadone may be diverted from treatment programs to the street, and not enough emphasis on protecting society from the epidemic of addiction (1996).

Nadelmann and McNeely (1996) cite a host of hindrances imposed by regulations that block effective employment of methadone. All methadone programs are subject to rigid staffing, security, documentation, and treatment requirements that have little to do with quality treatment. Decisions usually left to physicians and their clients, such as dosage and time spent in treatment, are instead dictated by federal, state, and local regulations. Methadone clients cannot fill prescriptions in a pharmacy but rather must visit a methadone clinic at least weekly, usually daily (1996).

SUMMARY AND FUTURE DIRECTIONS

Methadone maintenance, the most widely available treatment for heroin addiction, appears to be highly effective. According to Sees et al. (2000), the infusion of psychosocial interventions into a treatment plan for heroin addiction is essential for assisting individuals. Treating only one aspect of the addiction could neglect the treatment of the other aspects. The heroin abuser's psychological functioning, employment status, legal issues, family issues, and history of other drug use are all areas that must be addressed in the fight against addiction.

A combination of intense detoxification, the assignment of a case manager at the drug treatment facility, the establishment of psychosocial sessions that include individual counseling and group therapy, and an appropriate treatment method would be a suitable plan for treating heroin-addicted individuals. The case manager provides a sense of support that the heroin-dependent individual will need in combating his or her addiction. Individual and group counseling therapy assists the client in exploring the cause of the addiction, discovering ways of combating the addiction, initiating self-reflection, finding a starting point for life change, and resolving life issues (for example, unemployment) as well as providing overall support through the treatment process.

Methadone is an alternative opiate that provides the same effect as heroin but without the withdrawal symptoms and the euphoric rush. Methadone maintenance treatment may introduce an addiction to methadone, which is harder to discontinue than heroin. Although methadone blocks the effects of heroin, it does not prevent the addicted individual from consuming heroin while taking methadone or from selling take-home treatments in order to buy heroin. Most research on effective MMT has determined that numerous other components are necessary for successful treatment outcomes. These components include the provision of case management services, participation in psychotherapy, monitoring of illicit drug use, and effective methadone dosage.

Case management duties can include ensuring that the client has access to transportation in order to attend clinic treatments, a link to vocational training or other employment services, and legal assistance (if the client has past criminal offenses due to addiction behaviors). Ensuring that the client's basic needs are being met is essential; housing and food provision can be an important aspect of case management.

Psychotherapy consists of individual, group, and family counseling and support networks. Cognitive behavioral approaches have been proven helpful in individual therapeutic approaches. Family counseling provides educational tools to family members as well as avenues of support for the client. Group support networks have demonstrated their utility in providing a sense of community and social encouragement to individuals recovering from addiction.

Abstention from illicit drug use and correct methadone dosage are both important to the success of MMT. Several studies herald the benefits of higher methadone doses in assisting clients to abstain from illicit drug use. Improper methadone doses can lead to adverse health effects and even death. Because one of the goals of drug treatment is to abstain from substance use, it is important that methadone dosage be monitored for effectiveness in reaching that goal.

The goal for MMT should be to provide the most effective treatment options for opiate-addicted individuals. One way to increase the effectiveness of treatment is to reduce the stigma associated with MMT and with drug addiction in general. Educating the public about the national health problem of drug addiction may begin to accomplish this. There is a large discrepancy between the number of people addicted to heroin and the number seeking drug abuse treatment. More MMT clinics should be available in every state to give addicted individuals more valid treatment options.

New regulations such as the Drug Abuse Treatment Act (DATA) of 2000 may help somewhat to reduce the strict guidelines for how opiate-dependent clients are treated by the medical community. DATA allows physicians to prescribe narcotic drugs for heroin addiction and allows for moving the treatment of heroin addiction from the clinic to the private physician's office (Boatwright, 2002). But this is only a beginning, and office-based methadone maintenance is just one way to expand treatment options. Other viable treatment alternatives such as additional pharmacological methods, as well as effective methods for methadone detoxification, should be extensively studied and made available.

Finally, more studies of MMT need to be conducted, especially among special populations. Few studies to date address the specific needs of women, pregnant women, Latinos, African Americans, and other minorities in effective treatment of opioid addiction. Prognosis and successful long-term outcomes of MMT for these populations are correlated to factors unique to these groups, such as oppression, lack of resources, discrimination, lack of societal support, and institutional racism.

The authors would like to thank Nita Pierre for her contributions to previous versions of this chapter.

References

American Psychiatric Association. (2000). *Diagnostic and statistical manual of mental disorders* (4th ed., text rev.). Washington, DC: Author.

Bach, P. B., & Lantos, J. (1999). Methadone dosing, heroin affordability, and the severity of addiction. *American Journal of Public Health, 89*(5), 662–65.

Barnett, P. G., Rodgers, J. H., & Bloch, D. A. (2001). A meta-analysis comparing buprenorphine to methadone for treatment of opiate dependence. *Addiction, 96*, 683–90.

Beaini, A. Y., Johnson, T. S., Langstaff, P., Carr, M. P., Crossfield, J. N., & Sweeney, R. C. (2000). A compressed opiate detoxification regime with naltrexone maintenance: Patient tolerance, risk assessment and abstinence rates. *Addiction Biology, 5*, 451–62.

Boatwright, D. E. (2002). Buprenorphine and addiction: Challenges for the pharmacist. *Journal of American Pharmaceutical Association, 42*, 3, 432–38.

Carroll, C. R. (2000). *Drugs in modern society*. Boston: McGraw-Hill.

Chutuape, M. A., Silverman, K., & Stitzer, M. (1998). Survey assessment of methadone treatment serves as reinforcers. *American Journal of Drug and Alcohol Abuse, 24*(1), 1–16.

Curran, H., Bolton, J., Wanigaratne, S., & Smyth, C. (1999). Additional methadone increases craving for heroin: A double blind, placebo-controlled study of chronic opiate users receiving methadone substitution treatment. *Addiction, 94*(5), 665–75.

Fiellin, D., O'Connor, P., Chawarski, M., Pakes, J., Pantalon, M., & Schottenfeld, R. (2001a). Methadone maintenance in primary care. *Journal of the American Medical Association, 286*, 14.

Fiellin, D. A., Rosenheck, R. A., & Kosten, T. R. (2001b). Office-based treatment for opioid dependence: Reaching new patient populations. *American Journal of Psychiatry, 158*(8), 1200–04.

Friedman, P., D'Aunno, T., Jin, L., & Alexander, J. (2000). Medical and psychosocial services in drug abuse treatment: Do stronger linkages promote client utilization? *Health Services Research, 35*(2), 443–65.

Glass, R. (2000). Treating drug dependency. *Journal of the American Medical Association, 283*(10), 1378.

Hall, W. (2000). Transcending methadone. *Lancet, 355*, 9203.

Hall, W., Mattick, R., & Ward, J. (1999). Role of maintenance treatment in opioid dependence. *Lancet, 353*, 9148.

Lenne, M., Lintzeris, N., Breen, C., Harris, S., and associates. (2001). Withdrawal from methadone maintenance treatment: Prognosis and participant perspectives. *Australian and New Zealand Journal of Public Health, 25*(2), 121–25.

Mark, T. L., Woody, G. E., Judary, T., & Kleber, H. D. (2001). The economic costs of heroin addiction in the United States. *Drug and Alcohol Dependence, 61*, 195–206.

Marks, J. (1998). Mayor vs. drug czar: New York's Giuliani claims that methadone is merely another form of addiction. *U.S. News & World Report, 125*(14), 31.

McCaffrey, B. (2000). Methadone treatment. *Vital Speeches of the Day, 66*(15), 450–54.

McNeece, C. A. & DiNitto, D. M. (1998). *Chemical dependency: A systems approach* (2nd ed.). Needham Heights, MA: Allyn & Bacon.

Meier, B. (2002, April 15). OxyContin deaths may top early count. *New York Times*, A3.

Meulenbeek, P.A. (2000). Addiction problems and methadone treatment. *Journal of Substance Abuse & Treatment, 19*, 171–74.

Nadelmann, E., & McNeely, J. (1996). Doing methadone right. *The Public Interest, 123*, 83-94.

National Institute on Drug Abuse. (n.d. a). *Behavioral change through treatment*. Retrieved March 4, 2002, from http://www.nida.nih.gov/infofax/behavchange.html

National Institute on Drug Abuse. (n.d. b). *Effective drug abuse treatment approaches.* (2001). Retrieved March 4, 2002, from http://165.112.78.61/BTDP/Effective/Silverman.html

National Institute on Drug Abuse. (2001a). *Drug abuse treatment medications*. Retrieved March 4, 2002, from http://www.nida.nih.gov/infofax/treatmed.html

National Institute on Drug Abuse. (2001b). *Drug addiction treatment methods*. Retrieved March 4, 2002, from http://www.nida.nih.gov/infofax/treatmeth.html

National Institute on Drug Abuse. (2001c). *Principles of drug addiction treatment: Scientifically based approaches to drug addiction treatment*. Retrieved March 4, 2002, from http://www.nida.nih.gov/PODAT/PODAT9.html

National Institute on Drug Abuse. (2002, February 21). *Heroin: Abuse and addiction*. Retrieved February 25, 2002, from http://165.112.78.61/ResearchReports/Heroin/heroin5.html

Office of National Drug Control Policy. (2002). *Drug facts: Heroin*. Retrieved February 25, 2002, from http://www.whitehousedrugpolicy.gov/drugfact/heroin/heroin_b.html

Pani, P. P., Maremmani, I., Pirastu, R., Tagliamonte, A., & Gessa, G. L. (2000). Buprenorphine: A controlled clinical trial in the treatment of opioid dependence. *Drug and Alcohol Dependence, 60*, 39–50.

Psychotherapy for methadone patients. (1996). *Harvard Mental Health Letter, 12*(9), 7.

Sadovsky, R. (2000). Public health issue: Methadone maintenance therapy. *American Family Physician, 62*(2), 428.

Sees, K. L., Delucchi, K. L., Masson, C., Rosen, A., Westley, A., Clark, H., Robillard, H., Banys, P., & Hall, S. M. (2000). Methadone maintenance vs. 180-day psychosocially enriched detoxification for treatment of opioid dependence: A randomized controlled trail. *Journal of the American Medical Association, 283*(10), 1303–10.

Sloves, H. (2000). Drug treatment for drug addiction: Surmounting the barriers. *Behavioral Health Management, 20*(4), 42.

Strain, E., Bigelow, G., Liebson, I., & Stitzer, M. (1999). Moderate vs. high-dose methadone in the treatment of opioid dependence: A randomized trial. *Journal of American Medical Association, 281*(11), 1498.

Texas Commission on Alcohol and Drug Abuse. (1997, December). *Heroin: Just the facts.* Retrieved February 25, 2002, from http://www.tcada.state.tx.us/research/facts/heroin.html

Vastag, B. (2001). Methadone regulations overhauled. (Health agencies update). *Journal of the American Medical Association, 285*(11), 1435.

Ward, J., Hall, W., & Mattick, R. P. (1999). Role maintenance treatment in opioid dependence. *Lancet, 353*, 221–26.

Yarmolinsky, A., & Pechura, C. (1996). Methadone revisited (Government regulations make use of methadone for treatment of heroin addicts difficult). *Issues in Science and Technology, 12*(3), 38–43.

Zajdow, G. (1999). Learning to live without it: Women, biography and methadone. *Hecate, 25*(2), 63.

Chapter 9

Prescription Drugs: Sedatives, Hypnotics, and Painkillers

Cheryl E. Green, Tamara Blickem, Sophia F. Dziegielewski, and Barbara F. Turnage

DEPRESSANTS SUCH AS SEDATIVES, HYPNOTICS, AND PAINKILLERS ARE licit drugs that, when used properly, have therapeutic value. Sedatives, hypnotics, and painkillers do exactly what their names suggest. These substances work quickly to relax or sedate the body. The slowed breathing that often results because of their depressant effect on the central nervous system creates a hypnotic, slowed response. Pain killers, often referred to as narcotics, help to depress the pain centers of the brain, preventing the individual from feeling the true effect of an unpleasant stimulus. When these substances are given in small doses, they can help to relieve emotional stress. When given in larger doses, a more hypnotic effect is obtained, which can alleviate conditions such as insomnia and pain. Whether the individual is experiencing an acute headache or chronic pain, the belief that potential relief of these symptoms exists can be very seductive. When these substances are misused or abused, the outcome is dangerous and sometimes fatal. Prolonged use contributes to abuse and physical dependence on these drugs (Drug Enforcement Administration [DEA], n.d. a). Addiction to these substances often occurs in conjunction with the abuse of other drugs such as stimulants (e.g., heroin or cocaine), other depressants, or both. Why some individuals are more prone to develop an addiction to these licit drugs remains unclear (Segal, Gerdes, & Steiner, 2004).

Benzodiazepines, prescription sedatives traditionally referred to as antianxiety medications, or anxiolytics, provide a calming effect and allow the client to function in a more relaxed state or may induce sleep. Some examples of benzodiazepines include Xanax, Valium, Klonopin, and Ativan. Barbiturates, prescribed to treat anxiety and insomnia, are hypnotics that suppress central nervous system activity, which can result in mild sedation or severe reactions such as coma (DEA, n.d. a). These drugs can take effect dangerously fast and stay in the system for long periods. Amobarbital, pentobarbital, and secobarbital are a few forms of barbiturates preferred by abusers. The high fatality rate associated with the misuse of these and other barbiturates has contributed to the push for the development of safer alternatives (DEA, n.d. b). Unfortunately, such attempts have not been successful. Narcotics, particularly the painkillers, also tend to be of particular concern for abuse because, in addition to blocking pain receptors, they create feelings of pleasure and well-being. Generally, the substances most likely to create these pleasurable effects are opium, morphine, heroin, and codeine. One recently developed narcotic used primarily as a painkiller is the synthetic opiate OxyContin (discussed in chapter 8). OxyContin has become a popular drug among abusers and its misuse continues to be on the rise (Meadows, 2001; Corliss, Park, & Ressner, 2001).

This chapter explores current information regarding the abuse of and addiction to sedatives, hypnotics, and painkillers and describes the intervention options available. An integrated treatment approach that addresses the physiological and psychological aspects of addiction to these legal, prescription medications is recommended. Cognitive-behavioral therapy protocols are considered essential for assisting those who suffer from anxiety (Stein, 1998). Recent literature reviews support the usefulness of brief treatment models to help diminish anxiety (Barlow, Esler, & Vitali, 1998; Roth & Fonagy, 1996).

The chapter emphasizes the importance of practitioner familiarity with psychotropic medications as well as supplemental psychosocial interventions effective in treating prescription substance abuse. A successful multidisciplinary or interdisciplinary team approach will incorporate (1) a recognition of the problems that can occur with this type of abuse; (2) an understanding of how the belief that these substances are completely safe or medically necessary can easily lead to addiction; (3) brief treatment models using cognitive-behavior modification (including skills training and systematic desensitization); and (4) social support (professional encouragement and assistance).

ADDICTION TO SEDATIVES, HYPNOTICS, AND PAINKILLERS

Sedatives and hypnotics are prescription medications used therapeutically to decrease anxiety-related symptoms and improve sleep. Anxiety is a subjective emotional and physical state experienced by all people that becomes problematic when it is not controlled and interferes with an individual's ability to work, sleep, or concentrate. More than one-third of all clients who seek mental health treatment present with some type of anxiety-related problem. Due to diagnostic errors, only one in four people with anxiety disorders receive adequate intervention (Hales, 1995). Many individuals are misdiagnosed, an unfortunate finding because anxiety disorders are amenable to intervention, with short-term success rates as high as 70 percent (Roth & Fonagy, 1996).

A common assumption is that because prescription medications are tested and prescribed in medical settings, they must be safe (Dziegielewski & Leon, 2001). Furthermore, antianxiety medications need to be taken regularly because symptoms can occur with random frequency (Koemer, 1999; Nordenberg, 1999). This assumption of safety and a regular pattern of use, along with withdrawal and dependence issues, make for a fertile ground for the development of an addictive disorder.

Benzodiazepines are commonly used to treat anxiety and insomnia. These drugs have fast absorption rates and quickly produce an intoxicated feeling. The more rapidly the drug is absorbed, the higher the potential for abuse (Frances & Miller, 1998). This mode of alleviation is seductive, and clients should be monitored closely for the development of tolerance and any serious symptoms related to withdrawal.

When working with clients who are taking prescribed benzodiazepines, barbiturates, or narcotics, the potential for medication addiction and abuse should always be a concern. Benzodiazepines are central nervous system depressants that, when combined with another ingredient such as alcohol (also a depressant), can result in significant depression and may have a lethal effect (Dulcan, 1999; Kaplan & Sadock, 1990). It has been estimated that 70 to 90 percent of all people who attempt suicide use benzodiazepines in their attempts (Dulcan, 1999). The drug most notably involved is Valium (diazepam), which is used by 51 percent of individuals attempting suicide. Professionals prescribing these types of medications need to be aware of the problems associated with use, especially if a past history of substance abuse is evident. Clients between the ages of eighteen and twenty-five have a greater tendency to attempt suicide using these drugs. It is illegal for anyone to give or sell these medications to someone to whom the medication has not been prescribed (Dulcan, 1999).

According to Rassool (1998), there are three primary groups of long-term benzodiazepine users. The first group consists of individuals with physical problems who tend to be cautious and do not misuse their prescriptions. In a study by Vissers, van der Grinten, van der Horst, Kester, & Knottnerus (2003), health problems rather than social problems increase the use of this drug among this group. The second group consists of individuals with psychiatric problems, such as anxiety or depression. This group generally experiences more difficulties and withdrawal symptoms.

The third and largest group comprises individuals with chronic sleep problems, particularly the elderly (Curran et al., 2003). It appears that many elderly individuals complaining of difficulty sleeping are often administered prescription medications rather than natural or complementary remedies (Dziegielewski, 2003). Benzodiazepines are now the most widely prescribed medications for the elderly (Curran et al., 2003; Frances & Miller, 1998). The potential for misuse of these drugs among this age group is greater due to the high distribution and the decreased metabolism that occurs in the elderly population (Dziegielewski & Leon, 2001; Rassool, 1998). Misuse of these drugs among the elderly can be intentional, such as when the client purposely increases the drug dose, or unintentional, such as when the user is unable to decipher the doctor's instructions (Francis & Miller, 1998). Regardless, the prescribing physician is responsible for assessing the client's abuse potential and ability to understand the instructions.

The last group Rassool (1998) identifies is illicit drug users. These individuals are younger and more "socially disorganized" (p. 201). They often take higher drug doses than those in the other three groups.

The narcotics are generally related to opium, which is extracted directly from the opium poppy or synthetically altered in the laboratory. Opium has clear pain-relieving properties and can be smoked, eaten, or injected. Opium is very expensive, so it is not uncommon to combine it with other substances to increase its market value. Morphine, an opium derivative, can be very quickly absorbed into the system, especially when injected, and is used as an analgesic, anesthetic, or sedative. Morphine is considered central to pain relief and often creates euphoria while decreasing the symptoms of pain. This euphoria is probably the primary reason morphine can be so addictive. A second type of pain reliever that is also an opium derivative is codeine. Codeine is less habit forming than morphine, but it also produces less analgesia (pain relief). Today, morphine and codeine are primarily used to relieve pain, but because of their high potential for abuse, they have been classified as controlled substances.

PREVALENCE

According to the Substance Abuse and Mental Health Services Administration (SAMHSA, 2002), the use of tranquilizers has been increasing steadily since 1986 (SAMHSA, 2002). The 2001 National Household Survey on Drug Abuse (NHSDA) reported that, between 2000 and 2001, nonmedical pain reliever use increased. Related to this is the fourfold increase in the number of persons reporting use of OxyContin from 1999 to 2001 (SAMHSA, 2002). The Federal Drug Enforcement Administration reported an increase in OxyContin use as well (DEA, n.d. b). U.S. Department of Justice statistics indicated that approximately six million people used this drug for nonmedical purposes in 2000.

Ciraulo and Nace (2000) reported that 1.2 percent of the general population could qualify for a clinical diagnosis of anxiolytic, sedative, or hypnotic dependence. They also noted that sons of alcoholics are twenty-five times more likely to use benzodiazepines than men without a family history of alcohol abuse. According to the American Psychiatric Association (APA; 2000), 6 percent of the population has used sedatives illicitly, and the highest prevalence occurs among people ages twenty-six to thirty-four. Women and the elderly are most at risk for benzodiazepine misuse or abuse (National Institute on Drug Abuse [NIDA], 2002). In 1999, 87 percent of the individuals admitted for prescription drug abuse were Caucasian (SAMHSA, 2002).

CASE EXAMPLE

Case History

V is a thirty-three-year-old Caucasian female of average height (5' 5") who weighs approximately 130 pounds. She is a registered nurse and works for a traveling nurses' association. She was referred to the social worker in the public defender's office regarding her substance abuse and current incarceration. V was married at age seventeen after discovering she was pregnant. She reports that her husband is verbally and emotionally abusive. They have been separated for almost two years. Her husband lives a couple of hours away with another woman.

V lives with two of her children, a ten-year-old son and a twelve-year-old daughter. She relocated to the area a year and a half ago after the separation from her husband. She indicates that she has felt depressed for many years and relates this to the trouble in her marriage. V also reports feeling hopeless, experiencing low energy, and having poor concentration and a fluctuating appetite. She states she has been dealing with these feelings for about four years. She denies any history of mental health treatment in the past. Since her incarceration, her husband has been threatening to take her children away from her.

V has a very supportive and concerned family that is willing to participate in her treatment plan. Her mother lives a few hours away, and her father and brother live in different states. Her father views V as an intelligent, caring, and sweet person who has "recently fallen onto some difficult times."

V indicates that her addiction problem began with a prescription for Tussionex for bronchitis a year ago. Tussionex is a cough suppressant whose major ingredient is hydrocodone. V admits that she felt uncomfortable taking the medication initially because of the way it made her feel. She reports being prescribed other painkillers in the past for medical reasons and that all of them had uncomfortable side effects. She states that, once she got used to it, the Tussionex did not have these negative effects for her.

V notes that she began calling doctors after hours for prescriptions. For more than a year, she dodged the police by using false names along with the names of friends, family, and acquaintances. She went to numerous pharmacies in the area to obtain the drug and learned to leave the pharmacy when too many questions were being asked. V admits to having her daughter retrieve medication from the pharmacist on one occasion. She also admits trying to buy these medications on the Internet.

When V began working the night shift at a local hospital, her drug abuse began to increase. She states that her abuse of the drug helped her to sleep all day when she worked at night. She describes experiencing withdrawal symptoms when she awoke, such as extreme stomach pains, sweating, dizziness, and nausea. V states that she answered her children's questions regarding her drug-related activities by telling them it was okay because the medications were prescribed from the doctor. She expresses regret and becomes teary-eyed when discussing her children.

V provided information about her arrest, medical clearance, and booking into the jail. Her arrest occurred at a local pharmacy after she attempted to have a prescription filled. Dressed in only her nightgown, V was apprehended at the entrance of the store. Her first stop was a police substation, where her withdrawal symptoms began. She describes lying on the floor of the cell, dry-heaving and doubled over with abdominal cramps. The police transported her to the emergency room for medical clearance. While there, she was given Ativan, an antianxiety drug, to curb the painful withdrawal.

V states that she remembers little about being booked into the jail. Her last memory is clouded by dizziness and the memory of someone grabbing her arm. She was told that she suffered a seizure. V states that she has no memory of the seizure but reports that she felt "out of it" for a few hours afterward. V believes that she has fully detoxed from the hydrocodone because now she can think more clearly and has no more physical discomforts. V reports sleeping frequently and has lost fifteen pounds in thirty-five days.

Multiaxial Diagnostic Assessment

Taking into consideration the information provided by V, her family, the medical records from the jail, and the *DSM-IV-TR*, V's diagnosis is the following:

Axis I: Opioid Dependence (304.00)
          Dysthymic Disorder (300.4)
Axis II: Deferred
Axis III: None
Axis IV: 1. Marital separation from her husband and her children.
          2. Current incarceration secondary to substance use.
          3. Legal issues secondary to substance use.
          4. Lack of financial resources due to loss of job and substance use.
          5. Substance abuse problems.
Axis V: 60

In the recovery process, it will be crucial to help this client understand that anxiety, unless it is excessive, is a natural part of an individual's life and development. In the rehabilitation process, V will need to be prepared for the fact that some degree of anxiety is expected. She will need to learn that this anxiety can help her prepare for taking action or accepting life situations.

The first step in the diagnostic assessment is to make sure that the client has had a complete physical exam. This exam serves three purposes: (1) it identifies whether a medication is needed to help with the tapering process; (2) it rules out problems from any medical conditions; and, (3) it detects other medical problems. Because the symptoms of the individuals who take these medications can be as varied as their perceptions of anxiety (cognitive, behavioral, or somatic presentation), a proper medical assessment to rule out physical causes of the anxiety or medical complications provides the foundation for intervention.

An accurate medication history will assist the doctor in determining the need for continuance of medications during the recovery process. This history should include information about any drug (e.g., prescribed medications, over-the-counter medications, and alternate therapies such as herbal preparations) that the client may have used to control or avoid feelings of anxiety, depression, or stress (American Neuropsychiatric Association Committee on Research, 2000). It is also critical to assess whether the client has a history of substance abuse. If substance abuse has occurred or is occurring, it may be more effective to recommend a medication such as BuSpar (buspirone) that does not have the same addiction profile.

While gathering client information, practitioners should explore the client's current and past potential for substance abuse, especially substance use activities that support or result in addiction (e.g., use of stimulants such as caffeine) that the client may be engaged in without realizing the side effects.

The intervention process for V will begin by assisting V in recognizing the problems that can occur when tapering off of the medications while dealing with the uncomfortable feelings that are also bound to occur. V has learned from her active addiction that taking a benzodiazepine results in feeling better quickly. This knowledge contributes to her resistance to verbal therapy and the application of specific problem-solving techniques (Dziegielewski & Leon, 2001). Furthermore, V may have learned that "feeling better" is related to medicine use only. Individualized counseling, problem-solving techniques, and skill-building strategies help a person recognize and prepare for future anxiety-provoking situations and resistance to these interventions should be addressed openly (Dowd & Rugle, 1999). Interventions such as cognitive behavioral therapy and applied relaxation can be used to address anxiety and resistance.

V's intervention plan must address her immediate and long-term needs while satisfying her legal obligations. The first consideration will always be detoxification from the sedative, hypnotic, or painkiller addiction due to the severity of the physical dependence. V's detoxification process combined close monitoring by the medical staff at the jail and pharmacological treatment. In order to reduce the severe symptoms, Ativan was prescribed in small doses. Once detoxification was complete, V was ready to begin psychosocial intervention as a way to help her continue her sobriety.

Intervention Plan: Sedatives or Hypnotics Dependence Disorder

Definition.   A pattern of substance use that leads to significant impairments in social and occupational spheres, as well as marked psychological and physiological dependence. These symptoms manifest as tolerance, withdrawal, and compulsive behaviors that are related to the use of the substance. Continued use despite adverse consequences.

Signs and Symptoms.   Nausea; confusion; withdrawal from social activities; neglect of responsibilities; relationship problems; anxiety, insomnia; paranoia; depression; severe withdrawal symptoms.

Withdrawal Symptoms.   Abdominal cramps; anxiety; breathing difficulty; blurred vision; dizziness; heart palpitations; irritability; lack of concentration; lack of coordination; loss of memory; muscle aches and pains; severe headaches; seizures; tightness in chest.

Goals for Treatment.
1. Abstain from using substances (after a period of medically monitored detoxification).
2. Acquire a medical examination and a psychosocial assessment.
3. Educate client on the hazards of using these substances and discuss new coping skills.
4. Address underlying issues that relate to chemical dependency.
5. Link client to an inpatient treatment facility in the community.
6. Follow up with an aftercare plan upon release from program.

Objectives	Interventions
Client will attend and participate in an inpatient substance abuse treatment program.	Client will attend and participate in the treatment milieu of the program. This will include individual sessions three times a week in addition to daily group sessions.
Client will discuss issues related to her substance dependence and the negative consequences of substance-related behaviors.	Client and therapist will identify motivators for client to stop using the associated substance. Practitioner will assist client with recognizing how substance abuse is affecting client's life, friends, and family.
Client will discuss triggers that facilitate dependency, particularly anxiety.	Client and therapist will identify previous coping skills and modify these processes to include techniques that promote the client's well-being. Relaxation techniques, such as meditation, yoga, and imagery are utilized to reduce anxiety levels.
Client will discuss withdrawal symptoms and how they relate to the recovery process.	Client will recognize the types and severity of withdrawal symptoms related to anxiolytic, sedative, and hypnotic dependence.
Client will take prescription medication as instructed by physician.	Client and practitioner will monitor prescription use or misuse.
Client will participate in an aftercare program upon completion of inpatient treatment.	Client will attend weekly meetings with therapist to discuss the effectiveness of newly learned coping skills.

BEST PRACTICES

Treatment for people with addictions to sedatives, hypnotics, and painkillers is complex. Because of the severity of the withdrawal symptoms, detoxification can be dangerous and demands close monitoring. Rassool (1998) outlined a management plan for withdrawal from benzodiazepines. First, the client must be advised of the benefits of becoming clean and educated on the symptoms of withdrawal. Psychopharmacology is recommended to curb extreme anxiety (Ciraulo & Nace, 2000; SAMHSA, 2001, 2002). Alternative medications include buspirone, trazodone, venlafaxine, nefazodone, and paroxetine (Ciraulo & Nace, 2000). The next step is a closely monitored, gradual decrease of the addictive substance. Rassool stressed the importance of implementing coping skills and support for the anxiety. Complementary therapies include aromatherapy, acupuncture, and reflexology.

A well-integrated, individualized program that includes individual, group, and family counseling as well as contingency management appears most effective for those addicted to prescription medications (NIDA, 2002). Cognitive-behavioral therapy, in combination with a twelve-step program, is recommended for treatment of addiction to these drugs (Ciraulo & Nace, 2000). Cognitive-behavioral interventions are considered the primary supportive intervention for those who suffer from anxiety-related conditions (Reid, 1997). A 1991 consensus statement from the National Institute of Health recommended referrals to cognitive-behavioral or medication treatments if changes were not observed within the first six to eight weeks of alternative treatment (including hypnotherapy or psychoanalytic therapy). The individual who is addicted to these substances can benefit from cognitive restructuring, breathing retraining, and in vivo exposure components (Craske & Waikar, 1994). Although opinions vary as to exactly how these techniques should be implemented, their combination as a "treatment package" has proved useful to those in clinical settings (Reid, 1997).

In cognitive restructuring, misinterpretation or misappraisal of bodily sensations as being threatening are targeted. This therapy is based on the concept that cognitions precede (or trigger) anxiety and panic, so the identification of aberrant cognitive structures, and the challenging of misinterpretations and biases through reasoning and experience, can eliminate the anxiety. As part of the cognitive-behavioral intervention, relaxation training provides an important component for dealing with clients troubled by the fear of, and the anxiety that will develop in, discontinuing the substance. In recovery, those addicted to prescription medications fear giving up the drugs secondary to withdrawal. Teaching a client relaxation techniques can lead to the client learning how to direct personal energy in a more productive manner, thereby reducing anxiety levels (Ost, Salkovskis, & Hellstrom, 1991). Learning to identify the indicators of stress and how to reduce the physiological manifestations of stress serve as important precursors to exposing the client to the original target of his or her anxiety.

Applied relaxation will help the client address symptoms of panic; nearly 50 percent of clients with anxiety disorders report hyperventilation (Craske & Waikar, 1994). In applied relaxation, the client learns progressive relaxation skills such as breathing retraining and applies these in situations when he or she feels anxiety and apprehension (Dziegielewski & Wolfe, 2000). This method requires that the client identify stress cues and apply relaxing thoughts in stressful situations. To begin the process, the individual is instructed to assume a restful position. In breathing retraining, it is important to educate the client about diaphragmatic breathing, and taking deep, slow breaths should be encouraged. With each inhalation, the client is instructed to breathe in relaxing energy and exhale away tension. Many clients prefer to use a mantra or saying to assist them in this process. The relaxed state allows for restful suggestions to be made (Alfonso & Dziegielewski, 2001). These suggestions help the client become aware of phenomena in the body: feelings of heaviness, warmth and tingling, and calmness. Generally, a minute or so is spent on each sensation, allowing the individual to notice how the sensation feels. The individual is then asked to focus on the overall feeling of being relaxed (Feltman, 1996; Gottlieb, 1995). The chosen relaxation phrase should be used continually to anchor further relaxation training.

The client is instructed to repeat the diaphragmatic breathing and relaxation phrase procedures at home. Generally clients contract to practice deep breathing and to perform this exercise five times a day (Dziegielewski & MacNeil, 1999). Because clients sometimes weaken the effectiveness of the relaxation phrase by engaging in negative self-defeating statements, the use of a stress reduction tape can be an effective supplement to the exercises. Learning and practicing this technique is essential because the client will use it at each stage of the systematic desensitization and the cognitive restructuring process (Alfonso & Dziegielewski, 2001). Initiating the relaxation sequence in this order helps clients to learn the process quickly and to realize the significance of their adherence to the tasks of treatment.

Systematic desensitization and exposure techniques can also be used to assist those in recovery from an addiction to anxiety-reducing medications. Using these techniques in combination with in vivo techniques (real-life experiences) appears to have an even greater effect than simulating an experience in the office setting only (Marshall, 1988). Behavioral therapy that involves exposure and response prevention can be particularly effective in reducing panic symptoms (O'Sullivan & Marks, 1990). Treatment of this type requires that the client be systematically exposed to the object or situation that provokes the fear (and subsequent avoidance). Some clients who have used systematic desensitization have found it particularly helpful when the exposure is long enough to allow the anxiety to be markedly reduced (Marshall, 1996). Similarly, exposure techniques are thought to be most effective when internal and external distractions from the stressful objects or situations are minimized (Foa & Kozak, 1986).

There are many variations of in vivo exposure treatment, and no single model has emerged as superior to others; however, long sessions are generally thought to be more successful than shorter or interrupted sessions (Chaplin & Levine, 1981; Marshall, 1985). Establishing a plan in which sessions or exercises are conducted daily is considered superior to spacing the sessions out on a weekly schedule (Foa, Jameson, Turner, & Payne, 1980). Although Feigenbaum (1988) found a high-intensity (flooding) method to be effective, most practitioners favor the progressive model. Research suggests that exposure-based interventions can be administered by the practitioner or by the client in the outpatient setting

(Dziegielewski & MacNeil, 1999; Al-Kubaisy, Marks, Logsdail, & Marks, 1992). Cost savings can result by having the client continue with self-directed strategy on an outpatient basis.

In this type of systematic desensitization, three phases are suggested: relaxation training; the visualization of increasingly stressful, anxiety-producing scenes while maintaining good relaxation; and actually confronting and coping with the anxiety-arousing situation. Triggering events can be based on either internal or external physical sensations, which the client identifies as being associated with situations that produce feelings of panic. In systematic desensitization, the client and the practitioner develop a schedule of anxiety-producing situations relating to the panic symptoms. Usually, the practitioner tries to help the client find five to ten situations that represent progressively more exposure to the target of the anxiety. These situations are rank-ordered by the client from the least anxiety producing response to the greatest and can range from seeing the target to touching or handling it. These situations form the hierarchical steps that the client will use to overcome the phobic reaction (Beck, Stanley & Baldwin, 1984). Relaxation training and cognitive restructuring components of treatment address the internal sensations.

To facilitate this process, it is possible to develop a summative rating, which identifies the degree of fear that each of the situations elicits. Scales usually range from 1 (no fear) to 7 (extreme, paralyzing fear). It is common for clients to indicate that the least severe situation causes them extreme fear. When this happens, it is best not to rate the other situations; instead, just begin work on the least severe one (Alfonso & Dziegielewski, 2001). Having established the situations of interest and a means of evaluating how anxious the client feels about each objective, a plan for gradual exposure to the feared stimulus is developed.

The client is asked how much anxiety he or she would be willing to tolerate. Generally, clients are willing to endure anxiety ratings of 3 to 5 (Dziegielewski & MacNeil, 1999). When this level has been obtained, the practitioner establishes a contract with the client that stipulates the level of anxiety experienced, and the client monitors and records it. The contract clearly establishes anxiety levels for continued participation. For example, if a client indicates willingness to endure anxiety at a level of 4, it will be expected that the least severe situation that produces that level of anxiety will be selected. If the current task produces more anxiety than that, the client is given permission to return to the previous situation. When anxiety levels diminish to a manageable level (according to self-rated scoring), the client is able to proceed to the next task in the progression. Clients report their scores in weekly sessions and are encouraged to elaborate on the patterns that evolved. Clients are praised for their courage and the significant progress that they make.

Based on client readiness to proceed to more difficult situations, the practitioner continues the steps in the hierarchy. Each successive step is addressed until the client is able to complete the task at or below the contracted level of anxiety. The entire sequence of events is completed primarily through homework exercise and is typically accomplished in six to eight individual sessions.

In summary, when trying to help an individual taper off of a medication, minimal anxiety at the time of the withdrawal will lead to better treatment outcomes (Posternak & Mueller, 2001). Applied relaxation allows the person in treatment to gain a sense of control. Through this method, the symptoms related to substance addiction that can cause stress or weakness for relapse can be identified and clearly related to other areas of functioning. Treatment is then focused on the presenting problem. Oftentimes people enter treatment due to the negative consequences that result from the behaviors they exhibit, not because of the behaviors themselves. It is the practitioner's job to assist the client in making the connection between the behaviors and the resulting negative consequences and to feel as if control without abusing the substance is possible.

SUMMARY AND FUTURE DIRECTIONS

In treating individuals addicted to sedatives, hypnotics, or painkillers, practitioners should consider the following factors. First, a medical exam and assistance with detoxification are critical to the success of intervention. Second, psychotropic medications as the sole treatment modality are not sufficient in dealing with these events or the environmental situations that support problematic behaviors. Anxiety-producing events occur and are experienced daily in the lives of clients, and everyone has some difficulty dealing with such situations. The practitioner must be able to identify psychosocial intervention strategies, such as those described in this chapter, that clearly assist clients who have difficulties adjusting to stress and anxiety. The practitioner must be prepared to question the client's assumption that prescription medications are neither harmful nor addictive. Third, a comprehensive medication history (e.g., past substance abuse history and all drugs employed by client, including over-the-counter prescriptions, herbal remedies, and prescribed medications) will help the intervention team in prescribing appropriate treatment protocols. And finally, the practitioner should screen and identify the client's abuse patterns and recognize the possible need to taper off the client's use of anxiety-reducing medications.

Practitioners should be aware of the client's use and abuse of other substances such as alcohol when he or she presents with an addiction to sedatives, hypnotics, or painkillers. Alcohol and other recreational street drugs stimulate the release of certain neurochemicals in the brain that can inhibit anxiety. "Subjectively, the result of this biochemical process is social ease, experienced as pleasure, that seduces the users of chemical intoxicants to continue to use despite the side effects: slurred speech, slowed thoughts, memory failure, poor motor control, and the possibility of addiction" (Marshall, 1994, p. 152).

Medications used to reduce feelings of anxiety can also lead to the development of a false sense of security (Dziegielewski & Leon, 2001; Marshall, 1994). When clients feel better quickly, they may not want to commit the time and energy required to utilize relaxation or cognitive therapy interventions. To address possible noncompliance with treatment, the client should agree to continued psychosocial treatment with prescribed medication (Dziegielewski, 2002; Dziegielewski & Leon, 2001). Ideally, the practitioner should ask the client to contract to participate in psychosocial treatment prior to taking any tapering medications. If premedication contracting is not possible, the practitioner should ask the prescribing physician to address with the client the importance of continued psychosocial interventions in order to identify current and future psychosocial stressors disturbing functioning. The psychosocial counseling interventions employed, supplementary to psychotropic medication, help clients to recognize and prepare for anxiety-provoking and relapse situations.

Practitioners need to complete both an accurate assessment and a referral process for all clients served, regardless of the substance employed. This requires that practitioners take an active role in advocating for clients, particularly when medications will supplement interventions in the time-limited setting. The confounding nature of the anxiety and depression clients experience requires that practitioners remain aware of the psychological, sociological, and physiological implications of interventions when treating individuals recovering from addictions to sedatives, hypnotics, or painkillers. The practitioner should recognize potential problem areas related to this type of prescribed drug abuse and misuse, as well as effective psychosocial interventions recommended in the client's course of treatment.

Practitioners and clients should hope for long-lasting therapeutic effects yet acknowledge potential relapses as a part of the treatment process. The practitioner should prepare the client for possible relapses as part of his or her intervention. Relapse is always a possibility; interventions are not curative by nature. Physicians provide medical services and are not distressed when clients return for additional services. Likewise, substance abuse practitioners should be prepared for clients who return for repeat treatment or booster sessions, by way of office visits or telephone consultations. These types of follow-ups should be expected and provided.

References

Alfonso, S., & Dziegielewski, S. F. (2001). Self-directed treatment for panic disorder: A holistic approach. *Journal of Research and Social Work Evaluation: An International Publication, 2*(1), 5–18.

Al-Kubaisy, T., Marks, I. M., Logsdail, S., & Marks, M. P. (1992). Role of exposure homework in phobia reduction: A controlled study. *Behavior Therapy, 23*(4), 599–621.

American Neuropsychiatric Association Committee on Research. (2000). The use of herbal alternative medicines in neuropsychiatry. *Journal of Neuropsychiatry, 12*, 177–92.

American Psychiatric Association. (2000). *Diagnostic and statistical manual of mental disorders* (4th ed., text rev.). Washington, DC: Author.

Barlow, D. H., Esler, J. L., & Vitali, A. E. (1998). Psychosocial treatments for panic disorders, phobias, and generalized anxiety disorder. In P. E. Nathan & J. M. Gorman (Eds.), *A guide to treatments that work* (pp. 288–318). New York: Oxford University Press.

Beck, J. G., Stanley, M. A., & Baldwin, L. E. (1994). Comparison of cognitive therapy and relaxation training for panic disorder. *Journal of Consulting Clinical Psychology, 64*(4), 818–26.

Chaplin, E. W., & Levine, B. A. (1981). The effects of total exposure duration and interrupted versus continued exposure in flooding therapy. *Behavior Therapy, 12,* 360–68.

Ciraulo, D., & Nace, E. (2000). Benzodiazepine treatment of anxiety or insomnia in substance abuse patients. *American Journal of Addictions, 9,* 276–84.

Corliss, R., Park, A., & Ressner, J. (2001). Who's feeling no pain? *Time, 157*(11), 69.

Craske, M. G., & Waikar, S. V. (1994). Panic disorder. In M. Hersen & R. T. Ammerman (Eds.), *Handbook of prescriptive treatments for adults* (pp. 135–55). New York: Plenum Press.

Curran, H. V., Collins, R., Fletcher, S., Kee, S. C., Woods, B., & Iliffe, S. (2003). Older adults and withdrawal from benzodiazepine hypnotics in general practice: Effects on cognitive function, sleep, mood, and quality of life. *Psychological Medicine, 33*(7), 1223–37.

Dowd, E., & Rugle, L. (1999). *Comparative treatments in substance abuse.* New York: Springer.

Drug Enforcement Administration. (n.d. a). *DEA briefs and background, drugs and drug abuse, drug descriptions.* Retrieved January 5, 2003, from http://www.usdof.gov/dea/concern

Drug Enforcement Administration. (n.d. b). *OxyContin FAQs.* Retrieved January 6, 2003, from http://www.deadiversion.usdoj.gov/drugs_concern/oxycodone/oxycontin_faq.htm

Dulcan, M. K. (1999). *Helping parents, youth, and teachers understand medications for behavioral and emotional problems: A resource book for medication information handouts.* Washington, DC: American Psychiatric Press.

Dziegielewski, S. F. (2002). *DSM-IV-TR in action.* New York: John Wiley & Sons.

Dziegielewski, S. F. (2003). *The changing face of health care social work: Professional practice in the era of managed care.* New York: Springer.

Dziegielewski, S. F., & Leon, A. M. (2001). *Social work practice and psychopharmacology.* New York: Springer.

Dziegielewski, S. F., & MacNeil, G. (1999). Time limited treatment considerations and strategy for specific phobias. *Crisis Intervention and Time-Limited Treatment, 5*(1/2), 133–50.

Dziegielewski, S. F., & Wolfe, P. (2000). EMDR as a time-limited intervention for body image disturbance and self-esteem: A single subject case study design. *Journal of Psychotherapy in Independent Practice, 1*(3), 1–16.

Feigenbaum, W. (1988). Long-term efficacy of ungraded versus graded massed exposure in agoraphobias. In I. Hand & H. Wittchen (Eds.), *Panic and phobias: Treatments and variables affecting course and outcome.* Berlin: Springer-Verlag.

Feltman, J. (1996). *The* Prevention *how-to dictionary of healing remedies and techniques.* New York: Berkley Books.

Foa, E. B., Jameson, J. S., Turner, R. M., & Payne, L. L. (1980). Massed vs. spaced exposure sessions in the treatment of agoraphobia. *Behaviour Research and Therapy, 18,* 333–38.

Foa, E. B., & Kozak, M. S. (1986). Emotional processing of fear: Exposure to corrective information. *Psychological Bulletin, 99,* 20–35.

Frances, R., & Miller, S. (1998). *Clinical textbook of addictive disorders* (2nd ed.). New York: Guilford Press.

Gottlieb, B. (1995). *New choices in natural healing.* Emmaus, PA: Rodale.

Hales, R. (1995). Anxiety disorders. In D. Hales & R. Hales (Eds.), *Caring for the mind* (pp. 119–53). New York: Bantam Books.

Kaplan, H. I., & Sadock, B. J. (1990). *Pocket handbook of clinical psychiatry.* Baltimore: Williams & Wilkins.

Koemer, B. I. (1999, June 21). Coming to you direct (social anxiety disorder medication). *U.S. News and World Report, 126,* 24, 54.

Marshall, J. R. (1994). *Social phobia: From stage fright to shyness.* New York: Basic Books.

Marshall, J. R. (1996). Comorbidity and its effects on panic disorder. *Bulletin of the Menninger Clinic, 60*(2, Suppl. A), A39–A53.

Marshall, W. L. (1985). The effects of variable exposure in flooding therapy. *Behavior Therapy, 16*, 117–35.

Marshall, W. L. (1988). Behavioural indices of habituation and sensitization during exposure to phobic stimuli. *Behaviour Research and Therapy, 26*, 67–77.

Meadows, M. (2001). Prescription drug use and abuse. *FDA Consumer, 35*(5), 18–24.

National Institute on Drug Abuse. (2002). *Hearing before the Health, Education, Labor, and Pensions Committee, United States Senate: OxyContin: Balancing risks and benefits.* Retrieved January 6, 2003, from http://www.drugabuse.gov/Testimony/2-12-02Testimony.html

Nordenberg, T. (1999). Social phobias: Traumas and treatments. *FDA Consumer, 33*, 6, 27–33.

Ost, L. G., Salkovskis, P., & Hellstrom, K. (1991). One session therapist directed exposure vs. self-exposure in the treatment of spider phobia. *Behavior Therapy, 22*, 407–22.

O'Sullivan, G., & Marks, I. M. (1990). Long-term outcome of phobic and obsessive-compulsive disorders after treatment. In R. Hoyes, M. Roth, & G. D. Burrows (Eds.), *Handbook of anxiety: Vol. 4. The treatment of anxiety*. Amsterdam: Elsevier Science.

Posternak, M., & Mueller, T. (2001). Assessing the risks and benefits of benzodiazepines for anxiety disorders in-patients with a history of substance abuse or dependence. *American Journal of Addictions, 10*, 48–68.

Rassool, G. (1998). *Substance use and misuse: Nature, context, and clinical interventions*. Oxford: Blackwell Science.

Reid, W. H. (1997). Anxiety disorders. In W. H. Reid, G. U. Balis, & B. J. Sutton (Eds.), *The treatment of psychiatric disorders* (3rd ed., pp. 239–62). Bristol, PA: Brunner/Mazel.

Roth, A., & Fonagy, P. (1996). Anxiety disorders I: Phobias, generalized anxiety disorder, and panic disorder with and without agoraphobia. In A. Roth & P. Fonagy (Eds.), *What works for whom? A critical review of psychotherapy research* (pp. 113–44). New York: Guilford Press.

Segal, E. A., Gerdes, K. E., & Steiner, S. (2004). *Social work: An introduction to the profession*. Belmont, CA: Thomson/Brooks Cole.

Stein, M. D. (1998). Paroxetine treatment of generalized social phobia (social anxiety disorder). *Journal of the American Medical Association, 280*(8), 708.

Substance Abuse and Mental Health Services Administration. (2001). *National Household Survey on Drug Abuse (NHSDA)*. Retrieved January 7, 2003, from http://www.samhsa.gov/oas/nhsda/2k1nhsda/vol1.htm

Substance and Mental Health Services Administration. (2002). *The DASIS Report: Prescription and over-the-counter drug abuse admissions*. Retrieved January 5, 2003, from http://www.samhsa.gov/oas/2k2/OTCtx/OTCtx.pdf

Vissers, F., van der Grinten, R., van der Horst, F., Kester, A., & Knottnerus, J.A. (2003). Use of hypnotic and tranquilizing drugs in general practice. *Scandinavian Journal of Primary Health Care, 21*(3), 159–61.

Other Addictive Substances

Chapter 10

Cannabis

Sophia F. Dziegielewski and Cathy A. Van Bibber

CANNABIS, COMMONLY REFERRED TO AS MARIJUANA, IS THE MOST WIDELY used illicit drug in the United States. Most professionals agree that marijuana has the potential for abuse and dependence. As growing conditions and plant harvesting techniques continue to be refined, there is no question that the marijuana available today is far more potent than that available a few decades ago. Furthermore, most marijuana sold in the United States currently is considerably stronger than what is available in other countries. There has been little violence associated with marijuana use; however, there is evidence of violence associated with the trafficking of marijuana.

Currently, there is debate over the usefulness of marijuana for medicinal purposes; many health care professionals worry that marijuana's harmful physical and psychological effects outweigh its benefits. Marijuana was used in ancient times for medicinal purposes for various ailments as well as in religious rituals. Marijuana affects the respiratory system and cognitive processes. Intoxication from the drug interferes with the user's performance at work or school.

This chapter discusses the significance of marijuana use and the potential for abuse and dependence. A case study is included, and the most current interventions are discussed. Cognitive-behavioral treatments (CBT) appear the most promising intervention for decreasing marijuana use; however, more outcomes-based studies are needed in the area of marijuana abuse and dependence in order to determine the best possible treatment strategies for the diverse population of marijuana users.

THE HISTORY OF CANNABIS USE

Marijuana use was first recorded in China as early as 2737 BC, and the spread of this substance can be traced from China to India, North Africa, and later to Europe as early as AD 500. Exactly when it was discovered in America is uncertain; however, it had clearly made an impact in the early twentieth century. Initially, the early settlers used hemp as a fiber crop for making rope.

After World War II, Mexican laborers were influential in introducing marijuana smoking to the working class in America. During Prohibition, in the 1920s and early 1930s, marijuana use gained popularity as a substitute for the consumption of alcohol. The drug was widely available at hundreds of "tea pads," establishments comparable to opium dens, operating in New York City at that time (Inaba & Cohen, 2000).

In 1970, with the passage of the Controlled Substances Act, marijuana was categorized as a Schedule I drug—that is, a drug having a high potential for abuse and no accepted medical use (National Academy of Sciences, 1999). As of 1998, eight states had passed laws that allowed physicians to prescribe marijuana for medical necessity, and five other states passed ballot initiatives to that effect (National Academy of Sciences, 1999). Currently, marijuana is still classified as a controlled substance. "Under federal law, Congress defined marijuana to focus on those parts of the cannabis plant that are the source of tetrahydrocannabinols (THC). THC is the hallucinogenic substance in marijuana that causes the psychoactive effect or 'high'" (Drug Enforcement Administration [DEA], 2001, p. 1). THC from the marijuana available today can be detected more than thirty days after the last use (National Drug Intelligence Center [NDIC], 2003). Generally, cannabinoids show promise as a medicine but require a great deal of additional study. This additional study could result in improved treatments for those who suffer from medical conditions such as glaucoma and AIDS (Earleywine, 2002). But according to Iversen (2000), although therapeutic indications for cannabis-based medicines are possible, the "evidence for the clinical effectiveness of the drug is woefully inadequate by modern standards" (p. 174).

Recently, marijuana has been called the most widely used illicit drug in many societies (Hall & Solowij, 1998; Iversen, 2000) and has been referred to as the most widely available illicit drug in the United States (NDIC, 2003). Its popularity seems especially prominent among adolescents and young adults (Marijuana, 1999; National Institute on Drug Abuse [NIDA], n.d.). One reason for this popularity is the simple fact that it is so easy to grow and so readily available. A second reason is that so many adults, as well as youth, believe that marijuana use is harmless. Lastly, the price of marijuana has stayed relatively stable (NDIC, 2003).

Today, public debate continues over the harmful effects and possible benefits of marijuana. The latest developments in the medical use of cannabis and its derivatives involve the treatment of nausea and weight loss associated with chemotherapy and AIDS. Drobinal, a synthetic version of THC sold under the brand name Marinol, mimics some of marijuana's therapeutic effects, including increased appetite and decreased nausea (Earleywine, 2002; Iverson, 2000). Marinol is also prescribed for the treatment of glaucoma.

Those who advocate for marijuana to be legalized for medicinal purposes believe that the natural form of marijuana is superior to the synthetic Marinol because the effect is faster. Furthermore, users of the natural form can regulate how much or how little they require in order to relieve their symptoms. With Marinol, users are unable to control the effect once they have taken the prescribed dosage (Inaba & Cohen, 2000).

In contrast, others have growing concerns about the physical and psychological effects that can occur from marijuana use (Marijuana, 1999), especially when it is smoked versus taken orally (Mao & Oh, 1998). Unfortunately, there is no way to control the differences between what is produced in government-regulated laboratories and what is grown in a basement or an open field.

BIOCHEMICAL COMPOSITION AND PSYCHOPHYSIOLOGICAL EFFECTS

Marijuana contains several hundred chemicals. One type, known as cannabinoids, continues to be studied for psychoactive effects. The most highly potent cannabinoid is delta-9-tetrahydrocannabinol (THC) (Inaba & Cohen, 2000). The strength of marijuana depends on the amount of THC it contains, which is affected by the plant type, how it is cultivated, and numerous other factors (American Council for Drug Education, 1999). It appears that the potency of marijuana has risen from 1.5 percent in 1970 to a current average of approximately 7.6 percent (DEA, n.d.). Furthermore, in 1974, the average THC content of illicit marijuana was less than 1 percent; in early 1994, potency averaged 5 percent and today's sinsemilla ranges up to 17 percent" (DEA, n.d.). *Sinsemilla*, which means "without seeds," refers to a potent form of marijuana harvested from plants specially cultivated to prevent pollination. The resulting absence of seeds increases the psychoactive effect of the drug.

Marijuana is typically smoked, and when rolled it is commonly referred to as a *joint* or a *blunt*. When taken in this form, its effect can last two to four hours (Iversen, 2000). Within minutes of smoking marijuana, the psychoactive effects occur. The intoxication heightens sensitivity to external stimuli (i.e., distorted perception such as a distorted sense of time) and causes euphoria, reduced short-term memory, changes in visual perception (which slows reaction time), and impaired attention and coordination. Acute reactions can include anxiety and panic attacks and an impaired ability to carry out complex, goal-oriented tasks (Miller, Gold & Smith, 1997). Some of the common side effects include dry mouth, dizziness, disinhibition, time distortions, impaired judgment, reduced coordination, and ataxia. Some other perceived effects may be relaxation, happiness, enhanced sensory perception, and a heightened sense of awareness and imagination (U.S. Department of Justice, 2001).

Marijuana's impact on users' cognitive, neurological, and emotional development is more dangerous than that of nicotine. Marijuana users also risk damage to liver and lungs, as with alcohol and tobacco. Regardless of THC content, the amount of tar inhaled by marijuana smokers and the level of carbon monoxide absorbed are three to five times greater than among tobacco smokers. This may be due to marijuana users inhaling more deeply and holding the unfiltered smoke in their lungs (NIDA, 2003).

The National Academy of Sciences (1999) indicates that, among heavy users of marijuana, subtle defects in cognitive tasks have been reported after nineteen hours of abstinence from the drug and that longer-term cognitive deficits have also been reported. Marijuana use increases the likelihood of respiratory illness such as bronchitis (National Academy of Sciences, 1999). Research shows that many known carcinogens are found in marijuana smoke (Mao & Oh, 1998). Therefore, smokers can develop lung cancer from smoking marijuana. There has been some support to show that marijuana lowers immunity. This can make users more susceptible to colds, flu, and other infections (Inaba & Cohen, 2000). Legal consequences and health issues aside, "periodic cannabis use and intoxication can interfere with performance at work or school and may be physically hazardous in situations such as operating heavy machinery, or even driving a car" (Miller, Gold, & Smith, 1997).

In the *DSM-IV-TR* (American Psychiatric Association [APA], 2000), under substance-related disorders, diagnoses involving cannabis include cannabis use disorders and cannabis-induced disorders. Cannabis use disorders include cannabis abuse and cannabis dependence. Cannabis-induced disorders include cannabis intoxication, cannabis intoxication delirium, cannabis-induced psychotic disorder, and cannabis-induced anxiety disorders. Current medical and scientific evidence continues to demonstrate that marijuana has a high potential for abuse, and the current user population is more frequently exposed to higher potency marijuana than in previous years, which may increase the risk of dependence (NDIC, 2003). As noted in the *DSM-IV-TR*, "Individuals with Cannabis Dependence have a compulsive use and associated problems. Tolerance to most of the effects of cannabis has been reported in individuals who use cannabis chronically" (p. 236).

The clinical significance of withdrawal has not been verified with marijuana, although there have been reports of withdrawal symptoms. Withdrawal symptoms are not noticeable immediately and may be delayed because THC is stored in the body's fat cells and takes longer to leave the system. Some withdrawal effects are changes in sleeping and eating patterns, irritability, depression, cravings for the drug, and an inability to concentrate.

PREVALENCE

The National Drug Threat Assessment 2002 (NDIC, 2001) reported that the demand for marijuana far exceeds that of any other illicit drug. In describing the extent of marijuana use, the report stated that

> 76 million individuals aged 12 and older had tried marijuana in their lifetime; more than 18 million had used in the past year; and nearly 11 million in the past month; and on an average day, 5,556 individuals try marijuana for the first time, of which 3,814 are aged 12 to 17. (p. 4)

An overview of the findings from the 2001 Monitoring the Future survey (Johnston, O' Malley, & Bachman, 2002) stated that marijuana use among students in grades 10 and 12 has held steady since their peak in 1997. Additionally, "Eighth graders, who had shown a slow steady decline in marijuana use after their recent peak in 1996, also showed no further improvement this year" (p. 4).

Young adults have been shown to be at a great risk for trying marijuana when they leave home. Results of three national surveys (Gledhill-Hoyt, Hang, Strote, & Wechsler, 2000) on marijuana and other illicit drug use among college students in the 1990s concluded that "29% of past 30-day marijuana users first used marijuana and 34% began to use marijuana regularly at or after the age of 18, when most were in college" (p. 1655). The majority of violence and increased crime associated with marijuana appears to be related to trafficking of the drug. Law enforcement reports link marijuana distribution to kidnappings, shootings, and homicides, which often occur over unpaid drug debts (NDIC, 2003).

In a report of the collective statistics on drug use for the year 2000, the DEA (2001), using data from the National Household Survey on Drug Abuse, concluded that "76% of current illicit drug users use marijuana" and that "approximately 59% of current illicit drug users consumed only marijuana" (p. 2). Using statistics from the Drug Abuse Warning Network Survey for the year 2001, which reports emergency room episodes of illicit drugs, the DEA estimated that, "adjusting for population, young adults age 18 to 25 had the highest rate of marijuana-related ER episodes: 105 episodes per 100,000. The next highest rate was for individuals age 12 to 17." (p. 3).

Florida substance abuse treatment admissions for marijuana, the primary substance of abuse for the year 2000, totaled 19.6 percent (14,391). The majority of these admissions were for individuals aged fifteen to seventeen (36.5 percent) and eighteen to twenty (15.4 percent) (Substance Abuse and Mental Health Services Administration [SAMHSA], 2001). According to the Office of National Drug Control Policy (2002a), in 1998 marijuana accounted for 49 percent of admissions for individuals under the age of eighteen, with 71 percent of the admissions being Caucasian and 77 percent being male.

In summary, the research indicates that cannabis use is rising (particularly among American youth) and remains a very serious health concern in the area of addictions. Public perception that marijuana is safe for use can complicate efforts to curb or control the resulting problems that emerge from misuse of this substance.

CASE EXAMPLE

Case History

S reported that her first use of marijuana was at age twelve. She admitted to smoking marijuana every day for the past two months after relapsing. She says she used cocaine between the ages of twenty-two and twenty-six and stopped in 1988. She denies experimenting with or using any other mind-altering substances. She is aware of preoccupation, solitary use, and self-medicating with marijuana.

Psychological Functioning. S was oriented to person, place, and time and her memory was within average limits. Her thought processes appeared logical, coherent, and spontaneous. She made no reference to suicidal or homicidal ideations. She denies experiencing any type of hallucinations. She disclosed that she is depressed and suffers from mood swings all the time.

Her insight and judgment seem fair. She self-disclosed she has a substance abuse dependency problem. She seems to struggle with her self-image as well as impulse control. Her affect was within normal limits.

Educational/Vocational/Financial History. S started skipping school in grade 10 because she was not interested. She dropped out after that because she wanted to have a baby. She obtained her GED in 1989. She has worked several jobs doing production/assembly work. She likes to sit down and be busy with her hands.

S lives with her second husband in a modest apartment. Their combined income is in the mid-twenties. At this time, her son is in the custody of the Department of Children and Families and lives in a foster home.

Legal History. S was arrested in 1988 for trafficking in cocaine and spent time in prison. She was on probation, absconded for four years, turned herself in, and was restored to probation. She has a pending aggravated child abuse charge. She has been involved with the legal system since 1988.

Family and Social History. S states that she remembers her parents verbally and physically fighting, which ended in divorce when she was four years old. She related that she was separated from her younger sister and placed in a children's home at about age six and later went to various foster homes. Her mother reclaimed her at about age thirteen. She knows who her father is but has no contact with him.

S married at a young age and had a son and a daughter. The marriage was dissolved and the husband retained custody of the children. She became involved in another relationship and gave birth to another son. She had a tubal ligation afterward. Knowing she had a cocaine addiction, she allowed others to care for her son. She became involved in regaining custody when the child was eleven years old and she was residing with the child's father. The child had behavioral problems and, after six months and numerous requests for assistance, S lost her temper and hit the child with an extension cord. The Department of Children and Families removed the child, and a court case ensued. The final disposition required that she be placed on community control for two years. She is not able to regain custody of her son during this period.

Physical History. S relates that she experiences headaches occasionally. She denies having any sexually transmitted diseases. She says she had been hospitalized to give birth and had Cesarean sections.

Treatment History. S reported that she has tried to stop smoking marijuana on her own but has been unsuccessful. She stated that she made a decision to stop the use of cocaine and was successful in 1988. In 1993, S was in an inpatient substance abuse treatment facility for four months. She felt the program was somewhat helpful, although she did not complete the program.

S attended a drug education program and a basic outpatient treatment program from November 1997 to February 1998. She says she did not smoke marijuana while in those programs or for the couple of months after.

Rationale for Diagnosis. S has undergone recent prior attempts at treatment for cannabis dependence. She is aware that chemical dependency has affected her life. This will make self-help meetings fundamental, allowing her to benefit from twelve-step support. She appears to struggle with honestly identifying her feelings and being able to express them in an appropriate manner.

S appears to be deficient in her coping skills and tends to rationalize her behavior or blame others for her problems. When she believes she has lost control, she becomes aggressive or turns to substance abuse to cope with her situation.

Expected outcome and level of client involvement in treatment is better than average. She seems willing to make an effort in her treatment program.

Intervention Plan: Cannabis Dependence Disorder

Treatment focused on the client's inability to abstain from marijuana, her need to develop a positive support system to assist her in maintaining abstinence, and her need to develop the ability to identify and express her feelings in an appropriate way. Her addiction had led to her inability to remain gainfully employed. Low self-esteem issues were addressed along with past and present legal issues and substance abuse history.

Short-term goals were attendance and participation in all group sessions while learning more about the disease of addiction, learning techniques to live drug and alcohol free, and improving her communication skills through sharing and giving feedback. S was also to attend at least two self-help meetings a week and monthly individual appointments. She was to become gainfully employed within thirty days of treatment.

In order to learn to identify her feelings, S kept a daily log of her feelings and described what events brought her to those feelings. While in treatment, she was to learn how recovery would be instrumental in helping her to live within the confines of the law.

The counseling theories used with S were rational emotive therapy and reality therapy as well as the twelve-step model. Treatment included two group sessions a week, at least two self-help meetings a week, and monthly individual sessions. In group sessions she learned about the progressiveness of the disease of addiction; being accountable for her behavior; focusing on the present and learning the positive and negatives about her self-concept; and ways to improve her coping skills and change problematic behaviors.

The more her appropriate behavior was reinforced, the more responsible and serious S became about her recovery. She maintained abstinence throughout her treatment program. All her urine samples tested free from mind-altering substances. She also appeared to begin living the twelve steps and said that she was starting to understand the concept of being responsible and believing in a higher power.

Problem 1.   Client has used mind-altering substances within the last ninety days.

Manifestations.   Positive urinalysis for THC at probation; difficulties with employment.

Goals for Treatment.   Become abstinent within thirty days. Begin to participate in a recovery program. Become gainfully employed.

Objectives	Interventions
Client will abstain from all mind-altering substances.	Client will submit to random urine testing.
Client will identify various ways her life was negatively affected by continued substance use.	Client will attend and participate in all group and individual sessions. She will list and discuss her experiences with substance abuse, noting how her disease progressed along with the negative consequences in her life.
Client will become gainfully employed.	Using classified ads and placement agencies, client will submit three job applications per week.

Review of Treatment Plan for Problem 1. The client entered group therapy after the introduction process. She observed the first session. She submitted and shared a list of ways her life had been unmanageable, as was directed by the counselor, and heard feedback from the group. She attended and participated in all treatment groups and attended at least three self-help meetings per week. She reported for individual sessions with her primary counselor, where she reported her progress on finding employment through a placement agency.

Problem 2. Poor communication skills.

Manifestations. Client does not listen well and sends unclear messages.

Goals for Treatment. Learn how to transmit messages more clearly. Develop and improve listening skills.

Objectives	Interventions
Practice sharing in groups with emphasis on message transmission using "I" statements.	Client will share in every session and receive feedback from counselor and group members. As client listens to group members, she will feedback to various members what she heard from their transmission.
Practice active listening in groups.	

Review of Treatment Plan for Problem 2. Client actively participated in all group sessions. She communicated about herself using "I" statements and received feedback from the group when her statements became unclear. She practiced her listening skills by feeding back to group members what she heard them say. As she continued in treatment, her communication skills improved to the point where she was effectively confrontational with others.

Problem 3. Inability to identify and share feelings appropriately.

Manifestations. Using mind-altering substances to medicate self feelings (demonstrating confusion between thoughts and feelings).

Goal for Treatment. Identify and share feelings appropriately.

Objectives	Interventions
Client will develop a "feeling" vocabulary.	Using the feelings wheel, client will share feelings with counselor and group and receive feedback as needed.
Client will identify her feelings.	Using the feelings wheel, client will keep a daily journal of her feelings and share them with counselor and group.
Client will identify feelings she medicated in the past.	Client will identify feelings she described in her journal that used to be masked by the substance.

Review of Treatment Plan for Problem 3. Client used the feelings wheel and shared openly in group using "I feel" statements. She was receptive to group feedback. She shared her experiences of using thoughts and what she felt at the time. She also shared her feelings journal as instructed. She learned to identify feelings that she previously medicated through substance abuse.

Problem 4. Low self-esteem.

Manifestations. Negative remarks directed at self; lack of goals and no desire to identify her positive attributes.

Goals for Treatment. Identify positive attributes. Set realistic goals.

Objectives	Interventions
Decrease frequency of negative self-statements.	Client will read self-esteem affirmations aloud daily. She will share progress with counselor and groups and discuss statements that she struggles with understanding and accepting.
Use positive remarks about self to build and enhance self-esteem.	Client will listen to feedback from counselor and group.
Create realistic, attainable goals that will build and enhance self-esteem.	Counselor will work with client to establish reachable short-term goals and discuss possible long-term goals.

Review of Treatment Plan for Problem 4. When client shared any negative self remarks in group, she was redirected. This learned behavior eventually decreased. She shared self-esteem statements that she struggled with and heard feedback and insights from the counselor and group. As she received compliments and praise, she began to develop a self-affirmation system. Counselor worked with client to establish some short-term goals (gainful employment, improved communication skills, and a self reward system) and to look at long-term goals (remain abstinent, maintain employment, and return to school).

Problem 5. Serious legal involvement as a result of substance use.

Manifestations. Client is presently on probation for trafficking in cocaine and is facing a new charge that is not drug related.

Goal for Treatment. Learn to live within the confines of the law without further substance use.

Objectives	Interventions
Remain abstinent from all mind-altering substances.	Client will follow all counselor's directions and submit clean urine samples, both in treatment and at probation.
Attend court for pending charge and not go to jail or prison.	Client will share in individual and group sessions how her drug use resulted in legal involvement.
Prevent any further legal involvement.	Client will have legal representation in court along with counselor. She will accept responsibility for actions and present to the court the positive turn made in life.
	Obtain and maintain recovery and live within the confines of the law.

Review of Treatment Plan for Problem 5. Client maintained abstinence, as demonstrated by her clean urinalysis results. She shared in group and individual sessions the relationship between her drug use and her legal involvement. She used her knowledge of this relationship to change her behavior in order to live within the confines of the law.

Discharge Summary. S successfully completed the treatment program without any occurrence of relapse. She worked on her issues and seemed to make progress. She completed all her treatment plan goals. Her prognosis is good as long as she continues to abstain from mind-altering substances, continues to attend self-help meetings regularly, and continues to live the twelve steps with the help of a sponsor.

BEST PRACTICES

Stephens, Roffman, & Curtin (2000) conducted a study comparing brief and extended cognitive-behavioral therapy for marijuana users. Eligibility for inclusion in the Stephens et al. (2000) study required completion of a questionnaire—a self-report measuring perceived acute effects of marijuana intoxication, reasons for wanting to stop using marijuana, drug use, psychiatric symptoms, psychological distress, and sociodemographic characteristics. Cognitive-behavioral therapy for substance abusers focuses on altering environments, thoughts, and actions associated with drugs (Earleywine, 2002). The 291 study participants averaged thirty-four years of age, were mostly male (77 percent), and almost entirely Caucasian (95 percent). Participants were randomly assigned to a delayed-treatment control (DTC) group, an individualized assessment and intervention group (IAI), or a relapse prevention support group (RPSG). The RPSG treatment consisted of fourteen, two-hour group sessions for marijuana cessation using cognitive-behavioral and social support processes. The members of the RPSG were invited to attend an optional four-session support group with a spouse, partner, relative, or close friend. The IAI group treatment consisted of two, ninety-minute individual sessions spaced four weeks apart and concentrated on intervention techniques with motivational interviewing and cognitive-behavioral techniques. The members of the IAI group were invited to bring a spouse, partner, or significant other to the second session.

There were no significant outcome differences at the one-, four-, seven-, thirteen-, or sixteen-month follow-up between the extended cognitive-behavioral treatment (RPSG) and the brief cognitive-behavioral treatment (IAI group). Further, during the first month of follow-up, the IAI group reduced their marijuana use more than the RPSG group did. At the four-month follow-up, the IAI group and the RPSG were using marijuana at 30 percent of their pretreatment rate versus 70 percent for the DTC group. The researchers noted, however, that the generalizability of their study is limited due to the similar sociodemographic characteristics of the participants (Stephens et al., 2000).

In another study, Copeland, Swift, Roffman, and Stephens (2001) conducted a clinical trial in Australia to determine treatment effectiveness of brief cognitive-behavioral therapy (CBT) interventions of varying lengths for cannabis dependence. The cognitive-behavioral interventions (Copeland et al., 2001) for cannabis dependence in the previous year were measured using the Composite International Diagnostic Interview. Marijuana consumption was measured by using an adapted version of the Opiate Treatment Index and the Severity of Dependence Scale (SDS). Participants also completed a questionnaire designed for this study, the Cannabis Problems Questionnaire. The goal of treatment was total abstinence from marijuana, but other outcomes were also assessed. To be eligible for the study, participants had to be at least eighteen years old and express a desire to abstain from cannabis. The 229 participants had been using cannabis at least weekly for a mean of 13.9 years. Each was randomly assigned to a six-session cognitive-behavioral therapy (6CBT) program, a single-session cognitive-behavioral therapy (1CBT) group, or a delayed-treatment control (DTC) group. The 6CBT group sessions were one hour in length each week and included motivational interviewing and relapse prevention. The 1CBT group received a ninety-minute brief introduction to planning strategies for quitting, dealing with cravings, and behavioral self-management.

The twenty-four-week posttreatment follow-up included a urinalysis of cannabis levels to validate participant self-reports. At follow-up, 15.1 percent of the 6CBT group was continuously abstinent, 4.9 percent in the 1CBT group was continuously abstinent, and 0 percent of the DTC group was abstinent. Of those participants who did not remain abstinent, those in the 6CBT intervention group reported a greater overall decrease in the amount of marijuana use than did the control group. Treatment compliance also was associated with decreased dependence and fewer cannabis-related problems. The researchers noted that this study gives further support for the need for effective interventions for cannabis use disorder (Copeland et al., 2001).

A four-year longitudinal study of cannabis use, abuse, and dependence (Sydow et al., 2001) was conducted in Germany to establish the prevalence and patterns of cannabis use among adolescents and young adults. The 2,446 participants were assessed at baseline according to the *DSM-IV* and the Munich version of the Composite International Diagnostic Interview (M-CIDI). Over the four-year study, the youngest sample of respondents, aged fourteen to seventeen years at baseline, had two yearly follow-up interviews. The second and third samples of respondents, aged sixteen to twenty-one and twenty-two to twenty-four years at baseline, had only one follow-up interview, which was completed at the same time as the second post-treatment interview with the youngest respondents.

Of the users fulfilling the *DSM-IV* criteria for cannabis abuse or dependence within the first twelve months of the study, 40 percent still met the criteria for abuse and dependence. Whereas the younger participants (fourteen- to seventeen-year-olds) reported more frequent use of cannabis upon follow-up, the eighteen- to twenty-four-year-old group had reduced their use. In the final follow-up phase of the study, the cumulative lifetime incidence was 47 percent for cannabis use, 5.5 percent for cannabis abuse, and 2.2 percent for cannabis dependence. According to this study, the likelihood of developing cannabis abuse or dependence was low (8 percent), and the natural course of cannabis use was "quite variable" (Sydow et al., 2001, p. 347).

Swift, Hall, & Copeland (1999) conducted a one-year follow-up study on cannabis dependence in Australia and found that the largest predictor of cannabis use and dependence at follow-up was the severity of cannabis use and dependence upon initial assessment. Swift et al. (1999) assessed cannabis dependence using the *ICD-10* dependence scale, the short version of the University of Michigan Composite International Diagnostic Interview (UM-CIDI), and the Severity of Dependence Scale (SDS). At the one-year follow-up, 51 percent were still using cannabis daily, 30 percent were using one to six days a week, and 19 percent were using cannabis less than weekly or not at all. Factors that participants noted as reasons for increased cannabis use were enjoyment (18 percent), availability (25 percent), and stress (29 percent), while reasons noted for decreasing cannabis use were change of life circumstance (20 percent), lack of money (23 percent), and boredom with smoking (35 percent). The researchers noted that remission was much more common than dependence.

Liddle (2001) conducted a clinical trial on adolescent substance abuse to report on the usefulness of multidimensional family therapy in reducing adolescents' drug use and associated problems such as school failure and poor family functioning. Participants were thirteen to eighteen years old and had either used marijuana at least three times a week over the past thirty days or had a single episode of hard drug use within the past thirty days. Alcohol use was not a criterion for participation in the study. To determine the relationship of coping and stress to adolescent marijuana use, Siqueira, Diab, Bodian, & Rolnitzky (2001) asked respondents to rate their marijuana use on a four-point scale: 1 = never tried marijuana; 2 = smoked a few times in the past; 3 = now smoke a few times a week or more; and 4 = used to smoke frequently but quit. In addition, respondents completed the Perceived Stress Scale (PSS) and the Negative Life Events Scale (LES). The coping measures scale used was a Likert scale with forty-seven items assessing eight dimensions of coping. Of the participants, 49 percent used marijuana and alcohol only, and 51 percent were polysubstance users. Participants were assigned to multidimensional family therapy (MDFT), multifamily education intervention (MEI), or adolescent group therapy (AGT).

MDFT included sixteen individual and family sessions emphasizing the developmental-ecological and multiple-systems approaches. MEI emphasized psychoeducational and multifamily interventions, which involved three to four families per group over a sixteen-week period. AGT participants received two individual family sessions, one individual session for history gathering, and five group therapy sessions centered on social skills building. Results at termination indicated that the MDFT group had a significant reduction in drug use (42 percent) as compared to the MEI group (32 percent), and the AGT group (25 percent). Although all three treatment modalities appear to be beneficial, overall the MDFT intervention had the greatest success rate. At the one-year follow-up, MDFT still proved most beneficial in drug use reduction (45 percent); however, the AGT group had the next highest rate of drug reduction (32 percent), followed by the MEI group (26 percent).

Siqueira et al. (2001) found that stress and coping methods were directly related to adolescent marijuana use. Of the 918 adolescents (aged twelve to twenty-one) surveyed, 59 percent were long-term constant users and 18.4 percent were frequent weekly users. Adolescents who had more trouble coping with anger and whose parents had less ability to apply positive coping methods were found to be at significantly higher risk of marijuana use.

In another study, by Bray, Zarkin, Ringwalt, and Qi (2000), marijuana initiation and dropping out of high school were positively correlated. The data from the study's non–nationally representative sample suggest that "an individual who has initiated marijuana use is approximately 2.3 times more likely to drop out of school than an individual who has not initiated marijuana use" (p. 16).

In a review of adolescent substance abuse treatment outcomes, Williams and Chang (2000) found several variables related to positive treatment outcome. Pretreatment variables leading to positive outcomes included lower incidence of substance abuse, peer and parental support, higher school functioning, less conduct disorder, more motivation for treatment, and fewer prior substance abuse treatments. Treatment completion was found to be the most constant variable related to positive treatment outcome. Still, aftercare was related to the most positive treatment outcome at posttreatment. In comparing fifty-three studies on adolescent substance abuse treatment outcome, these researchers found that the average rate of abstinence was 38 percent immediately after treatment and at six-month follow-up, and 32 percent at twelve-month follow-up.

Chacin (1996) pointed out that "women's problems with marijuana are largely unexplored in drug addiction and treatment" (p. 130). She suggested that marijuana is a large factor in women's chemical dependency problems even though the overall rates of marijuana abuse and dependence are lower in women than in men.

Breaking through the denial of having a marijuana problem can be especially difficult for women. Chacin recommended that "recovery services should take into account women's needs for support in coping with addiction-related problems. These include histories of rape, battering and childhood abuse" (p. 167).

In a study (Best et al., 2001) comparing experiences with and attitudes toward Alcoholics Anonymous (AA) and Narcotics Anonymous (NA) among two hundred substance abusers in an inpatient detoxification center, the drug users reported more willingness and positive attitudes toward attending AA/NA inpatient meetings than did the alcohol users. Similarly, the drug users were more likely to report a desire to attend AA/NA meetings upon release from their inpatient treatment. The alcohol users reported a longer history with AA/NA than the drug users.

Substance abuse treatment may be obtained through various settings including the criminal justice system, private counseling, halfway houses, outpatient treatment centers, and residential treatment centers (Office of National Drug Control Policy, 2002b). Regardless of the setting, practitioners and researchers generally agree that the treatment of marijuana problems, should include individual therapy, inpatient hospital stays when needed, increasing the number of sessions, and medications to help with abstinence (Earleywine, 2002).

Overall, individuals with substance use disorders have diverse needs and often require a variety of treatments along a continuum of care. Polcin (2000) suggested that the substance abuse treatment field become aware of and integrate individualized models of abuse treatment relevant to the different needs commonly found among the substance-abusing population. Today, various licensing and supervising agencies require specifically individualized treatment plans. In most agencies, problem checklists are used in combination with a detailed medical history and a biopsychosocial questionnaire. These materials supply not only physical and addictions information but also important symptoms of mental health disorders, family history, and indications of various social issues.

In terms of treatment efficacy, the words of Alan Leshner, director of the National Institute on Drug Abuse, seem most relevant. He believes the treatment of drug abuse and addiction is most effective when practitioners treat the whole person, with the person's environment being a critical aspect of the treatment process. He further comments:

> The clear and unambiguous message from 25 years of scientific research is that drug abuse and addiction are complex, dynamic processes. No aspect will be explained or resolved simply by choosing from a list of either/or options. There are no simple solutions. The correct answer is: "All of the above." (Lasher, 2001, p. 1)

SUMMARY AND FUTURE DIRECTIONS

Marijuana has been used medicinally and recreationally for centuries. Its widespread use started in the East and moved west. Marijuana came to America via Mexico. It grew in popularity during Prohibition, when tea pads rivaled opium dens. It is currently the most widely used illicit drug in the United States.

THC, one of several cannabinoids in marijuana, creates the drug's psychoactive effects. Over the years, marijuana has been cultivated and processed in new ways that increase the amount of THC in the plant, which increases its potency. Government-grown marijuana is not as potent as illicitly grown marijuana due to lower levels of THC.

Research shows that millions of individuals have used marijuana at least once. Its use tends to be most prevalent among young American males. Violence associated with marijuana centers in the selling and trafficking of the drug. In most states, possession of marijuana is a crime.

Treatment intervention options are as diverse as the population that uses marijuana. Most studies indicate the use of various treatment theories including individual sessions, group sessions, family sessions, and relapse prevention groups. It appears that cognitive behavioral therapy is one of the more successful theories. Self-help groups such as Alcoholics Anonymous or Narcotics Anonymous may further the success of the treatment experience.

Steps in the intervention process that are essential for the treatment of all addictive disorders are establishing or maintaining abstinence, stabilizing the client's emotional/mental state, and providing support and education to enhance self-empowerment and self-determination. The treatment experience is the beginning of the recovery process. This process takes place over an extended period, which could be a lifetime. In order to maintain recovery, clients must develop a support network outside of treatment. This is where the importance of the twelve-step program becomes relevant.

As this chapter highlights, there are few recent controlled studies within the adult population of marijuana users and even fewer individualized studies dealing specifically with adolescents. Often the same models for treating other substance-related disorders are used to treat marijuana abuse and dependence. Yet, it is unclear exactly what the similarities and differences are between those individuals who use more than one substance and those who use only marijuana. With the lack of controlled studies specific to marijuana users, the question remains whether the treatment modalities being used need to be restructured to suit more specifically those who use only marijuana or if this particular population can be treated with mainstream treatment modalities.

Regardless, it appears that specialized training of any type in the areas of addictions can improve practitioners' attitudes toward treating this population (Amodeo & Fassler, 2001). Therefore, the importance of professional training in this area can be viewed as critical to the development of the therapeutic relationship and any subsequent interventions. Knowledge of addictions is also important for use in family services, administration, and public policy.

In closing, in terms of formalized intervention, cognitive-behavioral therapy appears to be the most promising for marijuana users. Twelve-step programs that take into account cannabis, such as Marijuana Anonymous, can only enhance an individual's recovery process. More studies are needed, however, to establish outcome effectiveness of standard treatment modalities when working with those who suffer specifically from marijuana abuse and dependence.

References

American Council for Drug Education. (1999). *Basic facts about drugs: Marijuana.* Retrieved March 22, 2002, from http://www.acde.org/common/Marijuana.html

American Psychiatric Association. (2000). *Diagnostic and statistical manual of mental disorders* (4th ed., text rev.). Washington, DC: Author.

Amodeo, M., & Fassler, I. (2001). Training helps social workers with substance-abusing clients. *Brown University Digest of Addiction Theory & Application, 20*(3), 3–5.

Best, D. W., Harris, J. C., Gossop, M., Manning, V. C., Man, L. H., Marshall, J., et al. (2001). Are the twelve steps more acceptable to drug users than to drinkers? *Alcohol Addiction Treatment, 7,* 69–77.

Bray, J. W., Zarkin, G. A., Ringwalt, C., & Qi, J. (2000). The relationship between marijuana initiation and dropping out of high school. *Health Economics, 9,* 9–18.

Chacin, S. (1996). Women's marijuana problems: An overview with implications for outreach, intervention, treatment, and research. *Journal of Chemical Dependency, 6*(12), 129–67.

Copeland, J., Swift, W., Roffman, R., & Stephens, R. (2001). A randomized controlled trial of brief cognitive-behavioral interventions for cannabis use disorder. *Journal of Substance Abuse Treatment, 21*(2), 55–64.

Drug Enforcement Administration. (n.d.). *Drugs of abuse: Marijuana.* Retrieved March 23, 2002, from http://www.usdoj.gov/dea/concern/abuse/chp6/marijuana.htm

Drug Enforcement Administration. (2001, October). *Collective statistics concerning drug use.* Retrieved April 12, 2002, from http//www.dea.gov/stats/drugsurvey.htm

Drug Enforcement Administration. (2002, March). *The latest news forms the nations only single mission, 1*(2). Retrieved April 19, 2002, from http://www.usdoj.gov/dea/pubs/update/030102.html

Earleywine, M. (2002). *Understanding marijuana: A new look at the scientific evidence.* New York: Oxford University Press.

Gledhill-Hoyt, J., Hang, L., Strote, J., & Wechsler, H. (2000). Increased marijuana use and other illicit drugs at U.S. colleges in the 1990s: Results of three national surveys. *Addiction, 95,* 1655–68.

Hall, W., & Solowij, N. (1998). Adverse effects of cannabis. *Lancet, 352,* (9140), 1611–16.

Inaba, D. S., & Cohen, W. E. (2000). *Uppers, downers, all arounders: Physical and mental effects of psychoactive drugs* (4th ed.). Ashland, OR: CNS Publications.

Iversen, L. L. (2000). *The science of marijuana.* New York: Oxford University Press.

Johnston, L. D., O' Malley, P. M., & Bachman, J. G. (2002). *Monitoring the future: National results on adolescent drug use overview of key findings 2001.* University of Michigan Institute for Social Research. Retrieved March 13, 2002, from http//monitoringthefuture.org/pubs/monographs/overview2001.pdf

Lasher, A. (2001, May). When the question is drug abuse and addiction, the answer is "all of the above." *NIDA Notes, 16*(2), 1. Retrieved April 24, 2002, from http://165.112.78.61/NIDA_Notes/NNVol16N2/DirRepVoll6N2.html

Liddle, H. (2001). Multimodal family therapy for adolescent drug abuse: Results of a randomized clinical trial. *American Journal of Drug Abuse, 27*(4), 651–88.

Mao, L., & Oh, Y. (1998). Does marijuana or crack cocaine cause cancer? *Journal of the National Cancer Institute, 90,* 1182–84.

Marijuana: A continuing concern for pediatricians. (1999). *Pediatrics, 104,* 982–85.

Miller, N. S., Gold, M. S., & Smith, D. E. (1997). *Manual of therapeutics for addictions.* New York: Wiley-Liss.

National Academy of Sciences (1999). *Marijuana and medicine: Assessing the science base.* Institute of Medicine. Retrieved April 19, 2002, from http://search.nap.edu/html/marimed/

National Drug Intelligence Center. (2001). *National drug threat assessment 2002: Marijuana.* Retrieved March 13, 2002, from http://www.usdoj.gov/ndic/pubs/716/marijuana.htm

National Drug Intelligence Center. (2003). *National drug threat assessment 2003.* Retrieved November 17, 2003, from http://www.usdoj.gov/ndic/pubs3/3300/marijuana.htm

National Institute on Drug Abuse. (n.d.). *Principles of drug addiction treatment: A research based guide.* Retrieved April 12, 2002, from http://165.112.78.61/podat/PODAT10.html

National Institute on Drug Abuse. (2003). *Marijuana.* Retrieved March 9, 2003, from http://www.nida.nih.gov/Infofax/marijuana.html

Office of National Drug Control Policy. (2002a). *Pulse check trends in drug abuse Winter 98.* Retrieved March 23, 2002, from http://www.whitehousedrugpolicy.gov/publications/drugfact/pulsechk/winter98/tab07.html

Office of National Drug Control Policy. (2002b). *Treatment: Types of treatment.* Retrieved April 12, 2002, from www.whitehousedrugpolicy.gov/treat/treatment.html

Polcin, D. L. (2000). Professional counseling versus specialized programs for alcohol and drug abuse treatment. *Journal of Addictions & Offender Counseling, 21,* 1–11.

Siqueira, L., Diab, M., Bodian, C., & Rolnitzky, L. (2001). The relationship of stress and coping methods to adolescent marijuana use. *Substance Abuse, 22*(3), 157–66.

Stephens, R. S., Roffman, R. A., & Curtin, L. (2000). Comparison of extended versus brief treatments for marijuana use. *Journal of Consulting and Clinical Psychology, 68*(5), 898–908.

Substance Abuse and Mental Health Services Administration. (2001). *Quick statistics: Florida 2000.* Retrieved March 17, 2002, from http://www.dasis.samhsa.gov/webt/quicklink/LF00.htm

Swift, W., Hall, W., & Copeland, J. (1999). One-year follow-up of cannabis dependence among long-term users in Sydney, Australia. *Drug and Alcohol Dependence, 59,* 309–18.

Sydow, K., Roselind, L., Pfister, H., Hofler, M., Sonntag, H., & Wittchen, H. U. (2001). The natural course of cannabis use, abuse, and dependence over four years: A longitudinal community study of adolescents and young adults. *Drug and Alcohol Dependence, 64,* 347–61.

U.S. Department of Justice. (2001). *Notices 2001: Denial of petition.* Retrieved April 13, 2002, from http://www.deadversion.usdoj.gov/fed_regs/notices/2001/fr0418/fr00418b.htm

Williams, R. J., & Chang, S. Y. (2000). A comprehensive and comparative review of adolescent substance abuse treatment outcome. *Clinical Psychology: Science and Practice, 7*(2), 138–66.

Chapter 11

LSD, Ecstasy, and PCP

Sophia F. Dziegielewski and Tracey A. Bersch

THREE OF THE MOST COMMON PSYCHEDELICS OR HALLUCINOGENS ARE lysergic acid diethylamide (LSD), methylenedioxy-methamphetamine (MDMA, or ecstasy), and phencyclidine (PCP). LSD's psychedelic effects were discovered serendipitously in 1947, and abuse reached epidemic proportions in the 1960s. Whether use of LSD and PCP has increased since that time remains controversial; ecstasy use, however, appears to be increasing at a notable rate (Holland, 2001). The primary reason proposed for the possible decrease of LSD and PCP use has been the public's fear of the damage these drugs can cause the individual and the developing infant (American Pregnancy Association, n.d; Office of National Drug Control Policy, 2001b). The same may prove true for ecstasy as public concern about its use continues to grow and the danger it poses becomes the subject of heated controversy.

All three of these substances have stringent legal and regulatory restrictions placed on their manufacture. The Food and Drug Administration (FDA) has classified LSD, ecstasy, and PCP as Schedule I controlled substances, indicating that the drugs have no medical use and a high potential for abuse. As will be discussed in this chapter, this classification remains controversial, particularly for ecstasy.

This chapter discusses these substances and the side effects that can result from misuse. Abuse of these psychedelic drugs is a serious concern—one of the potential side effects is death; however, based on the rarity of this occurrence, individuals can be lulled into believing these substances are not life threatening. Although all of these substances are currently illegal, pilot studies suggest that this view may change in the future, especially in regard to using ecstasy in the treatment of patients with posttraumatic stress disorder or end-stage cancer.

LYSERGIC ACID DIETHYLAMIDE (LSD)

The use of hallucinogens dates back thousands of years, from those found naturally in plants to those synthesized in a laboratory. Lysergic acid diethylamide (LSD) is one of the most potent synthetic hallucinogens. Originally synthesized in

1938 by Albert Hofmann, a chemist who worked for Sandoz Laboratories in Switzerland, LSD's popularity as a recreational drug peaked in the 1960s. LSD is manufactured from lysergic acid, which is found in ergot, a fungus that grows on rye and other grains. It is odorless, colorless, and tasteless and is usually sold after being dosed onto impregnated paper (blotter acid). LSD can also be sold as a pill (microdot), a capsule, or as thin squares of gelatin (windowpanes). On the street, LSD has many names, with some of the most recognizable ones being "acid," "boomers," "electric Kool-Aid," "Lucy in the sky with diamonds," and "yellow sunshine" (Drug Enforcement Administration [DEA], 2003b).

An oral dose of as little as 0.025 mg (or 25 micrograms, equal to a few grains of salt) of LSD is capable of producing rich and vivid hallucinations (DEA, 2003a, 2003b). The average effective oral dose of LSD is from 25 to 80 micrograms, with the effects of higher doses lasting for ten to twelve hours; the user experiences onset of action from LSD within thirty to forty minutes (Perry, 1996). The clinical manifestations of LSD intoxication often include an early stage of nausea, followed forty-five to sixty minutes after dosage by a confused state in which delusions and hallucinations may occur (DEA, 2003c). Some individuals report that they can delay the effect of LSD, at least for a time, with sheer determination to continue their present activity levels or by having a nonintoxicated associate help them to maintain contact with reality.

Many individuals using LSD show evidence of sympathetic stimulation (rapid heart rate, sweating palms, dilated pupils, and cold extremities), mental excitation (nervousness, trembling or spasms, anxiety, euphoria), and inability to relax or sleep. In addition, LSD users may experience subjective feelings of tension, heightened awareness, exhilaration, kaleidoscopic imagery, hilarity, and exultation. An addiction to LSD is considered to be a problem when the user continues its use despite significant substance-related problems (American Psychiatric Association [APA], 2000). When an individual is addicted to LSD, he or she will often rapidly develop a tolerance to the euphoric and psychedelic effects. Once under the influence of LSD, the user may spend hours to days recovering from the effects of most hallucinogens due to the drug's long half-life. Adverse effects include memory impairment, panic reactions ("bad trips"), and the re-experiencing of one or more of the perceptual symptoms that occurred during intoxication ("flashbacks"). Some individuals may manifest dangerous behavioral reactions (e.g., jumping out of a window in the belief that he or she can fly) due to lack of insight and judgment.

Other clinically significant maladaptive behavioral and psychological changes include marked anxiety or depression, difficulty focusing attention, fear of losing one's mind, paranoid ideation, impaired judgment, or impaired social or occupational functioning (American Psychiatric Association, 2000). Physiological symptoms include dilated pupils, tachycardia, sweating, palpitations, blurred vision, tremors, and lack of coordination. When an individual is under the influence of LSD, he or she might experience an intensification of perceptions, depersonalizations, de-realization, illusions, and hallucinations. Hallucinations are usually visual, and the person may report seeing geometric forms, persons, and objects that are not really there. It is common for individuals using any of the psychedelics to report feeling nauseated as the drug wears off. Some users, especially highly suggestible individuals, may also develop increasingly paranoid ideas and experience profound states of terror or ecstasy.

Of all the side effects from LSD use, flashbacks are considered the most dangerous. With flashbacks, images or effects experienced during LSD intoxication recur unexpectedly. These flashbacks can vary in frequency and duration (DEA, 2003c). These flashbacks can present as transient recurrences or disturbances in perception that are reminiscent of those experienced during one or more earlier episodes of substance use. It is difficult to say when or how long after substance use a flashback may occur. These perceptions may occur episodically and may be self-induced or triggered in various ways. The episodes usually abate after several months but can last longer.

LSD, like other hallucinogens, distorts the user's sense of reality, producing images, sounds, and sensations that do not really exist. These hallucinations can be pleasurable and—for some people—even intellectually stimulating, but they can also be disorienting or disturbing and result in a negative emotional experience (a "bad trip"). It is difficult to determine what kind of experience a person will have on LSD because the same person can have very different experiences each time. As with all drugs, but especially with LSD, previous drug experience, expectations, and setting as well as the neurological effects of the drug will shape a user's experience (Cambridge Educational, 2004).

LSD: Prevalence

The 2001 National Household Survey on Drug Abuse found that 320,000 Americans were current LSD users, representing 0.1 percent of the population ages twelve and older; 9 percent of those surveyed indicated using LSD at least once in their lifetime. Of those surveyed between the ages of twelve and seventeen, 3.1 percent reported the use of LSD at least once in their lifetime, whereas 15.3 percent of those surveyed between the ages of eighteen and twenty-five reported similar uses (DEA, 2003c). According to Johnston, O'Malley, and Bachman (2000), who reported data from the 1999 Monitoring the Future survey, the annual prevalence of LSD use among U.S. high school students has remained below 10 percent for the last twenty-five years. This same study reported that the availability of LSD has varied, declining considerably from 1975 to 1983 and then remaining level for a few years; the availability of LSD began a substantial rise after 1986, reaching a peak in 1995, with 53.8 percent of students in grade 12 reporting that LSD was fairly easy to obtain. LSD availability also rose among students in grades 8 and 10 in the early 1990s, reaching a peak in 1995 and 1996. Overall, in 2001, lifetime prevalence of LSD use for students in grades 8, 10, and 12 was 3.4 percent, 6.3 percent, and 10.9 percent, respectively.

One major reason for the increasing use of LSD is that it is now often being used in combination with ecstasy. According to the Office of National Drug Control Policy (2001b), cases of this dangerous combination of LSD and ecstasy use have been reported in Chicago, Denver, Honolulu, Memphis, Miami, Philadelphia, and Washington, DC. Using these drugs in combination is referred to as "candy flip-ping," "trolling," or "flipping." Another dangerous combination is the use of LSD with crack cocaine (DEA, 2003c).

LSD: Special Considerations

LSD is not considered an addictive drug because it does not appear to produce compulsive drug-seeking behavior, as occurs with use of cocaine, amphetamines, heroin, alcohol, and nicotine. Most LSD users voluntarily decrease use or self-initiate abstinence. The individual who uses LSD is also not expected to experience withdrawal when the substance is discontinued (American Psychiatric Association, 2000). However, like many of the addictive drugs, LSD produces tolerance, so some users who take the drug repeatedly must take progressively higher doses to achieve the same state of intoxication. This is an extremely dangerous practice, given the unpredictability of LSD. Tolerance develops rapidly when LSD is used one or more times per day over the course of four days or more.

The most frequent acute medical emergency associated with LSD use is panic episodes, which may persist for up to twenty-four hours (DEA, 2003c). A panic episode, or bad trip, is best managed by giving the person supportive reassurance ("talking down") and, if necessary, administering small doses of anxiolytic drugs. The adverse consequences of chronic LSD use include enhanced risk for psychosis and problems with memory function, problem solving, and abstract thinking. For an individual with a preexisting mental illness that involves psychosis, LSD use can cause intense exacerbation of symptoms, resulting in further loss of contact with reality. Persons who use LSD and experience persistent psychotic states or other psychological disorders require appropriate psychiatric care.

The potentially dangerous psychological changes produced by psychedelic chemicals have sometimes made users hypersuggestible, emotionally labile (unstable), and unusually aware of their own reactions and those of others. Users have also reported distortions in time perception (e.g., time may seem to slow down) and hallucinations. It is possible that use of the drug may affect sensory perceptions, giving the user a feeling of "hearing colors or seeing sounds."

Probably the most significant factor to keep in mind when treating individuals who use LSD is that, although some have suggested that relief is possible, the drug's effects are generally considered uncontrollable because there is no antidote (DEA, 2003c). Therefore, once the person has ingested LSD, treating the symptoms of its use becomes paramount. LSD is a very potent drug, and in some individuals very low doses may induce profound psychological and physiological effects.

Today, one of the most common interventions for assisting individuals intoxicated with some type of hallucinogen is the use of a sedative/hypnotic such as diazepam (Perry, 1996). Because LSD-related flashbacks, like those related to post-traumatic stress disorder, may be associated with excessive, sympathetic nervous activity, some physicians prescribe clonidine. This drug is documented to help reduce sympathetic outflow from the central nervous system, and for the most part, clonidine at low doses is well tolerated, has minimal side effects, and has no recognized potential for abuse (Physicians Desk Reference, 2002). Sometimes simply placing the client in a quiet room, thereby decreasing sensory input, can help to calm the individual (Perry, 1996). In many cases, establishing a verbal rapport with clients makes it possible to "talk them down," eliminating the need for pharmacological intervention.

METHYLENEDIOXY-METHAMPHETAMINE (MDMA, OR ECSTASY)

Use of MDMA, or ecstasy, has become widespread in the United States. Ecstasy is similar to LSD in that both are synthetic. Historically, its use stems from before 1912, when it was administered as a medication to stop bleeding (Holland, 2001). In 1912, ecstasy was synthesized by German chemists and considered for use as an appetite suppressant; however, due to potential side effects, it was not patented. In the 1970s, ecstasy was used in marital counseling, and it was not uncommon for American practitioners to refer to this substance as the "hug drug." These practitioners supported its use, citing ecstasy's unique ability to induce empathy and release buried emotions as being equal to months—if not years—of intensive therapy. Some therapists continued to support the use of ecstasy until 1985, when the DEA restricted its use. This restrictive action was based on the increasing popularity of this substance on college campuses and in dance clubs within the United States. Presently, the use of ecstasy is banned worldwide, with the exception of the Netherlands (Oh, 2000). Since 1985, however, it has been growing in popularity on college campuses and in nightclubs. Currently, the populations using ecstasy most extensively are adolescents and young adults.

Ecstasy is an amphetamine-like drug with hallucinogenic effects that is used illegally as a recreation drug ("FDA Gives Green Light," 2002). This recreational drug can be smoked, snorted, or injected; however, most frequently it is taken in a pill or tablet form. An average dose is 50 to 175 mg, and the psychological effects last two to four hours (MDMA [ecstasy] Effects, 2001). When experimenting with using ecstasy, individuals customarily ingest three tablets or more at one time, referred to as "stacking." Others consume a series of pills within a brief time, referred to as "piggy-backing." Being high from taking ecstasy is labeled "rolling."

Ecstasy's physiological effects are similar to those of a stimulant. They include increased heart rate, blood pressure, and body temperature, dilated pupils, decreased appetite, dry mouth, and occasional teeth grinding or clenching of the jaw. According to Wallace-Wells (2003), "Ecstasy seems to be linked to sudden heart attacks in healthy young people who do not appear to otherwise disposed to heart failure" (p. 14). The psychological effects of ecstasy include feelings of intense intimacy. Although ecstasy is not considered a sexual stimulant, these feelings of intimacy can result in impaired judgment, which could lead to unsafe sexual behaviors. For the most part, this substance has not been connected with any addictive or compulsive use; therefore, with repeated doses, the psychological effects typically become less appealing and the physiological effects become more unpleasant (MDMA [ecstasy] Effects, 2001). As a result, many users increase their dosage. But this practice is ineffective because "the quality of the MDMA experience decreases and the 'loved up effect' of ecstasy wanes with repeated use" (Zergoviannis, Weichers, & Bester, 2003, p. 166).

Today, MDMA is classified as a Schedule I drug—a drug having a high potential for abuse and no accepted medical use. This places ecstasy in the same category as marijuana and heroin. The only exception is when the drug is being used for federally approved research purposes. However, according to Oh (2000), "ecstasy is rivaling cocaine as the second most popular recreation drug—after marijuana—not only among ravers, but also club-goers, college partyers and even, perhaps that nice middle-class couple next door" (p. 44). Ecstasy is considered a widely abused "club drug," a term used for illicit drugs that are primarily synthetic and most prevalent in nightclubs. Some other names used for this particular club drug are XTC, go, disco biscuit, cristal, X, Adam, and hug drug (Office of National Drug Control Policy, 2002).

Because MDMA stimulates the central nervous system and produces mild hallucinatory effects, it has become the most popular club drug at raves . Raves are all-night dance parties driven by loud techno, industrial, or other forms of pulsating music. They also include special effects such as psychedelic lighting, smoke, and fog. Most typically, raves are held in warehouses, clubs, or fields that can accommodate a significant number of people.

The National Drug Intelligence Center (2001)also referred to ecstasy as the most popular drug within the rave culture and noted that this drug is increasingly combined with other substances such as marijuana, ketamine, GHB (gamma hydroxybutyrate), and heroin. Apparently, the pharmacological effects of MDMA provide the "raver" with enhanced sensory perception and the energy to dance throughout the rave. "It has been clearly demonstrated that the consumption of a single 100 mg tablet initiates brain cell death. Combined with the knowledge that all of these drugs are clandestinely produced in unsanitary laboratories which result in uncontrollable purity, the threat to public health and safety is immense."

The intense popularity of ecstasy at raves has resulted in increasing levels of dangerous misuse. According to Oh (2000), MDMA inhibits the body from regulating internal temperatures. Therefore, if users do not consume adequate amounts of water or take breaks from dancing, they may suffer a heat stroke. In turn, a heat stroke can lead to seizures, kidney and liver failure, and possibly death. Furthermore, putting the body into this condition can trigger an excessive release of serotonin, which can cause confusion, difficulty walking, and diarrhea. Also, muscle jerking, shivering, poor control of the heart rate, and blood pressure problems may occur. Under some circumstances, cardiac complications and liver abnormalities have been reported.

Ecstasy: Prevalence

DEA special agents invested approximately 250,000 hours in ecstasy investigations for the 2001 fiscal year alone. According to law enforcement officials, the manufacturing, smuggling, and availability of ecstasy are flourishing. Since January 2000, the DEA has confiscated more than three million doses of ecstasy.

Ecstasy is often used in combination with other drugs, and there has been an increasing trend among teenagers and young professionals to combine it with heroin. If this trend continues, ecstasy could become a "gateway" drug, leading to the consumption of other substances (Office of National Drug Control Policy, 2001a). In addition, ecstasy-related deaths are increasing (Oh, 2000). "According to the Drug Abuse Warning Network (DAWN), hospital emergency departments have seen MDMA cases quadruple over a three-year time span, from 1,143 in 1998 to 2,850 in 1999 to 4,511 in 2000" (DEA, 2001). "A number of deaths have resulted from malignant hyperthermia or idiosyncratic reactions to the drug, but these have been rare" (Boot, McGregor, & Hall, 2000, p. 1818). Because fatal complications of abusing this drug are rare, many individuals consider ecstasy to be a safe drug.

According to the 2000 National Household Survey on Drug Abuse, "more than 6.4 million people 12 years of age and older reported that they had used MDMA at least once in their lifetime. Among 12 year olds and 17 year olds, 2.6% reported using MDMA in their lifetime. 9.7% of 18 to 25 year olds reported MDMA lifetime use" (Office of National Drug Control Policy, 2001a, p. 2).

In a study conducted in the year 2000, the following results prevailed: Among high school students, 8.2 percent of students in grade 12, 5.4 percent of students in grade 10, and 3.1 percent of students in grade 8 stated that they had used MDMA in the past year. Among college students, 13.1 percent had used MDMA at least once in their lifetime. Among young adults ranging in age from nineteen to twenty-eight, 11.6 percent had used MDMA at least once in their lifetime. Reporting ecstasy use within thirty days prior to the survey were 2.5 percent of the college students and 1.9 percent of young adults (Office of National Drug Control Policy, 2002).

According to a national survey conducted by the Partnership for a Drug-Free America (2002), adolescent drug use has stayed constant with the exception of ecstasy consumption. In 2001, ecstasy consumption among the youth increased 20 percent. Stephen J. Pasierb, the president and CEO of the Partnership for a Drug-Free America, states, "Teen experimentation with ecstasy is now equal to or greater than adolescent consumption of cocaine, crack, heroin, LSD and methamphetamine. The rapid rise in ecstasy is strikingly similar to the country's experimentation with cocaine just one generation ago. In many respects, ecstasy has become the rave generation's cocaine" (p. 2).

According to data from 2001, ecstasy use among the adolescent population is rising. Use among eighth-grade students rose from 3.1 percent in 2000 to 3.5 percent in 2001; use among tenth-grade students rose from 5.4 percent to 6.2 percent; and use among twelfth-grade students rose from 8.2 percent to 9.2 percent. In 2001, ecstasy use in the adolescent population of the United States exceeded use of cocaine, LSD, crack, heroin, or methamphetamines (Partnership for a Drug-Free America, 2002). The availability of ecstasy also increased among high school seniors, from 51.4 percent to 61.5 percent. Dr. Glen Hanson, acting director of the National Institute of Drug Abuse, noted that the concerted effort to educate adolescents on the health risks of ecstasy and other drugs will contribute to future reductions in the use of drugs (U.S. Department of Health and Human Services, 2001).

Ecstasy: Controlled Studies Suggest Cognitive Impairment

Rodgers (2000) conducted a study to determine whether recreational use of ecstasy impairs cognitive performance—in particular, memory and attention span. Because users often combine ecstasy with cannabis, the study also explored the effects of cannabis use on cognitive performance. The study examined the cognitive functioning of three groups: fifteen regular users of ecstasy, fifteen regular users of cannabis who had never taken ecstasy, and fifteen control subjects who had never taken any illicit drugs. The Weschler Memory Scale (Revised) and a computerized reaction time task were administered to the participants. In addition, the Cognitive Failure Questionnaire was distributed to assess for cognitive slips. The results demonstrated significant impairment for both ecstasy and cannabis users on measures of verbal memory. On measures of delayed memory, the ecstasy users were found to have significant impairment in performance in contrast to the cannabis group and control group. Overall, there were no differences found in subjective ratings of cognitive failures between any of the three groups. These study results support the hypothesis that long-term neuropsychological effects are associated with ecstasy use.

Croft, Mackay, Mills, and Gruzelier (2001) further explained the association of ecstasy and cannabis in cognitive impairment. Three subject groups—nonusers (control group), cannabis users, and cannabis and ecstasy users—were evaluated on a series of neuropsychological tests. The results demonstrated that the ecstasy and cannabis group performed inadequately in comparison to the control group on the tests of memory, learning, word fluency, processing speed, and manual dexterity. In the area of processing speed, a covariate analysis revealed that deficits in the subjects' processing speed were more closely related to cannabis use than to ecstasy use. The results of this study suggest that cannabis constitutes a confounding variable, making it difficult to tell exactly how ecstasy relates to cognitive impairment. The study also noted that reports of cognitive impairment in persons who use ecstasy might coincide with the use of cannabis (Croft et al., 2001).

Wareing, Fisk, and Murphy (2000) also addressed the impairment of cognitive processing in relation to ecstasy use. Their study was executed to establish whether current and past users of ecstasy displayed impairments in fundamental levels of cognitive processing consisting of working memory functioning, information processing speed, anxiety, and arousal. The participants included ten nonusers, ten current users, and ten previous users. The participants were tested on word span, visual memory, and verbal fluency. The experiment also included random letter–generating tasks and an information processing speed measure. The results of this study indicated that people who use ecstasy exhibit an inability to deal with high levels of cognitive demand. Also, it appeared that current users and previous users were both cognitively impaired by the substance, even after abstinence.

Zanakis and Young (2001) also studied impairments in the memory of ecstasy users. This study differs from those mentioned previously in that the participants were examined over the course of a year. The fifteen participants in this longitudinal study were asked to maintain abstinence from drugs for the two weeks prior to being examined. The neuropsychological measures used in this particular study were the Weschler Adult Intelligence Scale III (WAIS-III) Vocabulary Block Design subtests and the Rivermead Behavior Memory Test (RBMT). The researchers used a paired sample t test that demonstrated a large decline effect in terms of total RBMT score. The results of this study indicated a significant relationship in terms of the participants' performance on the WAIS-III vocabulary subtests and frequency of ecstasy use. The study concluded that frequent use of ecstasy could result in the deterioration of both immediate and delayed memory recall.

Morgan (2001) conducted a study to determine which effects, including psychopathology, elevated behavioral impulsivity, and persistent impairment of memory performance, were still observed after a minimum of six months abstinence from ecstasy use. Participants included eighteen current heavy recreational ecstasy users, fifteen heavy recreational ecstasy users who had not used ecstasy for at least six months but were still using other illicit drugs, sixteen polydrug participants who had never used ecstasy but used other drugs, and fifteen drug-naive control subjects. All the candidates were mandated to refrain from using alcohol for ten hours, cannabis for at least twenty-four hours, and any other illicit drugs for at least one week prior to participating in this experiment. The results of this study established that ecstasy users, including both current and past users, exhibited elevated psychopathology and behavioral impulsivity in comparison to the polydrug users and the drug-naive control group. All the participants who used ecstasy either in the past or presently also displayed impaired working memory and verbal recall performance in comparison to the control group. Individuals who used ecstasy in the past were the only group that demonstrated impaired verbal recall relative to polydrug users. The researchers concluded that "selective impairments of neurological performance associated with regular ecstasy use are not reversed by prolonged abstinence" (p. 1).

According to Gamma (2001), "the most controversial area of research with MDMA . . . involves the issue of MDMA neurotoxicity and the possibility of functional or behavioral consequences that may result from such neurotoxicity, if it does indeed occur at the dose levels actually consumed" (p. 1). As a contribution to the research efforts of the Multidisciplinary Association for Psychedelic Studies (MAPS), Gamma reviewed different studies comparing memory functions of poly-drug users who self-administered ecstasy with those who did not use ecstasy. Gamma concluded that there is a likelihood that regular use of ecstasy may have a harmful effect on certain areas of memory functioning.

The studies mentioned here all support a connection between the use of ec-stasy and cognitive decline such as memory impairment that should be taken into account when planning subsequent intervention.

Ecstasy Use in Clinical Treatment

Historically, ecstasy has no medical purpose or use, but this may be changing. A shift may be occurring because of efforts such as those of Rick Doblin, the founder and director of MAPS. This nonprofit research and educational organiza-tion supports the use of ecstasy and other psychedelic drugs for therapy (Doblin, 2001). MAPS applied for government approval to assist in conducting studies on ec-stasy's potential use for clinical treatment. In November 2001 and the spring of 2004, the U.S. Food and Drug Administration approved a MAPS pilot study on ec-stasy used as treatment in posttraumatic stress disorder.

This approval caught the attention of many in the field of addiction treatment. The director of the National Institute of Drug Abuse, Alan I. Leshner, responded to the news by telling the *Wall Street Journal*, "I know of no evidence in the scientific literature that demonstrates the efficacy of ecstasy for any clinical indication. We don't give drugs of abuse to naïve subjects except under extraordinary circum-stances" ("FDA Gives Green Light," 2001, p. 1). Yet studies of this nature could lead to using ecstasy as a means to better treatment for clients suffering from chronic PTSD.

Another projected area of study is the use of ecstasy to modify the physical pain and psychological distress of patients in the final stages of cancer, determining whether using ecstasy as an analgesic for the pain associated with end-stage cancer or other terminal illnesses can stimulate a person's immune system in a safe and effective manner (Grob, 1995).

Ecstasy: Case Examples

The following two case examples from a study of MDMA use in therapeutic set-tings (Greer & Tolbert, 1998) highlight the use of ecstasy for medical purposes. The first case involved a man in his early seventies who was among the longest-lived survivors of multiple myeloma (a cancerous condition of the bone marrow). The goals of his MDMA treatment sessions were to help him deal with the pain he was experiencing and to help him acclimate to his lifestyle changes. In his elated state, he became free of pain. This was the first time he had been free of pain since his most recent relapse of myeloma. Two weeks after his session, the pain recurred, but he was able to cope by eliciting to some extent the pain-free state he experienced in his MDMA therapy sessions. He continued with MDMA therapy sessions over the subsequent nine months and reported continued satisfaction in dealing with his pain.

The second case involved a woman in her mid-thirties who was the child of two Holocaust survivors. She was suffering from anxiety and wanted to increase her awareness and personal expansion by participating in the MDMA therapy sessions. Initially her feelings of happiness while in the MDMA-induced state were intruded upon by disturbing thoughts and fears associated with concentration camps. She was able to recognize that her emotional pain and many aspects of her life were affected by the Holocaust. The use of ecstasy gave her a better understanding of her emotions, and she reported, "I am a different person."

LSD AND ECSTASY: BEST PRACTICES

Acute interventions should include supportive, dynamic, behavioral, cognitive, and relaxation therapies; these methods are often used in combination with long-term antidepressant medications. Clients who suffer from this type of addictive disorder will need significant support, and often these individuals have very limited tolerance for anxiety and depression. In intervention, the emphasis should be on supporting recovery, attending twelve-step meetings, and participating in other self-help and group therapies. Supportive interventions that focus on the development of insight need to be carefully evaluated because these types of treatments may increase anxiety and, thereby, inadvertently trigger relapse. When psychotherapy is required, clients should be referred to addictions specialists or recovery-oriented psychotherapists who know about these synthetic psychedelics and hallucinogens and are aware of the effects that these substances can have on the body. Practitioners need to make every attempt to help define reality for the client, making it clear that the client's hallucinations are from the drug and that these perceptions are not real.

PHENCYCLIDINE (PCP)

In the 1950s, phencyclidine (PCP) was investigated as an anesthetic. However, because patients experienced delirium, development of PCP for human use was discontinued (Perry, 1996). This gave rise to increased interest in this medication as a veterinary anesthetic (called Semylan), but in 1978, due to considerable abuse, its use was once again discontinued (Golden, Sokol, & Rubin, 1980).

PCP, known most commonly as "angel dust," is available in its purest form as a white, crystal-like powder or as a tablet or capsule. Some other common names for PCP include "peace pill," "super weed," "super grass," "killer weed," "embalming fluid," "KJ," "elephant tranquilizer," and "rocket fuel." PCP is also sold as a leaf mixture, rock crystal, and liquid; it is commonly applied to a leafy material such as parsley, mint, or oregano and smoked. PCP remains an important drug of abuse in some metropolitan areas, and among certain sociodemographic groups, because it can be taken alone or with other illicit drugs such as marijuana ("primos," "wac," "zoom") or cocaine ("space base," "space cadet," "tragic magic"). A new trend for PCP use involves marijuana cigarettes, marijuana-laced cigars, or tobacco cigarettes/cigars soaked in embalming fluid that is laced with PCP, referred to as "fry" (Elwood, 1998). This type of polysubstance abuse further complicates efforts to identify the effects of PCP from studies of clinical populations and to describe how to best address this drug in treatment.

PCP: Prevalence

In the late 1980s and early 1990s, the widespread use of crack cocaine helped to reduce the demand for PCP. In the late 1990s, PCP made a comeback. By 1997, an estimated 6.5 million people (3 percent of the surveyed population) reported having used PCP, and 369,000 people (0.2 percent) reported using PCP in the past year (Drug Test Center, n.d.). Between 1996 and 1997, no statistically significant differences were found for any age group for lifetime, past year, and past month use of PCP. Lifetime PCP use was reported about equally as often by twenty-six- to thirty-four-year olds and by those thirty-five or older (3 percent), and least often by youths ages twelve to seventeen (1 percent). In terms of gender, for individuals ages thirty-five or older, males were significantly more likely than their female counterparts to report having used PCP.

Johnston et al. (2000), reporting information from the 1999 Monitoring the Future survey, found that prevalence of lifetime use was around 14 percent among high school seniors and young adults eighteen to twenty-five years old, and prevalence of recent use (within the past thirty days) was 2.4 percent for high school seniors. Johnston and colleagues reported that the increased use of PCP was associated with the growing use of marijuana cigarettes and marijuana-laced cigars laced with PCP. At the same time, Los Angeles reported PCP-sprayed tobacco, parsley, and marijuana, and Chicago reported the use of "sherm sticks" (cigarettes dipped in PCP) and "happy sticks" (home-rolled marijuana or tobacco cigarettes sprayed with PCP). PCP was known on the street as "water" (National Institute on Drug Abuse [NIDA], n.d.). PCP can be sprinkled on mint or parsley leaves and sold by the bag, or dealers may allow individuals to dip a cigarette into a small container of PCP-laced embalming fluid.

According to the National Institute on Drug Abuse, data from the 2002 Monitoring the Future survey showed that the percentage of high school seniors who had used PCP remained stable at 3.1 percent in 2002, and past-year use remained stable at 1.1 percent. PCP use within the past month among students in grade 12 has declined significantly in the last few years, from 1.0 percent in 1998 to 0.4 percent in 2002. PCP mentions in emergency departments increased 28 percent from 1995 to 2002. There was a 42 percent increase from the 5,404 mentions in 2000 to the 7,648 mentions in 2002. There were significant increases in PCP mentions in

Washington, DC; Newark; Philadelphia; Baltimore; and Dallas. Chicago, however, had a decrease in mentions of PCP, declining 48 percent from 874 in 2001 to 459 in 2002 (NIDA, n.d.).

Because PCP can be made easily and inexpensively in the lab, it has gained popularity as a means of boosting the effects of other drugs (Strauss, Mondanlou, & Bosu, 1981). For example, illegal manufacturers and dealers have been mixing PCP with ecstasy, thereby improving their ability to increase the potency of these substances and yet lower the cost (Smalley & Rosenberg, 2002). Today, almost all of the PCP on the illicit market in the United States is produced in illegal laboratories.

Similar to LSD and ecstasy addictions, addiction to phencyclidine (PCP) and the less potent but similarly acting compounds such as ketamine, cyclohexamine, and dizocilpine is indicated by the individual's continued use of the substance despite substance-related problems. After smoking PCP or taking it orally or intravenously, individuals can become belligerent, assaultive, impulsive, and unpredictable. Lower doses of these substances can produce vertigo, ataxia, nystagmus, mild hypertension, abnormal involuntary movements, slurred speech, nausea, weakness, slowed reaction times, euphoria, or affective dulling or lack of concern. With use there is often a great deal of disorganized thinking, and when this is coupled with difficulties in sensory perception, a loss of reality can occur. When PCP is taken in higher doses, amnesia and coma, seizures and respiratory suppression can result. Many times, individuals using this substance will also use other substances, especially cocaine, alcohol, and the amphetamines.

PCP: Best Practices

Assisting the individual abusing PCP is difficult, especially when recognizing the potential for PCP overdose, because the client's initial symptoms may suggest an acute schizophrenic reaction. Confirmation of PCP use is possible by determination of PCP levels in serum or urine. (Large quantities of PCP remain in urine for one to five days following high-dosage PCP intake.) PCP overdose requires prompt life-support measures, including treatment of coma, convulsions, and respiratory depression in a hospital intensive care unit. There is no specific antidote or antagonist for PCP, though excretion of PCP from the body can be enhanced by acidification of urine and gastric lavage. If not carefully medically evaluated, death from PCP overdose can occur (Perry, 1996).

Overall, acute psychosis associated with PCP use should be considered a psychiatric emergency because patients may be at high risk for suicide or extreme violence toward others. Chronic PCP use has been shown to induce insomnia, anorexia, severe social and behavioral changes, and psychotic episodes. Many clinicians recommend sensory isolation to treat the behavioral effects while observing medical complications. Diminished psychotic activity has been demonstrated after a client is secluded in a quiet and dimly lit room (Perry, 1996).

Acute PCP intoxication can be one of the most challenging toxicological emergencies for the physician because the client may be experiencing a myriad of reactions to the drug, ranging from a having a bad trip to seizures and coma. For a client admitted to the inpatient setting, it is critical that the medical professionals be made aware of the potential problem so that they can evaluate and stabilize the client's airway, breathing, and circulation (ABCs). Because there is a potential for unpredictable client behavior, healthcare providers should protect themselves and the client from harm. Therefore, physical and chemical restraints may be necessary. According to Graham (2000), when a moderate amount of PCP is used, it causes the user to feel detached, distant, and estranged from his or her surroundings. Although the client may also experience numbness, slurred speech, and loss of coordination, these symptoms could be accompanied by displays of strength and unpredictable excitable energy. In addition, a blank stare, rapid and involuntary eye movements, and exaggerated gait are the more observable effects. Auditory hallucinations, distortion, severe mood disorders, and amnesia may occur. In some clients, acute anxiety, paranoia, hostility, and a feeling of impending doom may be observed (Perry, 1996). PCP produces many effects similar to those produced by classical depressant drugs, such as barbiturates, benzodiazepines, and ethanol. These include problems with motor coordination and muscle relaxation, anticonvulsant effects, and enhancement of the toxic, anesthetic, and behavioral effects of depressant drugs (Perry, 1996).

To date, little data on clinical trials and the treatment of PCP abuse/dependence are available. Most published studies describe psychiatric/psychosocial treatment methods such as outpatient group therapy (cognitive therapy and behavior modification) and long-term residential treatment, primarily with adolescents and young adults. Clinical experience and the available outcome data suggest that current treatment methods tend to have low long-term success rates. Even fewer data are available on pharmacological treatment of PCP abuse/dependence.

SUMMARY AND FUTURE DIRECTIONS

One of the issues inhibiting research on LSD, PCP, and, in particular, ecstasy is that there are serious side effects associated with these drugs, although there are no definitive determinations as to whether there are any long-term medical illnesses associated with using them. For example, some believe ecstasy causes memory loss and reduces one's ability to concentrate, whereas others report it to be a more benign drug. For the most part, given the conflicting statements in the professional literature, the long-term effects of all the psychedelics remain disputable. To end this debate, more controlled research is needed.

To address specific changes in memory, Gamma (2001) suggested a study design that would be useful in obtaining information about the effects of multiple doses of ecstasy on memory. The design entails administering memory tests to hundreds of young adults who have never taken ecstasy but have considered taking this substance in the future. The participants would be identified as at risk and be administered memory tests to obtain a baseline of their memory performance. After three to five years, these same individuals would be tested again. Each participant would be required to identify when they first consumed ecstasy, and their new memory test scores would be compared to their baseline scores.

From an ethical standpoint, it is difficult to design better controlled studies on the hallucinogens. The fear that hallucinogen use puts study participants at some level of risk for memory impairment makes voluntary implementation of such a study nearly impossible. Yet, Gamma (2001) predicts that people identified as being at risk for use will probably use these substances anyway, disregarding the warnings published by government entities.

Thus far, the evidence supporting the addictiveness of these substances is also limited. Current information on the effects of repeated use does not support the existence of an intense desire to use, as is found with repeated use of other substances such as heroin. If such an effect does occur, it is still questionable whether that would promote violent crime, given that these hallucinogens can costas little as seven dollars a pill.

Regardless, hallucinogen use is currently illegal. Generally, it is assumed that these substances have no medical purpose, yet the studies related to the therapeutic value of ecstasy are particularly interesting. Using these substances in a controlled setting can changes in the public's perception of hallucinogens. If these pilot studies yield favorable results, there is great potential that ecstasy could be openly recognized for medicinal purposes and thereby become the next prescribed medication in the treatment of posttraumatic stress disorder and end-stage cancer.

References

American Pregnancy Association. (n.d.). *Using illegal street drugs during pregnancy.* Retrieved November 9, 2003, from http://www.americanpregnancy.org/pregnancyhealth/illegal drugs.html

American Psychiatric Association. (2000). *Diagnostic and statistical manual of mental disorders* (4th ed., text rev.). Washington, DC: Author.

Boot, B. P., McGregor, I. S., & Hall, W. (2000). MDMA (ecstasy) neurotoxicity: Assessing and communicating the risks. *Lancet, 355,* 1818.

Cambridge Educational (Producer). (2004). *Drug uses and abuses: Psychedelics and hallucinogens* [Video]. Lawrenceville, NJ: Author.

Croft, R. J., Mackay, A. J., Mills, A. T. D., & Gruzelier, J. H. G. (2001). The relative contributions of ecstasy and cannabis on cognitive impairment. *Psychopharmacology, 153*(3), 373–79.

Doblin, R. (2001). A clinical plan for MDMA (ecstasy) in the treatment of post-traumatic stress disorder (PTSD): Partnering with the FDA. *Journal of Psychoactive Drugs, 34*(2), 185–94. Retrieved September 2, 2003, from http://www.maps.org/research/mdmaplan.html

Drug Enforcement Administration. (2003a). *LSD: The drug.* Retrieved January 4, 2004, from www.usdoj.gov/dea/pubs/lsd/lsd-4.htm

Drug Enforcement Administration. (2003b). *LSD: Related street terminology.* Retrieved January 4, 2004, from www.usdoj.gov/dea/pubs/lsd/lsd-4.htm

Drug Enforcement Administration. (2003c). *LSD: Use and effects.* Retrieved January 4, 2004, from www.usdoj.gov/dea/pubs/lsd/lsd-4.htm

Drug Test Center. (n.d.). *Phencyclidine (PCP) and related drugs.* Retrieved January 16, 2003, from http://www.drugtestcenter.com

Elwood, W. N. (1998). *"Fry": A study of adolescents' use of embalming fluid with marijuana and tobacco* (TCADA Research Brief). Retrieved January 14, 2003, from http://www.tcada.state.tx.us/research/populations/fry.pdf

FDA gives green light to ecstasy research. (2002). *Nursing, 32*, 1.

Gamma, A. (2001). *Does ecstasy cause memory deficits? A review of studies of memory function in ecstasy users.* Retrieved September 3, 2003, from http://www.maps.org/research/mdma/mdmamemory.html

Golden, N. L., Sokol, R. J., & Rubin, I. L. (1980). Angel dust: Possible effects on the fetus. *Pediatrics*, 65(1), 18–20.

Graham, S. (2000). *Toxicity: Phencyclidine.* Retrieved January 14, 2003, from http://www.emedicine.com/emerg/topic420.htm

Greer, G. R., & Tolbert, R. (1998). A method of conducting therapeutic sessions with MDMA. *Journal of Psychoactive Drugs, 30*(4), 371–79.

Grob, C. S. (1995). *A dose/response human pilot study: Safety and efficacy of methylene-dioxymethamphetamine (MDMA) in modification of physical pain and psychological distress in end-stage cancer patients.* Torrence, CA: Harbor-UCLA Medical Center.

Holland, J. (2001). MDMA myths and rumors dispelled. In J. Holland (Ed.), *Ecstasy: The complete guide* (pp. 54–57). Washington, DC: Helderf.

Johnston, L. D., O'Malley, P. M., & Bachman J. G. (2000). *The Monitoring the Future national survey results on adolescent drug use: Overview of key findings 1999.* Bethesda, MD: National Institute on Drug Abuse. Retrieved January 15, 2003, from http://www.monitoringthefuture.org/pubs.html

MDMA (ecstasy) effects. (2001). *Harvard Mental Health Letter, 18*, 1.

Morgan, M. J. (2001). Memory deficits associated with recreational use of "ecstasy" (MDMA). *Psychopharmacology, 141*, 30–36.

National Drug Intelligence Center. (2001). *National drug threat assessment 2002.* Retrieved September 3, 2003, from http://www.usdoj.gov/ndic/pubs/716/mdma.html

National Institute on Drug Abuse. (n.d.). *InfoFacts: PCP (phencyclidine).* Retrieved November 23, 2003, from http://165.112.78.61/infofax/pcp.html

Office of National Drug Control Policy. (2001a). *1999 America's drug use profile.* Washington, DC: Author. Retrieved November 21, 2003, from http://www.whitehousedrugpolicy.gov/publications/policy/ndcs01/chap2.html

Office of National Drug Control Policy. (2001b, November). *Pulse check: Trends in drug abuse.* Retrieved January 13, 2003, from www.whitehousedrugpolicy.gov/publications/drugfact/pulsechk/fall2001/club.html

Office of National Drug Control Policy. (2002, April). *Drug facts.* Washington, DC: Author. Retrieved January 4, 2004, from http://www.whitehousedrugpolicy.gov/publications/

Oh, S. (2000). The dark side of ecstasy. *Maclean's, 113*, 17.

Partnership for a Drug-Free America. (2002). *National survey: Ecstasy use continues rising among teens.* Washington, DC: Author. Retrieved January 4, 2004, from http://www.drugfreeamerica.org/Templates/pats_2002

Perry, P. (1996). *Phencyclidine intoxication. Clinical psychopharmacology seminar.* Retrieved September 3, 2003, from http://www.vh.org/adult/provider/psychiatry/CPS/29.html

Physicians' desk reference (56th ed.). (2002). Montvale, NJ: Medical Economics.

Rodgers, J. (2000). Cognitive performance amongst recreational users of ecstasy. *Psychopharmacology, 151*(1), 19–24.

Smalley, S., & Rosenberg, D. (2002, July 22). I felt like I wanted to hurt people: Emergency rooms report the violent return of PCP. *Newsweek*, p. 32. Retrieved January 4, 2004, from www.newsweek.com

Strauss, A. A., Modanlou, H. D., & Bosu, S. K. (1981). Neonatal manifestations of maternal phencyclidine (PCP) abuse. *Pediatrics*, 68(4), 550–52.

U.S. Department of Health and Human Services. (2001). *Monitoring the Future survey released: Smoking among teenagers decreases sharply and increase in ecstasy slows*. Washington, DC: National Institute of Drug Abuse.

Wallace-Wells, B. (2003). The agony of ecstasy. *Washington Monthly, 31*, 14–20.

Wareing, M., Fisk, J. E., & Murphy, J. E. (2000). Working memory deficits in current and previous users of MDMA (ecstasy). *British Journal of Psychology, 91*, 181–88.

Zanakis, K. K., & Young, D. A. (2001). Memory impairment in abstinent MDMA ("ecstasy") users: A longitudinal investigation. *Neurology, 56*, 966–69.

Zergoviannis, F. H., Weichers, E., & Bester, G. (2003). The "E" in rave: A profile of young ecstasy (MDMA) users. *South African Journal of Psychology, 33*, 162–70.

Chapter 12

Inhalants

Ilene J. VanGilder, Cheryl Green, and Sophia F. Dziegielewski

INHALANTS ARE USUALLY LIQUIDS FROM WHICH FUMES OR GASES CAN BE inhaled. Examples of products that can be used as inhalants include many household products such as correction fluid, glue, hair or deodorant sprays, felt-tip markers, and varnish. Although getting access to these products is easy, the abuse of inhalants can have devastating effects, including brain damage and death. Inhalant abuse is widespread among children and young adults in the United States. Inhalants are most commonly abused by those ages twelve to fourteen; an estimated 20 percent of all eighth graders in the United States have abused inhalants at least once (Gorny, 1994). Inhalants have been officially recognized as "gateway" drugs, meaning that their use has been documented as leading to the use of other substances of abuse.

This chapter provides an overview of the types and effects of inhalants as well as a review of the characteristics of users and the prevalence of use. A case example illustrates application of the multiaxial diagnostic assessment to inhalant abuse, and a treatment plan is suggested. Because the research literature provides little information on specific treatment approaches for abuse of inhalants, this chapter will explore potential options for more specialized interventions in this area.

THE HISTORY OF INHALANT ABUSE

The abuse of inhalants in the United States has been documented since the 1800s, when doctors and dentists who used ether and chloroform as anesthetics in their practices commonly abused these gases. The first mention in the research literature of children abusing inhalants was in the early 1950s—a case of two boys sniffing gasoline fumes to achieve intoxication (Gorny, 1994). Since the 1980s, research efforts have improved as the rate of inhalant abuse among children has increased, and there is hope that researchers will soon gain a better understanding of this type of substance abuse and identify implications for treatment.

The consensus in the literature is that there are three types of abusable inhalants: volatile solvents, aerosols, and nitrites (see table 8). Volatile solvents are

Table 8: Types of Inhalants

Volatile solvents	Aerosols	Nitrites
Gasoline	Spray paint	Amyl nitrite
Paint	Hair spray	("amies," "poppers," "snappers")
Paint thinner	Cooking spray	Butyl nitrite
Nail polish	Spray adhesive	("rush," "locker room," "bang,"
Nail polish remover	Shoe polish spray	"bolt," "bullet," "climax")
Glue	Underarm deodorant	Nitrous oxide
Lighter fluid		("laughing gas," "whippets")
Correction fluid		
Dry cleaning fluid		
Cleaning solutions		
Antifreeze		
Kerosene		
Oil		
Rubber cement		
Magic markers		
Superglue		
Rubbing alcohol		

Sources: Gorny (1994); Trotter, Rolf, & Baldwin (1997).

found in many household and industrial products. These are readily available to children in most homes and include chemicals such as gasoline, paint thinner, nail polish remover, and glue. (The term *volatile* means that these substances evaporate at room temperature and therefore emit fumes.) Aerosol products are essentially volatile solvents in a spray can form, such as spray paint and hair spray. The category of nitrites includes amyl and butyl nitrite and nitrous oxide ("laughing gas"). Amyl nitrate has been used in the past as a prescription drug for cardiac conditions, and butyl nitrite is a substance marketed as a commercial room deodorizer (Brouette & Anton, 2001; Gorny, 1994; Kurtzman, Otsuka, & Wahl, 2001; Stimmel, 2002).

Gorny (1994) estimates that there are more than seven hundred commonly available household substances that have been identified as abusable inhalants. Most of these products are legal, inexpensive, and common in most homes, which make them readily accessible to children. Only one product, amyl nitrite, must be obtained with a doctor's prescription. The ease of access and the wide variety of these products make this type of substance abuse unique. According to the American Academy of Pediatricians (1996), forty states have laws prohibiting the sale or use of inhalants to minors, but these laws are extremely difficult to enforce. The deterrence of inhalant abuse requires education about the signs of use and harmful effects addressed to all levels—children, parents, teachers, physicians, community leaders, and social service professionals.

PSYCHOPHYSIOLOGICAL EFFECTS

There are various terms used by abusers for the methods of introducing inhalants into the body, including "sniffing," "huffing" and "bagging." Volatile substances such as gasoline can be inhaled directly from a container, such as a gas can, or the substance may be poured into a soda can or cup of some kind. Aerosols are generally sprayed into a plastic or paper bag, and the fumes are inhaled through the nose or mouth from the bag. Some products can be poured onto a rag, from which the fumes are breathed in through the nose or mouth. This method allows for greater concentrations of the substance to be inhaled at one time (Kurtzman et al., 2001). The effects of inhalants occur relatively quickly, with euphoria resulting in minutes. The user will repeat inhalation of the toxic substances sometimes fifteen to twenty times within a one- to two-hour period.

Initially after inhalant use, the user may appear to be intoxicated, acting silly and giddy, and demonstrating disorientation, an unsteady gait, and uncoordinated movements. He or she may appear disheveled, and there often will be a conspicuous smell of the substance used on his or her breath or clothing. There may be a rash around the mouth or nose, with dry, cracked skin and possibly flecks of paint on the face. His or her eyes may appear irritated, and the pupils may be dilated. Typically there is a loss of appetite and weight loss among chronic users. The user may experience visual hallucinations and demonstrate delusional behavior, including irrational speech and uncontrollable, aggressive behavior. As the euphoric state progresses, drowsiness will set in, inhibiting further inhalant use. After the effect of the inhalant has worn off, there may be headaches and nausea, with mood swings including sudden, angry outbursts and depression.

According to the National Institute on Drug Abuse (NIDA; n.d.), solvents and aerosols containing solvents act primarily as depressants to the central nervous system, and essentially alter a person's moods. The solvent toluene, found in airplane glue and other products, is said to be the most damaging to the central nervous system (Kurtzman et al., 2001). Among inhalant users, silver and gold spray paint is preferred over colored paint because of the higher concentrations of toluene in these products. Nitrites, which are more commonly used by adults, dilate blood vessels and relax muscles, resulting in purposeful sexual enhancement among inhalant users. (NIDA, 2002).

Chronic use of inhalants may lead to brain damage and result in dementia. The International Institute for Inhalant Abuse estimates that chronic inhalant users may cause damage that can directly decrease their intelligence quotient (IQ) scores. Other organs of the body are also affected by chronic inhalant use. Possible complications include cardiac arrhythmias, hepatitis and liver damage, kidney damage, and hearing and visual impairments. Use of certain inhalants can lead to bone marrow damage and even leukemia (Kurtzman et al., 2001). Depending on the type of brain damage that occurs, some inhalant users may experience partial or permanent loss of muscle control and spasticity. Damage to the cerebral cortex and the cerebellum can be significant, resulting in personality changes, memory impairment, hallucinations, loss of coordination, and slurred speech (Office of National Drug Control Policy, 2002).

A serious concern for abusers of aerosols is a condition known as Sudden Sniffing Death (SSD), which may result in immediate death at even the first use. A component of aerosol products apparently causes a decrease in available oxygen in the body. If the user becomes startled or engages in sudden physical activity while oxygen deprived, he or she may suffer cardiac arrest. When this occurs, death can happen within minutes (Office of National Drug Control Policy, 2002).

DEMOGRAPHICS OF USERS AND PREVALENCE OF USE

Inhalant users are most commonly Caucasian males between the ages of twelve and fourteen, typically of lower socioeconomic levels. Various researchers have shown that there is increased likelihood of inhalant abuse in dysfunctional families with aggressive and hostile interactions among family members. Inhalant users are also more likely to be involved in criminal activity and gangs; these substance users tend to have general antisocial characteristics (Howard & Jenson, 1998; May & Del Vecchio, 1997). Poor academic achievers and high school dropouts also have increased rates of inhalant use (Bates, Plemons, Jumper-Thurman, & Beauvais, 1997).

The type of inhalant used varies depending on the frequency and duration of use. May and Del Vecchio (1997) divide users into three categories: experimental, acute, and chronic. Experimental users are in the fourteen- to seventeen-year-old range and have used inhalants sporadically for less than two years. Acute users are ages seventeen to twenty-one and have used for two to four years at least three times per week. Chronic users are twenty to twenty-eight years old and have used inhalants regularly for five to fifteen years. Based on the results from the annual National Household Survey on Drug Abuse performed by the National Institute on Drug Abuse (May & Del Vecchio, 1997), it is estimated that less than 2 percent of people ages twenty to twenty-eight are chronic users of inhalants.

The Substance Abuse and Mental Health Services Administration began collecting data on inhalant use with annual surveys in 1985. The highest rates occur among adolescents in the eighth grade, with approximately 20 percent having tried inhalants at least once. Another significant group of users were adolescent Native Americans who live on reservations, with rates between 25 and 30 percent, including females (Bates et al., 1997; Kurtzman et al., 2001; Novins, Beals, & Mitchell, 2001; Trotter, Rolf, & Baldwin, 1997; Howard, Walker, Silk, Cottler, and Compton, 1999) examined Native American youth who do not live on reservations to determine possible ethnic influence and concluded that peer influence and socioeconomic stressors were more indicative of potential inhalant abuse. Alvarez (2001) agrees with other researchers that Hispanic adolescents are just as likely as Caucasians to abuse inhalants, affirming that use is related to socioeconomic levels and is more common in isolated rural settings where other substances may be less accessible (Bates et al., 1997). This trend in which geographically and socioeconomically marginalized groups have higher incidence of inhalant use has been observed in other areas of the world as well (Howard et al., 1999).

Of serious concern to some researchers is the observation that inhalant use/abuse is occurring at very young ages and often leads to more serious problems. One report indicated that inhalant use occurs in children as young as six (American Academy of Pediatricians, 1996). Like marijuana and alcohol, inhalants are considered gateway drugs, with early first use of inhalants demonstrating a strong relationship with further substance use and polysubstance use in later years (Novins et al., 2001). Some young users indicated that they used inhalants even before smoking cigarettes (Young, Longstaffe, & Tenenbein, 1999). Early use of inhalants is often indicative of experimental or brief use, and rates of reported use typically decline among older adolescents. However, inhalant users frequently do not perform well in school and often dropout, making it difficult to accurately survey this population. For future research, it would be helpful to follow a group of adolescent inhalant users into adulthood to determine the rate of continued use.

CASE EXAMPLE

Case History

B is a thirteen-year-old boy who lives with his mother (who will be referred to as Mrs. Brown) in a rented apartment in a small town in central Florida. B is in seventh grade and attends a middle school in his community. He does not have any siblings. B's parents divorced within the last six months. B sees his father only on holidays because his father moved to another state. Before the divorce, B was very close to his father. B's father (who will be referred to as Mr. Brown) helped coach his son's baseball team and took B fishing frequently.

According to B's mother, Mr. Brown was a heavy drinker and became verbally and physically abusive with the family when he was drunk. Mrs. Brown eventually obtained a protection from abuse order and divorced her husband. Mrs. Brown was particularly concerned about the physical abuse that her husband inflicted on B, which motivated her to seek the divorce. Mr. Brown remarried within a few months of the divorce and moved away. Mrs. Brown is employed part-time as a retail store clerk and receives sporadic support payments from her ex-husband. B's mother is struggling financially to support herself and her son.

B has been in numerous fights in school with other boys and was referred to detention once recently. He also was caught stealing money from his grandparents' house, and his mother has noticed that he has possessions in his room that he could not have afforded to buy himself. B's grades in school are poor; he has several Ds and one F. His teachers report that he does not pay attention in class and often seems to be looking out the window or staring at the wall, oblivious to the class discussion.

Mrs. Brown is concerned that B does not talk to her about what is going on in his life, despite the repeated attempts she has made to talk with him. He becomes very angry with her, sometimes for no obvious reason. B has told her that he blames her for his father leaving. A counselor at school has talked with B a few times, and his anger seems to be centered on his father's absence from his life.

Recently, Mrs. Brown came home from work and found B on the floor in his bedroom, dazed and glassy-eyed, with a runny nose. There was a strong chemical odor in the room. When his mother entered the room, B became agitated with her, yelling obscenities and calling her names. He tried to get up but had trouble with his coordination and kept falling down. He knocked over a chair and suddenly burst into hysterical laughter. His mother called for an ambulance, and he was taken to the emergency room of the nearest hospital.

The doctor in the hospital examined B. He directed Mrs. Brown to wait outside the room because B became very agitated whenever his mother was present. The doctor observed gold paint flecks on B's face and hands. He also noted that B was underweight for his height and age and had a rash around his mouth, with dried, cracked skin. The doctor placed B on a cardiac monitor and ordered a variety of blood tests. About an hour after he was brought to the emergency room, B began to calm down and appeared very drowsy. He complained of being nauseated and also had a headache. The doctor gave him a mild sedative to help him calm down.

The hospital social worker made arrangements, with the consent of B's mother, for his admission to an adolescent drug treatment facility in the county. B was transferred to the facility by ambulance and admitted for treatment with the diagnosis of inhalant abuse. During the initial assessment at the facility, B admitted to huffing spray paint that he shoplifted from the local dollar store. He reported that he first began using inhalants with some friends at school, who used permanent markers, correction fluid, and nail polish. While working on the backstage crew for a school play, B soon discovered that spray paint was his preferred substance. A friend told him that the metallic paints, silver and gold, were the most effective. Because his mother worked until late in the evening and he was usually home alone, B soon began huffing at home as well as at school. B reported that he has had "visions" under the influence of inhalants, such as feeling that he was flying and seeing a monkey in his bedroom closet. He said that he likes the feeling of getting high from the spray paint because "it is like going on a journey," and he can forget about his life for a while.

B stayed in the adolescent substance abuse treatment unit for seven days. In treatment, he was involved in individual and group therapy and also attended a twelve-step support group in the community. B had some cravings to huff during the first few days and felt anxious about being in the treatment program. The counselors in the program encouraged B to talk to them when he was experiencing the cravings or anxiety, and within a few days, his symptoms subsided. In group therapy, he began to learn the harmful and toxic effects inhalants have on the mind and body. He also listened to other adolescents' stories of inhalant use and their difficult family situations. While B was in the program, he and his mother met with a family counselor to talk about their relationship and the conflicts between them. They both agreed to continue with family counseling after B's discharge from the program. B also made a commitment in his group, in front of his peers, to abstain from substance abuse and to develop healthier ways of dealing with his thoughts and feelings.

Mental Status

Presentation. Appearance: disheveled; mood: irritable; attitude: uncooperative; affect: flat; speech: loud, inappropriate; motor activity: restless; orientation: slightly disoriented.

Mental Functioning. Simple calculations: fair results; serial sevens: inaccurate; immediate memory: not intact; remote memory: intact; general knowledge: mostly accurate; proverb interpretation: unable to determine; similarities/differences: refused.

Higher-Order Abilities. Judgment: impulsive; insight: poor; intelligence: average.

Thought Form/Content. Thought processes: confused; delusions: none apparent; hallucinations: visual.

Multiaxial Diagnostic Assessment

Incorporating information from this case example and the *DSM-IV-TR* gives the following diagnostic impression:

Axis I: Inhalant Abuse (305.90)
Axis II: No diagnosis (v71.09)
            Antisocial traits
Axis III: Underweight for age and height
Axis IV: 1. Problems with primary support group—conflict with mother, father absent, history of verbal and physical abuse by father
            2. Problems with school—poor grades
            3. Economic problems—single-parent home
            4. Other psychosocial and environmental problems—fights with other boys in school, shoplifting from local store, stealing money from grandparents
Axis V: 32

B meets the *DSM-IV-TR* criteria for inhalant abuse based on his use of inhalants over the last several months. He has exhibited clinical impairment in his functioning through his hostile, disrespectful relationship with his mother; his frequent fights in school; his poor grades; and his continued use of inhalants with increasing tolerance to the substance. B has shown some signs of antisocial traits (stealing, fighting) and has been in detention at school, but thus far has not had legal consequences for his behavior. His GAF score is based on his aggressive behavior toward others and his poor school performance.

From the mental status examination, it appears that B could have some cognitive impairment, but this would need to be further assessed after the affect of the inhalant has worn off. In addition, he should have a full medical evaluation, including hearing and vision screening, to determine any significant impairments that may have occurred due to the sustained and increased use of inhalants over the past several months.

Intervention Plan: Inhalant Abuse

Definition. Deliberately breathing in vapors and fumes of various solvents to obtain the euphoric effect, despite knowledge of harmfulness and potential dangers of behavior.

Signs and Symptoms. Intoxication, euphoria, chemical odor on breath or clothing, unsteady gait/uncoordinated movements, disheveled appearance, irritated eyes, runny nose, rash around mouth or nose, sneezing, coughing, drowsiness, headaches, nausea.

Goals for Treatment.
1. Refrain from abuse of inhalants.
2. Find healthy ways to cope with social and emotional issues.
3. Improve relationship with mother.

Objectives	Interventions
Attend self-help program at least three times per week.	Provide list of meetings in community for client and his mother.
Identify negative aspects of substance abuse.	Provide educational material on inhalant abuse to client and his mother.
Avoid socializing with other users; develop schedule for after-school activities in community or possible part-time job.	Assist client in identifying trigger situations and people who have been part of his abusive lifestyle and encourage him to develop a plan to avoid these situations and choose healthier alternatives.
Identify emotions that trigger use.	Provide reflection of emotions in individual and group counseling sessions.
Identify three healthy ways to deal with anger and depressed mood.	Reinforce positive expression of anger and development of coping method/plan.
Develop relationship with adult male role model to improve communication.	Access information and refer to mentoring program for assignment of a mentor who will serve as a role model.

Objectives	Interventions
State thoughts and feelings to mother in weekly family therapy; mother will listen and restate/reflect.	Facilitate communication between mother and son through structural methods of interaction.
Spend fifteen minutes at the end of each day talking to mother about the events of the day; make a daily journal entry of the discussions.	Monitor communication patterns through reports in weekly therapy sessions and provide feedback and support.
Learn assertiveness techniques to improve ability to express needs to mother.	Teach assertiveness techniques in psychoeducational group setting, with adolescent peers.

BEST PRACTICES

Inhalant users often do not come to the attention of practitioners for treatment, unless discovered and interrupted during drug use, because most of the symptoms of their drug use abate in a short amount of time. With chronic use, others may begin to notice that the user is having a problem with drug use/abuse, including adults who may inadvertently interrupt the drug-taking behavior and discover that the adolescent is in a state of apparent intoxication. Because of the occasional uncontrollable behavior or alarming symptoms that may occur, users may be brought to hospital emergency rooms for examination. When an adolescent first presents at the hospital in the midst of an episode of inhalant use, the physician may prescribe benzodiazepines to decrease agitation and some of the withdrawal symptoms that may become evident.

The *DSM-IV-TR* (American Psychiatric Association [APA], 2000) does not include the diagnosis of inhalant withdrawal, due to lack of clinical significance. However, some users do report withdrawal-like symptoms such as ongoing cravings, increased irritability, and poor attention and concentration; these reactions may be due to psychological dependence or another underlying anxiety (Keriotis & Upadhyaya, 2000). Because of the risk of Sudden Sniffing Death, the person must be kept calm until the effects of the inhalant have worn off. The treating physician may perform blood work to determine possible organ damage from chronic inhalant abuse. According to the American Association of Pediatricians (1996), urine toxicology screenings typically do not detect inhalants, but they may detect other substances used in combination with inhalants.

Various substance abuse treatment options may be considered, but it is generally advisable, if possible, to refer the adolescent to a short-stay inpatient treatment program so he or she can achieve abstinence from the substance with the support and structure of a treatment regimen. Family involvement in treatment is crucial, in the inpatient phase and in subsequent outpatient therapies, to help the client to maintain abstinence from the substance and to address underlying social and emotional issues. One treatment method for substance abuse emphasizes teaching children responsible decision-making skills and helping them gain an understanding of the consequences for behavior. Enhancement of self-esteem and personal identity also appears to be a key focus in successful substance abuse treatment with adolescents (Ballard, 1998).

Tubman, Wagner, Gil, and Pate (2002) describe a particular technique for treating substance abuse in adolescents, which they label Guided Self-Change. This brief therapy model combines behavioral techniques and motivational enhancement in an individualized plan for change based on the adolescent's own situation and experiences. This treatment is divided into five sessions and includes techniques such as feedback, decision making and problem solving, goal setting, self-monitoring, homework assignments, social skills training, coping with stress, and identifying supports. In treatment, individuals monitor their thoughts and feelings about substance use, examine triggers for use, and increase their overall knowledge and awareness about substance use. This approach would be ideal in working with young children and adolescents, as many of these strategies are included in current prevention efforts.

DuPont (1996) stresses the importance of twelve-step programs for adolescent substance abuse treatment. The nature of these groups provides a necessary structure and a climate of honesty, which are vital factors in helping adolescents overcome addiction. Family members can also attend support groups to deal with codependency issues in order to avoid repeated cycles of addiction. In addition, parents or other family members may be dealing with their own addictions. In family therapy, it is important for the family to begin to establish boundaries and clear roles and for the family to have defined rules and consequences for the substance-abusing adolescent. Inpatient medical treatments are initially necessary to stabilize the substance abuse, but continued ongoing therapy is essential.

Springer and Orsbon (2002) use structural and solution-focused approaches in working with families with substance-abusing adolescents. The focus of the treatment is aimed at building on the strengths that families have to develop positive, future-oriented goals. Family composition and dynamics are considered important influences on the behavior of the adolescent. From the structural approach, families are encouraged to set limits and define roles to maintain stability and provide consequences for behavior.

Very little information is available in the current literature about specific treatment methods for inhalant abuse. Traditional substance abuse programs for adolescents are generally recommended. Prevention programs are stressed as essential for educating young people on the dangers of inhalant use and for deterring experimental users from prolonged inhalant or polysubstance use. Given the young ages of most inhalant users, children must be educated early about the problems and dangers of inhalant use. Some researchers emphasize the importance of family intervention, including accurate assessment strategies to determine family roles and influence in adolescent behavior, so parents, too, need to be educated to reinforce the information with their children.

SUMMARY AND FUTURE DIRECTIONS

Abuse of inhalants among individuals, particularly adolescents, is a serious problem that requires intervention by health workers, teachers, and social service professionals. The prevalence of abuse of these substances among young teens and grade school children is alarming. In addition, the potential for the use of these substances to lead to other, more serious substance abuse is cause for concern.

The enforced regulation of these common substances is impractical. Therefore, a focus on prevention programs is critical to increase knowledge and awareness about the dangers of inhalant abuse among children and parents and to stem the tide of adolescent substance abuse. Teachers, counselors, physicians, and other community officials need to become more aware of the signs of inhalant use and the effects of inhalant abuse in order to address the problem effectively.

Further research may be needed to determine the effectiveness of current substance abuse treatment programs for adolescents, with emphasis on long-term follow-up of identified inhalant users. The continuing existence of this type of drug abuse among children and adolescents, especially given the dangers of inhalant use, underscores the need for continued concern and increased efforts to eradicate the problem.

References

Alvarez, L. R. (2001). Substance abuse in the Hispanic population. In A. G. Lopez (Ed.), *The Latino psychiatric patient: Assessment and treatment*. Washington: American Psychiatric.

American Academy of Pediatricians. (1996). Inhalant abuse (American Academy of Pediatrics Committee on Substance Abuse and Committee on Native American Child Health). *Pediatrics*, *97*(3), 420–23.

American Psychiatric Association. (2000). *Diagnostic and statistical manual of mental disorders* (4th ed., text rev.). Washington, DC: Author.

Ballard, M. B. (1998). Inhalant abuse: A call for attention. *Journal of Addictions & Offender Counseling*, *19*, 28–32.

Bates, S. C., Plemons, B. W., Jumper-Thurman, P., & Beauvais, F. (1997). Volatile solvent use: Patterns of gender and ethnicity among school attendees and dropouts. *Drugs & Society*, *10*(1/2), 61–78.

Brouette, T., & Anton, R. (2001). Despite need for research, inhalants still misunderstood. *Brown University Digest of Addiction Theory & Application*, *20*(6), 2–4.

DuPont, R. L. (1996). Overcoming adolescent addiction: Working with families and the role of 12-step programs. In J. Lonsdale (Ed.), *The Hatherleigh guide to treating substance abuse, Part II*. New York: Hatherleigh Press.

Gorny, S. W. (1994). Inhalant abuse as an adolescent drug problem: An overview. *Child & Youth Care Forum*, *23*(3), 161–75.

Howard, M. O., & Jenson, J. M. (1998). Inhalant use among antisocial youth. *Addictive Behaviors*, *24*(1/2), 59–74.

Howard, M. O., Walker, R. D., Silk, P., Cottler, L. B., & Compton, W. M. (1999). Inhalant use among urban American Indian youth. *Addiction, 94*(1), 83–95.

Keriotis, A. A., & Upadhyaya, H. P. (2000). Inhalant dependence and withdrawal symptoms. *Journal of the American Academy of Child and Adolescent Psychiatry, 39*(6), 679–80.

Kurtzman, R. L., Otsuka, K. N., & Wahl, R. A. (2001). Inhalant abuse by adolescents. *Journal of Adolescent Health, 28*(3), 170–80.

May, P. A., & Del Vecchio, A. M. (1997). The three common behavioral patterns of inhalant/solvent abuse: Selected findings and research issues. *Drugs & Society, 10*(1/2), 3–37.

National Institute on Drug Abuse. (n.d.). *Inhalant abuse* (Research Report Series). Retrieved November 11, 2002, from http://165.112.78.61/PDF/RRInhalants.pdf

Novins, B. K., Beals, J., & Mitchell, C. M. (2001). Sequences of substance use among American Indian adolescents. *Journal of the American Academy of Child and Adolescent Psychiatry, 40*(10), 1168–85.

Office of National Drug Control Policy. (2002, April). *National drug control policy: Drug facts, inhalants*. Washington, DC: Author. Retrieved January 4, 2004, from http://www.whitehousedrugpolicy.gov/publications/

Springer, D. W., & Orsbon, S. H. (2002). Families helping families: Implementing a multifamily therapy group with substance-abusing adolescents. *Health and Social Work, 27*(3), 204–7.

Stimmel, B. (2002). Volatile solvents, anesthetics, and organic nitrites. In B. Stimmel (Ed.), *Alcoholism, drug addiction and the road to recovery: Life on the edge*. Binghamton, NY: Haworth Press.

Trotter, R. T., Rolf, J. E., & Baldwin, J. A. (1997). Cultural models of inhalant abuse among Navajo youth. *Drugs & Society, 10*(1/2), 39–59.

Tubman, J. G., Wagner, E. F., Gil, A. G., & Pate, K. N. (2002). Brief motivational intervention for substance-abusing delinquent adolescents: Guided self-change as a social work practice innovation. *Health and Social Work, 27*(3), 208–12.

Young, S. J., Longstaffe, S., & Tenenbein, M. (1999). Inhalant abuse and the abuse of other drugs. *American Journal of Drug & Alcohol Abuse, 25*(2), 371–75.

Complicating Factors

Chapter 13

Polysubstance Addiction

Sophia F. Dziegielewski and Sandra Lupo

AS EVIDENCED BY THE RESEARCH AND THE CASE EXAMPLES IN THIS TEXT, many individuals use more than one substance of abuse. Such polysubstance abuse has been gaining increased attention from researchers and practitioners in the area of addictions. Until recently, most of the attention in this area focused on illicit mood-altering substances. This has changed, however, and attention is now being directed toward over-the-counter prescription medications. These medications are often presumed to be safe and have slight mood-altering capabilities. But when used in combination with other substances such as alcohol, marijuana, cocaine, heroin, tobacco, ecstasy, or inhalant drugs, dangerous interactions can result (McNeece & DiNitto, 1998). Polysubstance abuse is unusually difficult to treat because of these interactions, which can cause numerous physiological, cognitive, behavioral, and interpersonal problems (Levin, 1999). Therefore, an accurate assessment is critical prior to beginning any type of treatment regime for the individual who engages in polysubstance abuse.

This chapter outlines the problem of polysubstance abuse and discusses the variety of substances used, in the most commonly used combinations, and how they are administered. Because there are so many substances that can be abused in combination, the bulk of information provided in this chapter is related directly to a case example.

POLYSUBSTANCE ABUSE

In polysubstance abuse, individuals develop problems in individual, social, and occupational functioning related directly to the use of more than one substance that results in some level of addictive behavior. Because there are multiple substances involved, the area of polysubstance abuse cannot be simply related to, say, alcohol abuse or stimulant abuse alone. By definition, polysubstance abuse is the involvement of several substances that act on the body in combination. It is this combined or synergistic effect that the individual experiences.

As might be expected, this combined effect also increases the number of risks associated with addiction (Gossop, Marsden, Stewart, & Rolfe, 2000). For example, the accumulated effects of the combined use of depressants such as alcohol and barbiturates can cause serious respiratory depression, decreased response to painful stimuli, severe confusion, and a decreased heart rate that can result in coma or even death (Naegle & D'Avanzo, 2001).

Tolerance also becomes of greater concern in polysubstance abuse. As tolerance increases, the natural reaction of the user is to increase the dosage levels or to switch to a more potent drug or a combination of drugs in order to feel the same effects. This can present some serious issues of toxicity, especially with the introduction of new substances (Naegle & D'Avanzo, 2001). Overdosing on stimulants alone, for example, can bring about extreme paranoia, agitation, increased body temperature, hallucinations, and death. Similarly, fatigue, paranoia, and a hallucinogen-like psychotic state reveal marijuana toxicity. If the user combines these substances of addiction, it could result in the development of serious physiological and psychological effects. Combining substances that have similar effects on the body can also be dangerous. Taking narcotics and depressants together, for example, could significantly depress metabolic body processes and thus cause serious damage and possibly death (Naegle & D'Avanzo, 2001). According to Iber (1991) and Naegle & D'Avanzo (2001), some common drug combinations include opiates, stimulants, and alcohol; amphetamines, sedatives, and alcohol; alcohol, sedatives, and tranquilizers; cocaine, sedatives, and alcohol; and Ritalin, marijuana, and alcohol.

Studies indicate that polysubstance abusers often require longer treatment, experience poorer social functioning, and are more likely to use illicit drugs and overdose (Hillebrand, Marsden, Finch, & Strang, 2001). According to the New York City Office of the Chief Medical Examiner, opiates, cocaine, and alcohol accounted for 98 percent of all accidental overdose deaths between 1990 and 1998; 58 percent of those deaths were attributed to two or more of these drugs in combination (Coffin, Galea, Leon, Vlahov, & Tardiff, 2003).

Identifying the polysubstance abuser is further complicated by the simple fact that so many over-the-counter (OTC) medications such as diet aids, laxatives, cough medicines, and inhalants, as well as prescription medications such as Xanax, Valium, Ritalin, and Percocet, contribute to polysubstance abuse. In addition, as the desire for a medication to address everything that ails an individual increases, so can the problems that result from such combinations (Dziegielewski & Leon, 2001).

According to the *DSM-IV-TR*, polysubstance abuse and dependence will also meet the general criteria for substance abuse; however, no one substance will be the predominant substance used over a twelve-month period. And, at least three types of substance will be present, excluding caffeine and nicotine. In addition, the polysubstance-dependent person will have social or occupational impairment related to each type of substance abused. For example, a polysubstance abuser may be so oblivious to the consequences of his behavior that he may drive his car with a suspended driver's license after being previously convicted for driving under the influence. Caution should be exercised, however. It is not the isolated incident that would qualify someone for a diagnosis of polysubstance abuse but rather the combination of events that have occurred as a direct result of the substances used. This combination of events or polysubstance use must be directly related as the cause of the social and occupational functioning impairments that result.

In polysubstance dependence, it is expected that the intake of a substance will cause cognitive, behavioral, and physiological changes in the body as well as adverse social and occupational functioning. The individual who is substance dependent will continue using the substances regardless of the negative consequences that can occur from this use. In most cases, there is tolerance to the substance. For most polysubstance abusers, evidence of withdrawal will determine whether they are suffering from dependence rather than from abuse. Numerous studies report demonstrated cognitive deficits associated with polysubstance abuse, including deficits in verbal and visual memory, problem solving, visuoperceptual and visuomotor skills, attention concentration, and psychomotor speed (Medina, Shear, Schafer, Armstrong, & Dyer, 2004).

Clinical studies have shown that individuals in methadone maintenance treatment, who are opiate-dependent, are often also concurrently dependent on alcohol, cocaine, or both (Hillebrand et al., 2001). Although these and other studies are presenting an increasing amount of data on polysubstance abuse, the serious lack of research directed specifically at polysubstance abuse results in an underestimation of the problem and thus inadequate efforts toward finding effective treatments.

Because of this lack of research directed specifically at polysubstance abuse, the development of effective intervention for the polysubstance abuser rests heavily on the individual practitioner's interpretation, taking into account which substances are involved. In this area, it is not uncommon for the addictions professional to use interventions based on his or her judgments of the cause of the problem, as well as evidence-based treatments. Such an approach requires careful assessment of the client and the formulation of an individualized intervention protocol.

CASE EXAMPLE

Case History

C, a thirty-six-year-old Caucasian woman, was admitted to the emergency room at the city hospital complaining of severe back pain. (During her evaluation, C was a poor historian, so most of the following information was gathered from previous admission records and a family friend.) C was intoxicated at admission, with a blood alcohol level of .28. C reports that she was having "a drink or two" with her boyfriend when an alarming pain shot through her lower back. C's boyfriend called for the paramedics but left the scene prior to their arrival. According to previous admission information, C reported that she regularly drinks alcohol each weekend, and increases this use during holidays. C also reports that because she often has trouble getting to sleep, she occasionally takes diazepam (Valium) to help her sleep. She reports on this admission that she was having trouble sleeping because she was concerned that she may be pregnant with her sixth child. C reports that her boyfriend is addicted to crack cocaine and is frequently unemployed. He is afraid of the police and of being arrested, and C believes this is probably why he left the apartment after calling for the paramedics. She is having severe financial difficulties and states that she expects to be evicted from her apartment next week because she has not paid her rent in two months. She also reports that she has no adequate day care for her children, which has prevented her from finding work.

C reports a long social and family history of substance use and abuse. She states that her mother was addicted to alcohol and that her father, who often was abusive when intoxicated, used to sell various drugs. Currently, her oldest brother is in jail and will be there for at least six months, and her younger sister is in an inpatient substance abuse program. In describing her relationships with men, C reports that either they also had substance abuse problems or they were violent toward her or her children. To date, she reports a strained relationship with her parents, and she doesn't communicate with them. She reports having no friends or outside social contact.

In terms of treatment, C has been in a detoxification program three times previously, with the longest period of sobriety being four months. Her most recent attempt at sobriety was after the birth of her third child, who was placed in foster care because of problems related to his being born with fetal alcohol syndrome. Upon C's admission to the hospital, it is discovered that she is in kidney failure. C has a long history of abusing various substances (including cocaine, heroin, and marijuana) that have been putting increased stress on her kidneys. She also has been diagnosed with gastrointestinal problems and a fatty liver, suggestive of alcohol abuse. She is considered at high risk for HIV, most likely due to unsafe drug use or unsafe sexual practices. Since her admission at the hospital, C has begun to experience some withdrawal symptoms. The results of the pregnancy test were negative, but the drug screen was positive for several substances including marijuana.

Multiaxial Diagnostic Assessment

An assessment is completed utilizing client self-report, medical findings, and completion of the McMullin Addiction Thought Scale and the Michigan Alcoholism Screening Test. The assessment reflected both substance abuse and dependence. C is diagnosed on Axis I with alcohol dependence (with physiological dependence), diazepam abuse, heroin abuse, and major depressive disorder (recurrent, severe, without psychotic features).

C best fits the diagnosis of polysubstance dependence disorder (304.80) because she has repeatedly used four different types of substances (alcohol, barbiturates, cocaine, and heroin) with no single substance being the most prominent. Because she also has a pattern of problems associated with using multiple drugs, she meets the criteria for alcohol dependence and heroin dependence. The diagnosis of alcohol dependence with physiological dependence is supported by evidence of tolerance and withdrawal. Other factors that support a diagnosis of dependence are her concurrent medical problems, including kidney failure and fatty liver as a result of alcohol consumption. She also has a long history of past unsuccessful attempts at sobriety with a strong desire for abstinence. In addition, her third child was born with fetal alcohol syndrome. She reports feeling guilty and shameful about the alcohol consumption during her third pregnancy, yet she continues to drink while currently concerned about being pregnant again.

The diagnosis of heroin abuse is justified because C reports using heroin to address the chronic pain in her stomach and back and has been using heroin for this pain (when she can get it) for two years. Other substances she has taken in excess include diazepam, which is reflected in her pattern of shopping for doctors to obtain additional prescriptions. She reports using heroin to help her get comfortable and diazepam as a sleep aid. This substance-induced sleep reportedly has been occurring for at least the past two and one-half years. Her financial situation is in crisis, but she continues to purchase heroin and diazepam. Because of her intense desire to find and use these substances, she has been unable to care for herself or her children, thereby failing to fulfill major role obligations at home.

For C, it will be important to monitor for depression and the possibility of a major depressive disorder. C reports feeling depressed and that this depression has lasted for several years, with few breaks of optimism in between the depressed episodes. C's psychomotor skills appear retarded, and she appears lethargic. She expresses feelings of hopelessness and a preoccupation with death. She has a diminished ability to concentrate and a flat affect. All of her symptoms affect her social functioning and reduce her self-esteem and self-confidence. There appears to be no indication of a manic episode from self-report and medical history. At this time, however, it is unclear if the symptoms she is feeling are related to the chronic polysubstance abuse or to depression. Although the diagnosis of major depressive disorder is deferred at this time, she will be monitored for this condition as she begins to recover from the effects of the substances.

There is no formal diagnosis on Axis II. C's defense mechanisms include denial, projection, rationalization, devaluation, and repression. C, like many substance abusers, may rely on these unhealthy defense mechanisms as a way to cope and therefore may not fully develop healthy coping styles.

Medical conditions coded on Axis III include kidney failure and HIV disease. Upon C's admission to the hospital, several tests were conducted. HIV testing was done because her reported history with heroin presented the possibility that she may have shared needles. Two separate tests confirmed that C is HIV positive. Her kidney failure will be addressed with surgery. The actual treatment for the kidney failure will not be known until the medical staff determines the severity of the damage. Tests reveal damage to C's liver. Should she discontinue her alcohol abuse, the damage to her liver will not cause any further complications. Should she continue to consume alcohol, her liver will continue to deteriorate and be subject to disease (McNeece & DiNitto, 1998).

Axis IV reflects several issues associated with environmental stressors. C has several medical issues to confront. She will need to have surgery for her kidneys. Her children have no support system other than herself. Her boyfriend has not been seen for several days and is not likely to return. She suffers from severe financial stressors—her utilities were shut off two days ago; she is about to be evicted from her apartment; she has no transportation; and she cannot afford day care. A referral to the Department of Children and Families was made, and her children have been placed in temporary foster care. C is in a great deal of pain, both physically and emotionally.

On Axis V, C's GAF score is currently 21 because of her inability to care for herself, her risk of complications from withdrawal, and her immediate need for surgery. Withdrawal symptoms from alcohol can be life threatening and require constant supervision by a medical professional. For C's treatment, it will be critical to determine other substances used and medical conditions that may complicate the withdrawal process.

Intervention Strategy

Practitioners in the area of addictions have the complicated task of determining the appropriate and most beneficial treatments for their clients. When developing a treatment plan for the polysubstance-abusing clients, it is imperative that each substance is clearly identified and the goals and objectives are clear and attainable (Laban, 1997). Many clients will already have made unsuccessful attempts at overall sobriety but may have succeeded at one time or another in giving up at least one substance. The fact that there are multiple substances involved will tend to complicate the process and frustrate the client. The helping professional should be prepared for resistant behaviors and intact defense mechanisms. When support systems are strained, the helping professional will need to find or establish support for the client. This is especially important when multiple substances are involved because oftentimes family and friends do not know where to start and will also become frustrated.

A common defense mechanism used by substance abusers is denial. There are several levels of defense mechanisms described in the *DSM-IV-TR*. C most often uses defense mechanisms located at what is termed the disavowal level, where unpleasant or unacceptable stressors, impulses, ideas, affect, or responsibilities are kept from awareness, with or without a misattribution of these feelings to external reasons or causes. It is at this level that denial, projection, and rationalization are used (American Psychiatric Association, 2000). For C, taking into account each individual substance and assessing her motivation for change is key to treatment.

The first step for an individual with several active substance addictions is clear identification of the substances of abuse and the general interactions that can result. Once assessed, the detoxification and withdrawal from the substances must occur. In the case of C, she is already at the hospital for severe medical problems, but her alcohol and drug withdrawal could warrant hospitalization regardless of the medical complications. Withdrawal syndromes are characterized by a continuum of signs and symptoms usually beginning twelve to forty-eight hours after cessation of intake that accompany alcohol withdrawal. Not all withdrawal symptoms are life threatening. They may include agitation, irritability, sweating, and weakness (Kaufman, 1994). Many of the withdrawal symptoms, however, are not only extremely uncomfortable but also dangerous. These include hallucinations, delusions, profuse sweating, extreme gastrointestinal discomfort, tremors, extreme depression, anxiety, and fear (Dziegielewski, 2002; Kaufman, 1994). Most of the physiological withdrawal processes are completed after one week, at which time the process of getting well can begin (Kaufman, 1994). With polysubstance abuse, each substance must be identified. Those that result in a complicated or dangerous physical withdrawal will need to be addressed first. Therefore, before any type of behavioral intervention is implemented, the potential for withdrawal from each substance involved must be assessed.

The second phase of treatment usually enlists a variety of behavioral and cognitive techniques for the purpose of maintaining sobriety (Kaufman, 1994). This phase of treatment helps the client identify triggers for his or her substance abuse, secure support systems for abstinence, and rebuild his or her everyday life without the use of substances. The client's main goal is to develop a life that is rewarding and substance free. New coping mechanisms are beginning to replace the unhealthy defenses that are familiar. Substances abused over extended periods retard the user's spectrum of emotions. A client may feel very overwhelmed with new emotions and a sense of unfamiliarity.

The third phase, according to Kaufman (1994), enlists the higher-level functioning and self-actualization process. A client, now sober for years, can learn to form intimate, healthy relationships without overuse of defense mechanisms. He or she can learn to care for self and others and cope with all of the negative and positive attributes that each person brings to the relationship. Intervention can provide a window for personal growth, moving the client beyond the substance dictating and shaping his or her existence.

Intervention Plan: Polysubstance Abuse Disorder

Definition. A physiological, psychological, and emotional dependence on three or more substances that alter mood. Severe impairment of social, occupational, or recreational functioning helps to define this disorder.

Signs and Symptoms. Inability to discontinue use of three or more substances; impaired social, occupational, or recreational functioning; neglected responsibilities; difficulty with interpersonal relationships; overuse of defense mechanisms; unsuccessful attempts to discontinue use through treatment; medical issues; financial difficulties; impaired psychomotor skills; history of victimization related to substance use.

Goals for Treatment.
1. Complete safe detoxification from all substances.
2. Maintain abstinence from all substances (exception as recommended by a doctor for treatment).

3. Follow and participate in medical treatments deemed necessary by hospital staff.
4. Learn about drug interaction and how this relates to the process of addiction and recovery.
5. Learn and implement relapse prevention skills.
6. Increase problem-solving skills.
7. Build a clean and sober support system for self and family.

Objective 1.   Client will spend a minimum of five to ten days in a detoxification facility under the supervision of medical and detoxification professionals. Client will identify all substances used and the frequency, duration, and amounts of consumption. Medical and counseling staff will identify any coexisting conditions and how they are reflected in current behaviors.

Intervention 1.   Client will comply with all medical and counseling interventions required by the detoxification facility. Client will honestly disclose how often and how much money was spent on alcohol (using receipts and canceled checks from bars, grocery stores, etc.) and identify how much money was spent on drugs. Once obtained, the information will be discussed with the practitioner and related to problems that she has experienced. Client and counselor will explore how depression affects her life, how often she feels depressed, and how she handles this depression. Strategies for coping with depression will be explored and implemented if needed.

Objective 2.   Work toward developing a social support system that supports positive attitudes and behaviors consistent with abstinence.

Intervention 2.   Client will contact social service professionals and others in the community to help identify and utilize possible sources of support. Client will develop a list of possible support providers and those in her support system that can help her. Client will contact and join a recovery group for persons with similar polysubstance abuse issues.

Objective 3.   Initiate the identification and development of effective coping skills to remain abstinent from drug and alcohol use.

Intervention 3.   Client will generate a list of what she feels are the biggest barriers to her recovery. This list will be discussed with the practitioner and with peer supports during group sessions. Client will generate a list of people, places, situations, and feelings that are triggers for the urge to use substances. Client will avoid people, places and situations on this list. Client will participate in discussion on relapse prevention and develop tools for coping with triggers. Client will participate in an intervention process designed to increase the coping skills required to lead a drug- and alcohol-free life, such as stress and anger management, self-esteem and self-awareness, communication, and other life skills.

Intervention Summary.   Stabilizing C's health has to be the number one priority in her treatment. Supervised detoxification should occur simultaneously with her medical treatment. While the client is being stabilized, the practitioner must make a referral to a social service professional to ensure that her children have adequate care. Upon discharge from the medical and detoxification facility, C should enter a substance abuse program to receive specific treatment for her polysubstance abuse. Given C's current indigence and her past, unsuccessful attempts at abstinence, inpatient treatment, which would surround her with a stable residence and a drug-free environment, is indicated. Once in the facility, she would be assigned a case manager. Upon C's discharge, this case manager could assist with services such as securing transportation and housing, locating outpatient support groups that will help C with her continued abstinence and her HIV status, and assisting C in making the appropriate connections in order to be reunited with her children.

Because C has a history of being unable to apply the skills necessary to remain abstinent on her own after discharge from a substance abuse facility, the practitioner will need to give her special attention at that time to discourage her from relapsing into drug and alcohol use. During treatment, C will need to learn problem-solving skills and coping skills and cognitive restructuring will need to be implemented to ensure that she will have the skills to remain abstinent. Plans for continued aftercare should be in place prior to discharge. Substance abuse narrows the range of emotions that the user experiences. C will need to learn to identify, process, and cope with feelings that are unfamiliar to her. Assignments that help C get in touch with her own feelings will improve her ability to identify emotional triggers. Making a list of barriers to recovery will give C and the helping professional other specific areas to explore and address. For example, individuals who are addicted to a substance often hold on to irrational beliefs. Once these are identified, the practitioner can restructure these thinking patterns to more accurately reflect the reality of the situation (Lewis, Dana, & Blevins, 1994).

The use of medications to treat substance abuse has shown some positive results; however, a very thorough assessment of substances used and existing medical/health issues is critical for ensuring that the treatment will be helpful and not harmful. Especially in the case of polysubstance abuse, one needs to be very cautious when mixing in more substances. In the case of C, she may also suffer from major depressive disorder. Because this comorbidity is common, the therapist must take into account the possibility of this dual diagnosis when making treatment decisions (McNeece & DiNitto, 1998). The treatment plan will help C report on the frequency, intensity, and duration of her depressed feelings when she is substance free. Once C is substance free, a clear determination can be made as to whether she indeed has major depressive disorder as originally hypothesized. Regardless, most of the cognitive and behavioral techniques are also helpful with depression, but in the case of major depressive disorder, antidepressant medication therapy will need to be considered as an adjunct to the intervention process.

BEST PRACTICES

For substance disorder interventions, many professionals agree that a group treatment experience is preferred because it allows the client to gain a sense of belonging. It is reassuring for the individual suffering from substance abuse to know that he or she has peers who are suffering some of the same problems. In this context, problems and solutions can be addressed by peers as well as by professionals. Peers have firsthand knowledge of the unhealthy techniques commonly used to deny or blame others for the problem, and with practitioner facilitation, they can openly confront the individual using these techniques (Stevens & Smith, 2001).

Stevens and Smith (2001) believe that it is critical to understand the effects that vicarious learning can have in the intervention setting. For the practitioner, it is crucial to identify key factors and experiences such as the client's perceptions of hope, safety, and support because these factors are central to developing cohesiveness and a sense of belonging. By understanding how the client perceives these factors, the practitioner can facilitate interpersonal and vicarious learning. Because all of these factors and the integration of these experiences contribute to a client's self-esteem and self-worth, developing this type of learning can increase the client's ability to accept that he or she is not alone with his or her substance addiction problems. Group treatments offer a wealth of vicarious learning opportunities. In group settings, clients learn the structure and rules of the group, how to set goals, a sense of belonging and safety, use of constructive confrontation, and modeling and role playing, and they acquire an increased knowledge of each individual's problem (Stevens & Smith, 2001).

One type of intervention strategy, mentioned in almost every chapter of this book because of its popularity when treating individuals with addictive disorders, is cognitive-behavioral therapy (CBT). The theory behind CBT postulates that individuals are active participants and have control over their behaviors and thoughts. Because individuals are assumed to have the ability to make decisions for themselves, CBT techniques are used to challenge the former learning and expectations of the substance abuser (Copeland, Swift, Roffman, & Stephens, 2001; Velleman, 1991).

According to a model developed by Heather and Robertson (1989), there are nine basic assumptions for effective substance abuse counseling: (1) understanding and treating drinking and/or substance abuse in context; (2) problem solving; (3) utilizing more concrete action strategy with less words; (4) inviting family, friends, and community for participation and involvement; (5) helping clients to realize that change is both productive and worthwhile and will achieve concrete positive results; (6) helping clients to master and recognize cues that can lead to problematic substance abusing behavior; (7) developing self-management and identify target behaviors with subsequent goal setting; (8) utilizing practitioners and counselors well-versed in the methods of CBT; and (9) always emphasizing and encouraging client choice. These nine interventive ingredients mix practice strategy with a strong theoretical grounding (Velleman, 1991).

To best assist the individual who suffers from addiction, the counseling relationship should exemplify qualities of empathy, genuineness, and respect (Lewis et al., 1994). As is clear from Heather and Robertson's nine basic assumptions, the role of the practitioner in facilitating this process is paramount. Here the practitioner needs to be aware of and proficient in a variety of skills. This requires that the practitioner be well versed in CBT, behavioral techniques, or other psychodynamic perspectives that might provide the foundation of the treatment strategy.

One behavioral technique that appears to be gaining in popularity is systematic desensitization (Dziegielewski & MacNeil, 1999). This technique has been used in a variety of settings with good potential for the substance-addicted individual. For example, an addicted individual may fear certain social situations in which there is a pronounced fear that relapse may occur. This could make individuals avoid parties or other places where substance-abusing behaviors have occurred in the past. It may also prompt the substance-abusing individual to avoid family or friends, thereby disrupting the development of what could be a healthy support system. When using this type of intervention with the substance-abusing individual, the practitioner and the client develop a hierarchy of anxiety-provoking situations and utilize relaxation techniques in order to reduce the anxiety. This can be particularly helpful when this in-vivo learning can be transferred to real-life situations (Lewis et al., 1994).

Two other areas of treatment beneficial for individuals with addictions are learning to use refusal skills and building assertion skills. Learning and developing refusal skills is helpful for all individuals who suffer from addictions, with particular applicability for adolescent substance abusers. Refusal and assertion skills should be developed together because these skills are somewhat complementary. The development of these skills can help the client to identify feelings, desires, and coping strategies. In addition, it can assist the client in learning to take responsibility for his or her behaviors. In the therapeutic process, emphasis is placed on developing and using scripts for handling problematic situations and providing the client with instruction and compromise strategies as a means of problem solving (Lewis et al., 1994).

Another important area in addictions intervention is education, including instruction on how to apply the knowledge gained to individual problem solving. Clients need to know what substances they are taking and link the use of these substances with the resulting problematic behavioral, mental, and physical symptoms or effects. For example, if an addicted client reports drinking alcohol to numb the senses and avoid depression, the practitioner can help the client to understand the effect alcohol can have on the body when used in this way. That is, the practitioner would explain that alcohol is a central nervous system depressant that, if used to address depressive symptoms, will only exacerbate the problem. Initially, the alcohol may serve as an anesthetic, numbing some of the current effects, but once it wears off, all the previously dulled feelings will resurface (Levin, 1999).

From a cognitive perspective, the practitioner can help the client to view the self in a more positive light, highlighting the strengths and abilities that encourage self-efficacy. If an individual who suffers from an addictive disorder has unrealistic perceptions of the world and these thoughts go unchallenged, he or she may incorporate these thoughts into his or her cognitive processes. Once illogical thought processes are identified, the practitioner can help the client identify and clarify them while suggesting alternate and more productive courses of action (Lewis et al., 1994).

Research also suggests that substance-abusing individuals very often have limited problem-solving ability (Faulkner, 2002). Studies have shown that the ability to solve both interpersonal and emotional problems is relevant to the recovery of those addicted to narcotics (Collier & Marlatt, 1995; Faulkner, 2002). One example of an intervention strategy that enhances this ability is enrollment in a ropes course. Ropes courses are designed to encourage teamwork and thereby improve problem-solving ability, self-esteem, self-control, and self-efficacy. All of these skills are considered important in the recovery process (Aubrey & MacLeod, 1994; Boyle, 1985; Davis, Ray, & Sayles, 1995; Mann, 1994). To date, most practitioners agree that assessing and improving problem-solving ability does play an extremely important role in maintaining sobriety (Velleman, 1991).

Waltman (1995), similar to Heather and Robertson (1989), suggested several key ingredients to effective addictions treatment. Waltman proposed that addicts cannot successfully recover without being able to have easy accessibility to care and that the care provided needs to be individualized and flexible. This model highlights the importance of the practitioner in facilitating and guiding the process, recognizing and integrating various ways to motivate clients as a means of increasing their investment in treatment. In this individualized setting, clients need to be matched with treatment goals that are directly related to identified, salient variables. The client must also be motivated to try new courses of action as well as take full responsibility for his or her behavior in and out of the treatment process. The logic behind this is that the more strongly clients are motivated for change, the better their prognosis for recovery. Furthermore, the involvement of collaterals (or a support system) is essential for building and rebuilding ties within the social and family contexts. At the end of treatment, programs need to provide follow-up and outline reasons for program failure as well as program success. Once these outcome measures are assessed, they need to be anticipated and reintroduced into the treatment process to assist with program betterment (Waltman, 1995).

Contingency management (CM) offers another treatment opportunity. The basic principle of CM is to reward a client for a desired behavior. For example, as part of the intervention strategy, the client could be given the opportunity to win money in a drawing, with the criterion for eligibility being a certain number of consecutive substance-free urine specimens (Kadden, 2001). Studies examining the efficacy of CM suggest positive effects, especially with drug use, which is relevant to the area of polysubstance use. It has also been claimed that CM can help to increase clinic attendance and naltrexone compliance. In terms of the future, community reinforcement (CR) combined with CM strategies appears promising (Schottenfeld, Pantalon, Chawarski, & Pakes, 1999). Although the combination of CR and CM did not show direct improvement with substance abusers, it did show increased levels of behaviors that are incompatible with substance abuse behaviors. More research in this area is needed to draw more conclusive links to effectiveness.

The use of medications to supplement interventions of any type continues to be a key part of most treatment experiences. Medications are often considered critical to safe detoxification as well as to maintenance. Although most practitioners in the area of addictions are unable to prescribe medications themselves, current practice strategy dictates a need for knowledge in this area (Dziegielewski & Leon, 2001). Through increased knowledge in this area, practitioners can help to monitor side effect profiles and ensure compliance.

Again, when multiple substances are used, special attention must be given to the initial assessment. In this assessment, it is critical to examine each of the substances being taken, regardless of whether it is legal or illegal. Such an examination requires that an assessment include in-depth questions regarding the person's history of substance use. The person needs to be asked about his or her use of each specific illicit drug or legal medication. For example, begin with asking clients the age they first used a specific drug and how many years have they used steadily, then pay particular attention to the previous six months down to the previous thirty days (e.g., "In the past month, how many days did you use cocaine? How much did you use each time?" and "In the last six months, would you say you used more, less, or the same amount of cocaine than you used in the last month?"). Because persons who abuse drugs are likely to underreport or deny their use, a urinalysis should be taken as part of the assessment. Include information regarding the person's substance use from friends and family if possible, as well as a comprehensive medical, legal, and treatment history.

Once the client has been assessed, the practitioner needs to help the client prepare for possible synergistic responses (where one substance enhances the effect of another) or interaction effects (where one substance complicates and or blocks the action of another) involving the prescribed treatment medication (Dziegielewski, 2002). For example, one of the most common medications used to combat alcohol dependence is disulfiram (Antabuse). If prescribed this medication, it is important for the client to take disulfiram regularly. While taking the medication, the individual must refrain from drinking any alcohol. If alcohol is combined with this medication, the user can become violently ill, and possible side effects may include skin rash, depression, fatigue, nausea, vomiting, increased blood pressure and heart rate, psychosis, and even death (Stevens & Smith, 2001).

Methadone, another commonly prescribed medication, is commonly used with heroin abusers who also have problems with polysubstance abuse. Methadone blocks the receptor sites that heroin would normally occupy, satisfying the cravings for the drug without the psychoactive results; but the problem behaviors, along with tolerance and withdrawal from other substances besides the heroin that the polysubstance user may be addicted to, will occur.

In summary, when assisting individuals who suffer from polysubstance abuse, individualized, combination approaches provide a cornerstone for linking all types of intervention strategies. Because these clients often abuse multiple substances that can have very different effects, a multidimensional diagnostic assessment is needed (Dziegielewski, 2002). After completion of this assessment, a combination approach that takes into account the unique presentation of the individual is advocated.

Special Considerations: Family Involvement in Treatment

Substance abuse does not affect only the user. The affects of polysubstance abuse can strain even the most supportive of family and friends. These strained relations often contribute to the client's feeling lost and alone and thus negatively affect his or her recovery. The optimal treatment plan would include the client's family and other supportive figures in the client's life in the treatment process. Both the client and the client's family need to understand the complexity of addiction. Furthermore, each client must understand his or her role in maintaining the addiction and the consequences it has for everyone in the family (McNeece & DiNitto, 1998).

When the individual recovering from a substance addiction is discharged from treatment, special attention needs to be given to make sure that the client does not fall back into the same problematic behavior patterns. Both the individual who suffers from polysubstance abuse and the family and friends who constitute the support system need to have acquired new skills to deal with the new situation. New ways of handling familiar cues are needed. Recovery can be enhanced by the simple presence of a supportive atmosphere. Inclusion of the family in the treatment process allows for examination of practices within the family that may contribute to unhealthy coping practices. When possible, it is important to assess family dynamics because often there are specific roles that each family member takes which foster or maintain addictive behaviors (McNeece & DiNitto, 1998).

Often the addicted client does not have contact with a supportive family. Regardless, it is a therapeutic necessity to help the client discover and incorporate a social support network of persons who are in recovery themselves and who will support the client's recovery. This activity may be as simple as referring the individual to a support group for polysubstance abusers. Or the individual may choose to seek out spiritual support. However it is done, fostering a support system is essential to treatment success.

SUMMARY AND FUTURE DIRECTIONS

Research in the field of addictions is extensive, yet specific research related to polysubstance abuse is extremely limited. This is ironic because it is well known in the field that substance addiction often involves more than just one substance. As stressed in this chapter and throughout this book, the best practice for the treatment of the substance abuser must include a comprehensive assessment that incorporates a multifaceted practice and intervention approach. The synergistic and interactive effects of several substances ingested in combination make polysubstance abusers more difficult to assess. This in turn makes the required treatment longer and more complicated. Individual planning and flexibility in the treatment regimen are therefore paramount.

Drug treatment facilities are faced with an increasing number of polysubstance abusers. In these cases, the facilities cannot identify one drug as the single source of the problem and focus on that drug for treatment. Cognitive-behavioral approaches appear to have some success with many different substances, but until the knowledge behind the usage of multiple substances is understood, CBT alone will offer limited success.

In all of the discussions of addictive substance disorders presented in this book, the emphasis has been on the development of individualized assessment, practice strategy, and intervention. This individualized approach is particularly important for the treatment of polysubstance disorders. Each of the substances a client is using must be assessed and incorporated into an individualized plan to ensure that the intervention strategy fits the client's specific needs and the substance use profile presented.

Every practitioner who works with addicted populations must always remember the importance of a complete and accurate diagnostic assessment because the diagnostic assessment will set the tone for practice. In the assessment, practitioners must be sure to include any prescription medications, and over-the-counter medications, herbal preparations, or tinctures the client may be using (Dziegielewski & Leon, 2001). A complete physical to rule out the potential for medical complications is always needed prior to any intervention. Every piece of information collected about the individual who suffers from polysubstance use can provide valuable clues to his or her particular substance abuse patterns and need for treatment.

Many professionals are still debating whether an individual with a substance problem such as alcohol abuse or dependence has to stay 100 percent abstinent for recovery to occur. The same debate applies to the polysubstance abuser. More research is needed to address this and other issues relevant to polysubstance abuse, as current studies simply do not offer enough controls for accurate generalizability (Faulkner, 2002). Current treatments offer promise for polysubstance abusers, with CBT appearing to be one of the stronger behavioral treatments, but more longitudinal studies are needed to better evaluate treatment efficacy. Indeed, additional research in general is required for the full development of the most beneficial individualized, integrated, and comprehensive treatments for this population.

References

American Psychiatric Association. (2000). *Diagnostic and statistical manual of mental disorders* (4th ed., text rev.). Washington, DC: Author.

Aubrey, A., & MacLeod, M. J. (1994). What does rock climbing have to do with career planning? *Women & Therapy, 15*(3/4), 205–16.

Boyle, S. (1985). *The effects of a ropes course experience on locus of control and self-efficacy.* Unpublished doctoral dissertation, Oklahoma State University, Stillwater.

Coffin, P.O., Galea, S., Leon, A. C., Vlahov, D., & Tardiff, K. (2003). Opiates, cocaine and alcohol combinations in accidental drug overdose deaths in New York City, 1990–1998. *Addiction, 98*(6), 739–47.

Collier, C., & Marlatt, G. (1995). Relapse prevention. In A. J. Goreczyny (Ed.), *Handbook of health and rehabilitation psychology.* New York: Plenum Press.

Copeland, J., Swift, W., Roffman, R., & Stephens, R. (2001). A randomized controlled trial of brief cognitive-behavioral interventions for cannabis use disorder. *Journal of Substance Abuse Treatment, 21,* 55–64.

Davis, D., Ray, J., & Sayles, C. (1995). Ropes course training for youth in a rural setting. *Child and Adolescent Social Work Journal, 12*(6), 445–63.

Dziegielewski, S. F., (2002). *DSM-IV-TR in action.* New York: John Wiley & Sons.

Dziegielewski, S. F., & Leon, A. M. (2001). *Social work practice and psychopharmacology.* New York: Springer.

Dziegielewski, S. F., & MacNeil, G. (1999). Time limited treatment considerations and strategy for specific phobias. *Crisis Intervention and Time-Limited Treatment, 5*(1/2), 133–50.

Faulkner, S., (2002). Low-elements ropes course as an intervention tool with alcohol/other drug dependent adults: A case study. *Alcoholism Treatment Quarterly, 20*(2).

Gossop, M., Marsden, J., Stewart, D., & Rolfe, A., (2000). Patterns of drinking and drinking outcomes among drug misusers: One-year follow-up results. *Journal of Substance Abuse Treatment, 19,* 45–50.

Heather, N., & Robertson, I. (1989). *Problem drinking.* Oxford: Oxford University Press.

Hillebrand, J., Marsden, J., Finch, E., & Strang, J. (2001). Excessive alcohol consumption and drinking expectations among clients in methadone maintenance. *Journal of Substance Abuse Treatment, 21,* 155–60.

Iber, F. (1991). *Alcohol and drug abuse: As encountered in office practice.* Boca Raton, FL: CRC Press.

Kadden, R. (2001). Behavioral and cognitive-behavioral treatments for alcoholism: Research opportunities. *Addictive Behaviors, 26,* 489–507.

Kaufman, E. (1994). *Psychotherapy for addicted persons.* New York: Guilford Press.

Laban, R. (1997). *Chemical dependency treatment planning handbook.* Kenner, LA: Charles C. Thomas.

Levin, J. (1999). *Primer for treating substance abusers.* Northvale, NJ: Jason Aronson.

Lewis, J., Dana, R., & Blevins, G., (1994). *Substance abuse counseling: An individualized approach* (2nd ed.). Pacific Grove, CA: Brooks/Cole.

Mann, D. (1994). *The effect of a ropes course program on high-risk adolescent self-esteem.* Unpublished master's thesis, California State University.

McNeece, C., & DiNitto, D., (1998). *Chemical dependency: A systems approach* (2nd ed.). Boston: Allyn & Bacon.

Medina, K. L., Shear, P. K., Schafer, J., Armstrong, T. G., & Dyer, P. (2004). Cognitive functioning and length of abstinence in polysubstance dependent men. *Archives of Clinical Neuropsychology, 19*(2), 248–58.

Naegle, M., & D'Avanzo, C. E., (2001). *Addictions and substance abuse: Strategies for advanced practice nursing.* Upper Saddle River, NJ: Prentice Hall.

Schottenfeld, R., Pantalon, M., Chawarski, M., & Pakes, J. (1999). Community reinforcement approach for combined opioid and cocaine dependence: Patterns of engagement in alternate activities. *Journal of Substance Abuse Treatment, 18,* 255–61.

Stevens, P., & Smith, R., (2001). *Substance abuse counseling: Theory and practice* (2nd ed.). Upper Saddle River, NJ: Merrill/Prentice Hall.

Velleman, R. (1991). Applications of cognitive behavioral therapy. In W. Dryden & R. Rentoul (Eds.), *Adult clinical problems: A cognitive-behavioral approach* (pp. 138–70). New York: Routledge.

Waltman, D. (1995). Key ingredients to effective addictions treatment. *Journal of Substance Abuse Treatment, 12*(6), 429–39.

Chapter 14

Dual Diagnosis: Mental Illness and Substance Addiction

Valorey Baron Young, Melodee Mcafee,
Sophia F. Dziegielewski, Cheryl Green, and Reginald Deaton

NO MATTER WHAT POPULATION OR FIELD OF PRACTICE IN WHICH PRACTI-tioners are employed, they are increasingly confronted with the dually diagnosed client. In the therapeutic setting, clinicians often encounter clients presenting with comorbid Axis I and Axis II disorders who also meet the criteria for chemical dependency (Ellason & Ross, 1996). Many professionals believe that attempting to do psychotherapy with clients who have this type of dual diagnoses can be problematic (McCann & Pearlman, 1990). In order for practitioners to work successfully with dually diagnosed clients, they must be cognizant of client problems, diagnostic assessments, clinical interventions, and current case studies. Clients with comorbid psychiatric and substance use disorders often exhibit extremely poor compliance to outpatient treatment (Booth, Cook, & Blow, 1992; Carey & Carey, 1990; Daley & Zuckoff, 1998; Matas, Staley, & Griffin, 1992). This leaves these individuals vulnerable to a variety of negative clinical ramifications including problems with relapse and rehospitalization that, in turn, could relate to higher service utilization and cost (Bartels et al., 1993; Clark, 1994; Bartels, Drake, & McHugo, 1992; Cournos et al., 1991).

This chapter gives special attention to the dually diagnosed client to ensure that he or she is not lost in a labyrinth of interdisciplinary conflicts and ineffective standard service delivery practices. This chapter advocates that treatment models be modified, integrated, and applied together in order to fully address the client's problems and needs. Practitioners from either a psychiatric or an addictions background should be fully versed and proficient in the treatment of persons with dual diagnoses. Therefore, this chapter provides an overview of the common problems related to the dually diagnosed client, as well as practice strategies, interventions, and measurement scales. A case example shows how a severe mental disorder can occur with a substance addiction, outlines treatment possibilities, and notes the problems that can arise.

OVERVIEW OF DUAL DIAGNOSIS

Often individuals who suffer from mental health diagnoses such as the depressive and anxiety disorders are not automatically screened for substance addictions. The opposite is also true; individuals who suffer from the substance addiction disorders are frequently not evaluated for co-occurring mental illness. This disconnect is puzzling because almost all professionals agree that these disorders can and often do coexist. It has been estimated that approximately 50 percent of the individuals who suffer from a chronic mental illness also suffer from alcoholism and other drug dependence, while 75 percent of adolescent mentally ill clients either abuse or are addicted to alcohol or other drugs (Buelow & Buelow, 1998).

DiNitto and Webb (1998) summarized previous research and reported that, according to comorbidity surveys, as many as 51 percent of the clients with lifetime disorders were dually diagnosed with an addictive substance disorder and a mental disorder. Furthermore, epidemiological studies over the past fifteen years have indicated that individuals with mental disorders are at least three times more likely to have an addictive disorder (Mowbray et al., 1999). Due to the complexity of assisting individuals who meet the criteria for more than one mental health diagnosis and the limitations of the health care system, these dually diagnosed individuals can be given inadequate or less than comprehensive treatment (Orlin & Davis, 1993). In today's managed behavioral healthcare environment, resources are often shaped and influenced by cost containment with an emphasis placed on time-limited, outcome-oriented interventions (Moggi, Ouimette, Finney, & Moos, 1999; Dziegielewski, 2002, 2004).

In managed healthcare, funds are rarely made available for treatment programs specializing in integrated treatment models. This places clients in an "all or nothing" position because they are required to meet criteria for placement in either a mental health facility or a substance abuse clinic. In addition, clients in inadequate or inappropriate treatment programs might combine legal and illegal medications and other drugs, resulting in potentially deadly consequences. Responsible clinical assessment starts with understanding that problems with more than one diagnostic condition can occur, and active intervention must always take these factors into account.

According to Sciacca (1991) many programs specializing in the treatment of mental health problems shy away from or refer individuals who also have problems with substance abuse. Conversely, clients may be reluctant to self-disclose about possible substance use patterns or psychiatric disorders for fear of being refused help (Ekleberry, 1996). This nondisclosure of information could hinder the practitioner's ability to render an accurate diagnosis. Without diagnostic clarity, the client's symptomology and impairment will not be sufficiently treated, thus putting the client at risk. Unaddressed needs could force the client to seek immediate treatment in expensive emergency rooms, or they may end up in detoxification programs.

Oftentimes, psychiatric clients are recalcitrant to treatment interventions because they maintain behaviors that are self-destructive through the misuse of drugs and alcohol (Horevitz & Loewenstein, 1994). Clients may depend on substances as a means of self-help or self-soothing (McCann & Pearlman, 1990). According to Herman (1997), in order to eliminate chronic dysphoria, clients may attempt to stimulate an internal state of well-being and comfort through the use of psychoactive drugs. Practitioners should be alert to warning signs that indicate possible substance misuse. According to Gray (1993), some of these signs are anger, defensiveness, impulsivity, dishonesty, impatience, and self-pity. In addition, clients may habitually miss sessions, cancel sessions, or be extremely late for sessions (Newman & Wright, 1994).

Noncompliance can cause a domino effect of adverse consequences, which can significantly decrease the client's ability to complete treatment. In a quality assurance study, Daley and Zuckoff (1998) compared 38 inpatients who had both a psychiatric disorder and a comorbid substance use disorder with 104 inpatients who suffered from major depression alone. Of the former, 43.5 percent were compliant with initial outpatient session; of the latter, 86 percent were compliant.

Daley and Zuckoff (1998) highlight the following adverse effects that can transpire for noncompliant, dually diagnosed clients:

- ◆ Relapse rates are higher for poorly compliant clients are more likely to experience clinical deterioration of their psychiatric condition, to relapse to alcohol or other drug use, and to return to the hospital as a result of severe depression, suicidality, homicidality, mania, or psychotic decompensation.

- ◆ These individuals are more likely to miss outpatient appointments, which can lead to failure to renew medication prescriptions, which in turn exacerbates the psychiatric and substance use symptoms.

- ◆ The complicating factors related to impaired mental health contribute to poor treatment compliance and cause the loss of supportive relationships while contributing to frustration among family members and professionals, who find themselves watching helplessly as the client deteriorates.

- ◆ Due to increased risk of hospitalization, poor outpatient compliance leads to increased costs of care as a result of more days spent in expensive inpatient treatment facilities.

The impairments and risks linked with substance abuse can have grim results for clients with dual disorders and clinicians alike. Professionals often encounter crisis situations, medical emergencies, and legal crises related to their clients' substance abuse (Horevitz & Loewenstein, 1994).

Unfortunately, "despite the substantial overlap between psychopathology and substance use problems, many clinicians feel ill-prepared to assess and manage substance abuse" (Myers, Brown, Tate, Abrantes, & Tomlinson, 2001, p. 275). Sciacca (1991) reported that when mental health professionals lack training in substance abuse, they may present as judgmental and critical toward dually diagnosed clients, and this could inhibit the practitioner's ability to recognize alcoholism and drug addiction as physiological diseases. Problematically, clients at this juncture may stop discussing their substance abuse and withdraw, becoming uncomfortable with the therapeutic setting.

ASSESSMENT

Effective assessment must distinguish whether the client's primary condition is psychiatric or related to substance use (Orlin & Davis, 1993). Furthermore, the assessment must acknowledge that there can be specific subgroups in which the types and levels of substance and mental disorder criteria are defined (Hendrickson, Schmal, Ekleberry, & Bullock, 1999; Moggi et al., 1999). Lehman (1996) proposes that dually diagnosed clients should be categorized into five subgroups indicating levels of substance involvement and mental illness symptoms:

1. Individuals with a substance use disorder and a substance-induced disorder such as depression.
2. Individuals with a substance use disorder and an independent mental disorder, known as co-occurring addictive and mental disorders (COAMD).
3. Individuals with a substance use disorder and an Axis II personality disorder.
4. Individuals with COAMD who have associated major medical problems.
5. Individuals with COAMD who have major social problems.

Practitioners need to consider the dimensions of comorbid substance abuse in connection with mental illness when attempting to subjectively measure typical consequences of substance use by clients. Mueser, Drake, and Miles (1997) note that the Michigan Alcohol Screening Test (Selzer, 1971), the Alcohol Dependence Scale (Skinner & Horn, 1984), and other standard instruments such as the Addiction Severity Index (McLellan, Luborsky, Woody, & O'Brien, 1980) are not that sensitive to clinically important levels of drug abuse among clients who may also have psychiatric disorders. To begin the assessment, Hendrickson et al. (1999) presented a seven-stage model for working with clients who suffer from comorbid disorders. They stated that practitioners should first identify the client's problem and expect the client to initially deny that the problem exists. Once this denial is addressed, the client will be able to move forward and develop self-awareness of the problem, thereby acknowledging to self and others that a problem does exist. Once the problem is acknowledged, the client needs to express a willingness to modify or completely change problematic behaviors while continuing to express interest and motivation toward maintenance of lifestyle changes.

To maximize the reliability and validity of the proposed diagnosis, Kranzler and Kadden (1996) suggest using several different interview formats such as the Diagnostic Interview Schedule (Robins, Helzer, Croughan, & Ratcliff, 1981) and the Structural Clinical Interview for *DSM-III-R* (SCID) (Spitzer, Williams, Gibbon, & First, 1992). To test whether the SCID could accurately assess diagnostic conditions, Kranzler and Kadden recruited one hundred clients from an inpatient alcohol and drug abuse treatment center. Results showed that discriminate validity for the alcohol and drug dependence was excellent; while the validity for lifetime comorbid disorders was more modest. Based on the research, it is obvious that the difficulty of measuring this complex phenomenon remains a therapeutic challenge (Schuckit, 1973; Grande, Wolf, Schubert, Patterson, & Brocco, 1984; Kranzler & Liebowitz, 1988).

Because brief interventions are generally the practice strategy utilized, the supporting assessment must be comprehensive. Myers et al. (2001) proposed that all assessment information be gathered using a systematic approach and that all assessment devices provide self-report assessments that can be reviewed with the client. When initially assessing substance disorders among individuals diagnosed with severe mental illness, numerous difficulties can occur (Drake, Alterman, & Rosenberg, 1993; Drake & Mercer-McFadden, 1995; Stone, Greenstein, Gamble, & McLellan, 1993). These can include incomplete histories (Ananth et al., 1989), clients' use of denial, distortion, and minimization in connection with self-reports (Aiken, 1986; Galletly, Field, & Prior, 1993; Stone et al., 1993), and distortions of cognitive and emotional frame of reference due to mental illness (Mueser, Bellack, & Blanchard, 1992). Another important issue that can obscure an accurate appraisal involves the qualitative difference found between clients with a substance disorder and those diagnosed with a mental disorder and a comorbid substance disorder (Drake et al., 1990; Lehman, Myers, Thompson, & Corty, 1994; McHugo, Paskus, & Drake, 1993). According to Mueser et al. (1997), compared with non–mentally ill substance abusers, those with dual disorders use lower amounts of alcohol and drugs, experience different consequences, are less likely to develop a dependence syndrome, and have less subjective distress. For example, the typical consequences of substance abuse among people with a mental disorder are difficulties with money management, destabilization of illness, unstable housing, and an inability to participate in rehabilitation. Therefore, Mueser et al., like others, support the contention that explicit assessment at each stage of the treatment process is needed and that to facilitate this, multiple administrations and multimodal testing instruments need to be considered (Carey, 1989; Drake et al., 1990; McHugo, Drake, Burton, & Ackerson, 1995; Stone et al., 1993).

CASE EXAMPLE

Case History

G, a thirty-year-old Caucasian woman, was admitted to the intensive care unit at the behavioral health center on a Baker Act (Florida) 52 basis, secondary to suicidal ideation with a plan. G was intoxicated upon admission with a blood alcohol level of .436. Upon admission, G's affect was sad and blunted, her speech was normal to slightly slurred, and her motor activity was retarded. G was slow to respond to questions and needed prompts to stay on task during the initial interview. She denied any previous psychiatric hospitalization. G reported that she has been using alcohol regularly to self-medicate instead of taking the Zoloft that her psychiatrist prescribed for her. She denied using any other substances or illegal drugs. G reported that she has been diagnosed in the past with dissociative identity disorder and alcohol use disorder.

G reported a long history of experiencing spells of forgetfulness, precipitated by headaches, after which she finds herself involved in situations and places she does not remember initiating. G stated that she meets people who call her by other names and finds new clothes in her closet that she does not remember buying. She also noted that she finds charges on her credit card that she cannot account for. G reported often losing time and experiencing nightmares and flashbacks. G identified the precipitating events that led to her admission as feelings of anxiety, depression, and hopelessness. G attributed these feelings to seeing her psychiatrist and doing Eye Movement Desensitization and Reprocessing (EMDR). G indicated the EMDR process brought up terrible memories of her father sexually assaulting her. G reported that two of her alter personalities had been integrated, but she also noted that having to feel emotions for the first time and to face the ugly things that happened to her was too much to bear.

G reported that when she left the psychiatrist's office, she went to a bar she frequented before she joined Alcoholics Anonymous. She intended to get one martini to feel better, but she needed more drinks to achieve feeling numb. G stated that this often happened. After a while, G became more and more depressed and decided to try to kill herself by overdose and went to a store purchase some over-the-counter pain relievers. The store manager apprehended G when she walked out of the store without paying for the pills, and the police were called. When questioned by the police, G admitted that she wanted to "off herself."

G was the only child of a Georgia farmer and his wife. Her mother died in a car accident when she was seven years old and her father, a recovering alcoholic, passed away four years ago from lung cancer. She was born in a rural farming community. She was unable to recall much of her childhood after her mother's death. She reported that soon after her mother passed away, her father would get drunk and come into her room in the middle of the night and rape her. G attempted to tell her second-grade teacher, but the teacher called her father, and G was beaten and left in a hall closet for two days without food or water. When her father realized no one was going to stop him, G reported that he had sex with her whenever he wanted. Outside the home, G was only allowed to socialize with people from her church (where her father was a deacon). However, once she became a teenager, her father kept a tight reign on her social contacts. G reported not minding due to feeling anxious with her peers. She stated that she was not allowed to attend any extracurricular activities after school, so she concentrated on her studies and graduated with honors from high school. Her tendency to isolate herself continued through college. G graduated with a degree in computer science and currently holds an executive position with a large company.

G admitted that, in the last several years, she has distanced herself from friends and extended family members; she also tends to isolate herself from outside functions. She indicated that she does not trust herself around others nor does she trust their response to her if one of her alter personalities were to come out. G does not have a strong support system. Her extended family members consist of an aunt and uncle, who own a peanut farm in Georgia, and a married cousin who also lives in Georgia.

Multiaxial Diagnostic Assessment

Incorporating information from the client and the *DSM-IV-TR* resulted in the following diagnostic impression:

Axis I: Dissociative identity disorder (300.14)
           Alcohol dependence with psychological dependence (303. 90)
Axis II: No diagnosis (V7.09)
Axis III: Allergy to sulfa drugs and penicillin
Axis IV: Problems with primary support group: childhood sexual and physical abuse
           Problems related to social environment: inadequate support system.
           Inability to maintain relationships.
           Legal charges pending for shoplifting.
Axis V: 40

On Axis I, G met the *DSM-IV-TR* criteria for dissociative identity disorder because of her inability to remember past events of personal significance and because two distinct alter personalities assume control of her behavior at different times. The assessment showed that G was alcohol dependent, although she had not experienced alcoholic blackouts. There were other disorders that needed to be considered and discounted, such as schizophrenia (i.e., dissociative disorder misinterpreted as thought disorder), affective disorder, and malingering disorder.

On Axis II, there was no diagnosis. However, G's avoidant and antisocial traits with her extended family and friends were noted.

On Axis III, there was no diagnosis. However, it was noted that G was allergic to certain drugs. Therefore, in order to differentiate this diagnosis from any other medical or neurological condition, the practitioner referred G for a complete physical and neurological examination. This was critical in ruling out other diagnoses such as seizure disorders.

On Axis IV, in considering the client's psychological and environmental issues, it was important to consider her primary support group (i.e., aunt, uncle, cousin, and coworkers). G stated that she had been sexually abused and that when she attempted to get help from her schoolteacher, her father started physically abusing her as well. The Axis IV diagnoses were (a) problems with primary support group: childhood sexual and physical abuse; and (b) problems related to social environment: G did not see her extended family very often and did not socialize with her coworkers, thus she had an inadequate support system and inability to maintain relationships. G also had legal charges pending for shoplifting.

On Axis V, G was given a GAF score of 40 based on her suicidal ideation.

Intervention Plan

G has been dually diagnosed with a mental disorder and an addictive disorder. She also uses alcohol to medicate herself and experience relief from the difficulties resulting from inadequate self-capacities and impaired functioning. Her noncompliance with the medication regimen prescribed by her psychiatrist has resulted in a domino effect of adverse consequences: clinical deterioration of her psychiatric condition; a relapse to alcohol; suicidal ideation; shoplifting with legal charges pending; and psychiatric hospitalization. In order to establish and foster a strong therapeutic alliance with G, it is important for the practitioner to remember that G's alcoholism is a physiological disease and to not express a critical or judgmental attitude toward her. Also, it is imperative that the practitioner not stifle her willingness to talk about her substance use.

G's primary diagnostic category is psychiatric categorized in the subgroup of individuals who have co-occurring mental and addictive disorders with major social problems. G has an awareness of her problems but her feelings of hopelessness handicap her ability to recognize that she can change her responses and behaviors toward her dissociative identity disorder and thus change her lifestyle. This is evidenced by distortions of her cognitive and emotional frame of reference due to her mental illness.

There are four questions that must be answered when working with G: (1) How many of the personalities have the addiction? (2) Can the strongest nonaddicted personality take the lead and the power away from the other alters? (3) G uses alcohol to forget, so what should be done to help her cope with remembering? and (4) Is alcohol abuse giving G permission to be the opposite of the primary personality (i.e., to exhibit wild, impulsive, extroverted, grandiose behavior)? Treatment of the addicted personalities will have to be framed in such a way as to give hope that these personality are not being repressed but rather will be able to find expression in creative and life-enhancing ways.

G's depression and anxiety may be effectively treated with psychotropic medication for a time. Neuroleptics (e.g., Seroquel, Zyprexa, Risperdal) will be utilized temporarily to banish the voices or other personalities to the background. This reprieve may make G very reluctant to allow the other personalities to resurface in therapy for fear that they will stay. However, their temporary suppression may provide an opportunity for more intense substance abuse treatment and support. G should be encouraged to participate in substance abuse treatment.

Intervention Strategy: Comorbid Dissociative Identity Disorder and Alcohol Dependence Disorder

The following intervention plan is suggested to address both the identity disorder and alcohol dependence:

Step 1: As far as possible, develop a map of primary and secondary personalities, defining the role of each.

Step 2: Identify which personality is not addicted to alcohol. Determine whether this personality can be recruited to captain the rest in sobriety. If the primary personality is alcohol dependent, the client should be *encouraged* to split if she is about to drink.

Step 3: Encourage the temporary use of psychotropic medications, which will banish the alters, and have the client work exclusively on recovery from the alcohol dependence. Encourage the client's medication compliance and recovery program while accessing alters through use of hypnosis. Note that a history of noncompliance to medications may lead to relapse and that the use of hypnosis may cause a risk of relapse because of the disturbance to the system that the recall of suppressed memories may create.

In some cases a client may be able to progress without medication, though overcoming his or her anxiety will demand tremendous commitment to recovery disciplines. Often, anxiety simply leads a person to an easy option such as alcohol use. This use of alcohol is the client's misguided attempt to feel well. But not only does this choice endanger the client's overall health, it makes it almost impossible for the practitioner to do good work with the alter personalities (when one of them has a drink, all of them feel the effects). Anxiolytics (e.g., Ativan) are an alternative to alcohol but can just as easily be abused. In the case of dissociative identity disorder, such medications should be used to provide brief periods of respite from the disorder for the purpose of focusing on substance abuse treatment rather than as a long-term solution to the identity disorder. Eventually, the alter personalities need to be heard because they have an important role in the process of personality integration. They should not be viewed simply as a problem to be eliminated.

The process of therapy then becomes an art rather like juggling. The first ball is helping the client become sober. The second is reducing anxiety, which could lead to relapse, through the use of medications, relaxation response, and hypnotic suggestion. The third is accessing alters and enabling them to reveal their purpose and their needs. The fourth is dealing with abreactions and the overwhelming anxiety that normally drives the client to alcohol. The successful outcome of this juggling art is the gradual fusing of the alter personalities with the primary personality. But even after this integration, the client will need to maintain sobriety. Years of practice in responding to life as a whole person is needed for full recovery. The reality is that one of the balls will be dropped from time to time, and ad hoc solutions will be needed to restart the process. The practitioner needs to be resilient, consistent, and optimistic, having hope when the client has none.

To facilitate intervention, the practitioner should encourage the following therapeutic action steps:

◆ G will attend an Alcoholics Anonymous meeting each day for ninety days (and continue less frequently thereafter). G may attend more than one a day if she feels the urge to drink. G will have a sponsor. The sponsor may be one who knows about her dissociative identity disorder, but this is not necessary.

◆ G will comply with medication management. G will see her psychiatrist for medication management once per month. Her psychiatrist and therapist will need to communicate to provide the most consistent treatment for her. G may experience an increase of symptoms, which may be necessary for the therapeutic process. Increasing or changing medications at this time may have contrary outcomes for the psychotherapy process.

◆ G will see her therapist for sixty-minute sessions twice per week (the first session my be considerably longer). The therapist will use relaxation response and hypnotic suggestion therapy to alleviate symptoms of anxiety. The therapist may make tapes for G to use outside the session.

◆ G's therapist will access and work with the alters in therapy. The therapist will have developed a map of the different alters and will have noted, as far as possible, the roles they play in helping the client survive. Each alter has been created for a purpose and protects G in some way. Some do not like each other and may want to cause harm, which results in harm to G. Strong boundaries need to be designated so that each alter has a place of protection from the others where he or she can be placed while the therapist is working with another. Gradual fusion of G's alters will come when they are heard and they can carry out their purpose without needing to be apart from the primary personality. Eventual fusion of all the alters with the primary personality comes when the primary and the alters that remain agree to the union.

Dealing with abreactions will require the therapist to calmly reassure G, to help her to feel safe, and to help her access her own calming skills or those she has learned in therapy.

The therapist must also successfully deal with several possible misconceptions the alters may have: that the therapist is going to kill the alters; that the past abuse is still occurring; that it is wrong to show any strong emotion (especially anger); that the victim is responsible for the abuse; that the primary personality must be punished; that the primary personality cannot handle the memories; that no one can be trusted. These misconceptions can increase anxiety and trigger a relapse (Ross, 1989; Ross & Gahan, 1988).

BEST PRACTICES

Professionals have several options to explore when dealing with clients who cannot utilize psychotherapy due to substance abuse. Herman (1997) cautions that clinicians must recognize that primary psychiatric clients' treatment can be fragmented and incomplete due to their complex symptoms. Therefore, a strong theoretical underpinning that can be employed in a flexible manner by the clinician is advocated.

Gray (1993) suggested that, in recovery, a behavioral and emotional change that leads to increased health and growth must occur. When relapse occurs, the client simply reverts to the previous state of dysfunction. A client cannot be in recovery and relapse at the same time. Brief therapeutic techniques can enhance the client's motivation to change as the practitioner gives feedback and referrals when necessary (Monti, Colby, & O'Leary, 2001).

Pape (1993) recommended that, in the case of dual diagnosis, treatment should begin by addressing the chemical dependency, with the primary goal being total abstinence from all mood-altering substances. From that stage, the client's ability to focus on treatment goals and sustain behavioral self-control will dictate the treatment pace (Horevitz & Loewenstein, 1994). As professionals encounter the multifaceted problems associated with comorbid disorders, it is imperative to have clear and operative goals. Hendrickson et al. (1999) advocate that the following treatment goals are essential when working with dual diagnosis clients:

♦ *Stabilization*: The client is helped to achieve abstinence and psychiatric stability.
♦ *Adaptive behavior change*: The client is encouraged to develop behaviors that promote abstinence and psychiatric stability.
♦ *Relapse prevention*: The client is monitored for signs and behaviors that can lead to alcohol and drug use or increased psychiatric symptoms.
♦ *Community maintenance*: Attachment to and involvement in long-term community supports such as self-help groups and psychosocial support programs such as clubhouses are encouraged.

Moggi et al. (1999) and other researchers advocate for practitioners to make use of the following treatment techniques when dealing with dual diagnoses:

♦ Liberal use of psychotropic medications in order to address psychiatric symptoms.
♦ Active participation in program activities (Franco, Galanter, Castaneda, & Patterson, 1995; Lehman et al., 1994, Minkoff, 1991, Osher & Kofoed, 1989).
♦ Maintaining well-organized program structure and providing clear rules (Drake, Bartels, Teague, Noordsy, & Clark, 1993; Mowbray et al., 1995, Osher & Kofoed, 1989).
♦ Supportive approaches rather than confrontation (Mueser et al., 1992, Osher & Kofoed, 1989).
♦ Practical orientation in terms of working on future goals.

According to Wenglinsky and Dziegielewski (2002), it is critical for the client in treatment to participate in formulating the intervention plan. In creating the intervention plan, special attention needs to be given to maintaining abstinence. Problems that need to be considered include how to improve social and coping skills while enhancing self-esteem. In the treatment planning process, all goals should match the assessment and the desires of the client.

It has become increasingly apparent since the late 1980s that the use of traditional methods for treating dually diagnosed clients has proved inadequate (Minkoff & Drake, 1991; Mueser et al. 1997; Polcin, 1992). In addition, the use of parallel and sequential approaches have been proven unproductive for meeting the needs of clients with psychiatric disorders and comorbid substance disorders (Baekeland, Lundwall, & Shanahan, 1973; LaPorte, McLellan, O'Brien, & Marshall, 1981; Mueser et al., 1997; Rounsaville, Dolinsky, Babor, & Meyer, 1987; Woody, McLellan, & O'Brien, 1990). According to Mueser et al. (1997), poor treatment outcomes can be directly linked to problems within the traditional service system, in which mental health and substance abuse services are viewed as separate, parallel programs. This creates a dual perspective in terms of staff training, the models of treatment and recovery, and funding sources.

As defined by Ekleberry (1996), dual-diagnosis treatment needs to be accessible, comprehensive, and integrated for both the psychiatric and the substance abuse disorders. An integrated approach offers flexibility while incorporating the knowledge base and treatment techniques of both the mental health and the addictions fields. Mueser et al. (1997) suggest ten common ingredients of integrated mental health and substance abuse treatment programs that clinicians can utilize with dual-diagnosis clients (see table 9).

SUMMARY AND FUTURE DIRECTIONS

As previously stated, statistics indicate that 51 percent of the clients practitioners treat have an addictive disorder paired with a mental disorder. Sadly, clients are often left to struggle in a morass of brief managed care without having their needs met. Recidivism to hospitals and rehab treatment facilities becomes a frustrating way of life for much of the dually diagnosed population. This "swinging door" existence is detrimental to clients and practitioners alike and often causes practitioners to become hardened to the plight of their dually diagnosed clients. Communication between healthcare givers and the varied disciplines they represent must start at the most basic level of assessment and admission to treatment programs. The responsibility of study and research into community resources and the specialized skills of other professionals needed for dually diagnosed clients rests on the practitioner.

In conclusion, there is still considerable need for research in the areas of treatment and recovery concerning the case example presented. The individual who is diagnosed with dissociative identity disorder is apt to encounter disbelief and disagreement among the very professionals to whom he or she goes for help. This contention in the professional community violates the client's right to proper treatment, starting with an inaccurate or incomplete diagnostic assessment. Misdiagnosis can also hamper the client's ability to reconnect with significant others, family members, and social systems. Added to these problems, the dually diagnosed client is often confused and unable to adapt to the parallel treatment that

---

Table 9: Helping the Dually Diagnosed

Ingredient	Function
The same professionals provide mental health and substance abuse treatment	Coordinating mental health and substance abuse treatments; avoiding sending "mixed messages" or failing to treat relevant problem areas.
Case management	Attending to the range of clinical, housing, social, and other needs that may be affected by either substance abuse or mental health problems.
Assertive outreach	Providing services directly in the community to engage clients, address pressing needs, follow up and re-engage relapsing clients.
Group interventions	Providing peer support, persuading clients to address substance use behavior, promoting sharing of coping strategies for managing urges to use substances and for social situations.
Education about substance abuse and mental illness	Informing clients about the nature of their psychiatric disorders and the effects of substance abuse to highlight negative effects of drugs/alcohol.
Motivational techniques	Engaging clients in working toward substance use reduction and abstinence by identifying personally relevant goals that become a focus for treatment.
Behavioral strategies	Using techniques such as social skills training, training in coping skills to manage symptoms and high-risk situations, and relapse prevention to reduce substance use and vulnerability to relapse.
Family/social network factors	Working with members of client's social networks to reduce factors that may maintain substance use behavior, help client's progress toward personal goals, and bolster resistance to relapses.
Stage-wise treatment	Providing specific interventions based on the client's specific stage of recovery: engagement, persuasion, active treatment, or relapse prevention.
Long-term perspective	Recognizing that dual disorders are chronic conditions that may require long-term, rather than time-limited, intervention.

Source: Mueser et al. (1997).

artificially separates the psychiatric disorder from the comorbid substance disorder. To avoid these pitfalls, practitioners must educate and train themselves to comprehensively assess clients who are both mentally ill and substance abusers. For the dually diagnosed client, it is not only therapeutically unproductive but also professionally negligent for a practitioner to simply refer psychiatric clients to a substance abuse program without verifying whether or not that program is prepared to meet the special needs of these clients.

References

Aiken, L. S. (1986). Retrospective self-reports by clients differ from original reports: Implications for the evaluation of drug treatment programs. *International Journal of Addiction, 21,* 767–88.

Ananth, J., Vanderwater, S., Kamal, M., Brodsky, A., Gamal, R., & Miller, M. (1989). Mixed diagnosis of substance abuse in psychiatric patients. *Hospital and Community Psychiatry, 40,* 297–99.

Baekeland, F., Lundwall, L., & Shanahan, T. J. (1973). Correlates of patient attrition in the outpatient treatment of alcoholism. *Journal of Nervous Mental Diseases, 157,* 99–107.

Bartels, S. J., Drake, R. E., & McHugo, G. J. (1992). Alcohol abuse, depression, and suicidal behavior in schizophrenia. *American Journal of Psychiatry, 149,* 394–95.

Bartels, S. J., Teague, G. B., Drake, R. E., Clark, R. E., Bush, P., & Noordsy, D. L. (1993). Substance abuse in schizophrenia: Service utilization and costs. *Journal of Nervous Mental Diseases, 181,* 227–32.

Booth, B. M., Cook, C. A. L., & Blow, F. C. (1992). Comorbid mental disorders in patients with AMA discharges from alcoholism treatment. *Hospital and Community Psychiatry, 43,* 730–31.

Buelow, G. D., & Buelow, S. A. (1998). *Psychotherapy in chemical dependence treatment.* Pacific Grove, CA: Brooks/Cole.

Carey, K. B. (1989). Emerging treatment guidelines for mentally ill chemical abusers. *Hospital and Community Psychiatry, 40,* 341–42.

Carey, K. B., & Carey, M. P. (1990). Enhancing the treatment attendance of mentally ill chemical abusers. *Journal of Behavioral and Experimental Psychiatry, 21,* 205–9.

Clark, R. E. (1994). Family costs associated with severe mental illness and substance use: A comparison of families with and without dual disorders. *Hospital and Community Psychiatry, 45,* 808–13.

Cournos, F., Empfield, M., Horwath, E., McKinnon, K., Meyer, I., Schrage, H., et al. (1991). HIV seroprevalence among patients admitted to two psychiatric hospitals. *American Journal of Psychiatry, 148,* 1225–30.

Daley, D. C., & Zuckoff, A. (1998). Improving compliance with the initial outpatient session among discharged inpatient dual diagnosis clients. *Social Work, 43*(5), 470–74.

DiNitto, D. M., & Webb, D. K. (1998). Compounding the problem: Substance abuse and other disabilities. In C. A. McNeece & D. M. DiNitto (Eds.), *Chemical dependency: A systems approach.* Boston: Allyn & Bacon.

Drake, R. E., Alterman, A. I., & Rosenberg, S. R. (1993). Detection of substance use disorders in severely mentally ill patients. *Community Mental Health Journal, 29,* 175–92.

Drake, R. E., Bartels, S. J., Teague, G. B., Noordsy, D. L., & Clark, R. E. (1993). Treatment of substance abuse in severely mentally ill patients. *Journal of Mental Diseases, 181,* 606–11.

Drake, R. E., & Mercer-McFadden, C. (1995). Assessment of substance use among persons with severe mental disorders. In A. F. Lehman & L. Dixon (Eds.), *Double jeopardy: Chronic mental illness and substance abuse.* New York: Harwood Academic.

Drake, R. E., Osher, F. C., Noordsy, D., Hurlbut, S. C., Teague, G. B., & Beaudett, M. S. (1990). Diagnosis of alcohol use disorders in schizophrenia. *Schizophrenic Bulletin, 16,* 57–67.

Drake, R. E., Osher, F. C., & Wallach, M. A. (1989). Alcohol use and abuse in schizophrenia: A prospective community study. *Journal of Nervous Mental Diseases, 177,* 408–14.

Dziegielewski, S. F. (2002). *DSM-IV-TR in action.* New York: John Wiley & Sons.

Dziegielewski, S. F. (2004). *The changing face of health care social work: professional practice in managed behavioral health care* (2nd ed.). New York: Springer.

Ekleberry, S. (1996). Dual diagnosis: Addiction and Axis II personality disorders. *The Counselor, 3*, 7–13.

Ellason, J. W., & Ross, C. A. (1996). Axis I and II comorbidity and childhood trauma history in chemical dependency. *Bulletin of the Menninger Clinic, 60*(1), 39–52. Retrieved August 22, 2002, from http//web5.epnet.com/

Franco, N., Galanter, M., Castaneda, R. & Patterson, J. (1995). Combining behavioral and self-help approaches in the inpatient management of dually diagnosed patients. *Journal of Substance Abuse Treatment, 12*, 227–32.

Galletly, C. A., Field, C. D., & Prior, M. (1993). Urine drug screening of patients admitted to a state psychiatric hospital. *Hospital and Community, Psychiatry, 44*, 587–89.

Grande, T. P., Wolf, A. W., Schubert, D. S. P., Patterson, M. B., & Brocco, K. (1984). Associations among alcoholism, drug abuse, and antisocial personality disorder: A review of literature. *Psychological Reports, 55*, 455–74.

Gray, M. (1993). Relapse prevention. In S. L. A. Straussner (Ed.), *Clinical work with substance abusing clients*. New York: Guilford Press.

Hendrickson, E. L., Schmal, M. S., Ekleberry, S., & Bullock, J. (1999, March/April). Supervising staff treating the dually diagnosed. *The Counselor, 17*, 2.

Herman, J. (1997). *Trauma and recovery: The aftermath of violence from domestic abuse to political terror*. New York: Basic Books.

Horevitz, R., & Loewenstein, R. (1994). The rational treatment of multiple personality disorder. In S. J. Lynn & J. W. Rhue (Eds.), *Dissociation: Clinical and theoretical perspectives*. New York: Guilford Press.

Kranzler, H. R., & Kadden, R. M. (1996, June). Validity of the SCID in substance abuse patients. *Addiction, 91*(6), 859–69.

Kranzler, H. R., & Liebowitz, N. (1988). Depression and anxiety in substance abuse: Clinical implications. *Medical Clinics of North America, 72*, 867–85.

LaPorte, D. J., McLellan, A. T., O'Brien, C. P., & Marshall, J. R. (1981). Treatment response in psychiatrically impaired drug abusers. *Comprehensive Psychiatry, 22*, 411–19.

Lehman, A. F. (1996). Heterogeneity of person and place: Assessing co-occurring addictive and mental disorders. *American Journal of Orthopsychiatry, 66*, 32–41.

Lehman, A. F., Myers, C. P., Thompson, J. W., & Corty, E. (1994). Prevalence and patterns of "dual diagnosis" among psychiatric inpatients. *Comprehensive Psychiatry, 35*, 106–12.

Matas, M., Staley, D., & Griffin, W. (1992). A profile of the noncompliant patient: A thirty-month review of outpatient psychiatry referrals. *General Hospital Psychiatry, 14*, 124–30.

McCann, I. L., & Pearlman, L. A. (1990). *Psychological trauma and the adult survivor: Theory therapy, and transformation*. New York: Brunner/Mazel.

McHugo, G. J., Drake, R. E., Burton, H. L., & Ackerson, T. H. (1995). A scale for assessing the stage of substance abuse treatment in persons with severe mental illness. *Journal of Nervous Mental Diseases, 183*, 762–67.

McHugo, G. J., Paskus, T. S., & Drake, R. E. (1993). Detection of alcoholism in schizophrenia using the MAST. *Alcoholism: Clinical and Experimental Research, 17*, 187–91.

McLellan, A. T., Luborsky, L., Woody, G. E., & O'Brien, C. P. (1980). An improved diagnostic instrument for substance abuse patients: The addiction severity index. *Journal of Nervous Mental Diseases, 168*, 26–33.

Minkoff, K. (1991). Program components of a comprehensive integrated care system for serious mentally ill patients with substance disorders. *New Direction Mental Health Services, 50*, 13–27.

Minkoff, K., & Drake, R. E. (Eds.). (1991). Dual diagnosis of major mental illness and substance use disorder. *New Directions for Mental Health Services* (Vol. 50). San Francisco: Jossey-Bass.

Moggi, F., Ouimette, P. C., Finney, J. W., & Moos, R. H. (1999). Effectiveness of treatment for substance abuse and dependence for dual diagnosis patients: A model of treatment factors associated with one-year outcomes. *Journal of Studies on Alcohol, 60*(6), 856.

Monti, P. M., Colby, S. M., & O'Leary, T. A. (Eds.). (2001). *Adolescents, alcohol, and substance abuse: Reaching teens through brief interventions*. New York: Guilford Press.

Mowbray, C. T., Jordon, L. C., Ribisl, K. M., Kewalramani, A., Luke, D., Herman, S., & Bybee, D. (1999). Analysis of postdischarge change in a dual diagnosis population. *Health and Social Work, 24*(2), 91–101.

Mowbray, C. T., Solomon, M., Ribisl, K. M., Ebejer, M. A., Deiz, N., Brown, W., et al. (1995). Treatment for mental illness and substance abuse in a public psychiatric hospital: Successful strategies and challenging problems. *Journal of Substance Abuse Treatment, 12*, 129–39.

Mueser, K. T., Bellack, A. S., & Blanchard, J. J. (1992). Comorbidity of schizophrenia and substance abuse: Implications for treatment. *Journal Consult Clinical Psychology, 60*, 845–56.

Mueser, K. T., Drake, R. E., & Miles, K. M. (1997). *The course and treatment of substance use disorder in persons with severe mental illness* (NIDA Research Monograph No. 172). Retrieved December 12, 2002, from http://www.nida.nih.gov/

Myers, M., Brown, S., Tate, S., Abrantes, A., & Tomlinson, K. (2001). Toward brief interventions for adolescents with substance abuse and comorbid psychiatric problems. In P. M. Monti, S. M. Colby, & T. A. O'Leary (Eds.), *Adolescent, alcohol, and substance abuse: Reaching teens through brief interventions*. New York: Guilford Press.

Newman, C. F., & Wright, F. D. (1994). Substance abuse. In F. M. Dattilio & A. Freeman (Eds.), *Cognitive-behavioral strategies in crisis intervention*. New York: Guilford Press.

Orlin, L., & Davis, J. (1993). Assessment and intervention with drug and alcohol abusers in psychiatric settings. In S. L. A. Straussner (Ed.), *Clinical work with substance-abusing clients*. New York: Guilford Press.

Osher, F. C., & Kofoed, L. L. (1989). Treatment of patients with psychiatric and psychoactive substance abuse disorders. *Hospital and Community Psychiatry, 40*, 1025–30.

Pape, P. A. (1993). Issues in assessment and intervention with alcohol and drug abusing women. In S. L. A. Straussner (Ed.), *Clinical work with substance-abusing clients*. New York: Guilford Press.

Polcin, D. L. (1992). Issues in the treatment of dual diagnosis clients who have chronic mental illness. *Professional Psychology: Research and Practice, 23*, 30–37.

Robins, L. N., Helzer, J. E., Croughan, H., & Ratcliff, K. S. (1981). National institute of mental health diagnostic interview schedule: Its history, characteristics, and validity. *Archives of General Psychiatry, 38*, 381–89.

Ross, C. A. (1989). *Multiple personality disorder: Diagnosis, clinical features and treatment*. New York: John Wiley & Sons.

Ross, C. A., & Gahan, P. (1988). Cognitive analysis of multiple personality disorder. *American Journal of Psychotherapy, 42*, 229–39.

Rounsaville, B. J., Dolinsky, Z. S., Babor, T. F., & Meyer, R. E. (1987). Psychopathology as a predictor of treatment outcome in alcoholics. *Archives of General Psychiatry, 44*, 505–13.

Schuckit, M. A. (1973). Alcoholism and sociopathy-diagnostic confusion. *Journal of Studies on Alcohol, 34*, 157–64.

Sciacca, K. (1991). An integrated treatment approach for severely mentally ill individuals with substance disorders. *New Directions for Mental Health Services, 50*. Retrieved December, 29, 2002, from http://users.erols.com/ksciacca/innteg.htm

Selzer, M. L. (1971). The Michigan Alcoholism Screening Test: The quest for a new diagnostic instrument. *American Journal Psychiatry, 127,* 1653–58.

Skinner, H., & Horn, J. (1984). *Alcohol dependence scale user's guide.* Toronto, Canada: Addiction Research Foundation of Ontario.

Spitzer, R. L., Williams, J. B. W., Gibbon, M., & First, M. B. (1992). The structured clinical interview for *DSM-III-R*: I. History rationale and description. *Archives of General Psychiatry, 49,* 624–29.

Stone, A. M., Greenstein, R. A., Gamble, G., & McLellan, A. T. (1993). Cocaine use by schizophrenic outpatients who receive depot neuroleptic medication. *Hospital and Community Psychiatry, 44,* 176–77.

Wenglinsky, J., & Dziegielewski, S. F. (2002). Substance disorders: Alcoholism. In S. F. Dziegielewski (Ed.), *DSM-IV-TR in action.* New York: John Wiley & Sons.

Woody, G. E., McLellan, A. T., & O'Brien, C. P. (1990). Research on psychopathology and addiction: Treatment implications. *Drug Alcohol Dependence, 25,* 121–23.

Contributors

Tracey A. Bersch, MSW, RCSW Intern, is an Alpha Counselor with The Center for Drug Free Living. She provides life-skill instruction and counseling for elementary school students.

Tamara Blickem, MSW, is the manager of the Social Services Department with the Office of the Public Defender in Florida. She specializes in advocating for persons with mental illness within the criminal justice system.

Carmen P. Chang-Arratia, CSW, is a licensed social worker, employed with Community Healthcare Network in NYC, providing mental health services to the adult Hispanic population.

Reginald Deaton is a licensed mental health counselor with 25 years of experience. Currently, he is in private practice and on the administrative team of a behavioral health center.

Sophia F. Dziegielewski, Ph.D., LCSW, is Professor and Director of the School of Social Work at the University of Cincinnati. She is a licensed clinical social worker, specializing in health and mental health practice.

Cheryl Green, Ph.D., is an Associate Professor in the School of Social Work at the University of Central Florida. As a practitioner and an academic, she is active in the field and teaches in the area of substance abuse and intervention.

Kimberly Harvey, MSW, is a mental health/substance abuse therapist working with juveniles at a secured level six commitment program.

Sandra Binner Lupo, MSW, is a child and family therapist at the Florida United Methodist Children's Home in Central Florida. She specializes in substance abuse and mental health practice.

Melodee McAfee, MSW, is a Ph.D. candidate at the University of Central Florida who specializes in health public issues. Her practice and research interests focus on substance addictions and women's health.

Nancy Suris, MPH, MSW, is culminating with additional studies in the area of public health at the University of South Florida. Her professional interests are in international social and health issues and maternal and child health.

Jacqueline M. Swank, MSW, currently works in the partial hospitalization program at Halifax Behavioral Services, a psychiatric facility for children and adolescents in Daytona Beach, Florida. She is a Registered Clinical Social Work Intern working toward completing licensure requirements.

Barbara Turnage, Ph.D., is an Assistant Professor in the School of Social Work at the University of Central Florida. As a practitioner and an academic, she is active in the field and continues to present at regional, national, and international conferences.

Cathy A. Van Bibber, MSW, CAPP, is a certified addictions practitioner who works with adolescents in the area of drug and alcohol education and prevention.

Ilene J. VanGilder, MSW, is a Program Specialist/Mobile Therapist for Northwestern Human Services in Central Pennsylvania. She works with children and adolescents in therapeutic foster care and community wraparound services.

Barbara Ann Vunk, MSW, is a social worker with experience in the areas of health, mental health, and gerontology.

Sara Wienke, MSW, LCSW Intern, is working at Florida Hospital Center for Behavioral Health in Orlando, FL. She is employed as a Medical Psychiatric Social Worker.

Valorey Baron Young, MSW, LCSW Intern, is a clinical social worker who specializes in mental health, clinical hypnosis, and rapid trauma resolution.

Special Thank You for Earlier Drafts of Chapters

Elaine M. Hernandez, MSW, is a licensed social worker residing in the state of New York.

Nita Pierre, MSW, is currently a senior case planner providing prevention services to families in the New York City area. Her practice interests are primarily in the area of HIV/AIDS, health, and mental health.

Index

BEST PRACTICES IN MENTAL HEALTH
An International Journal

A new and innovative journal available Spring 2005

Best Practices in Mental Health:An International Journal is a refereed publication intended primarily for mental health teachers, researchers, and practitioners and which will also provide valuable guidance for students in the field. Best practices are high priorities of the U. S. National Institute of Mental Health (NIMH), and the journal will publish articles, commentary, and research reports that promote the latest developments. By having an international scope, the journal will be able to publish the best mental health practices and research from around the world. A distinguished international editorial board will insure that the journal publishes materials which seek to replicate and improve promising practices wherever found and to promote intervention research. The journal is published twice a year. A year's subscription is $40.00 for individuals and $60.00 for libraries and institutions. Online access is being developed for library/institutional subscribers. All subscription inquiries should be sent to: Best Practices in Mental Health, 341 N. Charlotte Street, Lombard, IL 60148. E-mail inquiries can be sent to **lyceumsubscribe@comcast.net**.

For up-to-date information see the Lyceum Web site, **www.lyceumbooks.com**.

SOCIAL DEVELOPMENT ISSUES JOURNAL

Social Development Issues, sponsored by the Inter-University Consortium for International Social Development (IUCISD), is a refereed journal published three times a year that serves as a scholarly forum linking multiple disciplines, nations, and cultures. The Journal's purpose is to promote consideration of issues that affect social justice as well as the development and well being of individuals and their communities. The Journal is committed to the advancement of social, cultural, political, and economic theories including policy and practice (and their interrelationship) within a global context.

Each issue includes reviews of noteworthy new books.

Individual Journal subscriptions include membership in IUCISD and the Consortium's newsletter. For more information about the Consortium see the Web site at **http://www.iucisd.org**.

A sample of recent topics in the Journal:

❙ Globalization and the social responsibility of the state in developing countries
❙ The links between education, employment, and demographic change
❙ Social development and the feminist tradition
❙ From social development to transformation
❙ South African nongovernmental organizations
❙ Income growth and inequality in Singapore
❙ Women and war: protection through empowerment in El Salvador

Social Development Issues Journal

Shanti K. Khinduka IUCISD President	**Frank Raymond** IUCISD President-Elect Journal Board President University of South Carolina

All SDI editorial team members listed below are affiliates of Washington University in Saint Louis

Michael Sherraden Editor	**Amanda Moore McBride** Associate Editor	**Timothy Broesamle** Managing Editor	**Anupama Jacob** Production Editor

Subscribe and join today. Libraries may order direct or through their subscription agency.

The *Social Development Issues Journal* is published three times a year by Lyceum Books. The subscription rate is $40.00 per year for individuals; $60.00 for institutions and libraries. There is a $21.00 fee for all foreign postage. All subscription inquiries should be sent to Social Development Issues Journal, 341 N. Charlotte Street, Lombard, Illinois 60148. Your e-mail inquiries can be sent to **lyceumsubscribe@comcast.net**

If you would like to join the Inter-University Consortium for International Social Development, please click on: **http://www.iassw.org**

SCHOOL SOCIAL WORK JOURNAL

School Social Work Journal is a refereed publication intended primarily for school social work practitioners, educators, and students in the public schools. Articles in the Journal are directly related to the improvement of social work practice in the schools. These articles report original research, integrative and comprehensive reviews, conceptual and practical positions, effective assessment and intervention methodologies, and model service delivery programs. Each issues includes reviews of noteworthy new books.

To learn more about the Illinois Association of School Social Workers, visit the Web site: **http://www.iassw.org**

A sample of recent topics in the Journal:

∎ Caring for Grandparent-Headed Families
∎ Junior high school predictors of high school dropout.
∎ Ethics and Confidentiality
∎ Youth Mentoring
∎ Drug traffic intervention through school and community centers.
∎ Abuse in adolescent dating relationships.
∎ Ecological Strategies and Socially Isolated Youth
∎ The impact of violence on school achievement and behavior.
∎ Challenges and service needs of urban children.
∎ The development of a tool for school social work collaboration.

Each issue includes reviews of noteworthy new books.

The *School Social Work Journal* is published fall and spring by the Illinois Association of School Social Workers. The subscription rate is $20.00 per year for individuals; $40.00 for institutions and libraries. There is a $10.00 fee for all foreign postage. All subscription inquiries should be sent to School Social Work Journal, 341 N. Charlotte Street, Lombard, Illinois 60148.

E-mail inquiries can be sent to **lyceumsubscribe@comcast.net**